Step By Step

Y0-CAX-977

2

Second Edition

Includes upgrade notes
for Visual Basic .NET

MICROSOFT

VISUAL BASIC 6.0
PROFESSIONAL
STEP BY STEP

Michael Halvorson

PUBLISHED BY
Microsoft Press
A Division of Microsoft Corporation
One Microsoft Way
Redmond, Washington 98052-6399

Library of Congress Cataloging-in-Publication Data
Halvorson, Michael.
    Microsoft Visual Basic 6.0 Professional Step by Step / Michael Halvorson.--2nd ed.
       p. cm.
    Includes index.
    ISBN 0-7356-1883-6
     1. Microsoft Visual Basic. 2. BASIC (Computer program language) I. Title.

QA76.73.B3 H338   2002
005.26'8--dc21   2002033818

Printed and bound in the United States of America.

1 2 3 4 5 6 7 8 9   QWT   7 6 5 4 3 2

Distributed in Canada by H.B. Fenn and Company Ltd.

A CIP catalogue record for this book is available from the British Library.

Microsoft Press books are available through booksellers and distributors worldwide. For further information about international editions, contact your local Microsoft Corporation office or contact Microsoft Press International directly at fax (425) 936-7329. Visit our Web site at www.microsoft.com/mspress. Send comments to *mspinput@microsoft.com*.

Acquisitions Editor: Danielle Bird
Project Editor: Denise Bankaitis
Technical Editor: Jim Fuchs

Body Part No. X09-06391

For my grandmother, Phyllis Evelyn Zell (1913-   )

Table of Contents

The Visual Basic Programming Environment 4 • The User Interface Form 10 • The Toolbox 10 • The Properties Window 11 • The Project Window 13 • Getting Help 15 • One Step Further: Exiting Visual Basic 18 • Upgrade Notes: What's Different in Visual Basic .NET? 18 • Lesson 1 Quick Reference 20

Lucky Seven: Your First Visual Basic Program 24 • Programming Steps 24 • Creating the User Interface 25 • Setting the Properties 31 • Writing the Code 37 • Saving the Program 44 • Building an Executable File 46 • One Step Further: Adding to a Program 50 • Using the Package Deployment Wizard 48 • Upgrade Notes: What's Different in Visual Basic .NET? 52 • Lesson 2 Quick Reference 53

Acknowledgments

This is my tenth book about Basic programming and the seventh devoted to developing Visual Basic applications for Microsoft Windows. Over the years, I have benefited greatly from the wisdom and experience of many talented software developers, teachers, publishing professionals, and friends, and this book is no exception. For their hard work, skill, and dedication to this project I warmly acknowledge the following individuals: acquisitions editors Casey Doyle and Eric Stroo, project editor Jenny Benson, technical editor Emma Gibson, project manager Peter Whitmer, copy editor Gina Russo, editorial assistant Asa Tomash, layout specialists Joanna Zito and Javier Amador-Peña, proofreaders Joanne Crerand and Bridget Leahy, indexer Joan Green, publishing support specialist Bill Teel, marketing manager Kathy Boullin, designer Barbara Remmele, buildmaster Anthony Williams, program manager Philip Borgnes, project manager Joan Lambert, Visual Basic program manager Chris Diaz, and Visual Basic documentation manager Ann Morris.

For the Second Edition, I thank, in particular, Danielle Bird, acquisitions editor, Denise Bankaitis, project editor, Jim Fuchs, technical editor, Cheryl Penner, copy editor, and Kerri DeVault and Dan Latimer, principal compositors. A number of enthusiastic readers of the First Edition have also sent me their ideas, comments, corrections, and code snippets, and I thank them for their interest in this project. I hope you enjoy the new edition!

Finally, I would like to thank my family—Kimberly, Henry, and Felix—for their continued support and understanding as I complete another programming book.

*Quick*Look Guide

Working with forms, see "Adding New Forms to a Program," Lesson 8, page 213

Running a program and creating a Windows executable file, see "Building an Executable File," Lesson 2, page 46

Creating objects by using the interface design tools, see "Creating the User Interface," Lesson 2, page 25

Adding artwork, see "The Shape Control," Lesson 9, page 242

Selecting properties, see "The Properties Window" Lesson 1, page 11

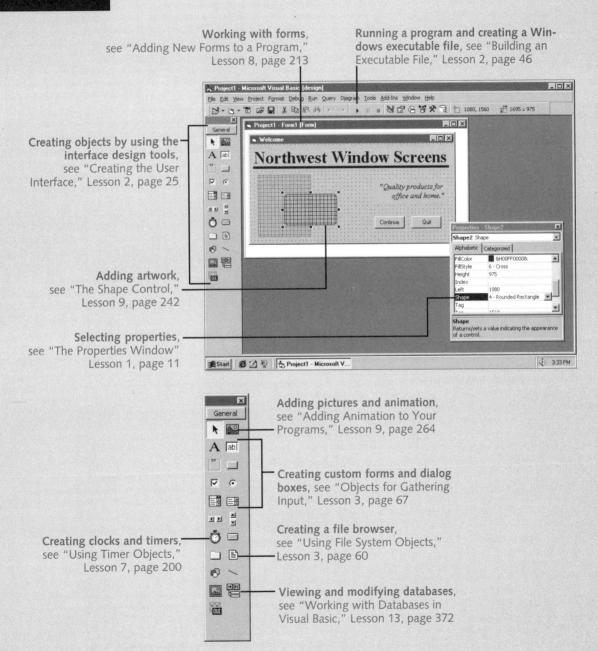

Adding pictures and animation, see "Adding Animation to Your Programs," Lesson 9, page 264

Creating custom forms and dialog boxes, see "Objects for Gathering Input," Lesson 3, page 67

Creating a file browser, see "Using File System Objects," Lesson 3, page 60

Creating clocks and timers, see "Using Timer Objects," Lesson 7, page 200

Viewing and modifying databases, see "Working with Databases in Visual Basic," Lesson 13, page 372

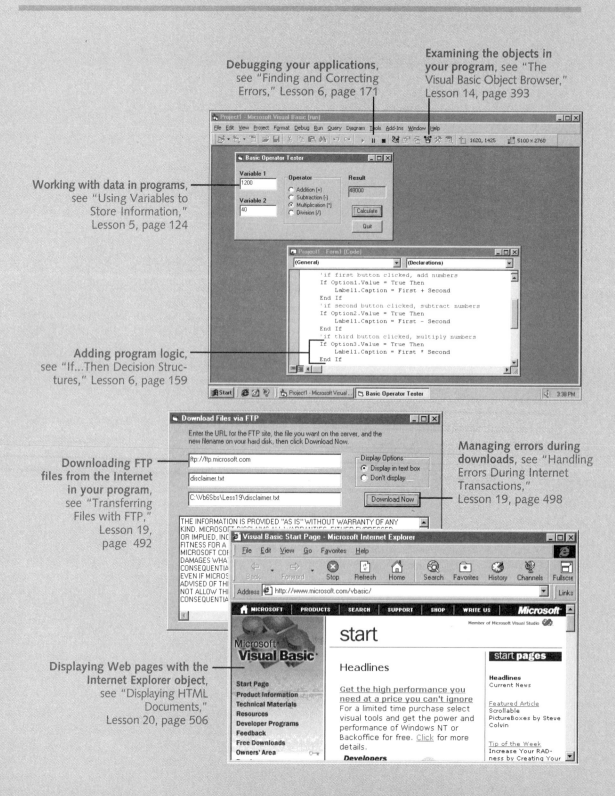

Debugging your applications, see "Finding and Correcting Errors," Lesson 6, page 171

Examining the objects in your program, see "The Visual Basic Object Browser," Lesson 14, page 393

Working with data in programs, see "Using Variables to Store Information," Lesson 5, page 124

Adding program logic, see "If...Then Decision Structures," Lesson 6, page 159

Downloading FTP files from the Internet in your program, see "Transferring Files with FTP," Lesson 19, page 492

Managing errors during downloads, see "Handling Errors During Internet Transactions," Lesson 19, page 498

Displaying Web pages with the Internet Explorer object, see "Displaying HTML Documents," Lesson 20, page 506

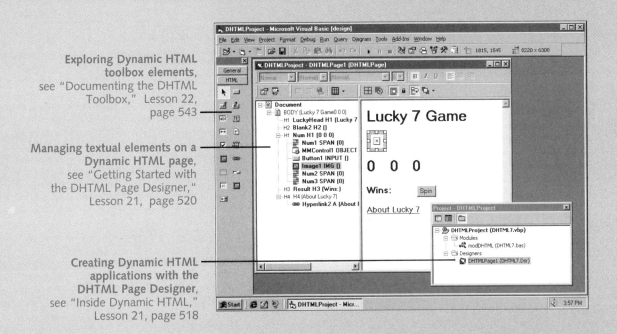

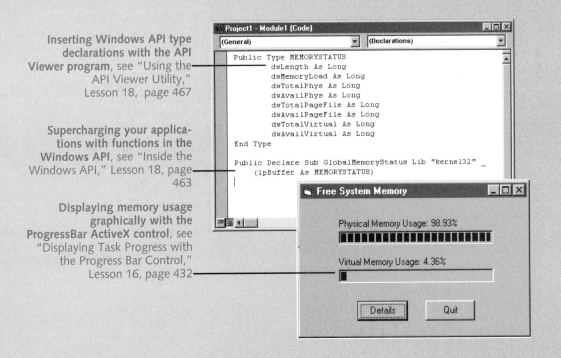

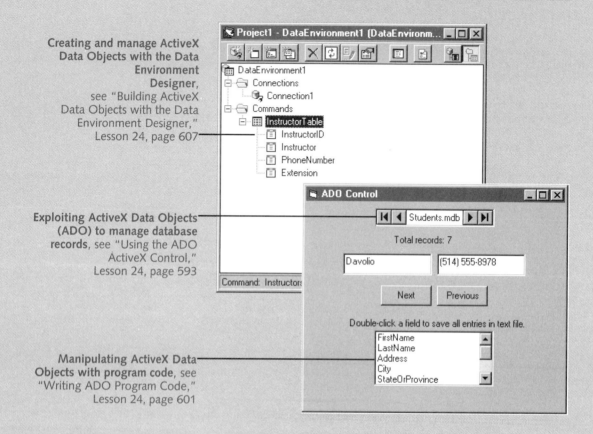

Finding Your Best Starting Point

Microsoft Visual Basic Professional 6.0 Step by Step, Second Edition, is a complete introductory programming course that teaches the Microsoft Visual Basic 6 Professional Edition software. I have designed this course with a variety of skill levels in mind so that new programmers can learn software development fundamentals in the context of useful real-world applications and so that experienced Visual Basic programmers can quickly master the essential tools and programming techniques offered in Visual Basic 6. I have also included information about how to smoothly upgrade to Visual Basic .NET—Microsoft's newest version of Visual Basic—if you eventually move along to that product.

Complementing the book's comprehensive approach is an organizational structure with 7 topically organized parts, 24 lessons, 2 appendices, and over 100 step-by-step exercises and sample programs. In this book, you'll quickly learn how to create professional-quality Visual Basic programs for Microsoft Windows and the World Wide Web. You'll also have fun!

important

Please note that the Microsoft Visual Basic 6 software isn't included with this book—you must purchase it separately and install it before you can complete the exercises I have created. You should also install Visual Studio 6 Service Pack 5, as I direct in "Installing Visual Studio 6 Service Packs." Microsoft Visual Basic 6 is sold in several different editions and product configurations, including Learning Edition, Professional Edition, Enterprise Edition, and Academic Edition. Visual Basic 6 is also distributed as a component in the Microsoft Visual Studio 6 programming suite, which includes (depending on product configuration) Microsoft Visual C++, Microsoft Visual FoxPro, Microsoft Visual InterDev, and Microsoft Visual SourceSafe. I have written this book to be compatible with the Visual Basic 6 Professional Edition and Enterprise Edition software. If your software installation is limited to Visual Basic 6 Learning Edition, you will be able to complete only Lessons 1–14 and 20.

Finding Your Best Starting Point in This Book

This book is designed to help you build skills in a number of essential areas. You can use this book if you are new to programming, switching from another programming language, or planning an eventual upgrade to Visual Basic .NET. Use the following table to find your best starting point in this book.

If you are	Follow these steps
New To programming	**1** Install the practice files as described in "Installing and Using the Practice Files" **2** Verify that you have the most recent version of Visual Basic 6 installed by reading "Installing Visual Studio 6 Service Packs." **3** Learn basic skills for using Microsoft Visual Basic by working sequentially through Lessons 1 through 14.

If you are	Follow these steps
Switching From Microsoft C++ to another Windows-based programming language	**1** Install the practice files as described in "Installing and Using the Practice Files." **2** Complete Lessons 1 and 2, skim Lessons 3 through 9, and then work through the lessons in Parts 4 and 5 sequentially. **3** For specific information about creating Internet and database programs, read Parts 6 and 7, respectively.

If you are	Follow these steps
Upgrading From Microsoft Visual Basic 5	**1** Install the practice files as described in "Installing and Using the Practice Files." **2** Skim through Lessons 1 through 13 to review the fundamentals of event-driven programming, and then work sequentially from Lessons 13 through 24. **3** For new information about creating Dynamic HTML Web pages, read Lessons 21 and 22. For critical information about ActiveX Data Objects, read Lesson 24.

If you are	Follow these steps
Planning An eventual upgrade to Microsoft Visual Basic .NET	**1** Install the practice files as described in "Installing and Using the Practice Files." **2** Skim "Visual Basic 6 vs. Visual Basic .NET" to learn about the major differences between Visual Basic 6 and Visual Basic .NET. **3** Work through Lessons 1 through 24 as your interests dictate. **4** Pay special attention to the "Upgrade Notes: What's Different in Visual Basic .NET?" sidebars near the end of each lesson, which highlight the significant differences between Visual Basic 6 and Visual Basic .NET. **5** Read Appendix A to learn about migration strategies and how to convert Visual Basic 5 programs to Visual Basic .NET using the Visual Basic Upgrade Wizard.

If you are	Follow these steps
Referencing This book after working through the lessons	**1** Use the index to locate information about specific topics, and use the table of contents and the *Quick*Look Guide to locate information about general topics. **2** Read the Quick Reference at the end of each lesson for a brief review of the major tasks in the lesson. The Quick Reference topics are listed in the same order as they are presented in the lessons.

New Features in Visual Basic 6

The following table lists the major new features in Microsoft Visual Basic that are covered in this book. The table shows the lesson in which you can learn how to use each feature. You can also use the index to find specific information about a feature or a task you want to perform.

To learn how to	See
Use the integrated Microsoft Developer Network (MSDN) online Help Library	Lesson 1
Jump-start your projects with one or more predefined forms	Lesson 8
Use Visual Basic for Applications collections	Lesson 11
Explore new sorting and encryption techniques	Lesson 12
Use Automation to integrate the features of Microsoft Office into your Visual Basic applications	Lesson 14
Play new media types with the Multimedia MCI control	Lesson 17
Use new Windows API functions	Lesson 18
Use Microsoft Internet Explorer to display HTML documents	Lesson 20
Create Dynamic HTML pages with the new DHTML Page Designer	Lesson 21
Use DHTML Toolbox Elements and ActiveX controls	Lesson 22
Distribute DHTML applications	Lesson 22
Use the new ActiveX Data Objects (ADO) control	Lesson 24
Create ADO command objects with the Data Environment Designer	Lesson 24

Corrections, Comments, and Help

Every effort has been made to ensure the accuracy of this book and the contents of the practice files CD-ROM. As corrections or changes are collected for this book, they will be integrated into the Microsoft online Help tool known as the Knowledge Base. To search the Knowledge Base and review your support options for this book or CD-ROM, click the "Search for Microsoft Press book and CD corrections" link on the Microsoft Press Support site at

http://www.microsoft.com/mspress/support

If you have problems, comments, or ideas regarding this book or the practice files CD-ROM, please send them to Microsoft Press.

Send e-mail to

mspinput@microsoft.com

Or send postal mail to

Microsoft Press
Attn:
Microsoft Visual Basic 6.0 Professional Step by Step, Second Edition, Editor
One Microsoft Way
Redmond, WA 98052-6399

Please note that support for the Visual Basic software product itself is not offered through the above addresses.

Visual Basic 6 Software Support

For help using Visual Basic in the United States, you can call the Microsoft Professional Support for Developers line at 1-800-936-5800. This service is currently available 24 hours per day and is a charge-based service. (Your version of Visual Basic or Visual Studio might provide free phone support for a limited time.) You will be connected to a real, trained Visual Studio professional when you call the support number, not an endless series of phone recordings. Check your Visual Basic product documentation for the details of your service agreement, or simply call the support number and be prepared to give them your product ID number (serial number), which you can locate by choosing the About Microsoft Visual Basic command on the Visual Basic Help menu.

Visit the Microsoft Press World Wide Web Site

You are also invited to visit the Microsoft Press World Wide Web site at the following location:

http://www.microsoft.com/mspress/

You'll find descriptions for the complete line of Microsoft Press books (including others by Michael Halvorson), information about ordering titles, notice of special features and events, additional content for Microsoft Press books, and much more.

You can also find out the latest in Visual Basic software developments and news from Microsoft Corporation by visiting the following World Wide Web site:

http://msdn.microsoft.com/vbasic/

Get online, and check it out!

Installing and Using the Practice Files

The CD-ROM inside the back cover of this book contains practice files that you'll use as you perform the exercises in the book. For example, when you're learning how to display database records with the Microsoft ActiveX Data Objects control, you'll open one of the practice files—a company database named Students.mdb—and then use the control to access the database. By using the practice files, you won't waste time creating all the samples used in the lessons. Instead, you can concentrate on learning how to master Microsoft Visual Basic programming techniques. With the files and the step-by-step instructions in the lessons, you'll also learn by doing, which is an easy and effective way to acquire and remember new skills.

important

Before you break the seal on the practice files CD-ROM, be sure that this book matches your version of the software. This book is designed for use with Microsoft Visual Basic 6 for the Microsoft Windows operating system. To find out what software you're running, you can check the product package, or you can start the software, and then on the Help menu at the top of the screen, click About Microsoft Visual Basic.

Install the Practice Files on Your Computer

Follow these steps to install the practice files on your computer's hard disk so that you can use them with the exercises in this book.

➊   Remove the CD-ROM from the package inside the back cover of this book.

➋   Insert the CD-ROM in your CD-ROM drive.

important

On many systems, Windows will automatically recognize that you have inserted a CD and start running the StartCD program. If this happens, skip to step 5.

❸ On the taskbar at the bottom of your screen, click the Start button and then click Run.

The Run dialog box appears.

❹ In the Open text box, type **d:startcd** and then click OK. Don't add spaces as you type. (If your CD-ROM drive is associated with a different drive letter, such as e, type it instead.)

❺ Click the Install Practice Files link, and follow the directions on the screen.

The setup program window appears with recommended options preselected for you. For best results in using the practice files with this book, accept these preselected settings. (If you change the installation location, you will need to manually adjust the pathnames in a few practice files to locate essential components—such as artwork and database files—when you use them.)

❻ When the files have been installed, remove the CD-ROM from your CD-ROM drive and replace it in the package inside the back cover of the book.

A folder named \Vb6Sbs has been created on your hard disk, and the practice files have been placed in that folder.

Using the Practice Files

Each lesson in this book explains when and how to use any practice files for that lesson. When it's time to use a practice file, the book will list instructions for how to open the file. The lessons are built around scenarios that simulate real programming projects, so you can easily apply the skills you learn to your own work.

For those of you who like to know all the details, the following table lists the Visual Basic projects (.vbp files) included on the practice disc.

Project	Description
Lesson 1	
StepUp	A simple animation program that welcomes you to the programming course
Lesson 2	
Lucky	Your first program—a Lucky 7 slot machine game that simulates a Las Vegas one-armed bandit
Lesson 3	
Hello	A "Hello, world!" program that demonstrates the Label and TextBox controls
Online	The user interface for an electronic shopping program, assembled using several powerful input controls
Browser	A bitmap browser tool that searches for artwork on any drive using the File System controls
Data	A simple database front end that demonstrates the efficient Data control
OleBid	A bid estimate tool that uses the OLE control to launch applications for Microsoft Windows
Lesson 4	
Menu	Shows how menus and commands are added to a form
Dialog	Uses the CommonDialog control to change the color of text on a form
Lesson 5	
VarTest	Declaring and using Variant variables to store information
MsgBox	Displaying output with the MsgBox function
InputBox	Receiving input with the InputBox function
Data	A demonstration of different fundamental data types
Constant	Using a constant to hold a fixed mathematical entity
BasicOp	Basic use of operators for addition, subtraction, multiplication, and division
AdvOp	Advanced use of operators for integer division, remainder division, exponentiation, and string concatenation
Lesson 6	
Login	Use of If...Then...Else to manage the logon process
Pass	Use of the And logical operator to check for logon password
Case	Statement used in a program to display an appropriate foreign-language welcome message
IfBug	A step-by-step debugging exercise (Can you find the logic error?)

Uninstalling the Practice Files

Use the following steps to delete the practice files added to your hard drive by the Microsoft Visual Basic Professional 6.0 Step by Step installation program:

1   Click Start, point to Settings, and then click Control Panel.

2   Double-click the Add/Remove Programs icon.

3   The Add/Remove Programs icon appears.

4 Select Microsoft Visual Basic 6 Professional Step by Step from the list, and then click Add/Remove. (Click Change/Remove if your computer is running Windows XP.)

A confirmation message appears.

5 Click Yes.

The practice files are uninstalled.

6 Click OK to close the Add/Remove Programs Properties dialog box.

7 Close the Control Panel window.

System Requirements

Microsoft Visual Basic 6 will install and run on any computer running Microsoft Windows 95 or later with 32 MB or more of memory. The Practice Files require about 12 MB of disk space.

Need Help with the Practice Files?

Every effort has been made to ensure the accuracy of this book and the contents of the practice files CD-ROM. As corrections or changes are collected for this book, they will be integrated into the Microsoft online Help tool known as the Knowledge Base. To search the Knowledge Base and review your support options for this book or CD-ROM, click the "Search for Microsoft Press book and CD corrections" link on the Microsoft Press Support site.

http://www.microsoft.com/mspress/support/search.asp

If you have problems, comments, or ideas regarding the book or the practice files CD-ROM, please send them to Microsoft Press at the following address:

mspinput@microsoft.com

Conventions and Features in This Book

You can save time when you use this book by understanding, before you start the exercises, how I offer instructions and the elements I use to communicate information about Microsoft Visual Basic programming. Please take a moment to read the following list, which identifies stylistic issues and discusses helpful features of the book that you might want to use. A few conventions are especially useful for readers who plan to upgrade Visual Basic 6 applications to Visual Basic .NET someday.

Conventions

- Hands-on exercises for you to follow are given in numbered lists of steps (1, 2, and so on). A round bullet (•) indicates an exercise that has only one step.

- Text that you are to type appears in boldface type.

- As you work through steps, you will occasionally see tables with lists of properties that you will type into Visual Basic. Text properties appear within quotes, but you do not need to type the quotes.

- A plus sign (+) between two key names means that you must press those keys at the same time. For example," "Press Alt+Tab" means that you hold down the Alt key while you press the Tab key.

- Notes labeled "tip" and accompanying text in the left margin provide additional information or alternative methods for a step.

- Control icons and buttons shown in the left margin provide visual hints as to which interface elements you should click in the Visual Basic programming environment to create application objects and execute commands.

■ Notes labeled "note" or "important" alert you to essential information that you should check before continuing with the lesson.

tip

important

note

Other Features of This Book

■ You can learn special programming techniques, background information, or features related to the information being discussed by reading the shaded sidebars that appear throughout the lessons. These sidebars often highlight difficult terminology or suggest future areas for exploration.

■ You can learn about options or techniques that build on what you learned in a lesson by trying the optional "One Step Further" exercise at the end of the lesson.

■ You can get a quick reminder of how to perform the tasks you learned by reading the Quick Reference at the end of a lesson.

Planning for Visual Basic .NET

If you plan to upgrade Visual Basic 6 programs to Visual Basic .NET eventually, you should be aware of the following three features in this book that are designed to help you evaluate and upgrade your existing projects quickly:

■ The next section of this book ("Visual Basic 6 vs. Visual Basic .NET"), which describes briefly how Visual Basic 6 differs from Visual Basic .NET and gives a few of the reasons you might—or might not—want to upgrade to Visual Basic .NET in the future.

■ "Upgrade Notes" sidebars, near the end of each lesson, which provide a basic overview or "executive summary" of the new features in Visual Basic .NET. Use these sidebars if you are interested in how Visual Basic .NET has changed in the context of an individual topic such as variable declaration, Toolbox controls, or database programming. The goal of these sidebars is not to convert you immediately to Visual Basic .NET programming, but to make you aware of pertinent features so that you can be ready when you eventually need to upgrade.

■ A special appendix, "Appendix A: Upgrading Visual Basic 6 Programs to Visual Basic .NET," which is located immediately after Lesson 24. This appendix describes how to evaluate your existing Visual Basic 6 programs and how to upgrade them to Visual Basic .NET using Internet resources and the new Visual Basic Upgrade Wizard (a tool supplied with Visual Basic .NET Professional Edition).

Visual Basic 6 vs.
Visual Basic .NET

Visual Basic 6 was released in September 1998, and it quickly became the world's most popular rapid application development (RAD) tool, enjoying an installed base of over 3.5 million programmers. In February 2002, Microsoft released a new version of the Visual Basic development system—Microsoft Visual Basic .NET—and this programming tool has also become popular, attracting many Visual Basic 6 developers, as well as programmers familiar with other development products, such as Java and Visual C++. Since Visual Basic 6 and Visual Basic .NET now coexist in the marketplace, one might ask what the differences are between the two development systems, and how smooth it is to upgrade from Visual Basic 6 to Visual Basic .NET. This section briefly addresses these questions.

Visual Basic 6.0 Features

Visual Basic 6.0 is a comprehensive development system designed to create graphical applications for both Microsoft Windows and the Web. In particular, Visual Basic 6 offers the following features:

- A fast native code compiler, which creates quick applications and components

- Familiar user interface components and tools that support drag-and-drop development techniques

- Support for Microsoft Internet Information Services applications

- Professional Visual Database Tools, so that you can view tables, modify data, and create SQL queries within the integrated development environment

- ActiveX Data Objects technology, for quickly accessing distributed data sources

- DHTML Page Designer, for creating fast and efficient Web applications

- Professional Edition tools and ActiveX controls, for creating fast, interesting, and useful applications that are commercial quality

- Professional setup and distributions tools, which quickly install Visual Basic applications on other systems

- Object Automation technology, which allows you to use the features of Automation-compatible applications (such as Microsoft Office) remotely

Although the .NET version of Visual Basic has been released, Microsoft remains firmly committed to the Visual Basic 6 programming language and has promised to sell and support the product through 2007. In addition, some developers have chosen to stick with the Visual Basic 6 Development System, either because their workgroup or company has not chosen to upgrade or because they are not currently running an operating system that supports Visual Basic .NET. (Visual Basic .NET development is supported only on Windows 2000 and Windows XP systems—Windows 98 and Windows Me are not supported as development platforms, although Windows 98 and Windows Me systems can run Visual Basic .NET applications.) For these and other reasons, Visual Basic 6 will continue to be a popular programming tool for years to come, and learning Visual Basic 6 development skills remains a very worthwhile activity.

Visual Basic .NET Features

Visual Basic .NET is a major upgrade to the Visual Basic 6 product, and it has been developed in conjunction with the full complement of tools in the Visual Studio .NET software suite. Because of this joint development, Visual Basic .NET shares a common user interface and integrated development environment with the Visual C++ .NET, Visual C# .NET, and Visual J# .NET languages, as well as the other development tools in Visual Studio .NET. Visual Basic .NET was also rewritten from scratch to support an elegant new programming model called the .NET Framework, and this model has brought numerous benefits, including full object-oriented capabilities, such as code inheritance; structured error handling; new threading models; and freedom from the constraints of COM. However, moving to a new programming model has also necessitated changes in how Visual Basic programmers build their code, including the removal of so-called "legacy" language features in Visual Basic (keywords such as GoTo), the replacement of the DHTML programming model with Web Forms programming, an upgrade of the ADO database programming paradigm to a related model called ADO.NET, and the addition of several new controls and tools.

Here's a list of the major new tools and features that await you in Visual Basic .NET:

- A shared development environment, which allows all of the Visual Studio .NET languages (Visual C++ .NET, Visual C# .NET, and Visual J# .NET) to be used together

- Two new forms packages (Windows Forms and Web Forms) for creating applications for Windows and the Web

- A new version of ADO (ADO.NET) for interacting with disconnected data sources on local computers, networks, and the Web

- An enhanced and streamlined Visual Basic programming language

- The .NET Framework, a collection of useful libraries and APIs that can be used to perform numerous system-level tasks and augment the Visual Basic programming language

- Full support for object-oriented programming, including such features as code inheritance, method overloading, and shared members

- Enhanced deployment options and tools, including the so-called "xcopy" deployment, in which program files are installed by simply copying them to a new folder on the user's system

- Rich support for XML (Extensible Markup Language), a method for describing structured data on the Web and other locations (The World Wide Web Consortium (W3C) defines XML standards so that structured data will be uniform and independent of applications.)

- The ability to create scalable Web sites with Web Forms and ADO.NET working in combination

- Rich support for external devices, such as printers

- Visual Basic .NET is now an" "equal player" in the Visual Studio .NET software suite, with application performance equivalent to Visual C++ .NET and Visual C# .NET programs

Upgrading to Visual Basic .NET

Upgrading to Visual Basic .NET is something that you can do gradually if you choose to purchase the Visual Basic .NET software. The purpose of this book is not to convince you to upgrade to Visual Basic .NET immediately, but to prepare you for the upgrade if you choose to migrate your code to Visual Basic .NET down the road. The first step in upgrading to Visual Basic .NET is usually running the Visual Basic .NET Upgrade Wizard, which starts automatically in Visual Basic .NET Professional Edition, Enterprise Developer Edition, or Enterprise Architect Edition when you open a Visual Basic 6 program. This tool is described in Appendix A: "Upgrading Visual Basic 6 Programs to Visual Basic .NET." Microsoft suggests that 95 percent of your upgrade tasks can be handled automatically when you run this tool.

When a Visual Basic project is upgraded, the program code is modified automatically to match the new syntax of Visual Basic .NET, and Visual Basic 6 Forms are converted to Windows Forms. After these preliminary steps, the Upgrade Wizard highlights the areas in your code where additional programming is required. This last step is necessary because certain objects and language features either have no equivalent in Visual Basic .NET or have an equivalent too dissimilar for an automatic upgrade. One interesting aspect of this code upgrade is that all languages in the Visual Studio .NET programming suite utilize the same variable types, arrays, user-defined types, classes, and interfaces as Visual Basic .NET. Once you learn the basics of Visual Basic .NET, you've gone a long way toward learning the remaining tools in Visual Studio .NET as well.

As you explore Visual Basic 6 programming techniques in this book, keep in mind that your new skills can immediately be applied in the Visual Basic .NET development system. As the lessons demonstrate, there are many aspects of Visual Basic 6 programming that are essentially identical in Visual Basic .NET. When there are significant differences, I'll mention them in a sidebar near the end of the lesson.

Installing Visual Studio 6 Service Packs

Since the first release of Visual Basic 6 in September 1998, Microsoft has updated the Visual Basic software with bug fixes, product enhancements, and additional software components such as drivers and administration tools. These updates are distributed periodically via service packs, which supplement your existing Visual Basic software and make it compatible with other programs, including recent tools distributed by Microsoft. For example, recent Visual Basic service packs enable the Visual Basic 6 database tools to work with Microsoft Access 2000 databases—something that was not possible when Visual Basic 6 was first released in 1998. Service packs are available for Visual Basic 6 alone and also for the entire Visual Studio 6 software suite. The service pack you need depends on the software that you have installed. Detailed information, including download instructions, can be found at the following Microsoft Web site at

http://support.microsoft.com/default.aspx?scid=kb;en-us;Q194022

The CD-ROM included with this book contains Visual Studio 6 Service Pack 5 (SP5), the service pack designed to upgrade all components of Visual Studio 6, including all versions of Visual Basic 6 (Learning Edition, Professional Edition, and Enterprise Edition). SP5 was the most recent service pack available when this book was printed in November 2002. To complete the lessons in this book and to get the most out of the Visual Basic programming system, you'll want to install SP5. Note that since SP5 contains all the previous service pack fixes and components, it is not necessary to install earlier versions. SP5 does not include the Visual Basic .NET development system, however, which is a separate upgrade to Visual Basic.

Checking the Current Service Pack Installation

Not all readers of this book will need to install SP5. Depending on when you purchased the Visual Basic 6 software and installed it, SP5 may have been a component in your original software installation, or someone in your workgroup or school might have installed it later. Before you install SP5, check your existing version of Visual Basic to see which service pack version you have installed, if any.

Complete these steps to check your service pack version:

① In Microsoft Windows, click the Start button, point to Programs, and point to the Microsoft Visual Basic 6.0 folder.

② Click the Microsoft Visual Basic 6.0 program icon.

The New Project dialog box appears, a feature that will be explained thoroughly in Lesson 1.

③ Click Open to open a new, default Visual Basic project.

A new project opens in the Visual Basic programming environment. Now you can check your Visual Basic version.

④ On the Help menu, click the About Microsoft Visual Basic command.

The About Microsoft Visual Basic dialog box appears, as shown in the following illustration:

The About dialog box describes the version of Visual Basic you are using, and the top line of the dialog box indicates the service pack version that is installed, if any. If you see the text "Visual Basic 6.0 (SP5)," you know the current service pack is installed and you won't need to install SP5 again. If you don't see SP5, however, you should install the most recent service pack.

① Click OK to close the About dialog box.

② On the File menu, click the Exit command.

When you are asked whether you want to save your changes to the new Visual Basic project you opened, click No.

Visual Basic closes, and you are ready to install the service pack. (Service packs can't be installed when the Visual Basic software is running.)

Installing Visual Studio 6.0 Service Pack 5

Follow these steps to upgrade Visual Basic 6 with the Visual Studio 6.0 Service Pack 5:

① Remove the CD-ROM from the package inside the back cover of this book, and insert the CD-ROM into your CD-ROM drive.

If you just installed this book's practice files, the CD-ROM might still be in the CD-ROM drive.

② In the StartCD window, click the Install Visual Studio 6 SP5 link.

③ Follow the directions on the screen to extract the Service Pack 5 files to a directory on your computer such as C:\VS6SP5.

④ On the Windows Taskbar, click the Start button and then click Run.

⑤ In the Run dialog box, type **c:\vs6sp5\setupsp5.exe** and then click OK. (If you installed the Service Pack 5 files to a directory other than C:\VS6SP5, use that directory instead.)

⑥ Follow the directions on the screen.

Service Pack 5 modifies your Visual Basic 6 program installation (and any other Visual Studio components you have installed) and then prompts you to restart your system.

⑦ When the installation is complete, remove the CD-ROM from the CD-ROM drive and replace it in the package inside the back cover of the book.

important

You should install Service Pack 5 before you compile and distribute any Visual Basic 6 applications. Feature enhancements are included in the service pack that will be important for the users of your applications. If additional service packs are released after Service Pack 5, you can locate and download them by monitoring the following Web site:

http://support.microsoft.com/default.aspx?scid=kb;en-us;Q194022

PART 1

Getting Started with Visual Basic

Opening and Running a Visual Basic Program

ESTIMATED TIME
30 min.

In this lesson you will learn how to:

- ✔ *Start Visual Basic.*
- ✔ *Use the Visual Basic programming environment.*
- ✔ *Open and run a Visual Basic program.*
- ✔ *Change a property setting.*
- ✔ *Use online Help and exit Visual Basic.*

Microsoft Visual Basic's ability to perform some impressive tasks rests on key fundamentals we'll cover carefully in the first part of this book. After a few lessons, you'll see that it's easy to use Visual Basic to write powerful Microsoft Windows–based programs. Even if you haven't written a program before, you'll find that programming uses many of the same reasoning abilities and computer skills you use every day. In this lesson, you'll learn how to start Visual Basic and how to use the Visual Basic Programming System to open and run a simple program. You'll learn the essential Visual Basic menu commands and programming procedures; you'll open and run a simple Visual Basic program called StepUp; and you'll get your feet wet by changing a programming setting called a property. You'll also learn how to get more information by using online Help and how to exit Visual Basic safely.

The Visual Basic Programming Environment

The Visual Basic programming environment contains all the tools you need to build powerful programs for Windows quickly and efficiently. Use the following procedures to start Visual Basic now.

important

If you haven't yet installed this book's practice files, work through "Finding Your Best Starting Point" and "Installing and Using the Practice Files" at the beginning of the book. Then return to this lesson.

Start Visual Basic

1 In Microsoft Windows, click the Start button, point to Programs, and point to the Microsoft Visual Basic 6.0 folder. The icons in the Microsoft Visual Basic 6.0 folder appear in a list.

tip

If your copy of Visual Basic is part of the Microsoft Visual Studio suite of development tools, point to the Microsoft Visual Studio folder to display the Visual Basic 6.0 program icon. The instructions in Parts 1–4 of this book apply equally to Visual Basic Learning Edition, Professional Edition, and Enterprise Edition.

2 Click the Microsoft Visual Basic 6.0 program icon.

The New Project dialog box appears. This dialog box prompts you for the type of programming project you want to create. (The exact contents of the dialog box depend on the edition of Visual Basic that you're using.)

3 Click Open to accept the default new project, a standard 32-bit Visual Basic application.

A new project opens in the Visual Basic programming environment, along with some of the windows and tools shown in the illustration on the following page.

The Visual Basic programming environment contains programming tools to help you construct your Visual Basic programs. The *menu bar* provides access to most of the commands that control the programming environment. Menus and commands work as they do in all Windows-based programs, and you can access them by using the keyboard or the mouse. Located below the menu bar is the *toolbar,* a collection of buttons that serve as shortcuts for executing commands and controlling the Visual Basic programming environment. If you've used Microsoft Excel or Microsoft Word, the toolbar should be a familiar concept. To activate a button on the toolbar, click the button using the mouse. Along the bottom of the screen is the Windows *taskbar.* You can use the taskbar to switch between various Visual Basic components and to activate other Windows-based programs. You may also see a taskbar icon for Microsoft Internet Explorer or another Internet browser program.

To display the function of a toolbar button, position the mouse pointer over the button for a few moments.

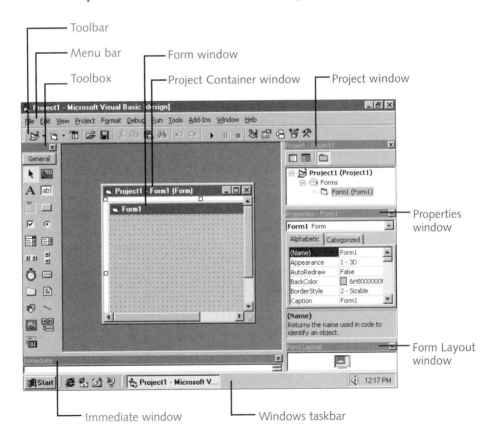

Other available features that you may see are the toolbox, the Project Container window, the Form window, the Project window, the Immediate window, the Properties window, and the Form Layout window. The exact size and shape of these windows depends on how your system has been configured. In Visual Basic versions 5 and 6, you can align and attach, or *dock*, windows to make all the elements of the programming system visible and accessible. You'll learn how to use these features to customize your programming environment in this way later in the lesson.

tip

The appearance of your Visual Basic programming environment will also depend on the version of Windows that you are using. For example, Windows XP forms might have a different button configuration on the title bar and slightly rounded windows. You can also see more of the Visual Basic programming environment if you set your Windows desktop properties to 800 x 600 or greater. To do this, right-click the Windows desktop, click Properties, click the Settings tab, and then move the Screen Resolution (or Desktop Area or Screen Area) slider to 800 x 600 or greater.

In the following exercise, you'll practice using the menu bar and toolbar to load and run a sample Visual Basic program called StepUp.

Use the menu bar to open an existing programming project

1 On the File menu, click the Open Project command.

The Open Project dialog box appears. This dialog box allows you to open any existing Visual Basic program on your hard disk, Internet connection or network drive, CD-ROM, or floppy disk:

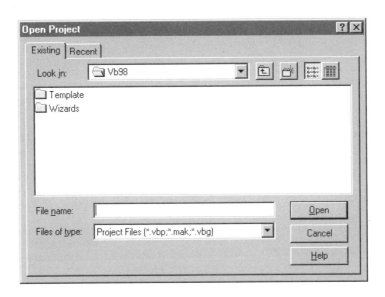

Visual Basic project files are distinguished by the .vbp, the .mak, or the .vbg filename extension.

Up One Level button

❷ Browse to the C:\Vb6Sbs\Less01 folder by clicking the Up One Level button three times, double-clicking the Vb6Sbs folder in the root directory, and then double-clicking the Less01 folder.

The \Vb6Sbs folder (the default folder created by the Visual Basic 6 Step by Step Practice Files installation program) contains all the practice and sample files for the book. You'll use the Less*xx* folder corresponding to each lesson as you work your way through this book.

❸ In the Less01 folder, click the StepUp.vbp project, and then click Open.

The StepUp project file loads the user interface form, the properties, the program code, and the standard module of the StepUp program.

❹ If the StepUp form is not visible, double-click the Forms folder in the Project window, and then click Form1 (StepUp.frm).

Before you can work with a component in a project, you must select it in the Project window.

View Object button

❺ Click the View Object button in the Project window to take a look at the program's user interface.

The program form appears, as shown in the illustration on the following page.

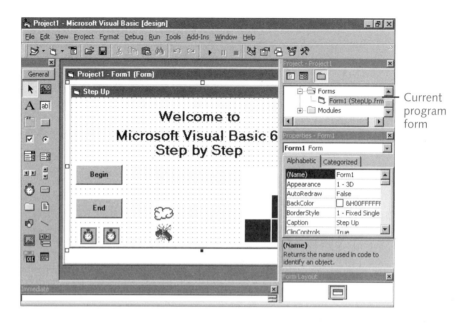

Current program form

If you don't see the project container around the form, it is maximized and you need to click the Restore Window button on the toolbar to view the project as shown.

StepUp is just a simple Visual Basic program designed to get you in the swing of things. Because StepUp contains several of the elements found in a typical Visual Basic program, you can use it to explore some of the fundamentals of the programming environment. When you run StepUp, it displays some animation and a message welcoming you to this book.

Start button

6 Click the Start button on the Visual Basic toolbar to run the StepUp program in the Visual Basic environment.

The toolbox and the Properties window disappear, and the StepUp program starts to run.

7 Click the Begin button to see some simple animation. Your screen will look like the following illustration.

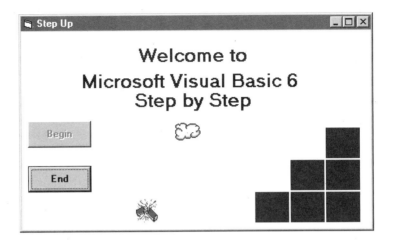

8 Click the End button to quit the program and return to the programming environment. That's all there is to it—you've just run your first program in Visual Basic!

Moving, Docking, and Resizing Tools

With seven programming tools to contend with on the screen, the Visual Basic development environment can become a pretty busy place. To give you complete control over the shape and size of the elements in the development environment, Visual Basic 6 lets you move, dock, and resize each of the programming tools.

In the Visual Basic development environment, you can use docking to organize your programming tools.

To move a window, the toolbox, or the toolbar, simply click the title bar and drag the object to a new location. If you align one window along the edge of another window, it will attach itself, or *dock*, to that window. Dockable windows are advantageous because they always remain visible. (They won't become hidden behind other windows.)

If you want to see more of a docked window, simply drag one of its borders to view more content. If you get tired of docking and want your tools to overlap each other, click the Options command on the Tools menu, click the Docking tab, and then remove the check mark from each tool you want to stand on its own (that is, make an overlapping window).

As you work through the following sections, practice moving, docking, and resizing the different tools in the Visual Basic programming environment until you feel comfortable arranging them to suit you.

The User Interface Form

Each form is a window in your user interface.

In Visual Basic, a *form* is a window you customize to create the user interface of your program. In the StepUp program, the form is the window you saw while the program was running. A form can contain menus, buttons, list boxes, scroll bars, and any of the other items you've seen in a typical Windows-based program. When you start the Visual Basic programming environment, a default form called Form1 appears. On this form is a standard grid (a group of regularly spaced dots) that you can use to create and line up the elements of your program's user interface. You can adjust the size of the form by using the mouse; the form can take up part or all of the screen. You can add additional forms by clicking the Add Form command on the Project menu.

If part of the form is covered by the programming tools, you can either close or resize the programming tools so that they take up less space, or you can click the form's title bar and drag the form until you can see the hidden parts. Moving the form around the screen in the development environment has no effect on the form's location on the screen when the program actually runs. This runtime characteristic is controlled by the Form Layout window. To set the starting place for a new form, simply drag the tiny preview form in the Form Layout window to the location you want.

The Toolbox

Toolbox button

You can move the toolbox to another location on the screen by clicking the toolbox title bar and dragging the toolbox.

You add the elements of a program's user interface to a form by using the tools, or *controls,* in the toolbox. To open the toolbox, click the Toolbox button on the toolbar. The toolbox is typically located along the left side of the screen. It contains controls that you can use to add artwork, labels, buttons, list boxes, scroll bars, menus, and geometric shapes to a user interface. Each control you add to a form becomes an *object,* or programmable user interface element, in your program. These elements will be visible to the user of your program when the program runs and will operate like the standard objects in any Windows-based application.

The toolbox also contains controls that you can use to create objects that perform special "behind the scenes" operations in a Visual Basic program. These powerful objects do useful work but are not visible to the user when the program is running; they include objects for manipulating information in databases, working with Windows-based applications, and tracking the passage of time in your programs.

You can display the name of a control in the toolbox by placing the mouse pointer over the control for a few moments. You'll start using the controls in the toolbox later on in Lesson 2.

The Properties Window

The Properties window lets you change the characteristics, or *property settings*, of the user interface elements on a form. A property setting is a quality of one of the objects in your user interface. For example, the welcome message the StepUp program displayed can be modified to appear in a different font or font size or with a different alignment. (With Visual Basic, you can display text in any font installed on your system, just as you would in Excel or Word.) You can change property settings by using the Properties window while you are creating your user interface or you can add program code via the Code window to change one or more property settings while your program is running.

The Properties window contains an object drop-down list box that itemizes all the user interface elements (objects) on the form; the Properties window also lists the property settings that can be changed for each object. (You can click one of two convenient tabs to view properties alphabetically or by category.) You'll practice changing the Caption property of the End button in the StepUp program now.

Change a property

1 Verify that the StepUp program has stopped running. (You'll see the word *design* in the title bar when the program has stopped.) Then click the End object on the form.

When the End object (a command button) appears surrounded by rectangles, it is *selected*. To work with an object on a Visual Basic form, you must select the object first.

Properties Window button

2 Click the Properties Window button on the toolbar.

The Properties window is activated in the programming environment. (If the Properties window was not open, it will appear now.)

3 Double-click the Properties window title bar to display it as a floating (non-docked) window.

You'll see a window similar to the illustration on the following page.

Caption property

The Properties window lists all the property settings for the second command button on the form. (In all, 33 properties are available to the command buttons.) Property names are listed in the left column of the window, and the current setting for each property is listed in the right column. On the Alphabetic tab, the properties are listed in alphabetical order.

④ Scroll in the list box until the Caption property is visible.

The Properties window scrolls like a regular list box.

⑤ Double-click the Caption property (in the left column).

The current caption ("End") is highlighted in the right column, and a cursor blinks to the right of it.

⑥ Press Del, type **Quit**, and then press Enter.

The setting of the Caption property is changed from "End" to "Quit." The caption changes on the form, and the next time you run the program, *Quit* will appear inside the command button.

⑦ Return the Properties window to a docked position above the Project window.

Thinking About Properties

In Visual Basic, each user interface element in a program (including the form itself) has a set of definable properties. You can set properties at design time by using the Properties window. Properties also can be referenced in code as the program runs to do meaningful work. (User interface elements that receive input often use properties to convey information to the program.) At first, you may find properties a difficult concept to grasp. Viewing them in terms of something from everyday life can help.

Consider this bicycle analogy: a bicycle is an object you use to ride from one place to another. Because a bicycle is a physical object, it has several inherent characteristics. It has a brand name, a color, gears, brakes, and wheels, and it is built in a particular style. (It may be a touring bike, a mountain bike, or a bicycle built for two.) In Visual Basic terminology, these characteristics are *properties* of the bicycle object. The mold that created the bicycle frame would be called the bicycle control. Most of the bicycle's properties would be defined while the bicycle was being built. But others (tires, travel speed, age, and options such as reflectors and mirrors) could be properties that changed as the bicycle is used. As you work with Visual Basic, you'll find object properties of both types.

This is a good time to practice your docking technique. Double-clicking the title bar is the quickest method, or you can fine-tune the window's position by dragging it above the edge of the Project window. Because there are so many windows close together, "manual docking" takes some practice and can be a little frustrating at first. But when you use these programming tools later, you'll benefit greatly from a well-organized workspace and your experimentation time will pay off.

The Project Window

A Visual Basic program is made up of several files that are assembled together, or *compiled,* when a program is complete. As you work on a project you will need to switch back and forth between these components. To help you, the designers of Visual Basic have included a *Project window* in the programming environment. (This tool is also known as the *Project Explorer* in some circles.) The Project window lists all the files used in the programming process and provides access to them via two special buttons: View Code and View Object. When you add and save individual files to and remove files from a project by using commands on the File and Project menus, these changes are reflected in the Project window.

The project file that maintains the list of all the supporting files in a programming project is called the *Visual Basic project (.vbp)* file. In Visual Basic versions 5 and 6, more than one project file can be loaded in the Project window at once. You can switch back and forth between them by clicking the project name. Beneath the project name, the Project window displays the components of each project in a tree structure similar to the outline view presented by Windows Explorer. You can expand and collapse its "branches," including Forms, Modules, and other categories, by clicking the plus and minus signs next to the folders.

In the next exercise, you'll examine the Project window for the StepUp program.

Display the Project window

Project Explorer button

1 Click the Project Explorer button on the toolbar.

The Project window (aka the Project Explorer) is activated in the programming environment. (If the window was not open, it will appear now.)

2 Double-click the Project window's title bar to display it as a floating (non-docked) window.

You'll see a Project window that looks like the illustration below.

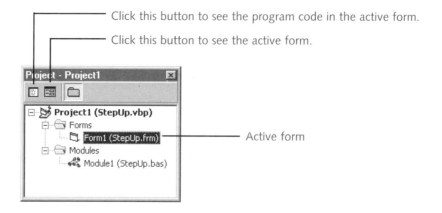

Click this button to see the program code in the active form.

Click this button to see the active form.

Active form

❸ Click the plus signs next to the Forms and Modules folders (if you haven't already) to view all the project's components.

The project file in this programming project is named StepUp.vbp. In the StepUp.vbp project, the files StepUp.frm and StepUp.bas are listed. StepUp.frm contains the user interface form and any program code associated with the objects on the form. StepUp.bas contains code shared by all parts of the program. Later on, when the program is compiled into an executable file (or prepared so that it can run under Windows), these files will be combined to form a single .exe file.

❹ Double-click the Project window's title bar to return it to its docked position.

Getting Help

Visual Basic includes an online reference that you can use to learn more about the programming environment, development tools, and programming language in the Visual Basic Programming System. Take a moment to explore your help resources before moving to the next lesson, where you will build your first program.

tip

Visual Basic online Help is provided by two Microsoft Developer Network (MSDN) Library CDs. If you have about 95 MB of extra disk space, you can copy all the Visual Basic documentation onto your system from these CDs. Alternatively, you can insert the required CD into your CD-ROM drive each time that you use the Visual Basic online Help.

You can access Help information in several ways.

To get Help information	Do this
By topic or activity	On the Visual Basic Help menu, click Contents to open the MSDN Library.
While working in the Code window	Click the keyword or program statement you're interested in and press F1.

(continued)

To get Help information	Do this
While working in a dialog box	Click the Help button in the dialog box.
By searching for a specific keyword	On the Help menu, click Search and type the term you're looking for in the MSDN Library Search tab.
By connecting to a Web page with information about Visual Basic or programming	On the Help menu, point to the Microsoft On The Web submenu, and then click the topic or location you're interested in.
About contacting Microsoft for product support	On the Help menu, click Technical Support.

Use the following steps to get help on a specific topic in Visual Basic. This practice exercise instructs you to search for information about the Project window, but you can substitute your own topic.

Get help on a specific topic

The Help menu is your door to the Visual Basic Help system.

1 Click the Help menu on the menu bar.

The contents of the Help menu appear.

2 On the Help menu, click Contents.

Visual Basic starts the MSDN Library. (Insert the appropriate MSDN Library CD if you are prompted to do so.)

3 Maximize the MSDN Library window.

The MSDN Library displays Help information in HTML format. When you first open the MSDN Library, the window on the right displays a few introductory topics of interest to software developers. The window on the left lets you navigate to a particular topic of interest. When you select a topic, the window on the right displays the associated Help file.

4 Click the Index tab in the MSDN Library.

5 Type **project explorer** (or another search topic) in the text box.

As you type the words *project explorer*, Help topics beginning with "p," then "pr," and so on appear in the list box. Continue typing until you see the topic Project Explorer.

6 Double-click the Project Explorer topic in the list box.

The MSDN Library searches for each occurrence of Project Explorer in the Help system and displays the results in the Topics Found dialog box.

7 Double-click the Project Explorer (Visual Basic Reference) topic.

The MSDN Library displays information about the Visual Basic Project Explorer in the right window. Scroll bars provide access to any information you can't see in the window. Take a few minutes to read the article, and to explore the other resources of the MSDN Library.

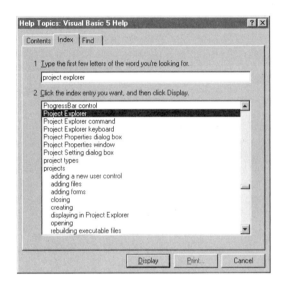

8 Click the Exit command on the MSDN Library File menu to exit the Help system.

The MSDN Library is a useful resource for learning about the programming environment or any topic related to Visual Basic programming. Be sure to use it if you have a question.

One Step Further   Exiting Visual Basic

When you're finished using Visual Basic for the day, save any projects that are open and close the programming system. Give it a try.

Exit Visual Basic

1 Save any changes you have made to your program by clicking the Save button on the toolbar. (If you are prompted for the name and location of your project's components, specify them as directed.)

2 On the File menu, click the Exit command.

The Visual Basic program exits. Nothing to it!

If you want to continue to the next lesson

● Fire up Visual Basic again and turn to Lesson 2.

If you want to stop using Visual Basic for now

● Simply walk away from your computer. Or, if you haven't quit yet, click the Exit command on the File menu to close Visual Basic.

If you see a Save dialog box, click Yes.

Upgrade Notes: What's Different in Visual Basic .NET?

Although this book focuses exclusively on Visual Basic 6.0 programming techniques, a newer version of Visual Basic is now available—Visual Basic .NET—and I want to make you aware of that product as you work through this book so that you can easily upgrade to Visual Basic .NET if you choose to do so in the future. Since Visual Basic .NET is a major upgrade, more than a few Visual Basic 6.0 tools and controls have changed, and there are also several new and exciting technologies to exploit. To address a few of these migration issues, I conclude each lesson in this book with a sidebar that highlights how Visual Basic .NET has diverged from the Visual Basic 6.0 that you are learning. For more specific details, see "Visual Basic 6.0 vs. Visual Basic .NET" in the front matter and "Appendix A: Upgrading Visual Basic 6 Programs to Visual Basic .NET."

Here are the Visual Basic .NET upgrade notes for this lesson:

- In Visual Basic .NET, the Visual Basic programming environment is now an integrated component in the Visual Studio .NET development environment—in other words, Visual Basic .NET shares a common development environment with Microsoft Visual C++ .NET, Microsoft Visual C# .NET, and several other programming tools. Although Visual Basic .NET and Visual C++ .NET are still different programming languages, they share the same programming tools, Code window, Toolbox controls, and so on.

- As part of its new development environment, Visual Studio .NET offers a new Get Started pane, which shows recently used projects and lets you open new or existing source files. Additional links on the Get Started pane provide you with access to Visual Studio Web sites, profile information, and contacts in the Visual Studio development community.

- The Visual Studio .NET development environment contains several new and modified programming tools. The Project window is now called the Solution Explorer, and there is a new context sensitive help window called Dynamic Help. You'll find that the toolbox has really changed— it is now subdivided into several functional categories, from Windows Forms to Web Forms to Data.

- Most of the programming tools can now be *pinned*, or attached, to other tool windows.

- Projects are now saved in a different way in Visual Studio .NET. You give your project a name *before* you create it. The project itself now is spread over several files and folders—even more than in Visual Basic 6.0.

Lesson 1 Quick Reference

To	Do this	Button
Start Visual Basic	Click the Start button on the taskbar. Then point to Programs, point to the Visual Basic 6.0 folder, and click the Visual Basic 6.0 program icon.	Start
Display a button's function	Place the mouse pointer over the button.	
Open an existing project	Start Visual Basic. On the File menu, click the Open Project command.	
Start a new project	Start Visual Basic. On the File menu, click the New Project command.	
Run a program	Click the Start button on the toolbar. *or* Press F5.	▶
Dock a programming tool	Click the title bar and drag the tool to the edge of another tool until it snaps into place. To see more of a docked tool, double-click the title bar or resize it with the mouse.	
Move the toolbox	Drag the toolbox by using the mouse.	
Set properties	Click the Properties Window button on the toolbar to display the Properties window (if it is not open), and then double-click the Properties window title bar. Open the object drop-down list box to display the user interface elements on your form, click the object you want to set properties for, and then click the property settings you want in the Properties list box.	

Lesson 1 Quick Reference

To	Do this	Button
Display the Project window	Click the Project Explorer button on the toolbar (if the Project window is not open), and then double-click the Project window's title bar.	
Quit Visual Basic	On the File menu, click Exit.	

2

Writing Your First Program

In this lesson you will learn how to:

- ✔ *Create the user interface for a new program.*
- ✔ *Set the properties for each object in your user interface.*
- ✔ *Write program code.*
- ✔ *Save and run the program.*
- ✔ *Build an executable file.*
- ✔ *Use the Package & Deployment Wizard.*

ESTIMATED
TIME
35 min.

As you learned in Lesson 1, the Microsoft Visual Basic programming environment contains several powerful tools to help you run and manage your programs. Visual Basic also contains everything you need to build your own applications for Windows from the ground up. In this lesson, you'll learn how to create a simple but attractive user interface with the controls in the Visual Basic toolbox. Next, you'll learn how to customize the operation of these controls with special characteristics called property settings. Then, you'll see how to identify just what your program should do with text-based program code. Finally, you'll learn how to save and run your new program (a Las Vegas–style slot machine) and how to compile it as an executable file.

Lucky Seven: Your First Visual Basic Program

The Windows-based application you're going to construct is Lucky Seven, a game program that simulates a lucky number slot machine. Lucky Seven has a simple user interface and can be created and compiled in just a few minutes using Visual Basic. (If you'd like to run a completed version of Lucky.exe before you start, you can find it in the \Vb6Sbs\Less02 folder on your hard disk.) Here's what your program will look like when it's finished:

Programming Steps

The Lucky Seven user interface contains two command buttons, three lucky number windows, a graphic of a stack of coins, and the label Lucky Seven. These elements were produced in the program by creating seven objects on the Lucky Seven form and then changing several properties for each object. After the interface was designed, program code for the Spin and End command buttons was added to the program to process the user's button clicks and produce the random numbers. To re-create Lucky Seven, you'll follow three essential programming steps in Visual Basic: creating the user interface, setting the properties, and writing the program code. The process for Lucky Seven is summarized in the table on the following page.

Programming step	Number of items
1. Create the user interface.	7 objects
2. Set the properties.	10 properties
3. Write the program code.	2 objects

Another way to think about the Lucky Seven program is to use the following *algorithm*, or list of programming steps. Creating an algorithm can be a useful starting point when developing a program.

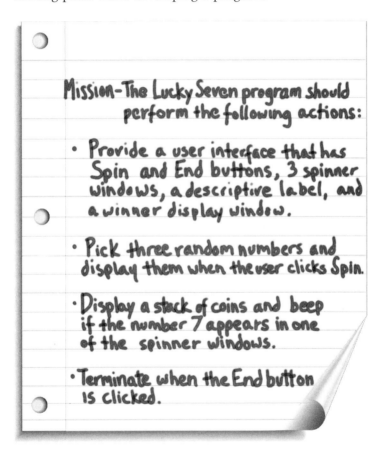

Mission-The Lucky Seven program should perform the following actions:

- Provide a user interface that has Spin and End buttons, 3 spinner windows, a descriptive label, and a winner display window.

- Pick three random numbers and display them when the user clicks Spin.

- Display a stack of coins and beep if the number 7 appears in one of the spinner windows.

- Terminate when the End button is clicked.

Creating the User Interface

In this exercise you'll start building Lucky Seven by creating a new project and then using controls in the toolbox to construct the user interface.

Create the user interface

You start a new programming project by clicking the New Project command on the File menu.

1 On the File menu, click the New Project command.

Click No if you are asked whether you want to save any changes to the StepUp program from Lesson 1. This removes the StepUp program from memory.

2 Click OK to create a standard 32-bit Visual Basic application.

Visual Basic cleans the slate for a new programming project and displays in the center of the screen a blank form you can use to build your user interface.

Now you'll enlarge this form, and then you'll create the two buttons in the interface.

3 Position the mouse pointer over the lower-right corner of the Form window (not the Project Container window) until the mouse changes into a sizing pointer, and then increase the size of the form to make room for the objects in your program.

As you resize the form, scroll bars appear in the Project window, as shown in the following illustration:

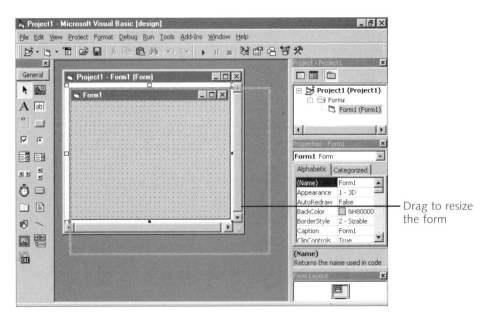

Drag to resize the form

To see the entire form without obstruction, resize the Project Container window to remove the scroll bars and move or close the Properties window, the Project window, and the Form Layout window.

Now you'll practice a command button object on the form.

tip

Confused by all this resizing? Don't sweat it. You're working with two windows here: the Project Container window and the Form window (which fits inside the Project Container window). The troublesome part is that you resize each window by using the resizing pointer in the lower-right corner of the frame, and these two corners tend to overlap a bit. To get more real estate for designing your projects, you may want to run Windows in 800 x 600 mode or greater.

CommandButton control

❹ Click the CommandButton control in the toolbox, and then place the mouse pointer over the form.

The CommandButton control is selected, and the mouse pointer changes to crosshairs when it rests on the form. The crosshairs are designed to help you draw the rectangular shape of a command button. When you hold down the left mouse button and drag, the command button object takes shape and snaps to the grid formed by the intersection of dots on the form.

Try creating your first command button now.

❺ Move the mouse pointer close to the upper-left corner of the form, hold down the left mouse button, and then drag down and to the right. Stop dragging and release the mouse button when you have a command button similar to the one shown here:

The name of the command button is Command1.

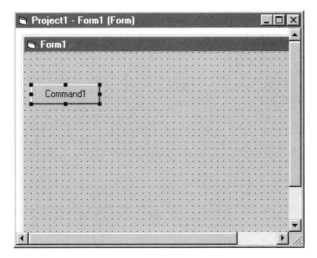

A command button with selection handles appears on the form. The button is named Command1, the first command button in the program. (You might make a mental note of this button name—you'll see it again later when you write your program code.)

You can move command buttons by dragging them with the mouse and you can resize them by using the selection handles whenever Visual Basic is in *design mode* (whenever the Visual Basic programming environment is active). When a program is running, however, the user will not be able to move interface elements unless you have changed a special property in the program to allow this. You'll practice moving and resizing the command button now.

Move and resize a command button

1 Drag the command button to the right by using the mouse.

The command button snaps to the grid when you release the mouse button. The form grid is designed to help you edit and align different user interface elements. You can change the size of the grid by clicking the Options command on the Tools menu and then clicking the General tab.

The grid helps you design your user interface.

2 Position the mouse pointer on the lower-right corner of the command button.

When the mouse pointer rests on a corner or a side of a selected object, it changes into a sizing pointer. You can use the sizing pointer to change the shape of an object.

3 Enlarge the object by holding down the left mouse button and dragging the pointer down and to the right.

When you release the mouse button, the command button changes size and snaps to the grid.

4 Use the sizing pointer to return the command button to its original size, and then move the button back to its original location on the form.

Now you'll add a second command button to the form, below the first button.

Add a second command button

Command-Button control

You can delete an object by selecting the object on the form and then pressing Del.

1 Click the CommandButton control in the toolbox.

2 Draw a command button below the first button on the form. (For consistency, create a command button of the same size.)

3 Move or resize the button as necessary after you place it. If you make a mistake, feel free to delete the command button and start over.

Add the number labels

Now add the labels used to display the numbers in the program. A *label* is a special user interface element designed to display text, numbers, or symbols when a program runs. When the user clicks the Lucky Seven program's Spin button, three random numbers appear in the label boxes. If one of the numbers is a seven, the user hits the jackpot.

Label control

① Click the Label control in the toolbox, and then place the mouse pointer over the form.

The Label control is selected, and the mouse pointer changes to crosshairs when it rests on the form.

② Create a small rectangular box like the one shown below.

The label object you have created is called Label1, the first label in the program. Now you'll create two more labels, named Label2 and Label3, on the form.

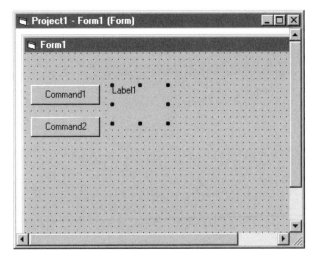

③ Click the Label control, and then draw a label box to the right of the first label.

Make this label the same size as the first. The caption "Label2" will appear in the label.

④ Click the Label control again and add a third label to the form, to the right of the second label.

The caption "Label3" will appear in the label.

tip

As you create labels in this exercise, take a look at the pop-up box that appears next to the labels as you draw them. This box, which contains horizontal and vertical measurements, is called a sizing box. The numbers give the horizontal and vertical dimensions, respectively, of the object you are creating. The numbers are in units of measure called *twips*; a twip is one-twentieth of a point. (A point is 1/72 inch, so a twip is 1/1440 inch.) You can use the sizing box to compare the relative sizes of objects you're creating. After you create the object, the same information is also displayed on the right side of the toolbar.

Now you'll use the Label control to add a descriptive label to your form. This will be the fourth and final label in the program.

5 Click the Label control in the toolbox.

6 Create a larger rectangle directly below the two command buttons.

When you've finished, your four labels should look like those in the following illustration. (You can resize the label objects if they don't look quite right.)

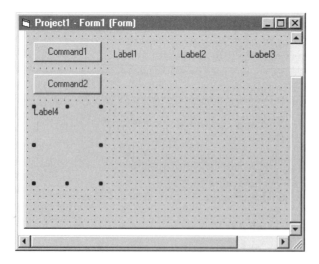

Now you'll add an *image box* to the form to display the stack of coins the user wins when he or she draws a seven and hits the jackpot. An image box is designed to display bitmaps, icons, and other artwork in a program. One of the best uses for an image box is to display a piece of Visual Basic clip art.

Add an image

Image control

❶ Click the Image control in the toolbox.

❷ Using the Image control, create a large rectangular box directly beneath the three number labels.

When you've finished, your image box object should look like the following:

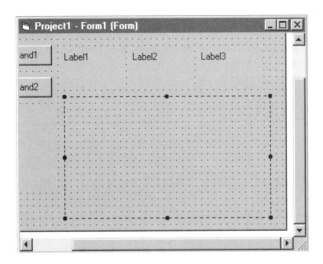

This object will be called Image1 in your program; you'll use this name later in the program code.

Now you're ready to customize your interface by setting a few properties.

Setting the Properties

As you discovered in Lesson 1, you can change properties by selecting objects on the form and changing their settings in the Properties window. You'll start setting the properties in this program by changing the caption settings for the two command buttons.

Set the command button properties

❶ Click the first command button (Command1) on the form.

The command button is surrounded by selection handles.

❷ Double-click the Properties window title bar.

The Properties window is enlarged to full size, as shown in the illustration on the following page.

The Properties window lists the settings for the first command button. These include settings for the background color, caption, font height, and width of the command button.

3 Double-click the Caption property in the left column of the Properties window.

The current Caption setting ("Command1") is highlighted in the Properties window.

4 Type **Spin** and press Enter.

The Caption property changes to "Spin" in the Properties window and on the form. Now change the caption of the second button to "End". (You'll select the second button in a new way this time.)

5 Open the object drop-down list box at the top of the Properties window.

A list of the interface objects in your program appears in the list box:

These properties for the objects on your form, and for the form itself, can be set with the object drop-down list box.

6 Click Command2 (the second command button) in the list box.

The property settings for the second command button appear in the Properties window.

7 Double-click the current Caption property ("Command2"), type **End**, and then press Enter.

The caption of the second command button changes to "End".

tip

Using the object drop-down list box is a handy way to switch between objects in your program. You can also switch between objects on the form by clicking each object.

Now you'll set the properties for the labels in the program. The first three labels will hold the random numbers generated by the program and will have identical property settings. (You'll set most of them as a group.) The descriptive label settings will be slightly different.

Set the number label properties

To select more than one object on a form, hold down the Shift key while clicking the objects.

1 Click the first number label, and then, holding down the Shift key, click the second and third number labels. (If the Properties window is in the way, move it to a new place.)

A set of selection rectangles appears around each label that you click. When you've selected all three labels, release the Shift key.

tip

Because more than one object is selected, only those properties that can be changed as a group are displayed in the Properties window. You'll change the Alignment, BorderStyle, and Font properties now so that the numbers that appear in the labels will be centered, boxed, and identical in font and point size.

2 Click the Alignment property, and then click the drop-down list box arrow that appears to the right.

A list of alignment options appears in the list box.

3   Click the 2 - Center option.

The Alignment property for each of the selected labels changes to 2 - Center.

Now you'll change the BorderStyle property.

4   Click the BorderStyle property, and then click the drop-down list box arrow that appears to the right.

A list of the valid property settings (0 - None and 1 - Fixed Single) appears in the list box.

5   Click 1 - Fixed Single in the list box to add a thin border around each label.

Now you'll change the font for the labels by changing settings for the Font property.

6   Double-click the Font property in the Properties window.

The Font dialog box appears, as shown here:

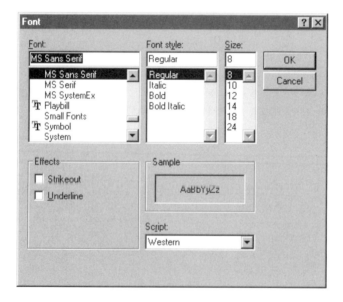

7   Change the font to Times New Roman, the font style to Bold, and the point size to 24, and then click OK.

The label captions appear in the font, style, and size you specified.

Now you'll delete the three captions so that the boxes will be empty when the program starts. (Your font selections will remain with the labels because they are stored as separate properties.) To complete this operation, you'll first need to select each of the labels individually.

8   Click the form to remove the selection handles from the three labels, and then click the first label.

9 Double-click the Caption property, and then press Del.

The caption of the Label1 object is deleted. You'll use program code to put a random "slot machine" number in this property later in this lesson.

10 Delete the captions in the second and third labels on the form.

You've finished with the first three labels. Now you'll change the Caption, Font, and ForeColor properties of the last label.

Set the descriptive label properties

1 Click the fourth label object on the form.

2 Change the Caption property to "Lucky Seven".

3 Double-click the Font property, and use the Font dialog box to change the font to Arial, the font style to Bold, and the point size to 20. Click OK.

The font in the label box is updated. Notice that the text in the box wrapped to two lines because it no longer fits on one. This is an important concept: the contents of an object must fit inside the object. If they don't, the contents will wrap or be truncated.

Now you'll change the foreground color of the text.

4 Double-click the ForeColor property in the Properties window.

A System tab and a Palette tab appear in a list box, providing you with two options to change the color of your object. The System tab displays the current colors used for user interface elements in your system. (The list reflects the current settings on the Appearance tab in your desktop's property sheet.) The Palette tab contains all the available colors in your system.

5 Click the Palette tab, and then click the box containing dark purple.

The text in the label box changes to dark purple. The selected color is translated into a hexadecimal (base 16) number in the Properties window. Most programmers won't have to deal with this format often, but it is interesting to see how Visual Basic actually records such information inside the program.

Now you're ready to set the properties for the last object.

The Image Box Properties

The image box object will contain the graphic of the stack of coins in your program. This graphic will appear when the user hits the jackpot (that is, when at least one seven appears in the number labels). You need to set the Stretch property to accurately size the graphic; the Picture property, which specifies the name of the graphics file to be loaded into the image box; and the Visible property, which specifies the picture state at the beginning of the program.

Set the image box properties

1. Click the image box object on the form.

2. Click the Stretch property in the Properties window, click the drop-down list box arrow, and then click True.

   Setting Stretch to True before you open a graphic will make Visual Basic resize the graphic to the exact dimensions of the image box. (Typically, you set this property before you set the Picture property.)

3. Double-click the Picture property in the Properties window.

   The Load Picture dialog box appears, as shown in the following illustration:

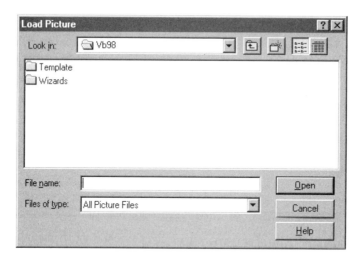

4. Navigate to the \Vb6Sbs folder in the Load Picture dialog box.

   The subfolders in the \Vb6Sbs folder appear.

5. Double-click the Less02 folder.

   The Windows metafile Coins.wmf appears in the Load Picture dialog box. Windows metafiles contain graphics objects that can be rendered in a variety of different sizes, so they look good in small and large boxes.

6. Select the file Coins.wmf in the dialog box, and then click Open.

   The Coins Windows metafile is loaded into the image box on the form.

   Now you'll change the Visible property to False so that the coins will be invisible when the program starts. (You'll make them appear later with program code.)

7 Click the Visible property. Click the Visible drop-down list box arrow.

The valid settings for the Visible property appear in a list box.

8 Click False to make the image invisible when the program starts.

The Visible property is set to False. This affects the image box when the program runs, but not now while you are designing it. Your completed form looks like this:

9 Double-click the Properties window's title bar to return it to the docked position.

Writing the Code

Now you're ready to write the code for the Lucky Seven program. Because most of the objects you've created already "know" how to work when the program runs, they're ready to receive input from the user and process it automatically. The inherent functionality of objects is one of the great strengths of Visual Basic—once objects are placed on a form and their properties are set, they're ready to run without any additional programming. However, the "meat" of the Lucky Seven game—the code that actually calculates random numbers, displays them in boxes, and detects a jackpot—is still missing from the program. This

Program code is entered in the Code window.

computing logic can be built into the application only by using program state-ments—code that clearly spells out what the program should do each step of the way. Because the program is driven by the Spin and End buttons, you'll associate the code for the game with those buttons. The *Code window* is a special window in the programming environment that you use to enter and edit Visual Basic program statements.

Reading Properties in Tables

In this lesson, you've set the properties for the Lucky Seven program step by step. In future lessons, the instructions to set properties will be presented in table format unless a setting is especially tricky. Here are the properties you've set so far in the Lucky Seven program in table format, as they'd look later in the book.

Object	Property	Setting
Command1	Caption	"Spin"
Command2	Caption	"End"
Label1, Label2, Label3	BorderStyle	1 – Fixed Single
	Alignment	2 – Center
	Font	Times New Roman, Bold, 24-point
	Caption	(Empty)
Label4	Caption	"Lucky Seven"
	Font	Arial, Bold, 20-point
	ForeColor	Dark purple (&H00800008)
Image1	Picture	"\Vb6Sbs\Less02\coins.wmf"
	Stretch	True
	Visible	False

In the following steps, you'll enter the program code for Lucky Seven in the Code window.

Use the Code window

1 Double-click the End command button on the form.

The Code window appears, as follows:

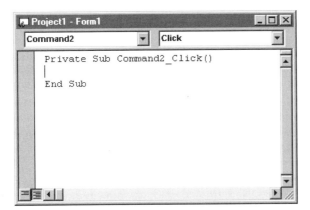

If the window is smaller than the one shown above, resize it with the mouse. (The exact size is not that important because the Code window includes scroll bars that you can use to examine long program statements.)

Inside the Code window are program statements that mark the beginning and the end of this particular Visual Basic subroutine, or *event procedure,* a block of code associated with a particular object in the interface:

```
Private Sub Command2_Click()
End Sub
```

The body of a procedure always fits between these lines and is executed whenever a user activates the interface element associated with the procedure. In this case, the event is a mouse click, but as you'll see later in the book, it could also be an event of a different type.

2 Type **End** and press the Down arrow key.

As you type the statement, the letters appear in black type in the Code window. When you press the Down arrow key (you could also press Enter or simply click a different line), the program statement turns blue, indicating that Visual Basic recognizes it as a valid statement, or *keyword,* in the program.

*The End state-
ment stops the
execution of a
program.*

You use the program statement End to stop your program and remove it from the screen. The Visual Basic programming system contains several hundred unique keywords such as this, complete with their associated operators and symbols. The spelling of and spacing between these items are critical to writing program code that will be accurately recognized by the Visual Basic compiler.

tip

Another name for the exact spelling, order, and spacing of keywords in a program is *statement syntax*.

③ Move the cursor to the beginning of the line with the End statement in it, and press the Spacebar four times.

The indent moves the End statement four spaces to the right to set the statement apart from the Private Sub and End Sub statements. This indenting scheme is one of the programming conventions you'll use throughout this book to keep your programs clear and readable. The group of conventions regarding how program code is organized in a program is often referred to as *program style*.

Now that you've written the code associated with the End button, you'll write code for the Spin button. These programming statements will be a little more extensive and will give you a chance to learn more about program syntax and style. You'll study each of the program statements later in the book, so you don't need to know everything about them now. Just focus on the general structure of the program code and on typing the program statements exactly as they are printed. (Visual Basic is fussy about spelling and the order in which keywords and operators appear.)

Write code for the Spin button

① Open the Object drop-down list box in the Code window.

The Lucky Seven interface objects appear in the list box, as shown below:

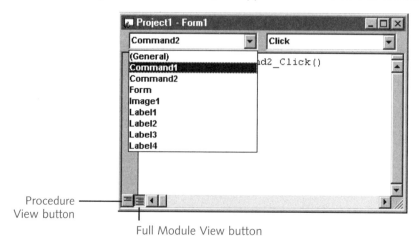

Procedure View button

Full Module View button

2 Click Command1 in the list box.

A procedure associated with the Command1 button appears above the first procedure.

By default, Visual Basic displays all the event procedures for a form in one window, so you can easily switch back and forth between them. (A horizontal line appears between the procedures so you can keep them apart.) Alternatively, you can view one procedure per window by clicking the tiny Procedure View button in the bottom-left corner of the Code window. To see all the procedures again in one window, click the Full Module View button located just to the right of the Procedure View button.

Although you changed the caption of this button to "Spin", its name in the program is still Command1. (The name and the caption of an interface element can be different to suit the needs of the programmer.) Each object can have several procedures associated with it, one for each event it recognizes. The click event is the one we're interested in now because users will click the Spin and End buttons when they operate the program.

3 Type the program lines shown on the following page between the Private Sub and End Sub statements, pressing Enter after each line and taking care to type the program statements exactly as they appear here. (The Code window will scroll to the left as you enter the longer lines.) If you make a mistake (usually identified by red type), delete the incorrect statements and try again.

tip

As you enter the program code, Visual Basic formats the text and displays different parts of the program in color to help you identify the various elements. When you begin to type a property, Visual Basic also displays the available properties for the object you're using in a list box, so you can double-click the property or keep typing to enter it yourself. If Visual Basic displays an error message, you may have misspelled a program statement. Check the line against the text in this book, make the necessary correction, and continue typing. (You can also delete a line and type it from scratch.) Readers of previous editions of this book have found this first typing exercise to be the toughest part of the lesson—"But Mr. Halvorson, I *know* I typed it just as written!"—so please give this program code your closest attention. I promise you, it works!

```
Image1.Visible = False           ' hide coins
Label1.Caption = Int(Rnd * 10) ' pick numbers
Label2.Caption = Int(Rnd * 10)
Label3.Caption = Int(Rnd * 10)
'if any caption is 7 display coin stack and beep
If (Label1.Caption = 7) Or (Label2.Caption = 7) _
  Or (Label3.Caption = 7) Then
    Image1.Visible = True
    Beep
End If
```

When you've finished, the Code window should look like the following:

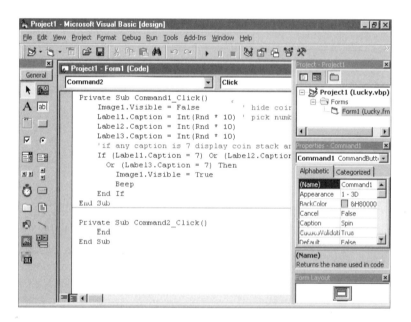

A Look at the Command1_Click Procedure

The Command1_Click procedure is executed when the user clicks the Spin button on the form. The procedure uses some pretty complicated statements, and because I haven't formally introduced them yet, the whole thing may look a little confusing. However, if you take a closer look you'll probably see a few things that look familiar. Taking a peek at the contents of the procedures will give you a feel for the type of program code you'll be creating later in this book. (If you'd rather not have a look, feel free to skip to the next section, "Saving the Program.")

The Command1_Click procedure is the heart of the Lucky Seven program.

The Command1_Click procedure performs three tasks: it hides the coin stack, creates three random numbers for the label windows, and displays the coin stack when the number seven appears. Let's look at each of these steps individually.

The first task in the procedure is accomplished by the line

```
Image1.Visible = False        ' hide coins
```

This line is made up of two parts: a program statement and a comment. The program statement (Image1.Visible = False) sets the Visible property of the first image box object (Image1) to False (one of two possible settings). You might remember that you set this property to False once before by using the Properties window. You're doing it again now in the program code because the first task is a spin and you need to clear away any coins that might have been displayed in a previous game. Because the property will be changed at runtime and not at design time, the property needs to be set by using program code. This is a handy feature of Visual Basic, and we'll talk about it more in Lesson 3.

Comments describe what program statements do.

The second part of the first line (the part displayed in green type on your screen) is called a *comment*. Comments are explanatory notes included in program code following a single quotation mark ('). Programmers use comments to describe how important statements work in a program. These notes aren't processed by Visual Basic when the program runs; they exist only to document what the program does. You'll want to use comments often when you write Visual Basic programs to leave a "plain English" record of what you're doing.

The next three lines handle the random number computations. The Rnd function in each line creates a random number between 0 and 1 (a number with a decimal point), and the Int function multiplies the numbers by 10 and rounds them to the nearest decimal place. This computation creates random numbers between 0 and 9 in the program. The numbers are then assigned to the Caption properties of the first three labels on the form, and the assignment causes the numbers to be displayed in boldface, 24-point, Times New Roman type in the three label windows.

The last group of statements in the program checks whether any of the random numbers is seven. If one or more of them is, the stack of coins is made visible on the form and a beep announces a jackpot. Each time the user clicks the Spin button, the Command1_Click procedure is called and the program statements in the procedure are executed.

Saving the Program

Now that you've completed the Lucky Seven program, you should save it to disk. Visual Basic saves your form's code and objects in one file and the "packing list" of project components in another file. (The project components are listed in the Project window.) You can use these component files individually in other programming projects by using the Add File command on the Project menu. To save a program in Visual Basic, click Save Project As on the File menu or click the Save Project button on the toolbar.

Save the Lucky Seven program

You can save your program at any time during the programming process.

❶ On the File menu, click the Save Project As command.

The Save File As dialog box appears, prompting you for the name and storage location for your form.

❷ Select the Less02 folder in the dialog box, if it's not already selected.

You'll save your project files in the practice folder that the Microsoft Visual Basic 6 Step by Step Practice Files installation program created on your hard disk. (You can specify a different folder if you like.)

❸ Type **MyLucky** in the File Name text box, and press Enter.

important

I recommend that you save each project you create in this book by using the My prefix to keep a record of your progress and to preserve the original practice files. That way you can check the original files if you have any problems.

The Lucky Seven form is saved under the name MyLucky.frm. The Save Project As dialog box then appears:

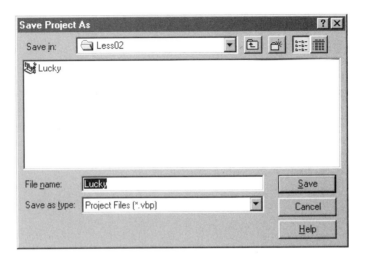

❹   Type **MyLucky** and press Enter.

The Lucky Seven project is saved under the name MyLucky.vbp. To load this project again later, click the Open Project command on the File menu and click MyLucky in the Open Project dialog box. You can also load a recently used project by clicking the project name at the bottom of the Visual Basic File menu.

The complete Lucky program is located in the \Vb6Sbs\Less02 folder.

Congratulations! You're ready to run your first real program. To run a Visual Basic program from the programming environment, you can click Start on the Run menu, click the Start button on the toolbar, or press F5. Try running your Lucky Seven program now. If Visual Basic displays an error message, you may still have a typing mistake or two in your program code. Try to fix it by comparing the printed version in this book with the one you typed, or load Lucky from your hard disk and run it.

Run the program

Start button

❶   Click the Start button on the toolbar.

The Lucky Seven program runs in the programming environment. The user interface appears, just as you designed it.

2 Click the Spin button.

The program picks three random numbers and displays them in the labels on the form, as follows:

Because a seven appears in the first label box, the stack of coins appears and the computer beeps. (The sound depends on your Windows Control Panel setting.) You win!

3 Click the Spin button 15 or 16 more times, watching the results of the spins in the number windows.

About half the time you spin, you hit the jackpot—pretty easy odds. (The actual odds are about 3 times out of 10; you're just lucky at first.) Later on you might want to make the game tougher by displaying the coins only when two or three sevens appear. (You'll see how to do this when you learn more about modules and public variables in Lesson 10.)

4 When you've finished experimenting with your new creation, click the End button.

The program stops, and the programming environment reappears on your screen.

Building an Executable File

An .exe file can run under any recent version of Microsoft Windows.

Your last task in this lesson is to complete the development process and create an application for Windows, or executable file. Applications for Windows created with Visual Basic have the filename extension .exe and can be run on any Windows 95, Windows 98, Windows Me, Windows NT 3.51 or later, Windows

2000, or Windows XP system that contains the necessary support files. Visual Basic installs these support files, including dynamic link libraries and ActiveX controls, when you use the Package & Deployment wizard, described later in the lesson.

Try creating MyLucky.exe now.

Create an executable file

1 On the File menu, click the Make MyLucky.exe command. (Visual Basic adds your program's name to the command automatically.)

The Make Project dialog box appears, as follows:

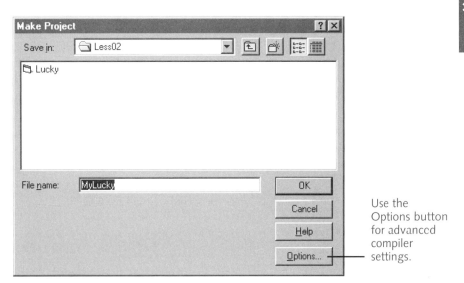

Use the Options button for advanced compiler settings.

tip

The Project Properties dialog box (accessed from the Project menu) contains a Compile tab that you can use to control advanced features related to your program's compilation. These include optimizations for fast, efficient code; small, compact code; debugging; and other specialized operating conditions. By adding these sophisticated features to the compilation process, Visual Basic makes available to the professional developer tools that have traditionally been associated with the most efficient compilers, such as Microsoft Visual C++.

The dialog box contains text boxes and list boxes that you can use to specify the name and location of your executable file on disk. It also contains an Options button that you can click to open the Project Properties dialog box. You can use the Project Properties dialog box to control the program icon and version information associated with the file. By default, Visual Basic suggests the Less02 folder for the location of your executable file.

2 Click OK to accept the default filename and location for the file.

Visual Basic creates an executable file on disk in the specified location.

To run this program later under Windows, use the Run command on the Start menu or double-click the filename in Windows Explorer. You can also create a shortcut icon for MyLucky on the Windows desktop by right-clicking the Windows desktop, pointing to New, and then clicking Shortcut. When you are prompted for the location of your application file, click Browse and select the MyLucky executable file in the \Vb6Sbs\Less02 folder. Click the Open, Next, and Finish buttons, and Windows will place an icon on the desktop that you can double-click to run your program. The shortcut icon will look like this:

3 On the File menu, click Exit to close Visual Basic and the MyLucky project.

The Visual Basic Programming System closes.

Using the Package & Deployment Wizard

Visual Basic Professional Edition includes a tool that assembles the files you need to run a Visual Basic program on computers that don't contain the Visual Basic 6.0 programming system. This tool is called the Package & Deployment Wizard, and it automatically builds a setup program for your application that handles the setup process. The wizard even organizes files so that they can be copied easily to installation disks.

To run the Package & Deployment wizard, follow these steps:

1 Click the Start button, point to Programs, point to the Microsoft Visual Basic 6.0 folder, and then point to the Microsoft Visual Basic 6.0 Tools folder.

2 Click the Package & Deployment Wizard program icon.

The Package & Deployment Wizard opens, and prompts you for the name of the project that you want to deploy, as shown here:

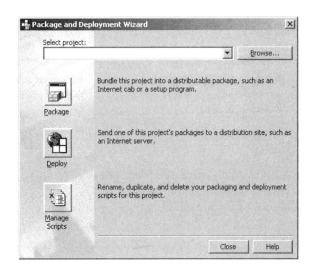

3 Click the Browse button, and then browse to the project (.vbp) file on which you want to base your deployment.

Feel free to specify the MyLucky project if you like.

4 Click the Package button to build setup files for your project.

If you haven't yet compiled your project into an executable file, you will be prompted to do so now.

5 Specify the package type, or way that the files will be distributed to your users, and then click Next.

The Standard Setup Package type, which will create a setup.exe file for installation, is recommended.

6 Specify a folder location for your package, and then click Next.

7 Review the support files that will be included in your setup package, and then click Next.

8 Identify the size of the installation (CAB) files you would like to use, and then click Next.

You can choose one large file (suitable for CD or network installation), or several smaller files that will fit on the type of floppy disk that you plan to use.

9 Specify the project name that will appear in the Setup program's title bar during installation, and then click Next.

10 Identify your preferences for the remaining options (folder structure, file location, and shared files), clicking Next after each selection.

It is usually fine to select the default values for these options.

When you're finished configuring the setup files, click Finish.

11 The Package & Deployment wizard builds the necessary files on your system and displays a packaging report.

12 Click Close twice to dispatch the report and close the wizard.

You now have the setup files you need to install your Visual Basic program on one or more computers. Simply copy the files you created to floppy disks or CDs and begin the installation process!

One Step Further   Adding to a Program

You can restart Visual Basic at any time and work on a programming project you have stored on disk. You'll restart Visual Basic now and add a special statement named Randomize to the Lucky Seven program.

Reload Lucky Seven

1 Click the Start button on the Windows taskbar, point to Programs, point to Visual Basic 6.0 (or Visual Studio), and then click the Visual Basic 6.0 program icon.

2 Click the Recent tab in the New Project dialog box.

A list of the most recent projects that you have worked on appears in a list box. Because you just finished working with Lucky Seven, MyLucky should be the first project on the list.

❸ Double-click MyLucky to load the Lucky Seven program from disk.

The Lucky Seven program loads from disk, and the MyLucky form appears in a window. (If you don't see it, click the MyLucky form in the Project window and then click the View Object button.)

Now you'll add the Randomize statement to the Form_Load procedure, a special procedure that is associated with the form and that is executed each time the program is started.

❹ Double-click the form (not one of the objects) to display the Form_Load procedure.

The Form_Load procedure appears in the Code window, as shown in the following illustration:

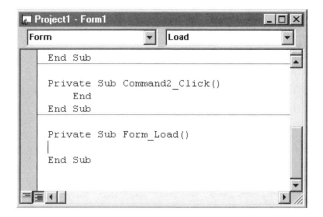

❺ Press the Spacebar four times, type **Randomize**, and press the Down Arrow key.

The Randomize statement is added to the program and will be executed each time the program starts. Randomize uses the system clock to create a truly random starting poinl, or "seed," for the Rnd statement used in the Command1_Click procedure. You may not have noticed, but without Randomize the Lucky Seven program produces the same string of random spins every time you restart the program. With Randomize in place, the program will spin randomly every time it runs. The numbers won't follow a recognizable pattern.

❻ Run the new version of Lucky Seven, and then save the project to disk. If you plan to use the new version a lot, you may want to create a new .exe file too. Visual Basic does not update executable files automatically when you change the source code.

If you want to continue to the next lesson

● Keep Visual Basic running, and turn to Lesson 3.

If you want to exit Visual Basic for now

● On the File menu, click Exit.
If you see a Save dialog box, click Yes.

Upgrade Notes: What's Different in Visual Basic .NET?

If you choose to upgrade to Visual Basic .NET in the future, you'll notice some new features related to the topics in this lesson, including the following:

■ The Visual Studio .NET development environment provides a few different menus and toolbars with which you can build your programs. For example, there are no longer Run, Format, or Add-Ins menus in Visual Studio .NET. Most of the commands on these menus have been relocated—you'll find many of the Run menu commands on the Debug menu.

■ The CommandButton control is called the Button control in Visual Studio .NET, and many of its properties and methods have changed. For example, the Caption property is now called the Text property.

■ The Label control has new properties and methods, including the Text and TextAlign properties.

■ The Image control has been removed from Visual Studio .NET. To display pictures, Visual Basic .NET programmers use the PictureBox control.

■ Visual Basic .NET code contains more compiler-generated statements than you see in Visual Basic 6.0. In particular, Visual Basic .NET adds a block of code called Windows Form Designer Generated Code to the top of each form, which defines important form characteristics and should not be modified. (You add your own program code below this code block.)

Lesson 2 Quick Reference

To	Do this	Button
Create a user interface	Use toolbox controls to place objects on your form, and then set the necessary properties. Resize the form and the objects as appropriate.	
Move an object	Drag the object on the form by using the mouse.	
Resize an object	Click the object, and then drag the selection handle attached to the part of the object you want to resize.	
Delete an object	Click the object, and then press Del.	
Open the Code window	Double-click an object on the form (or the form itself). *or* Click the View Code button in the Project window when a form or module name is highlighted in the Project window.	
Write program code	Type Visual Basic program statements associated with the object you want to program in the Code window.	
Save a program	On the File menu, click the Save Project As command. *or* Click the Save Project button on the toolbar.	
Create an .exe file	On the File menu, click the Make *filename*.exe command.	
Reload a project	On the File menu, click the Open Project command. *or* Double-click the file in the Recent tab of the New Project dialog box.	

LESSON

3

Working with Controls

ESTIMATED TIME
55 min.

In this lesson you will learn how to:

✔ Use text box and command button objects to create a "Hello World" program.

✔ Use file system objects and an image object to browse artwork on disk.

✔ Use option button, check box, and list box objects to process user input.

✔ Use an OLE object to launch Microsoft Windows–based applications on your system.

✔ Use a data object to view records in a Microsoft Access database.

✔ Install ActiveX controls.

As you learned in Lessons 1 and 2, Microsoft Visual Basic controls are the graphical tools you use to build the user interface of a Visual Basic program. Controls are located in the toolbox in the programming environment, and you use them to create objects on a form with a simple series of mouse clicks and dragging motions. In this lesson, you'll learn how to display information in a text box, browse drives and folders on your system, process user input, launch Windows-based applications, and view database records. The exercises in this lesson will help you design your own Visual Basic applications and will teach you more about objects, properties, and program code. You'll also learn how to add ActiveX controls to the toolbox so that you can extend the functionality of Visual Basic.

The Basic Use of Controls:
The "Hello World" Program

A great tradition in introductory programming books is the "Hello World" program. Hello World is the name given to a short program that demonstrates how the simplest utility can be built and run in a given programming language. In the days of character-based programming, Hello World was usually a two- or three-line program typed in a program editor and assembled with a stand-alone compiler. With the advent of graphical programming tools, however, the typical Hello World has grown into a complex program containing dozens of lines and requiring several programming tools for its construction. Fortunately, creating a Hello World program is still quite simple with Visual Basic. You can construct a complete user interface by creating two objects, setting two properties, and entering one line of code. Give it a try.

Create a Hello World program

1 Start Visual Basic, and click the the Open button to create a standard Visual Basic application.

   The Visual Basic programming environment appears, as shown in the following illustration. The two controls you'll use in this exercise, TextBox and CommandButton, are labeled in the toolbox.

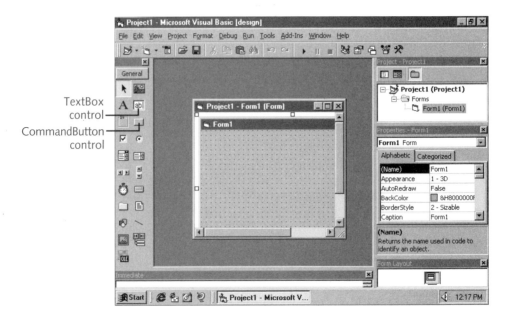

TextBox control

2 Click the TextBox control in the toolbox.

3 Move the mouse pointer to the center of the form. Note that the pointer turns into crosshairs as it passes over the form. Draw a text box similar to the following:

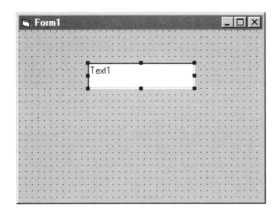

A *text box object* is used to display text on a form or to get user input while a Visual Basic program is running. How a text box works depends on how you set its properties and how you reference the text box in the program code. In this simple program, a text box object will be used to display the message "Hello, world!" when you click a command button on the form.

Now you'll add a command button to the form.

CommandButton control

4 Click the CommandButton control in the toolbox.

5 Move the mouse pointer below the text box on the form, and draw a command button.

Your form should look like the following:

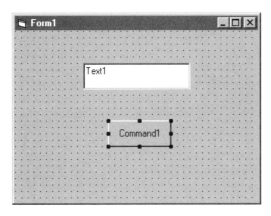

A *command button object* is used to get the most basic input from a user. When a user clicks a command button, he or she is requesting that the program perform a specific action immediately. In Visual Basic terms, the user is using the command button to create an *event* that needs to be processed in the program. Typical command buttons in a program are the OK button, which a user clicks to accept a list of options and indicate that he or she is ready to proceed; the Cancel button, which a user clicks to discard a list of options; and the Quit button, which a user clicks to exit the program. In each case, you should use command buttons in a recognizable way, so that they work as expected when the user clicks them. A command button's characteristics (like those of all objects) can be modified with property settings and references to the object in program code.

For more information about setting properties, see the section "Setting the Properties" in Lesson 1.

6 Set the following properties for the text box and command button objects, using the Properties window. The setting (Empty) means that you should delete the current setting and leave the property blank. Settings you need to type in are shown in quotation marks. You shouldn't type the quotation marks.

Control	Property	Setting
Text1	Text	(Empty)
Command1	Caption	"OK"

The complete Hello.vbp program is located on disk in the \Vb6Sbs\Less03 folder.

7 Double-click the OK command button, and type the following program statement between the Private Sub and End Sub statements in the Code window:

```
Text1.Text = "Hello, world!"
```

tip

After you type the Text1 object name and a period, Visual Basic displays a list box containing all the valid properties for text box objects, to jog your memory if you've forgotten the complete list. You can select a property from the list by double-clicking it, or you can continue typing and enter it yourself. (I usually just keep on typing, unless I'm exploring new features.)

The statement you've entered changes the Text property of the text box to "Hello, world!" when the user clicks the command button at runtime. (The equal sign assigns everything between the quotation marks to the Text property of the Text1 object.) This example changes a property at runtime—one of the most common uses of program code in a Visual Basic program. Your statement is in an *event procedure*—an instruction that is executed when the Command1 command button is clicked. It changes the property setting (and therefore the text box contents) immediately after the user clicks the command button.

Use the Form Layout window to control the placement of your form at runtime.

8 Use the Form Layout window to set the position of the form when the program runs. (If the Form Layout window is not visible, click the Form Layout Window command on the View menu.)

By default, the Form Layout window positions forms in the upper-left corner of the screen. However, you can customize this setting by dragging the tiny form icon within the Form Layout window. This feature is especially useful in programs that display more than one window.

Now you're ready to run the Hello World program and save it to disk.

Run the Hello World program

Start button

1 Click the Start button on the toolbar.

The Hello World program runs in the Visual Basic programming environment.

2 Click the OK command button.

The program displays the greeting "Hello, world!" in the text box, as shown here:

When you clicked the OK command button, the program code changed the Text property of the empty Text1 text box to "Hello, world!" and displayed this text in the box. If you didn't get this result, repeat the steps in the previous section and build the program again. You might have set a property incorrectly or made a typing mistake in the program code. (Syntax errors appear in red type on your screen.)

End button

3 Click the End button on the toolbar to stop the program.

You can also click the Close button on the program form to stop the program.

4 On the File menu, click the Save Project As command.

5 Select the \Vb6Sbs\Less03 folder, type **MyHello**, and click Save.

Visual Basic saves your form to disk with the name MyHello.frm. Because Visual Basic saves forms separately from project files, you can reuse forms and procedures in future programming projects without rebuilding them from scratch.

After you enter the form name, you are prompted for a project filename for the file that Visual Basic uses to build your program. This Visual Basic project file has a .vbp filename extension.

6 Type **MyHello** again, and click Save.

Visual Basic saves your project to disk under the name MyHello.vbp. To open the program again later, you can select this file by clicking the Open Project command on the File menu. Visual Basic then loads all the files in the project list.

Congratulations—you've joined the ranks of programmers who have written a Hello World program. Now let's move on to some other objects.

Using File System Objects

Visual Basic provides three very useful objects for gaining access to the file system. These are *drive list boxes*, which let you browse the valid drives on a system; *directory list boxes*, which let you navigate the folders on a particular drive; and *file list boxes*, which let you select a specific file in a folder. In the following exercise, you will use the three file system objects to build a program called Browser that locates and displays files containing artwork on your system.

tip
You will also use an *image object* in this program. An image object can display six kinds of graphics formats: bitmaps (.bmp files), Windows metafiles (.wmf files, which are electronic artwork files that you can size), icons (.ico files), cursors (.cur files), JPEG format (.jpg files), and GIF format (.gif files).

The Browser Program

The Browser program uses the three file system objects, an image object, and several lines of program code to create an artwork browser program. When you've finished creating Browser, you can use it routinely to examine the artwork on any floppy disk, hard disk, network drive, or CD-ROM. The file system objects support all drive types.

Build the Browser program

1   On the File menu, click New Project, and then click OK to create a new standard executable file.

The Hello World program disappears, and a blank form appears on the screen. (You have a chance to save any unsaved changes in Hello World before it closes.)

2   On the Tools menu, click Options, and then click the Editor tab. If a check mark appears in the Require Variable Declaration box, click the box to remove the check mark. (This option will be discussed in Lesson 4.) Click OK.

3   Increase the size of your form so that it is big enough to hold file system controls and a good-sized window for viewing images.

Scroll bars appear around your form so that you can view any hidden parts as you develop your program.

4   Click the DriveListBox control in the toolbox.

5   Move the mouse pointer to the upper-left corner of the form, and then draw a drive list box, as shown in the following illustration:

DriveListBox control

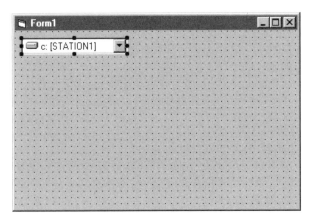

Visual Basic includes the current drive and volume label in the object when you create it. This information is displayed to help the user identify the currently selected drive when he or she is using the program. It also lets you verify at design time whether you can see all the drive and volume information so that you can resize your drive list box accordingly.

DirListBox controlC

6 Click the DirListBox control in the toolbox, and then add a directory list box to the form, below the drive list box. Allow room for at least four or five folders to appear in the list box.

A directory list box object provides access to the folders in the file system. When you place the object on a Visual Basic form, the folders appear as they will when the program runs. It's tempting to start clicking folders now, but because the list box isn't active, nothing will happen. Folders appear now only so that you can size the object appropriately.

FileListBox control

7 Click the FileListBox control in the toolbox, and then add a file list box to the form, below the directory list box. Allow room for at least four or five filenames to be displayed.

A file list box object lets a user select a specific file in the file system. When the user selects a file, Visual Basic puts the filename in the Filename property of the file list box object. In a similar manner, the Drive property of the drive list box object and the Path property of the directory list box object receive the drive and folder selections the user makes in the drive and directory list boxes. You'll use these three properties together in the Browser program to open the artwork file the user selects.

This is a typical use of objects and properties in a program. The user changes a setting in an object while the program is running, the change is reflected in a property, and the property is processed in the program code.

tip

The Drive, Path, and Filename properties are available only at runtime. (They contain values that are assigned when the file system list boxes are used.) You cannot set them by using the Properties window.

Image control

8 Click the Image control in the toolbox, and then add a large image box to the form, to the right of the drive, directory, and file list boxes.

After you add the image object, your screen should look similar to the following:

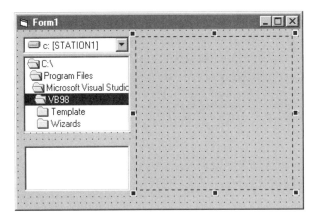

9 Now set the following properties by using the Properties window:

Object	Property	Setting
File1	Pattern	*.bmp;*.wmf;*.ico
Image1	Stretch	True
Image1	BorderStyle	1 – Fixed Single

The Pattern setting in the file list box is especially important in this case. It lists the valid graphics formats that Visual Basic can display in a program by using an image box. If the property were left blank, the file list box would list all file types in a folder, and if the user selected a graphics format that Visual Basic doesn't support (such as TIFF), the selection would result in a crash or a runtime error. If possible, it's best to eliminate such problems before they occur.

Now you'll add a few lines of program code to the procedures associated with the file system objects. These procedures are called *event procedures* because they are run when an event, such as a mouse click, occurs in the object.

Double-click an object to display its default event procedure.

10 Double-click the drive list box object on the form, and then type the following program statement between the Private Sub and End Sub statements in the Drive1_Change event procedure:

```
Dir1.Path = Drive1.Drive
```

This statement updates the Path property in the directory list box when the user selects a drive in the drive list box. The statement hooks the two objects together so that the directory list box lists folders for the correct drive.

11 Close the Code window (click the Close button in the upper-right corner). Then double-click the directory list box on the form and add the following program statement to the Dir1_Change event procedure:

```
File1.Path = Dir1.Path
```

This statement links the file list box to the directory list box so that the files in the list box match the selected folder.

12 Close the Code window. Now double-click the file list box on the form and add the following code to the File1_Click event procedure:

```
SelectedFile = File1.Path & "\" & File1.Filename
Image1.Picture = LoadPicture(SelectedFile)
```

You'll learn more about operators, variables, and functions in Lesson 4.

These two lines are the heart of the program. The first line uses the & operator to combine File1's Path property, the \ character, and File1's Filename property, and then stores the resulting pathname in the SelectedFile variable. A *variable* is a temporary storage space or holding tank for information in a program. In this case, the SelectedFile variable holds the complete name of the file that has been selected by the user (including drive and folder names). The second statement in the event procedure uses the SelectedFile variable when it loads the file into the image box (Image1) on the form with the LoadPicture function and the Picture property.

After you enter the code for the File1_Click event procedure, the Code window should look similar to the following illustration. (This screen shot shows an enlarged Code window.)

The complete Browser.vbp program is located on disk in the \Vb6Sbs\Less03 folder.

Now you're ready to run the Browser program and save it to disk.

Run the Browser program

Start button

1 Click the Start button on the toolbar.

The Browser program starts to run in the programming environment.

2 Open the folder \Vb6Sbs\Less03 by using the directory list box.

The Windows metafiles in the selected folder appear in the file list box.

3 Click the filename answmach.wmf.

The selected file (a picture of an answering machine) appears in the image box, as shown here:

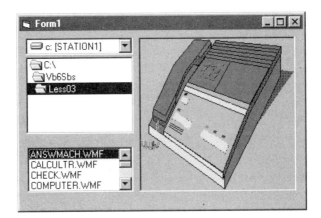

4 Scroll down the list, and click the poundbag.wmf filename.

A picture of an English money sack appears in the image box.

5 Use the drive, directory, and file list boxes to view other bitmaps, Windows metafiles, and icons on your system.

You'll probably find several interesting bitmaps in the \Windows folder.

When you've finished experimenting with Browser, stop the program and save it to disk.

6 Click the Close button on the form.

7 On the File menu, click Save Project As. Save the form as **MyBrowser** and the project as **MyBrowser**.

What If My Program Crashes?

If you use the Browser program a lot, you might notice that it produces a runtime error, or *crashes,* in two specific situations. Because this program was created quickly for demonstration purposes, you didn't add the code necessary to protect the program against out-of-the-ordinary problems. As you begin to write more complex programs, however, you'll want to test your code carefully to make sure you can't break it under either normal or extreme operating conditions.

The first problem with Browser is that it crashes if the user selects a drive in the drive list box that doesn't contain a disk or is otherwise unready for work. (An example of an unready drive would be a drive containing a floppy disk that isn't formatted or an offline network drive.) To watch this happen, verify that drive A in your system doesn't have a disk in it, and then select A: in the Browser drive list box. The program immediately stops, and Visual Basic displays the message "Run-time error '68': Device unavailable." This statement means that Visual Basic couldn't find the floppy disk and quit running the program because it didn't know how to proceed. The Browser program relies on the user not making any mistakes with disks, which is probably not a wise assumption.

The second problem Browser has is with viewing artwork located in the root folder. Because files in the root folder have a pathname of only the backward slash (\), the program statement

```
SelectedFile = File1.Path & "\" & File1.Filename
```

causes trouble because it creates a pathname containing two backward slashes. (For example, the statement would describe a file named Truck.wmf in the root folder as C:\\Truck.wmf.) When Visual Basic tries to load a file whose name contains two backward slashes side by side, it causes a runtime error and the program stops.

The way around these problems is to use program statements that avoid the error condition (you can do this with the pathname problem) or to create special routines called *error handlers* that will help your program recover if errors occur. Error handlers are beyond the scope of our current discussion, but for now you should note that although Visual Basic can handle most operating conditions, now and then users can create problems that make all but the sturdiest programs crash. We'll discuss tracking down and fixing bugs in Lessons 6 and 8.

Objects for Gathering Input

Visual Basic provides several objects for gathering input in a program. *Text boxes* accept typed input, *menus* present commands that can be clicked, and *dialog boxes* offer a variety of elements that can be chosen individually or selected in a group. In this exercise, you'll learn to use four important objects that will help you gather input in several different situations. You'll learn about option button objects, check box objects, list box objects, and combo box objects. You will explore each of these objects as you use a Visual Basic program called Online Shopper, the user interface for an Internet application or other online utility that allows you to order computers and office equipment graphically. As you run the program, you'll get some hands-on experience with the input objects. In the next lesson, we'll discuss how these objects can be used along with menus in a full-fledged program.

The Online Shopper Program

The Online Shopper program simulates an electronic ordering environment in which you see what you're ordering as you make your selection. If you work in a business that does a lot of order entry, you might want to expand this program into a full-featured graphical order entry program someday. (Graphical tools like this are popular on the Web.) As you experiment with Online Shopper, spend some time observing how the option button, check box, list box, and combo box elements work in the program. They were created in a few short steps by using Visual Basic.

Run the Online Shopper program

1. On the Visual Basic File menu, click Open Project.

    The Open Project dialog box appears.

2. Open the Online.vbp file in the \Vb6Sbs\Less03 folder.

3. In the Project window, select the Online form and click the View Object button.

View Object button

4. Close the Properties, Project, and Form Layout windows to see more of the Online Shopper form. If the Immediate window (a tool that is typically used only for debugging) is also open, close it now. You won't be using these tools in this exercise.

    The Online Shopper form appears, as shown in the illustration on the following page.

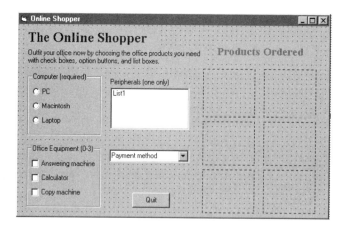

The Online Shopper form contains option button, check box, list box, combo box, image box, command button, and label objects. These objects work together to create a simple order entry program that demonstrates how the Visual Basic input objects work. When the Online Shopper program is run, it loads Windows metafiles from the \Vb6Sbs\Less03 folder on drive C and displays them in the six image boxes on the form.

tip

If you installed the practice files in a location other than the default C:\Vb6Sbs folder, the statements in the program that load the artwork from the disk will contain an incorrect pathname. (Each statement begins with c:\Vb6Sbs\less03, as you'll see soon.) If this is the case, you can make the program work by renaming the practice files folder to \Vb6Sbs or by changing the pathnames in the Code window using the editing keys or the Replace command on the Edit menu.

Start button

Option buttons allow the user to select one item from a list.

5 Click the Start button on the toolbar.

The program runs in the programming environment.

6 Click the Laptop option button in the Computer box.

The image of a laptop computer appears in the Products Ordered area on the right side of the form. In the Computer box, a group of *option buttons* is used to gather input from the user. Option buttons force the user to choose one (and only one) item from a list of possibilities. The user can click the various option buttons repeatedly. After each click, the current choice is graphically depicted in the order area to the right.

7 Click the Answering Machine, Calculator, and Copy Machine check boxes in the Office Equipment box.

Check boxes let the user select any number of items.

Check boxes are used in a program when more than one option at a time can be selected from a list. Click the Calculator check box again, and notice that the picture of the calculator disappears from the order area. Because each user interface element is live and responds to click events as they occur, order choices are reflected immediately.

8 Click Satellite Dish in the Peripherals list box.

List boxes let the user select one item from a variable-length list of choices.

A picture of a satellite dish is added to the order area. A *list box* is used to get a user's single response from a list of choices. List boxes can contain many items to choose from (scroll bars appear if the list is longer than the list box), and unlike option buttons, a default selection is not required. In a Visual Basic program, items can be added to, removed from, or sorted in a list box while the program is running.

9 Now choose U.S. Dollars (sorry, no credit) from the payment list in the Payment Method combo box.

Combo boxes take up less space than list boxes.

A *combo box,* or drop-down list box, is similar to a regular list box, but it takes up less space. Visual Basic automatically handles the opening, closing, and scrolling of the list box. All you do as a programmer is write code to add items to the list box before the program starts and to process the user's selection. You'll see examples of each task in the Online Shopper code.

After you make your order selections, your screen should look something like this:

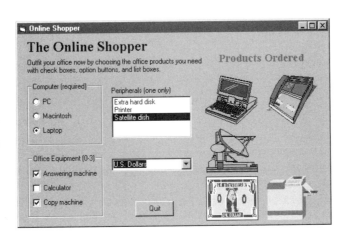

10   Practice making a few more changes to the order list in the program (try different computers, peripherals, and payment methods), and then click the Quit button in the program to exit.

The program closes when you click Quit, and the programming environment appears.

Lessons 5, 6, and 7 discuss program code in detail.

Looking at the Online Shopper Program Code

Although you haven't had much formal experience with program code yet, it's worth taking a quick look at a few event procedures in Online Shopper to see how the program processes input from the user interface elements. In these procedures, you'll see the If...Then and Select Case statements at work. You'll learn about these and other decision structures in Lesson 6. For now, concentrate on the Value property, which changes when a check box is selected, and the ListIndex property, which changes when a list box is selected.

Examine the check box code and list box code

1   Be sure the program has stopped running, and then double-click the Answering Machine check box in the Office Equipment box to display the Check1_Click event procedure in the Code window.

2   Resize the Code window, and you'll see the following program code:

In program code, an underscore (_) at the end of a line indicates that the program statement continues on the next line.

```
Private Sub Check1_Click()
    If Check1.Value = 1 Then
        Image2.Picture = _
            LoadPicture("c:\vb6sbs\less03\answmach.wmf")
        Image2.Visible = True
    Else
        Image2.Visible = False
    End If
End Sub
```

The Check1_Click event procedure contains the program code that is run when a user clicks the Answering Machine check box in the program. The important keyword here is Check1.Value, which should be read as "the Value property of the first check box object." Check1 is the name of the first check box created on a form; subsequent check boxes are named Check2, Check3, and so on. The Value property is the property that changes when a user clicks the check box on the form. When an "x" or a check mark appears in the check box, the Value property is set to 1; when the check box is blank, the Value property is set to 0 (zero).

The Value property can be set by using the Properties window when you are designing your check box (so that the check box can contain a default setting), or the property can be changed by the user when the program is running (when a check box is clicked). In the code above, the Value property is evaluated by an If...Then...Else decision structure. If the property evaluates to 1, the program loads the picture of an answering machine into the second image box on the form and makes the picture visible. Otherwise (if the Value property is 0), the answering machine picture is hidden from view. If this seems odd, don't worry. You'll learn about decision structures in detail in Lesson 6.

③ Close the Code window, and double-click the Peripherals list box on the form.

The List1_Click event procedure appears in the Code window. The following statements appear:

```
Private Sub List1_Click()
    Select Case List1.ListIndex
    Case 0
        Image3.Picture = _
            LoadPicture("c:\vb6sbs\less03\harddisk.wmf")
    Case 1
        Image3.Picture = _
            LoadPicture("c:\vb6sbs\less03\printer.wmf")
    Case 2
        Image3.Picture = _
            LoadPicture("c:\vb6sbs\less03\satedish.wmf")
    End Select
    Image3.Visible = True
End Sub
```

When the user clicks an item in a list box, Visual Basic returns the name of the item to the program in the List1.Text property.

Here you see code that executes when the user clicks an item in the Peripherals list box in the program. In this case, the important keyword is List1.ListIndex, which is read "the ListIndex property of the first list box object." After the user clicks an item in the list box, the ListIndex property returns a number that corresponds to the location of the item in the list box. (The first item is numbered 0, the second item is numbered 1, and so on.)

The actual text of the choice (the name of the list box item) is also returned in the List1.Text property. Visual Basic programmers often use this value in their programs. In the code above, List1.ListIndex is evaluated by the Select Case decision structure, and a different Windows metafile is loaded depending on the value of the ListIndex property. If the value is 0, a picture of a hard disk is loaded; if the value is 1, a picture of a printer is loaded; if the value is 2, a picture of a satellite dish (my dream peripheral) is loaded. You'll learn more about how the Select Case decision structure works in Lesson 6.

A Word About Terminology

So far in this book I've used several different terms to describe items in a Visual Basic program. Although I haven't defined each of them formally, it's worth listing several of them now to clear up any confusion. Can you tell the difference yet?

Control A control is a tool you use to create objects on a Visual Basic form. You select controls from the toolbox and use them to draw objects on a form by using the mouse. You use most controls to create user interface elements, such as command buttons, image boxes, and list boxes.

Object An object is the name of a user interface element you create on a Visual Basic form by using a toolbox control. You can move, resize, and customize objects by using property settings. Objects have what is known as *inherent functionality*—they know how to operate and can respond to certain situations on their own. (A list box "knows" how to scroll, for example.) You can program Visual Basic objects by using customized event procedures for different situations in a program. In Visual Basic, the form itself is also an object.

Property A property is a value or characteristic held by a Visual Basic object, such as Caption or ForeColor. Properties can be set at design time by using the Properties window or at runtime by using statements in the program code. In code, the format for setting a property is

```
Object.Property = Value
```

where *Object* is the name of the object you're customizing, *Property* is the characteristic you want to change, and *Value* is the new property setting. For example,

```
Command1.Caption = "Hello"
```

4   Close the Code window, and double-click the form (not any of the objects) to display the code associated with the form itself.

Statements in the Form_Load event procedure run when the program starts.

The Form_Load event procedure appears in the Code window. This is the procedure that is executed each time the Online Shopper program starts, or *loads*. Programmers put program statements in this special procedure when they want them executed every time a program loads. Often, as in the Online Shopper program, the statements define an aspect of the user interface that couldn't be created by using toolbox controls or the Properties window.

could be used in the program code to set the Caption property of the Command1 object to "Hello".

Event procedure An event procedure is a block of code that is executed when an object is manipulated in a program. For example, when the first command button in a program is clicked, the Command1_Click event procedure is executed. Event procedures typically evaluate and set properties and use other program statements to perform the work of the program.

Program statement A program statement is a keyword in the code that does the work of the program. Visual Basic program statements create storage space for data, open files, perform calculations, and do several other important tasks.

Variable A variable is a special container used to hold data temporarily in a program. The programmer creates variables to store the results of a calculation, create filenames, process input, and so on. Numbers, names, and property values can be stored in variables.

Method A method is a special statement that performs an action or a service for a particular object in a program. In program code, the notation for using a method is

Object.Method Value

where *Object* is the name of the object you want to change, *Method* is the command you want to use to change the object, and *Value* is an optional argument to be used by the method. For example, the statement

```
List1.AddItem "Check"
```

uses the AddItem method to put the word *Check* in the List1 list box.

The Form_Load code follows:

```
Image1.Picture = LoadPicture("c:\vb6sbs\less03\pcomputr.wmf")
List1.AddItem "Extra hard disk"
List1.AddItem "Printer"
List1.AddItem "Satellite dish"

Combo1.AddItem "U.S. Dollars"
Combo1.AddItem "Check"
Combo1.AddItem "English Pounds"
```

The first line loads the personal computer Windows metafile into the first image box. This is the default setting reflected in the Computer option button box. The next three lines add items to the Peripherals list box (List1) in the program. The words in quotes will appear in the list box when it appears on the form. Below the list box program statements, the items in the Payment Method combo box (Combo1) are specified. The important keyword in both these groups is AddItem, which is a special function, or *method,* for the list box and combo box objects.

Methods are special statements that perform an action or a service for a particular object, such as adding items to a list box. Methods differ from properties, which contain a value, and event procedures, which execute when a user manipulates an object. Methods can also be shared among objects, so when you learn how to use one method, you'll often be able to apply it to several circumstances. We'll discuss several important methods as you work through this book.

You're finished using the Online Shopper program. Take a few minutes to examine any other parts of the program you're interested in, and then move on to the next exercise.

Using an OLE Object to Launch Applications

One of the most exciting features of Visual Basic is its ability to work closely with other applications for Windows. Using an OLE object, you can launch applications or other components from your program while it is running and process several types of information. You can also run parts of other applications (such as the spelling checker in Microsoft Word) by using a special technology called *Automation* (formerly called OLE Automation).

An OLE object lets you start applications for Windows from inside a Visual Basic application.

We'll discuss Automation in detail in Lesson 14. In the next exercise, you'll learn how an OLE object works and how it can be used (without program code) to create an application named Bid Estimator that launches Word, Microsoft Excel, and Microsoft Paint documents so that the user can enter estimate and bid information and site drawings for a construction project.

To run the Bid Estimator program, you'll need copies of Word, Excel, and Paint on your hard disk. (Paint is included with Microsoft Windows.) When you first create an OLE object, an Insert Object dialog box appears, listing the available application objects you can use in your program. If you don't have Word, Excel, or Paint on your hard disk, the Insert Object dialog box won't list them, but feel free to choose another object instead. The purpose of this exercise is to practice using applications you'd like to start from a Visual Basic program. When you run it, the completed utility will look like the illustration shown on the following page.

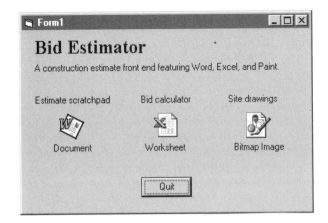

Create the Bid Estimator program

1 On the File menu, click New Project, and then click OK to create a standard .exe file.

The Online Shopper program closes, and a new form appears in the programming environment.

2 In the upper-left corner of the form, create a label that has the caption "Bid Estimator". Below the label, create a second label that has the caption "A construction estimate front end featuring Word, Excel, and Paint".

Leave some extra space in the first label—you'll increase the point size of the caption when you set properties later.

3 Below the second label, spaced equally across the form (see the illustration above), create three additional labels that have the captions "Estimate scratchpad", "Bid calculator", and "Site drawings".

These labels will be used to identify the OLE objects used to launch the Word, Excel, and Paint applications, respectively.

Now you'll add the objects to the form.

OLE control

4 Click the OLE control in the toolbox.

5 Below the Estimate Scratchpad label, create a rectangle about the size of a matchbox by using the OLE control.

When you release the mouse button, Visual Basic displays the Insert Object dialog box, shown on the following page, which contains a list of all the application objects you can use in your program. (This will take a moment or two, because Visual Basic needs to gather the information from your system registry.) The exact list will vary from system to system.

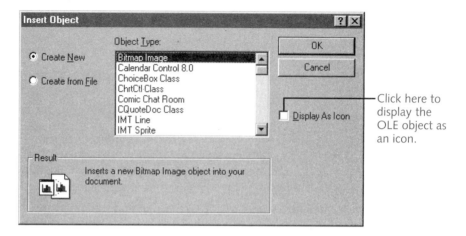

Click here to display the OLE object as an icon.

6 Scroll down the list of objects, and click the Microsoft Word Document object if you have Microsoft Word on your computer.

If you don't have Word, select another Windows-based word processor or a similar application in the dialog box.

7 Click the Display As Icon check box in the Insert Object dialog box so that the application will appear as an icon in your Visual Basic program.

If you don't click this check box, the application object (typically a document) will be displayed in a window in your application. You'll use this feature to considerable advantage later in this book. For now, however, just click Display As Icon.

8 Click OK to close the Insert Object dialog box and to open Word.

Word opens and displays a blank word processing document in a window. This document will become a *template* in the Bid Estimator program.

It should contain any information a contractor would find useful when using the program, such as information about the construction company, names, addresses, prices, materials, and so on.

9 For now just type **Estimate Notes—**. Then use the Date And Time command on the Insert menu to add today's date to the template.

The text appears in the Word document as it will when you run the program.

10 On the Word File menu, click Exit.

If you are asked whether you want to update the source document, click Yes. You will receive this prompt when you close certain application objects.

When you're finished with the first object, your form should look like the following illustration. Resize your object or label if any text is hidden from view.

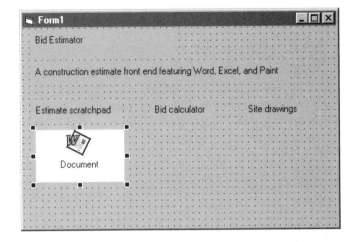

tip

The three-dimensional appearance of the OLE object is controlled by the Appearance property, which has 3D and Flat settings. In step 13, you will set the Appearance property of each OLE object to Flat and the BackColor property of each OLE object to light gray to make the objects match the form.

11 Repeat steps 4 through 10 to add a Microsoft Excel Worksheet object (or its equivalent) to the form below the Bid Calculator label and a Bitmap Image object to the form below the Site Drawings label.

Be sure to click the Display As Icon check box in the Insert Object dialog box both times, and add some template information (such as notes or instructions) to the Excel worksheet and the Paint canvas if you're comfortable using those programs. In the Excel worksheet, it is easy to imagine a well-organized contractor including several rows and columns of bidding information, including costs of lumber, paint, and labor. The beauty of using other Windows-based applications in your program is that you have access to all these applications' features automatically—you don't have to reinvent the wheel!

12 Place a command button at the bottom of the form. After you've added the button, double-click the object and type the statement **End** in the Command1_Click event procedure.

The End program statement will terminate the program when the user is finished using it.

13 Set the following properties for the objects on the form by using the Properties window:

Object	Property	Setting
Command1	Caption	"Quit"
Label1	Font	Times New Roman, Bold, 18-point
OLE1	BorderStyle	0 – None
	Appearance	0 – Flat
	BackColor	Light gray
OLE2	BorderStyle	0 – None
	Appearance	0 – Flat
	BackColor	Light gray
OLE3	BorderStyle	0 – None
	Appearance	0 – Flat
	BackColor	Light gray

14 On the File menu, click Save Project As, and save the form to disk with the name **MyOleBid**. Save the project to disk with the name **MyOleBid**.

When you've finished, your MyOleBid form should look similar to the following:

The complete OleBid program is located on disk in the \Vb6Sbs\Less03 folder.

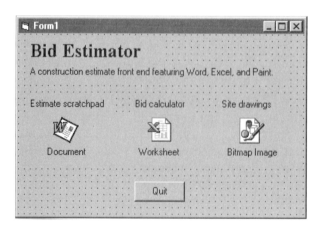

Now try running the program to see how the OLE objects operate at runtime.

Run the My Bid Estimator program

① Click the Start button on the toolbar.

The program runs in the programming environment. The OLE1 object (the Document icon) is surrounded by a dotted line, indicating that it has the attention, or *focus,* of the program.

tip

The focus is important for keyboard operations. When the user presses Enter, the object that has the focus is selected, or activated, in the program. The user can switch the focus to another object in the program by pressing the Tab key or by clicking the object. You can change the order in which objects receive the focus in the program by changing each object's TabIndex property.

② Double-click the Document icon in the program.

The word processor starts, and the Word template document appears in a window.

③ Type a few lines of text (pretend you're an important contractor), and then on the File menu, click Exit to return to the MyOleBid program.

④ Double-click the Worksheet icon in the program.

The spreadsheet starts, and the Excel template appears in a window.

⑤ Enter a few rows and columns of information in the spreadsheet (feel free to use Excel functions and formatting features if you like). Then on the File menu, click Exit to return to the MyOleBid program.

⑥ Double-click the Bitmap Image icon.

The Paint accessory program starts and appears in a window. Paint is a simple illustration program containing drawing tools and color palettes for creating rudimentary artwork.

⑦ Create a simple construction site sketch with the Paint accessory (or pretend you did), and then, on the File menu, click Exit & Return To.

⑧ Click the Quit button to end the program.

Congratulations! You've built your first program that uses Microsoft Office application objects. You can use this technique to include in a program any application object installed on your system. Now you'll try working with another type of file in the Windows environment—a preexisting database containing customer names and addresses.

Using a Data Object to View a Microsoft Access Database

If you work in a corporate setting or share information with other computer users regularly, you might use databases to track important information about clients, employees, or ongoing projects. A *database* is an organized collection of information stored electronically in a file. Database applications, such as Microsoft Access, dBASE, and Paradox, are special programs that create and process information stored in databases. They provide the tools to design the database, manipulate the information in it, and search for specific items. To enhance your work with databases, Visual Basic provides three objects that let you display and modify the information in database files. The primary object, data, gives you access to the fields and records of a database file directly on your form. You'll practice using a data object now to display information in an Access database named Students.mdb.

Fields and Records

Two important terms used to describe information in databases are *fields* and *records*. Fields are the categories of information stored in a database. Typical fields in a customer database might include customer names, addresses, phone numbers, and comments. All the information about a particular customer or business is called a record. When databases are created, information is entered in tables of fields and records. Often the records correspond to rows in the table, and the fields correspond to columns.

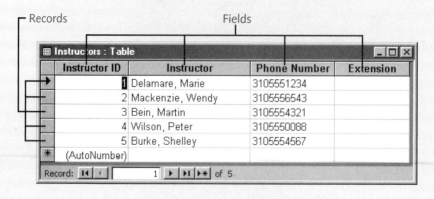

tip

The Access file used in this exercise is on disk in the Less03 folder, so you can try this exercise even if you don't have Access installed. You can also substitute one of your own database files for the Access file if you like

Create a data object

1 On the File menu, click New Project, and then click OK to create a standard .exe file.

The MyOleBid program closes, and a new form appears in the programming environment. Save any changes to the MyOleBid program if you are prompted to.

Data control

2 Click the Data control in the toolbox.

3 Move the mouse pointer to the center of the form, near the bottom, and draw a rectangular box by using the control.

A data object named Data1 appears on the form:

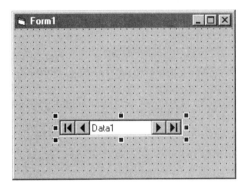

The object contains arrows that let you scroll through the records of your database when the program runs. The object also contains a caption (currently Data1) that you can use to describe the database you'll access by using the object. Typically, the caption is set to the name of the database. The second set of arrows near the outside edges of the object are used to move to the beginning or the end of the database.

You can perform many sophisticated operations with a database in Visual Basic. In this exercise, you will display the Instructor field of the Students.mdb database. (You'll actually be able to scroll through the database and view each name in the file.) To display the Instructor field on the form, an additional object is needed to hold the data. Because the data you want to display is text, you'll add a text box object to the form. (You'll also place a label above the text box to identify the database field.) Finally, you'll establish a connection between the data object and the text box object, or *bind* them together, by using several property settings.

Create text box and label objects

TextBox control

1 Click the TextBox control in the toolbox.

2 Create a text box on the form, above the data object.

The text box should be about the same size as the data object. The box should be wide enough to display instructor names (both first and last) up to 20 characters long.

Label control

3 Click the Label control in the toolbox.

4 Create a label above the text box on the form.

When you've finished creating the objects, your screen should look like this:

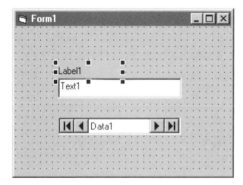

Now you'll set the properties for the objects.

Set object properties

1 Click the data object, and then click the Properties Window button on the toolbar.

2 In the Properties window, verify that the Connect property is set to Access (the default).

The Connect property records the database or spreadsheet format you'll be using. The formats Visual Basic can read include Access, Excel, Lotus 1-2-3, dBASE, FoxPro, and Paradox.

③   In the Properties window, set the DatabaseName property to c:\vb6sbs\
less03\students.mdb by selecting the file in the DatabaseName dialog box.

Students.mdb is the sample Access database you'll open in this exercise. It
contains a number of useful tables, fields, and records that an instructor or
administrator might use to track academic data, including student names,
teachers, classrooms, grades, and miscellaneous scheduling information. I've
made this a fairly sophisticated database so that you can continue to experiment on your own if you like.

④   In the Properties window, click the RecordSource property, and then click
the drop-down list box arrow. When a list of database tables appears, click
Instructors in the list box.

The RecordSource property lets you specify the table (the collection of data)
you want to open in the database.

⑤   In the Properties window, set the Caption property of the data object to
"Students.mdb".

The caption in the control changes to Students.mdb to identify the database
to the user.

Now you'll change the DataSource property of the text box to link the text
box to the data object.

⑥   Click the text box object, and then click the Properties Window button on
the toolbar.

⑦   In the Properties window, click the DataSource property, click the drop-
down list box arrow, and then click Data1.

⑧   In the Properties window, click the DataField property, click the drop-down
list box arrow, and then click Instructor (the field you want to display) in
the list.

⑨   Click the Label object, click the Properties button on the toolbar, and then
change the Caption property to "Instructor".

This will identify the database field in the text box when the program runs.
Adding labels to your form to explain what objects are is always a good
idea, especially when you're working with database fields.

⑩   Save your form as **MyData** and your project as **MyData**.

That's it! Now run your program.

Run the MyData program

1 Click the Start button on the toolbar.

The complete Data.vbp program is located on disk in the \Vb6Sbs\Less03 folder.

The program runs in the program environment, as shown in the following illustration:

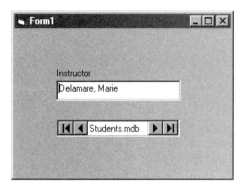

Visual Basic loads the Students.mdb database, opens the Instructor table, and places the first Instructor field in the text box. Examine other field entries now by clicking buttons in the data object.

2 Click the inner-right button in the data object.

The second name in the database appears in the text window.

3 Click the outer-right button in the data object.

Visual Basic displays the last name in the database.

4 Click the outer-left button in the data object.

Visual Basic displays the first name in the database.

5 Click the Close button on the form to stop the program.

Modifying a Database

A data object also lets you modify the information in databases. To change a name in the Students.mdb database, run the MyData program and scroll to the name you want to change. Then click in the Name text box, and edit the name as you see fit. When you change to a different record, the edit you made is copied to the original database immediately. Give it a try now.

Change a name in the database

1 Click Start on the toolbar to run the MyData program.

The first name in the database appears in the text box.

② Highlight the first name by using the mouse, press Del, and then type **Cocco, Sean.**

③ Click the inside right arrow in the data object to move to the next record.

The first name in the database is changed to Cocco, Sean.

④ Click the inside left arrow in the data object to move back to the first record.

The first name now appears as Cocco, Sean.

⑤ Click the Close button on the form to stop the program.

As you can see, a data object gives you quick access to preexisting databases. You can display any field in the database and process the information as you see fit. You'll learn more about data objects and how to manipulate database records in future lessons.

One Step Further   Installing ActiveX Controls

You can extend the functionality of Visual Basic by installing the ActiveX controls that come with Visual Basic or by installing ActiveX controls that you create yourself or acquire from third-party tool vendors. To conserve system resources and desktop space, Visual Basic only displays the basic set of interface controls in the toolbox when you open a new project. However, you can customize the toolbox for each project individually by using the Components command on the Project menu. The ActiveX controls you install take advantage of 32-bit ActiveX technology, a Microsoft standard for programmable objects in application programs, operating systems, and Internet tools. You can recognize ActiveX controls by their .ocx filename extension. They are added to the operating system automatically each time you install a new application program. (Visual Basic "learns" about new ActiveX controls by looking for those associated with specific programs in the Windows system registry.)

Install the Grid and the CommonDialog ActiveX controls

Each version of Visual Basic includes extra ActiveX controls you can use in your projects. (If you have the Professional or Enterprise Editions of Visual Basic, you'll have a variety of interesting ActiveX controls to choose from.) For example, if you're writing a program to display data in a table, you can install the FlexGrid control, located in the file Msflxgrd.ocx, and use it to create a grid of cells on a form. (A grid object looks a lot like an Excel worksheet.) Another useful ActiveX control, the CommonDialog control, which is located in the file Comdlg32.ocx, creates standard dialog boxes, such as Open and Save As.

Follow these steps to install the ActiveX controls:

① On the File menu, click New Project, and then click OK to create a standard .exe file.

Save any changes to the MyData program if you are prompted to.

② On the Project menu, click the Components command, and then click the Controls tab.

The Components dialog box appears.

The Controls tab presents an alphabetical list of the ActiveX controls in your system that can be added to your project's toolbox. To give you flexibility in how you create your programs, every project has its own unique toolbox containing the default Visual Basic controls and any ActiveX controls you select. Accordingly, any controls you add to this project now will appear only in this project's toolbox. In the following steps, you'll add the FlexGrid control (Msflxgrd.ocx) and the CommonDialog control (Comdlg32.ocx) to your toolbox.

tip

The Components dialog box also contains an Insertable Objects tab, which you can use to add application objects to your project's toolbox. An *insertable object* is a program component supplied by another application for Windows, such as a Word document or an Excel worksheet. You'll find these tools just as useful as ActiveX controls.

③ Click the check box next to the control named Microsoft Common Dialog Control 6.0.

The ActiveX control is selected, and the location of the .ocx file appears at the bottom of the dialog box.

④ As shown in the illustration on the following page, click the check box next to the control named Microsoft FlexGrid Control 6.0 to select it as well.

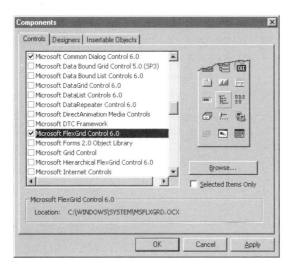

5 Click OK to add the selected ActiveX controls to this project's toolbox.

The toolbox displays two new controls, as shown in the following illustration:

CommonDialog control

FlexGrid control

The FlexGrid and CommonDialog controls work exactly like the rest of the Visual Basic controls in the toolbox. In fact, if you didn't know they were ActiveX controls, it would be difficult to tell them apart from the standard toolbox controls. You select the ActiveX controls by clicking them, and you use them to create objects on a form the same way you use the other controls. The ActiveX controls also have adjustable property settings and can be used in program code like the rest of the controls you've used in this lesson.

If you want to continue to the next lesson

● Keep Visual Basic running, and turn to Lesson 4.

If you are asked whether you want to save the changes to the current project later, click No.

If you want to quit Visual Basic for now

● On the File menu, click Exit.

If you see a Save dialog box, click No. You don't need to save this project and its list of ActiveX controls.

Upgrade Notes:
What's Different in Visual Basic .NET?

If you choose to upgrade to Visual Basic .NET in the future, you'll notice some new features related to the topics in this lesson, including the following:

■ Visual Studio .NET offers several controls that are not included in the Visual Basic 6.0 Toolbox, including the new LinkLabel control, which is designed to display and manage Web links on a form.

■ The Visual Basic 6.0 Frame control has been replaced with a new GroupBox control.

■ The OptionButton control has been replaced with a new RadioButton control.

■ There is no longer an Image control in Visual Basic .NET. In Visual Basic .NET you use the PictureBox control instead.

■ You use the System.Drawing.Image.FromFile method (not the LoadPicture function) to add images to picture box objects.

■ Message boxes are now displayed using the MessageBox.Show method.

■ The ListIndex property in the ListBox control has been replaced by a property called SelectedIndex. The same change was made to the ComboBox control.

■ The DriveListBox control, DirListBox control, and FileListBox control are no longer used for file system operations. Instead, Visual Basic .NET programmers use the OpenFileDialog control and the new StreamReader class in the .NET Framework library.

■ The OLE control is no longer supported in Visual Basic .NET.

■ The Data control is no longer part of the Visual Basic .NET Toolbox. Data access is now handled using ADO.NET data access tools and techniques.

■ ActiveX controls are added to the Toolbox in a new way, and are "wrapped" by Visual Studio so that they can be used in Visual Basic .NET applications

Lesson 3 Quick Reference

To	Do this	Button
Create a text box	Click the TextBox control, and draw the box.	
Create a command button	Click the CommandButton control, and draw the button.	
Change a property at runtime	Change the value of the property by using program code. For example: `Text1.Text = "Hello!"`	
Create a drive list box	Click the DriveListBox control, and draw the box.	
Create a directory list box	Click the DirListBox control, and draw the box.	
Create a file list box	Click the FileListBox control, and draw the box.	
Prevent a program crash	Write an error handler by using program code. (See Lesson 8.)	

Load a picture at runtime	Call the LoadPicture function, and assign the result to the Picture property of an image object or a picture box object. The syntax for this statement is
	
	`Object.Picture = _`
	`    LoadPicture(SelectedFile)`
	
	where *Object* is the name of the object and *SelectedFile* is a variable that	

(continued)

Working with Controls   3

Lesson 3 Quick Reference

To	Do this	Button
	holds the filename of a graphic. For example: ```SelectedFile = "c:\truck.bmp" Image1.Picture = _ LoadPicture(SelectedFile)```	
Create an option button	Use the OptionButton control. To create multiple option buttons, place more than one option button object inside a box you create by using the Frame control.	
Create a check box	Click the CheckBox control, and draw a check box.	
Create a list box	Click the ListBox control, and draw a list box.	
Create a drop-down list box	Click the ComboBox control, and draw a drop-down list box.	
Add items to a list box	Include statements with the AddItem method in the Form_Load procedure of your program. For example: ```List1.AddItem "Printer"```	
Launch applications for Windows	Use the OLE control to draw a box for the application on your form. Then select the desired application object in the Insert Object dialog box to include it in your program.	
Display existing databases within your program	Use the Data control to create an object to move through the database. Then bind the data object to an object that can display the database records (typically, a text box object).	
Modify records in a database	Display the database in the program. Edit the record in the text box object at runtime, and then click an arrow on the data control to save the change to disk.	
Install ActiveX controls	On the Project menu, click the Components command, and then click the Controls tab. Select the ActiveX controls you want to add to your project's toolbox, and then click the OK button.	

4

Working with Menus and Dialog Boxes

**ESTIMATED
TIME
45 min.**

In this lesson you will learn how to:

✔ *Add menus to your programs by using the Menu Editor.*

✔ *Process menu choices by using program code.*

✔ *Use common dialog objects to display standard dialog boxes.*

In Lesson 3, you used several Microsoft Visual Basic objects to gather input from the user while he or she was using a program. In this lesson, you'll learn to present choices to the user by using professional-looking menus and dialog boxes. A *menu* is located on the menu bar and contains a list of related commands. When you click a menu title, a list of the menu commands appears in a list box. Most menu commands are executed immediately after they are clicked; for example, when the user clicks the Copy command on the Edit menu, information is copied to the Clipboard immediately. If a menu command is followed by an ellipsis (...), however, Visual Basic displays a dialog box requesting more information before the command is carried out. In this lesson, you'll learn to use the Menu Editor and the CommonDialog control to add menus and standard dialog boxes to your programs.

Adding Menus by Using the Menu Editor

The Menu Editor is a graphical tool that manages menus in your programs. It lets you add new menus, modify and reorder existing menus, and delete old menus. It also lets you add special effects to your menus, such as access keys, check marks, and keyboard shortcuts. After you have added menus to your form, you can use event procedures to process the menu commands. In the following exercise, you'll use the Menu Editor to create a Clock menu containing commands that display the current date and time.

Create a menu

1 Start Visual Basic and open a new standard project.

If the programming environment is already running, on the File menu, click New Project to open a new standard project.

Menu Editor button

2 Click the Menu Editor button on the toolbar.

The Menu Editor appears, as shown in the following illustration:

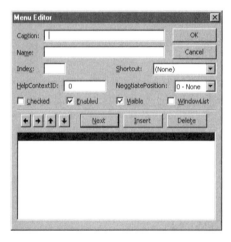

The Menu Editor helps you create and modify menus.

The Menu Editor displays menu-building commands and options in a dialog box. You specify the caption for a menu (the name of the menu on the screen) in the Caption text box. You specify the name for a menu (the name it will have in the program code) in the Name text box. These are the two most important settings for a menu. Additional settings, such as Index, HelpContextID, Shortcut, and Checked, are optional. You'll learn about the Shortcut setting at the end of this lesson.

When you click the Next button in the Menu Editor dialog box, the Menu Editor clears the dialog box so that you can enter specifications for the next menu item. The menu list box at the bottom of the dialog box displays menu items as you create them and shows the overall structure of the menu.

You'll use the Menu Editor now to create a Clock menu.

❸ Type **Clock** in the Caption text box, and then press Tab.

The word *Clock* is entered as the caption of your first menu, and the cursor moves to the Name text box. As you type the menu caption, the caption also appears in the menu list box at the bottom of the dialog box.

By convention, the prefix mnu is used to identify a menu.

❹ Type **mnuClock** in the Name text box.

The word *mnuClock* is entered as the name of your menu in the program.

By convention, the prefix *mnu* is used to identify a menu object in the program code. Prefixing user interface elements with a three-character label will help you differentiate event procedures as your programs get larger, and it will help you identify interface elements in the Code window.

tip

The "One Step Further" section in Lesson 9 lists the naming conventions for all Visual Basic objects.

❺ Click the Next button to add the Clock menu title to your program.

The Clock menu is added to the menu bar, and the Menu Editor clears the dialog box for your next menu item. The menu title still appears in the menu list box at the bottom of the dialog box. As you build your menu, each item will be added to the menu list box so that you can see the structure of the menu.

❻ Type **Date** in the Caption text box, press Tab, and then type **mnuDateItem** in the Name text box.

The Date command appears in the menu list box. Because you want to make Date a command rather than a menu title, you use another naming convention—you add the word *Item* to the end of the name in the Name text box. This will help you differentiate menu commands from menu titles in the Code window.

❼ With the Date item highlighted in the menu list box, click the right arrow button in the Menu Editor.

The Date command moves one indent (four spaces) to the right in the menu list box, indicating that the item is a menu command. The position of an item in the list box determines whether it is a menu title (flush left), a menu command (one indent), a submenu title (two indents), or a submenu command (three indents). You click the right arrow button in the Menu Editor dialog box to move items to the right, and you click the left arrow button to move items to the left.

Now you'll add a menu command named Time to the Clock menu.

8   Click the Next button, type **Time**, press Tab, and then type **mnuTimeItem**.

The Time command appears in the menu list box, as shown here:

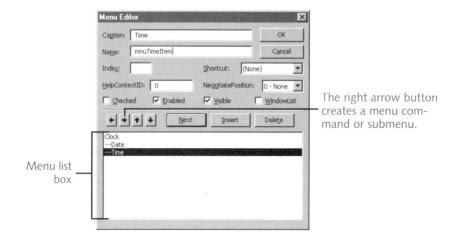

The right arrow button creates a menu command or submenu.

Menu list box

Notice that the Menu Editor assumed that the next item would be a menu command and indented Time one level. You've finished adding commands to the Clock menu, so you can close the Menu Editor.

9   Click OK to close the Menu Editor.

The Menu Editor closes, and your form appears in the programming environment with a menu bar and a Clock menu. Now you'll open the Clock menu to see its contents.

10   Click the Clock menu.

The Date and Time commands appear.

Clicking a menu command in the programming environment displays the event procedure that is executed when the menu command is chosen. You'll create event procedures for Date and Time a little later. First, you'll add keyboard support to the menus.

11   Click the form (or press Esc twice) to close the Clock menu.

Adding Access Keys to Menu Commands

You define an access key by placing an ampersand (&) before the letter.

Visual Basic makes it easy to provide *access key* support for menus and menu commands. The access key for a command is the keyboard key the user can press to execute the command. When the user opens a menu at runtime, the access key for a command is indicated by an underlined letter in the command name. To add an access key to a menu item, all you need to do is start the Menu Editor and prefix the access key letter in the menu item caption with an ampersand (&). From that time forward, your program will support the access key.

Try adding access keys to the Clock menu now.

Menu Conventions

By convention, each menu title and menu command in an application for Microsoft Windows has an initial capital letter. File and Edit are often the first two menu names on the menu bar, and Help is the last. Other common menu names are View, Format, and Window. No matter what menus and commands you use in your applications, take care to be clear and consistent with them. Menus and commands should be easy to use and should have as much in common with those in other Windows-based applications as possible. As you create menu items, use the following guidelines:

- Use short, specific captions consisting of one or two words at most.

- Assign each menu item in a program a unique access key. Use the first letter of the item if possible.

- If a command is used as an on/off toggle, place a check mark next to the item when it is active. You can add a check mark by clicking the Checked check box in the Menu Editor or by setting the menu item's Checked property to True.

- Place an ellipsis (...) after a menu command that requires the user to enter more information before the command can be executed.

- Use menu naming conventions such as the *mnu* prefix and the *Item* suffix when assigning menu names.

Add access keys

*Menu Editor
button*

1 Click the Menu Editor button on the toolbar.

The Menu Editor appears, and the menu list box displays the menu items that are in your program. The caption and name for the Clock menu appear in the dialog box.

2 Click in front of the word *Clock* in the Caption text box.

The cursor blinks before the letter "C" in *Clock*.

3 Type **&** to define the letter "C" as the access key for the Clock menu.

An ampersand appears in the text box.

4 Click the Date command in the menu list.

The caption and name for the Date command appear in the dialog box.

5 Type an ampersand before the letter "D" in the Caption text box.

The letter "D" is now defined as the access key for the Date command.

6 Click the Time command in the menu list.

The caption and name for the Time command appear in the dialog box.

7 Type an ampersand before the letter "T" in the Caption text box.

The letter "T" is now defined as the access key for the Time command.

8 Click OK in the dialog box to close the Menu Editor.

Now you'll run the program to see how the access keys look at runtime.

Start button

9 Click the Start button.

10 Press the Alt key, and then press the Down Arrow key.

The Clock menu and the menu commands are displayed with underlined access keys.

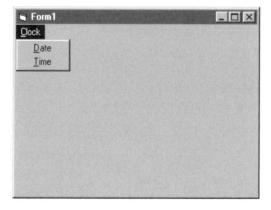

End button

11   Click the End button on the toolbar to quit the program.

Now you'll practice using the Menu Editor to switch the order of the Date and Time commands on the Clock menu. Changing the order of menu items is an important skill to have; at times you'll think better of a decision you made when you first defined your menus.

> ## note
> The Windows XP operating system has changed the way menus are displayed in some programs. For example, access keys are not always visible if you open menus by clicking them with the mouse. In Visual Basic 6.0 applications running under Windows XP, access keys appear only if you open menus using keyboard keys—they don't appear when you click the menus with the mouse. (This is not a bug, but an attempt to make the Windows user interface cleaner looking for people who rarely use access keys.) When you want access keys to appear in Windows XP, press the Alt key to activate the menu, and then the Down Arrow key to display the menu commands. If you're running Windows 98, Windows Me, or Windows 2000, however, you'll always see the access keys—Windows doesn't hide them. (You can also restore the old menu behavior in Windows XP. To do so, right-click the Desktop and choose Properties. In the Display Properties dialog box, click the Appearance tab and then click the Effects tab. In the Effects dialog box, uncheck the Hide Underlined Letters For Keyboard Navigation Until I Press The Alt Key checkbox, and then click OK twice.)

Change the order of menu items

1   Click the Menu Editor button on the toolbar.

       The Menu Editor appears.

2   Click the Time command in the menu list.

       The caption and name for the Time command appear in the dialog box.

3   Click the Up arrow button in the menu list.

       The Time menu item is moved above the Date menu item.

4   Click the OK button.

       The Menu Editor closes, and the order of the Date and Time commands is switched in the Clock menu. You can also use the Down arrow button in the Menu Editor to switch menu items; it moves commands down in the list.

You've finished creating the user interface for the Clock menu. Now you'll use the menu event procedures to process the user's menu selections in the program.

(sidebar) **4**   **Menus and Dialog Boxes**

tip

You can also insert new menu items and delete unwanted menu items by using the Menu Editor. To insert a new menu item, click the item in the menu list that should follow the new item and then click the Insert button. The Menu Editor will insert a blank item in the list. You can define this item by using the Caption and Name text boxes. To delete an unwanted menu item, click the unwanted item in the menu list and then click the Delete button.

Processing Menu Choices

A menu command is processed by an event procedure associated with the command.

After menu items are placed on the menu bar, they become objects in the program. To make the menu objects do meaningful work, you need to write event procedures for them. Menu event procedures typically contain program statements that display or process information on the user interface form and modify one or more menu properties. If more information is needed from the user to process the selected command, an event procedure will often display a dialog box by using a common dialog object or one of the input objects.

In the following exercise, you'll add a label object to your form to display the output of the Time and Date commands on the Clock menu.

Add a label object to the form

Label control

❶ Click the Label control in the toolbox.

❷ Create a small label in the top middle area of the form.

The label appears on the form. It is named Label1 in the program code. Your form should look like the following:

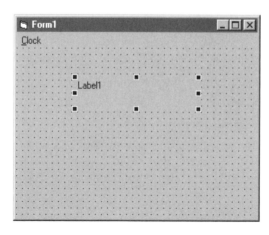

❸ Set the following properties for the label:

Set Label1 properties by using the Properties window.

Object	Property	Setting
Label1	Alignment	2 – Center
	Border Style	1 – Fixed Single
	Caption	(none)
	Font	MS Sans Serif, Bold, 14-point

tip

In the following exercises, you'll enter program code to process menu choices. Type in the program statements exactly as they are printed. You won't learn how program statements work yet—only how they are used to support a functional user interface. You'll learn how program statements work in Lessons 5 through 7.

Now you'll add program statements to the Time and Date event procedures to process the menu commands.

Edit the menu event procedures

❶ Click the View Code button in the Project window to open the Code window.

❷ Click the Object drop-down list box, and then click mnuTimeItem.

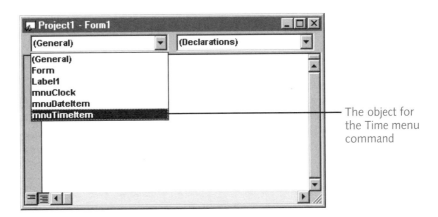

The object for the Time menu command

(side tab) Menus and Dialog Boxes 4

The mnuTimeItem_Click event procedure appears in the Code window. You assigned the name mnuTimeItem to the Time command in the Menu Editor. When the user clicks the Time command in the program, the mnuTimeItem_Click event procedure is executed.

3 Press the Spacebar four times, and then type

```
Label1.Caption = Time
```

This program statement displays the current time (from the system clock) in the caption of the Label1 object, replacing the previous Label1 caption. You can use the Time function at any time in your programs to display the time accurately down to the second.

tip

Visual Basic's Time function returns the current system time. You can set the system time by using the Date/Time option in Control Panel; you can change the system time format by using Control Panel's Regional Settings option.

4 Press the Down arrow key.

Visual Basic interprets the line and adjusts capitalization and spacing, if necessary. (Visual Basic checks each line for syntax errors as you enter it. You can enter a line by pressing Enter, Up arrow, or Down arrow.)

5 Click the mnuDateItem object in the Object drop-down list box.

The mnuDateItem_Click event procedure appears in the Code window. This event procedure is executed when the user clicks the Date command on the Clock menu.

6 Press the Spacebar four times, and then type

```
Label1.Caption = Date
```

This program statement displays the current date (from the system clock) in the caption of the Label1 object, replacing the previous Label1 caption. The Date function is also available for general use in your programs. Assign Date to an object caption whenever you want to display the current date on a form.

tip

Visual Basic's Date function returns the current system date. You can set the system date by using the Date/Time option in Control Panel; you can change the system date format by using Control Panel's Regional Settings option.

7 Press the Down arrow key to enter the line.

Your screen should look like the following:

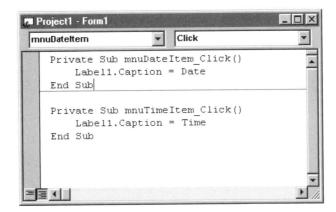

8 Close the Code window.

You've finished entering the menu demonstration program. Now you'll save the form and project to disk under the name MyMenu.

Save the MyMenu program

Save Project button

1 Click the Save Project button on the toolbar.

The Save Project button is the toolbar alternative to the Save Project command on the File menu.

2 To enter the name of your project form, select the \Vb6Sbs\Less04 folder, and then type **MyMenu** and press Enter.

The form is saved to disk with the name MyMenu.frm, and the Save Project As dialog box appears.

3 To enter the name of your project, type **MyMenu** and press Enter.

The project is saved to disk with the name MyMenu.vbp.

Now your program is ready to run.

Run the MyMenu program

Start button

1 Click the Start button on the toolbar.

The MyMenu program runs in the programming environment.

2 Click the Clock menu on the menu bar.

The contents of the Clock menu appear.

*The complete
Menu.vbp pro-
gram is located
on disk in the
\Vb6Sbs\Less04
folder.*

❸ Click the Time command.

The current system time appears in the label box, as shown in the following illustration:

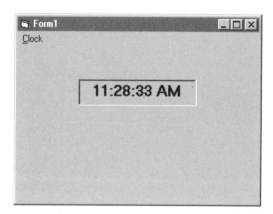

Your time will probably differ from what appears here.

Now you'll try displaying the current date by using the access keys on the menu.

❹ Press and release the Alt key.

The Clock menu on the menu bar is highlighted.

❺ Press C to display the Clock menu.

The contents of the Clock menu appear.

❻ Press D to display the current date.

The current date appears in the label box.

❼ Click the End button to stop the program.

End button

Congratulations! You've created a working program that makes use of menus and access keys. In the next exercise, you'll learn how to use menus to display standard dialog boxes.

System Clock Functions

You can use 10 functions to retrieve chronological values from the system clock. You can use these values to create custom calendars, clocks, and alarms in your programs. The following table lists the most useful system clock functions. For more information, check the Visual Basic online Help.

Function	Description
Time	Returns the current time from the system clock.
Date	Returns the current date from the system clock.
Now	Returns an encoded value representing the current date and time. This function is most useful as an argument for other system clock functions.
Hour (*time*)	Returns the hour portion of the specified time (0 through 23).
Minute (*time*)	Returns the minute portion of the specified time (0 through 59).
Second (*time*)	Returns the second portion of the specified time (0 through 59).
Day (*date*)	Returns a whole number representing the day of the month (1 through 31).
Month (*date*)	Returns a whole number representing the month (1 through 12).
Year (*date*)	Returns the year portion of the specified date.
Weekday (*date*)	Returns a whole number representing the day of the week (1 is Sunday, 2 is Monday, and so on).

Using Common Dialog Objects

A *common dialog object* allows you to display any of five standard dialog boxes in your programs. Each of these common dialog boxes can be displayed from a single common dialog object by using the common dialog object method corresponding to that particular box. (As mentioned earlier, a method is a command that performs an action or a service for an object.) You control the contents of a common dialog box by setting its associated properties. When the user fills out a common dialog box in a program, the results are returned through one or more properties in the common dialog object, which can then be used in the program to perform meaningful work.

The five common dialog boxes provided by the common dialog object are listed with the methods you use to specify them in the following table:

Dialog box	Purpose	Method
Open	Get the drive, folder name, and filename for an existing file	ShowOpen
Save As	Get the drive, folder name, and filename for a new file	ShowSave
Print	Let the user set printing options	ShowPrinter
Font	Let the user choose a new font type and style	ShowFont
Color	Let the user select a color from a palette	ShowColor

Save both the form and the project under a new name when you're renaming a project. Always save the form first.

In the following exercises, you'll add a new menu to the MyMenu program and practice using the Open and Color common dialog boxes. To retain a copy of the original MyMenu program, you'll save the MyMenu form and project with the name MyDialog before you start.

Save the MyMenu files as MyDialog

1 If MyMenu.vbp is not already open, load it from disk by clicking Open Project on the File menu.

   If you didn't create MyMenu, open Menu.vbp from the \Vb6Sbs\Less04 folder. Its contents should match those of MyMenu.

2 On the File menu, click the Save MyMenu.frm As command.

   The Save File As dialog box appears.

3 Specify the \Vb6Sbs\Less04 folder, type **MyDialog.frm**, and then press Enter.

   A copy of the MyMenu form is saved to disk under the name MyDialog.frm.

important

If you don't save the form under a new name first, the MyMenu and MyDialog programs will share the same form.

④ On the File menu, click the Save Project As command.

The Save Project As dialog box appears.

⑤ Specify the \Vb6Sbs\Less04 folder, type **MyDialog.vbp**, and then press Enter.

A copy of the MyMenu project file is saved to disk under the name MyDialog.vbp.

Adding a Common Dialog Object

A common dialog object is not visible to the user at runtime.

Now you'll use the CommonDialog control to add a common dialog object to the form. The common dialog object appears in only one size and is not visible to the user at runtime. (Because the object will not be visible, it can be placed anywhere on the form.) Placing the object on the form allows you to use any of the five common dialog boxes in your program.

Add the CommonDialog control to your toolbox

If the CommonDialog control is not in your toolbox, you can add it by clicking the Components command on the Project menu. Follow these steps:

① On the Project menu, click the Components command.

② Click the Controls tab, and place a check mark in the check box next to the Microsoft Common Dialog Control 6.0.

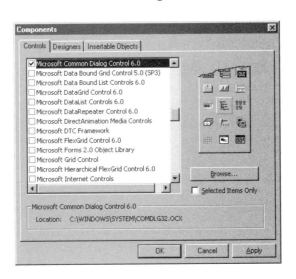

❸   Click OK.

The CommonDialog control appears in your toolbox, as shown in the following illustration:

CommonDialog control

Add a common dialog object

CommonDialog control

❶   Click the CommonDialog control in the toolbox.

❷   Draw a common dialog object in the lower-left corner of the form.

When you finish drawing the object, it resizes itself. The common dialog object is ready for use in your program.

Now you'll create an image object by using the Image control. The image object displays artwork the user selects in your program by using the Open common dialog box.

Add an image object

Image control

❶   Click the Image control in the toolbox.

❷   Add an image object to the form, below the label.

❸   Use the Properties window to set the image object's Stretch property to True.

When you've finished, your screen should look like the one shown here.

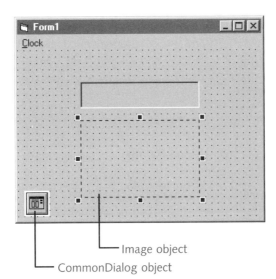

Image object
CommonDialog object

Now you'll use the Menu Editor to add a File menu to the MyDialog program.

Add a File menu

① Click the form to select the form object.

The form must be selected before you can add or modify menu items.

Menu Editor button

② Click the Menu Editor button on the toolbar.

The Menu Editor appears, and the current menu structure of the MyDialog program appears in the dialog box. Now you'll add to the program a File menu that includes Open, Close, and Exit commands.

③ Click the Insert button four times.

Four blank lines appear at the top of the menu item list. This creates space for the File menu commands you'll enter.

④ Click the Caption text box, type **&File**, press Tab, type **mnuFile**, and then click the Next button.

The File menu is added to the program. The letter "F" is specified as the access key.

⑤ Type **&Open...**, press Tab, type **mnuOpenItem**, click the Right arrow button, and then click Next.

The menu item Open—a command that will open Windows metafiles—is added to the menu list and indented one level. Because the command will display a dialog box, you added an ellipsis to the command caption.

⑥ Type **&Close**, press Tab, type **mnuCloseItem**, click the Right arrow button, and then click Next.

The menu item Close (a command that will close the open file) is added to the menu list.

⑦ Type **E&xit**, press Tab, type **mnuExitItem**, and then click the Right arrow button.

The menu item Exit—a command that will close the MyDialog application— is added to the menu list. It's traditional to use "x" as the access key for the Exit command. Your screen should look like the following:

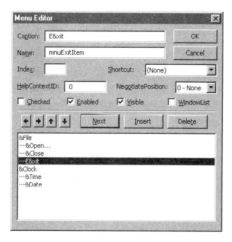

Disabling a Menu Command

In a typical application for Windows, not all menu commands are available at the same time. In a typical Edit menu, for example, the Paste command is available only when there is data on the Clipboard. You can disable a menu item by clearing the Enabled check box for that menu item in the Menu Editor. When a command is disabled, it appears in dimmed type on the menu bar.

In the following exercise, you'll disable the Close command. (Close is a command that can be used only after a file has been opened in the program.) Later in the lesson, you'll include a statement in the Open command event procedure that enables the Close command at the proper time.

Disable the Close command

1 Click the Close command in the menu list.

The caption and name of the command appear in the dialog box.

2 Click the Enabled check box in the Menu Editor to remove the check mark.

The check mark is removed from the check box, and the setting is disabled.

Now you'll add a TextColor command to the Clock menu to demonstrate the Color common dialog box. The Color common dialog box returns a color setting to the program through the CommonDialog1.Color property. You'll use that property to change the color of the text in the label caption.

Add the TextColor command to the Clock menu

1 Click Date, the last menu item in the menu list.

You'll place the TextColor command at the bottom of the Clock menu.

2 Click the Next button.

A blank line appears at the bottom of the menu list.

3 Type **TextCo&lor...**, press Tab, and type **mnuTextColorItem**.

The command TextColor is added to the Clock menu. The command contains a trailing ellipsis to indicate that it will display a dialog box when the user clicks it. The access key chosen for this command was "L" because "T" was already used in the menu, for Time. Your access keys won't behave correctly if you use duplicate keys at the same level within a particular menu or duplicate keys at the menu bar level.

4 Click OK to close the Menu Editor.

Event Procedures That Manage Common Dialog Boxes

To display a common dialog box in a program, you need to call the common dialog object by using the appropriate object method in an event procedure. If necessary, you must also set one or more common dialog box properties before the call by using program code. After the user makes his or her selections in the common dialog box, you process the choices by using program code in the event procedure.

In the following exercise, you'll type in the program code for the mnuOpenItem_ Click event procedure, the routine that executes when the Open command is clicked. You'll set the Filter property in the CommonDialog1 object to define the file type in the Open common dialog box. (You'll specify Windows metafiles.) Then you'll use the ShowOpen method to display the Open common dialog box. After the user has selected a file and closed the common dialog box, you'll display the file in the image object by setting the Picture property of the Image1 object to the filename the user selected. Finally you'll enable the Close command so that the user can unload the picture if he or she wants.

Edit the Open command event procedure

View Code button

1 Click the View Code button in the Project window.

2 Click the Object drop-down list box, and then click the mnuOpenItem object.

The mnuOpenItem_Click event procedure appears in the Code window.

3 Type the following program statements in the event procedure, between the Private Sub and End Sub statements. Indent each line four spaces to set the line off as the text of the event procedure. Be sure to type each line exactly as it is printed here, and press the Down arrow key after the last line.

```
CommonDialog1.Filter = "Metafiles (*.WMF)|*.WMF"
CommonDialog1.ShowOpen
Image1.Picture = LoadPicture(CommonDialog1.FileName)
mnuCloseItem.Enabled = True
```

Your screen should look like the following:

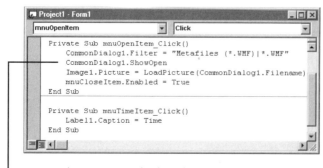

This statement displays the Open dialog box.

The first three lines in the event procedure refer to three different properties of the CommonDialog1 object. The first line uses the Filter property to define a list of valid files. (In this case, the list has only one item: *.WMF.) This is important for the Open dialog box because an image object, as you learned in Lesson 2, is designed for six types of files: bitmaps (.bmp files), Windows metafiles (.wmf files), icons (.ico files), cursors (.cur files), JPEG format (.jpg files), and GIF format (.gif files). (Attempting to display a .txt file in an image object would cause a runtime error, for example.)

The Filter property defines the file types that will be listed in the Open dialog box.

To add additional items to the Filter list, you can type a pipe symbol (|) between items. For example,

```
CommonDialog1.Filter = "Bitmaps (*.BMP)|*.BMP|Metafiles (*.WMF)|*.WMF"
```

allows both bitmaps and Windows metafiles to be chosen in the Open dialog box.

The second line in the event procedure displays the Open common dialog box in the program. Each common dialog box is displayed by using a different object method; the method for displaying the Open common dialog box is ShowOpen. (See the table earlier in this lesson for the methods that display other common dialog boxes.) This is the critical statement for the event procedure. Because the command's name is Open, the procedure needs to display an Open common dialog box and process the results.

The third line uses the filename selected in the dialog box by the user. When the user selects a drive, folder, and filename and then clicks OK, the complete pathname is passed to the program through the CommonDialog1.FileName property. The LoadPicture function, a routine that loads electronic artwork, is then used to copy the specified Windows metafile into the Image1 object.

The final line in the procedure enables the Close command on the File menu. Now that a file has been opened in the program, the Close command should be available so that users can close the file.

Now you'll type in the program code for the mnuTextColorItem_Click event procedure, the routine that runs when the TextColor command on the Clock menu is clicked.

Edit the TextColor command event procedure

➊ Click the mnuTextColorItem object in the Object drop-down list box.

The event procedure for the TextColor command appears in the Code window.

➋ Type the following program statements (indented four spaces) in the event procedure, between the Private Sub and End Sub statements.

```
CommonDialog1.Flags = &H1&
CommonDialog1.ShowColor
Label1.ForeColor = CommonDialog1.Color
```

Controlling Color Choices by Using Flags

The Flags property defines the type of Color common dialog box that will be displayed.

The mnuTextColorItem_Click event procedure makes use of the common dialog object's properties and methods. The first line sets a property named Flags to &H1&, a hexadecimal value that directs the Color common dialog box to present a list of standard color choices to the user, with custom colors as an option and a default color choice highlighted. The following table shows the four possible values for the Flags property.

Flag	Meaning
&H1&	Display a standard Color common dialog box (with custom colors as an option), and specify the current color as the default.
&H2&	Display a standard and custom Color common dialog box.
&H4&	Display a standard Color common dialog box with the Define Custom Colors button disabled.
&H8&	Display a Help button in the Color common dialog box.

You can use any combination of these values to prepare your Color common dialog box before you open it. To combine two or more values, use the Or operator. For example,

```
CommonDialog1.Flags = &H1& Or &H8&
```

displays the same Color common dialog box as before, but with an added Help button.

The second line in the event procedure uses the ShowColor method to open the Color common dialog box, and the third line assigns the selected color to the ForeColor property of the Label1 object. You might remember Label1 from the MyMenu program earlier in this lesson—it's the label box you used to display the current time and date on the form. You'll use the color returned from the Color common dialog box to set the color of the foreground text in the label.

tip

The Color common dialog box can be used to set the color of any user interface element that supports color. Other possibilities include the form background color, the colors of shapes on the form, and the foreground and background colors of objects.

Now you'll type in the program code for the mnuCloseItem_Click event procedure, the routine that closes the file displayed in the image object when the Close command on the File menu is clicked.

Edit the Close command event procedure

1 Click the Object drop-down list box in the Code window, and then click the mnuCloseItem object in the list box.

The event procedure for the File Close command appears in the Code window.

2 Type the following program statements (indented four spaces) in the event procedure, between the Private Sub and End Sub statements.

Use the LoadPicture function with empty quotes to clear an image or image box.

```
Image1.Picture = LoadPicture("")
mnuCloseItem.Enabled = False
```

The first line closes the open Windows metafile by loading a blank picture into the Image1 object. (This is the technique used to clear an image box or a picture box object.) The second line dims the Close command on the File menu because there is no longer an open file.

Now you'll type in the program code for the mnuExitItem_Click event procedure, the routine that stops the program when the Exit command on the File menu is clicked. This is the last event procedure in the program.

Edit the Exit command event procedure

1 Click the mnuExitItem object in the Object drop-down list box.

The event procedure for the File Exit command appears in the Code window.

2 Type the following program statement (indented four spaces) in the event procedure, between the Private Sub and End Sub statements.

```
End
```

This statement stops the program when the user is finished. (It might look familiar by now.)

3 Close the Code window.

4 Click the Save Project button on the toolbar to save the completed project to disk.

Visual Basic saves your changes in the MyDialog form and project files.

Save Project button

Now you'll run the MyDialog program and experiment with the menus and dialog boxes you've created.

Run the MyDialog program

Start button

The Dialog.vbp program is located in the \Vb6Sbs\Less04 folder.

1 Click the Start button on the toolbar.

The program runs, and both the File and Clock menus appear on the menu bar.

2 On the form's File menu, click Open.

The Open common dialog box appears. Notice the Metafiles (*.WMF) entry in the Files Of Type box. You defined this entry with the statement

```
CommonDialog1.Filter = "Metafiles (*.WMF)|*.WMF"
```

in the mnuOpenItem_Click event procedure. The first part of the text in quotes—Metafiles (*.WMF)—specifies which items are listed in the Files Of Type box. The second part—*.WMF—specifies the default filename extension of the files that are to be listed in the dialog box.

3 Open the \Vb6Sbs\Less03 folder on your hard disk.

The sample Windows metafiles in the Less03 folder appear in the file list box, as shown in the following illustration:

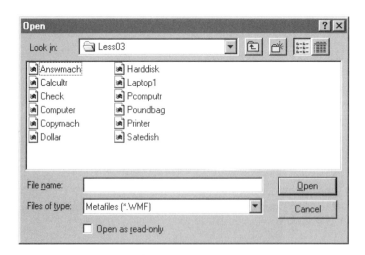

4 Double-click the file pcomputr.wmf.

A picture of a computer appears in the image box.

Now you'll practice using the Clock menu.

5 On the Clock menu, click the Time command.

The current time appears in the label box.

6 On the Clock menu, click the TextColor command.

The Color common dialog box appears, as shown here:

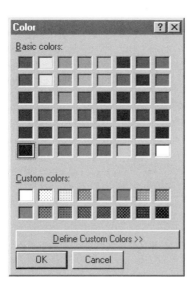

The Color common dialog box contains elements that let you change the color of the clock text in your program. The current color setting, black, is selected.

7 Click the light blue box, and then click the OK button.

The Color common dialog box closes, and the color of the text in the clock label changes to light blue.

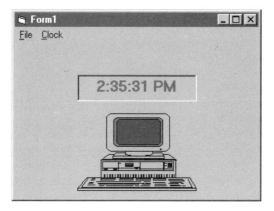

8 On the Clock menu, click the Date command.

The current date is displayed in light blue type. Now that the text color has been set in the label, it will remain light blue until the color is changed again or the program closes.

9 Click the File menu.

Notice that the Close command is now enabled. (You enabled it in the mnuOpenItem_Click event procedure by using the statement mnuCloseItem.Enabled = True.)

10 Press **C** to close the computer Windows metafile.

The file closes, and the Windows metafile is removed.

11 Click the File menu.

The Close command is now dimmed because there is no picture in the image box.

12 Click the Exit command.

The MyDialog program closes, and the Visual Basic programming environment appears.

Adding Nonstandard Dialog Boxes to Programs

What if you need to add a dialog box to your program that isn't one of the five common dialog box types? No problem—but you'll need to do a little extra design work. As you'll learn in future lessons, a Visual Basic program can use more than one form to receive and display information. To create nonstandard dialog boxes, you'll need to add new forms to your program, add input and output objects, and process the dialog box clicks in your program code. (These techniques will be introduced in Lesson 8.) In the next lesson, you'll learn how to use two handy dialog boxes that are specifically designed for receiving text input (InputBox) and displaying text output (MsgBox). These dialog boxes will help bridge the gap between the common dialog boxes and those that you need to create on your own.

That's it! You've learned several important commands and techniques for creating menus and dialog boxes in your programs. After you learn more about program code, you'll be able to put these skills to work in your own programs.

One Step Further **Assigning Shortcut Keys to Menus**

The Menu Editor also lets you assign *shortcut keys* to your menus. Shortcut keys are key combinations that a user can press to activate a command without using the menu bar. For example, on a typical Edit menu in an application for Windows (such as Visual Basic), you can copy selected text to the Clipboard by pressing Ctrl+C. Try assigning shortcut keys to the Clock menu in the MyDialog program now.

Assign shortcut keys to the Clock menu

Menu Editor button

❶ Click the Menu Editor button on the toolbar.

The Menu Editor appears.

❷ Click the Time command in the menu list box.

The caption and name of the Time command appear in the dialog box.

You assign a shortcut key by selecting the desired key combination in the Shortcut drop-down list box. You'll assign Ctrl+T as the shortcut key for the Time command.

You can't assign a shortcut key to a menu title.

❸ Click the Shortcut drop-down list box, scroll down in the list box, and then click Ctrl+T.

Ctrl+T is assigned as the shortcut key for the Time menu item, and the key combination appears in the menu list box.

❹ Click the Next button.

The caption and name of the Date command appear in the dialog box. You'll assign Ctrl+D as the shortcut key for this command.

5 Click the Shortcut drop-down list box, and then click Ctrl+D.

Your screen should look like the following:

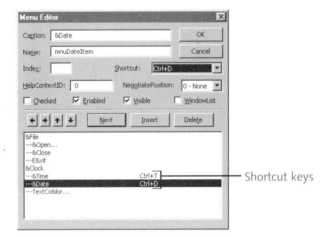

— Shortcut keys

6 Click OK to close the Menu Editor.

Now you'll run the program, and try the shortcut keys.

Start button

7 Click the Start button on the toolbar.

8 Press Ctrl+T to choose the Time command.

The current time appears in the program.

9 Press Ctrl+D to choose the Date command.

The current date appears in the program.

10 Click the Clock menu.

The shortcut keys are listed beside the Time and Date commands. Visual Basic adds these key combinations when you define the shortcuts by using the Menu Editor.

11 On the File menu, click the Exit command.

The program stops, and the programming environment appears.

Save Project button

12 Click the Save Project button to save your shortcut keys to disk.

If you want to boost your productivity

Spend a few minutes exploring the Magnify utility (magnify.vbp) in the \Vb6Sbs\Extras folder on your hard disk. I wrote this program as an extension of the Dialog program to give you a little more practice with the menu and dialog box concepts in this lesson. The application is a bitmap magnifier that lets you examine bitmaps up close on your system, in much closer detail than you can in a standard art program. I find it a useful tool for evaluating the dozens of bitmap (.bmp) files I routinely use in my programming projects for toolbars and other artwork. (Look in your \Windows folder for a few good examples.) If you like, you can try to expand the program yourself or simply use it as is for your daily work.

If you want to continue to the next lesson

● Keep Visual Basic running, and turn to Lesson 5.

If you want to quit Visual Basic for now

● From the File menu, click Exit.

  If you see a Save dialog box, click Yes.

Upgrade Notes: What's Different in Visual Basic .NET?

If you choose to upgrade to Visual Basic .NET in the future, you'll notice some new features related to the topics in this lesson, including the following:

■ Menus are no longer created using the Visual Basic 6.0 Menu Editor tool. Instead, you create a main menu object on your form using the MainMenu control in the Visual Studio .NET toolbox, and then customize the object using property settings and the Menu Designer. However, menu choices are still processed with program code—just like you're learning here with Visual Basic 6.0.

■ Standard dialog boxes are not created in Visual Basic .NET using the CommonDialog control. Instead, you use one of seven Windows Forms controls that add standard dialogs to your project. These controls include OpenFileDialog, SaveFileDialog, FontDialog, ColorDialog, PrintDialog, PrintPreviewDialog, and PageSetupDialog.

■ Forms in Visual Basic .NET now include the ShowDialog method and the DialogResult property, making it easier to create custom forms that look and act like standard dialog boxes.

Menus and Dialog Boxes

4

Lesson 4 Quick Reference

To	Do this	Button
Create a menu item	Click the Menu Editor button, and define the menu item's caption, name, and position.	
Add an access key to a menu item	Start the Menu Editor, click the menu item you want, and then click in the Caption text box. Type an ampersand (&) before the letter you want to use as an access key.	
Assign a shortcut key to a menu item	Start the Menu Editor, and click the menu item you want. Specify the shortcut key in the Shortcut drop-down list box.	
Change the order of menu items	Start the Menu Editor. Click the menu item you want to move, and click the Up arrow button or the Down arrow button to move the item.	
Use a standard dialog box in your program	Click the CommonDialog control, add a common dialog object to your form, and then use one of the five common dialog methods in your program code to display the dialog box.	
Disable a menu	Remove the check mark from the Enabled check command box associated with the menu command in the Menu Editor.	
Enable a menu command by using program code	Use the program statement `mnuCloseItem.Enabled = True` but substitute your command name for *mnuCloseItem*.	
Clear an image	Use the program statement `Image1.Picture = LoadPicture("")`	

PART 2

Programming Fundamentals

5

Visual Basic
Variables and Operators

ESTIMATED
TIME
50 min.

In this lesson you will learn how to:

✔ *Use variables to store data in your programs.*

✔ *Get input by using the InputBox function.*

✔ *Display messages by using the MsgBox function.*

✔ *Use mathematical operators and functions in formulas.*

In Part 1, you learned how to create the user interface of a Microsoft Visual Basic program and how to build and run a program in the Visual Basic programming environment. In the next three lessons, you'll learn more about Visual Basic program code—the statements and keywords that form the core of a Visual Basic program. After you complete Part 2, you'll be ready for more advanced topics.

In this lesson, you'll learn how to use variables to store data temporarily in your program and how to use mathematical operators to perform tasks such as addition and multiplication. You'll also learn how to use mathematical functions to perform calculations involving numbers, and you'll use the InputBox and MsgBox functions to gather and present information by using dialog boxes.

The Anatomy of a Visual Basic Program Statement

A program statement is a valid instruction for the Visual Basic compiler.

As you learned in Lesson 2, a line of code in a Visual Basic program is called a program statement. A *program statement* is any combination of Visual Basic keywords, properties, functions, operators, and symbols that collectively create a valid instruction recognized by the Visual Basic compiler. A complete program statement can be a simple keyword, such as

Beep

that sounds a note from your computer's speaker, or it can be a combination of elements, such as the following statement, which assigns the current system time to the Caption property of a label:

```
        Label1.Caption = Time
```
Object name   Property name   Assignment operator   Visual Basic function

The rules of construction that must be used when you build a programming statement are called statement *syntax*. Visual Basic shares many of its syntax rules with earlier versions of the Basic programming language and with other language compilers. The trick to writing good program statements is learning the syntax of the most useful language elements and then using those elements correctly to process the data in your program. Fortunately, Visual Basic does a lot of the toughest work for you, so the time you spend writing program code will be relatively short, and the results can be used again in future programs.

In the following lessons, you'll learn the most important Visual Basic keywords and program statements. You'll find that they will complement nicely the programming skills you've already learned and will help you to write powerful programs in the future. Variables and data types, the first topics, are critical features of nearly every program.

Using Variables to Store Information

A *variable* is a temporary storage location for data in your program. You can use one or many variables in your code, and they can contain words, numbers, dates, or properties. Variables are useful because they let you assign a short and easy-to-remember name to each piece of data you plan to work with. Variables can hold information entered by the user at runtime, the result of a specific calculation, or a piece of data you want to display on your form. In short, variables are simple tools you can use to track almost any type of information.

Using variables in a Visual Basic program is a little like getting a table at a fancy restaurant. You can start using one at any time, but the management is happiest if you make reservations for it in advance. I'll cover the process of making reservations for, or *declaring*, a variable in the next two sections.

Making Reservations for Variables: The Dim Statement

Dim reserves space for a variable.

To explicitly declare a variable before using it (typically, at the beginning of an event procedure), you type the variable name after the Dim statement. (Dim stands for *dimension*.) This declaration reserves room in memory for the variable when the program runs, and it lets Visual Basic know what type of data it should expect to see later. For example, the following statement creates space for a variable named LastName in a program:

```
Dim LastName
```

After the variable name, you can specify the variable type if you like. (You'll learn about several fundamental data types later in this lesson.) Visual Basic lets you identify the type in advance so that you can control how much memory your program uses. For example, if the variable will hold a small number without any decimal places (an integer), you can declare the variable as an integer and save some memory space. By default, however, Visual Basic reserves space for a variable type called a *variant*, which is a variable that can hold data of any size or format. The general-purpose variant variable is extremely flexible, and it may be the only variable you use in your programs.

You store data in a variable by using the assignment operator (=).

After you declare a variable, you are free to assign information to it in your code. For example, the following program statement assigns the last name "Jefferson" to the LastName variable:

```
LastName = "Jefferson"
```

After this assignment, the LastName variable can be used in place of the name "Jefferson" in your code. For example, the assignment statement

```
Label1.Caption = LastName
```

would display *Jefferson* in the first label (Label1) on your form.

Declaring Variables Without Dim

You can also declare a variable without the Dim statement; this process is called *implicit declaration*. To declare a variable in this way, you simply use the variable on its own, skipping the Dim statement altogether:

```
LastName = "Charles V"
```

Implicit declaration has the advantage of speed because you don't spend time typing the Dim statement. However, "the management" often discourages the use of implicit declaration because it doesn't force you to organize and list your variables in advance and because it prevents Visual Basic from displaying an error message if you mistype the variable name later. (See the following tip.) In this book, I'll declare variables by using both techniques.

tip

If you decide always to declare your variables by using the Dim statement, you might want to put the Option Explicit statement in the declarations section of your startup form for each new project. You can do this automatically by clicking the Options command on the Tools menu, clicking the Editor tab, and adding a check mark to the Require Variable Declaration check box.

When you use Option Explicit, Visual Basic generates an error message whenever it finds a variable that has not been explicitly declared in the code. (The likely cause is a spelling error in the variable name.) If you're worried about spelling errors, this statement can help you track them down.

Using Variables in a Program

Variables can maintain the same value throughout a program or they can change values several times, depending on your needs. The following exercise demonstrates how a variable named LastName can contain both text and a number and how the variable can be assigned to object properties.

Change the value of a variable

1   Start Visual Basic.

2   On the File menu, click the Open Project command.

The Open Project dialog box appears.

View Object button

3 Open the sample project VarTest in the \Vb6Sbs\Less05 folder.

The Variable Test project opens in the programming environment. Variable Test is a skeleton program—it contains a form with labels and buttons for displaying output, but little program code. You'll add code in this exercise.

4 If the Variable Test form is not visible, highlight the form name in the Project window, and then click the View Object button in the Project window.

The Variable Test form appears on the screen, as follows:

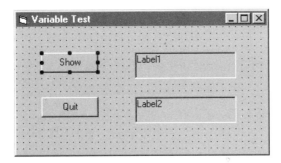

The form contains two labels and two command buttons. You'll use variables to display information in each of the labels.

5 Double-click the Show command button.

The Command1_Click event procedure appears in the Code window.

6 Type the following program statements to declare and use the LastName variable:

```
Dim LastName

LastName = "Smart"
Label1.Caption = LastName

LastName = 99
Label2.Caption = LastName
```

Variables can transfer information to a property.

The program statements are arranged in three groups. The first statement declares the LastName variable by using the Dim statement. Because no type was specified, the variable is declared as a variant type—a variable that can hold text or numbers. The second and third lines assign the name "Smart" to the LastName variable and then display this name in the first label on the form. This example demonstrates one of the most common uses of variables in a program—transferring information to a property.

The fourth line assigns the number 99 to the LastName variable (in other words, it changes the contents of the variable). This operation removes the text string from the variable and replaces it with a number. The number wasn't placed in quotation marks. Text strings require quotation marks, but numbers don't. (If you had placed quotation marks around the number, the number would be treated as a text string and couldn't be used in mathematical formulas.)

Your screen should look like the following:

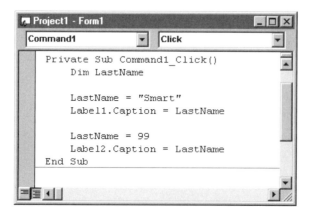

Start button

❼   Click the Start button on the toolbar to run the program.

The program runs in the programming environment.

❽   Click the Show button.

The program declares the variable, assigns two values to it, and copies each value to the appropriate label on the form. The program produces the following output:

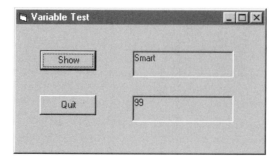

Variable Naming Conventions

Naming variables can be a little tricky because you need to use names that are short but intuitive and easy to remember. To avoid confusion, use the following conventions when naming variables:

- Begin each variable name with a letter. This is a Visual Basic requirement. Variable names must be fewer than 256 characters long and cannot contain periods.

- Make your variable names descriptive by combining one or more words when it makes sense to do so. For example, the variable name SalesTaxRate is much clearer than Tax or Rate.

- Use a combination of uppercase and lowercase characters and numbers if you wish. An accepted convention is to capitalize the first letter of each word in a variable; for example, DateOfBirth.

- Don't use Visual Basic keywords, objects, or properties as variable names.

- (Optional) Begin each variable name with a two- or three-character abbreviation corresponding to the type of data that is stored in the variable. For example, use strName to show that the Name variable contains string data. Although you don't need to worry too much about this detail now, you might make a note of this convention for later—you'll see it in the Visual Basic online Help and many of the advanced books about Visual Basic programming. (See "Working with Specific Data Types" later in this lesson for more information about data types.)

9. Click the Quit button to stop the program.

   The program stops, and the programming environment returns.

10. Save your form changes to disk under the name **MyVarTest.frm** by using the Save VarTest.frm As command. Save your project changes to disk under the name **MyVarTest.vbp** by using the Save Project As command.

Using a Variable to Store Input

You can get input from the user effectively by using the InputBox function and a variable.

One practical use for a variable is to hold information input from the user. Although you can often use an object such as a file list box or a text box to retrieve this information, at times you may want to deal directly with the user and save the input in a variable rather than in a property. One way to do this is to use the InputBox function to display a dialog box on the screen and then store the text the user types in a variable. You'll try this approach in the following example.

Get input by using InputBox

1 On the File menu, click the Open Project command.

The Open Project dialog box appears.

2 Open the project InputBox in the \Vb6Sbs\Less05 folder.

The InputBox project opens in the programming environment. InputBox is a skeleton program—it contains a form with buttons and a label for displaying output, but it contains little program code.

3 If the InputBox form is not visible, highlight the form in the Project window, and then click the View Object button in the Project window.

The form contains one label and two command buttons. You'll use the InputBox function to get input from the user, and then you'll display the input in the label on the form.

4 Double-click the InputBox command button.

The Command1_Click event procedure appears in the Code window.

5 Type the following program statements to declare two variables and call the InputBox function:

```
Dim Prompt, FullName
Prompt = "Please enter your name."

FullName = InputBox$(Prompt)
Label1.Caption = FullName
```

This time you're declaring two variables by using the Dim statement: Prompt and FullName. The second line in the event procedure assigns a group of characters, or a *text string,* to the Prompt variable. This message will be used as a text argument for the InputBox function. (An *argument* is a value or an expression passed to a subprocedure or a function.) The next line calls the InputBox function and assigns the result of the call (the text string the user enters) to the FullName variable. InputBox is a special Visual Basic function that displays a dialog box on the screen and prompts the user for input. In addition to a prompt string, the InputBox function supports other arguments you may want to use occasionally. Consult the Visual Basic online Help for details.

After InputBox has returned a text string to the program, the fourth statement in the procedure places the user's name in the Caption property of the Label1 object, which displays it on the form.

tip

In older versions of BASIC, the InputBox function was spelled with a $ character at the end to help programmers remember that the function returned information in the string ($) data type. You can call InputBox with or without the $ character in Visual Basic—I use it both ways in this book. (Sometimes I get sentimental for the old days.)

Start button

6 Click the Start button on the toolbar to run the program.

The program runs in the programming environment.

7 Click the Input Box button.

Visual Basic executes the Command1_Click event procedure, and the InputBox dialog box appears on your screen:

8 Type your full name, and click OK.

The InputBox function returns your name to the program and places it in the FullName variable. The program then uses the variable to display your name on the form as shown in the figure on the following page.

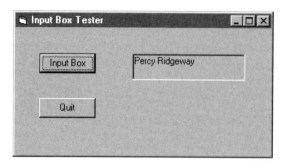

Use the InputBox function in your programs anytime you want to prompt the user for information. You can use this function in combination with the other input controls to regulate the flow of data into and out of a program. In the next exercise, you'll learn how to use a similar function to display text in a dialog box.

⑨ Click the Quit button on the form to stop the program.

The program stops, and the programming environment returns.

⑩ Save your form and project changes to your hard disk under the name **MyInputBox**.

What Is a Function?

InputBox is a special Visual Basic keyword known as a function. A *function* is a statement that performs meaningful work (such as prompting the user for information or calculating an equation) and then returns a result to the program. The value returned by a function can be assigned to a variable, as it was in the MyInputBox program, or it can be assigned to a property or another statement or function. Visual Basic functions often use one or more arguments to define their activities. For example, the InputBox function you just executed used the Prompt variable to display dialog box instructions for the user. When a function uses more than one argument, the arguments are separated by commas, and the whole group of arguments is enclosed in parentheses. The following statement shows a function call that has two arguments:

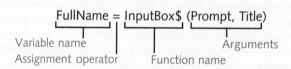

Using a Variable for Output

The MsgBox function uses text strings to display output in a dialog box. It supports a number of optional arguments.

You can display the contents of a variable by assigning the variable to a property (such as the Caption property of a label object) or by passing the variable as an argument to a dialog box function. One useful dialog box function for displaying output is the MsgBox function. Like InputBox, it takes one or more arguments as input, and the results of the function call can be assigned to a variable. The syntax for the MsgBox function is

```
ButtonClicked = MsgBox(Message, NumberOfButtons, Title)
```

where *Message* is the text to be displayed on the screen, *NumberOfButtons* is a button style number (1 through 5), and *Title* is the text displayed in the message box title bar. The variable *ButtonClicked* is assigned the result returned by the function, which indicates which button the user clicked in the dialog box.

If you're just displaying a message in MsgBox, the assignment operator (=), the *ButtonClicked* variable, and the *NumberOfButtons* argument are optional. You won't be using these in the following exercise; for more information about them (including the different buttons you can include in MsgBox and a few more options), search for *MsgBox* in the Visual Basic online Help.

Now you'll add a MsgBox function to the MyInputBox program to display the name the user enters in the InputBox dialog box.

Display a message by using MsgBox

1   If you don't see the Code window now, double-click the InputBox button on the MyInputBox form.

The event procedure for the Command1_Click procedure appears in the Code window. (This is the code you entered in the last exercise.)

2   Use the mouse to select the following statement in the event procedure (the last line):

```
Label1.Caption = FullName
```

This is the statement that displays the contents of the FullName variable in the label.

3   Press Del to delete the line.

The statement is removed from the Code window.

4 Type the following line into the event procedure as a replacement:

```
MsgBox (FullName), , "Input Results"
```

This new statement will call the MsgBox function, display the contents of the FullName variable in the dialog box, and place the words *Input Results* in the title bar. (The optional *NumberOfButtons* argument and the *ButtonClicked* variable are irrelevant here and have been omitted.) Your event procedure should look like the following:

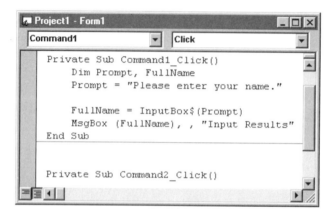

```
Private Sub Command1_Click()
    Dim Prompt, FullName
    Prompt = "Please enter your name."

    FullName = InputBox$(Prompt)
    MsgBox (FullName), , "Input Results"
End Sub


Private Sub Command2_Click()
```

tip

When no *ButtonClicked* variable is included, the parentheses enclose only the first argument.

Start button

5 Click the Start button on the toolbar.

6 Click the Input Box button, type your name in the input box, and then click OK.

The input is stored in the program in the FullName variable and is then displayed in a message box. Your screen should look similar to the following:

7 Click OK to close the message box. Then click Quit to close the program.

The program closes, and the programming environment returns.

8 Save the form and project as **MyMsgBox** to keep a copy of your program.

Working with Specific Data Types

In most cases, the variant data type will be the only data type you need. Variant variables can store all of Visual Basic's fundamental (predefined) data types and switch formats automatically. Variants are also easy to use and don't require you to give much thought to the eventual size of the variable when you declare it. If you want to create especially fast and concise code, however, you may want to use more specific data types when appropriate.

If a variable will always contain a specific data type, you can increase your program's efficiency by declaring the variable as that type.

For example, if a variable will always contain small integer values (numbers without a decimal point), you can save space in memory when your program runs by declaring the variable as an integer rather than as a variant. You'll also gain a small performance advantage if your program performs calculations, because an integer variable speeds up arithmetic operations, too.

The table on the following page lists the fundamental data types in Visual Basic. In the next exercise, you'll see how several of these data types work.

Variable storage size is measured in bytes—the amount of space required to store 8 bits (approximately 1 character).

> ## tip
> You can specify some fundamental data types by appending a type-declaration character to the variable's name. For example, you can declare a variable as type integer by adding a % character to the end of its name. So, in Visual Basic, the following two declaration statements are equivalent:
>
> ```
> Dim I As Integer
> Dim I%
> ```
>
> This is an older programming convention, but one that is still used by many programmers.

Variables and Operators

5

Data type	Size	Range	Sample usage
Integer	2 bytes	−32,768 through 32,767	`Dim Birds%` `Birds% = 37`
Long integer	4 bytes	−2,147,483,648 through 2,147,483,647	`Dim Loan&` `Loan& = 350,000`
Single-precision floating point	4 bytes	−3.402823E38 through 3.402823E38	`Dim Price!` `Price! = 899.99`
Double-precision floating point	8 bytes	−1.79769313486232D308 through 1.79769313486232D308	`Dim Pi#` `Pi# = 3.1415926535`
Currency	8 bytes	−922337203685477.5808 through 922337203685477.5807	`Dim Debt@` `Debt@ = 7600300.50`
String	1 byte per character	0 through 65,535 characters	`Dim Dog$` `Dog$ = "pointer"`
Boolean	2 bytes	True or False	`Dim Flag as Boolean` `Flag = True`
Date	8 bytes	January 1, 100, through December 31, 9999	`Dim Birthday as Date` `Birthday = #3-1-63#`
Variant	16 bytes (for numbers); 22 bytes + 1 byte per character (for strings)	All data type ranges	`Dim Total` `Total = 289.13`

tip

Variable storage size is measured in bytes—the amount of space required to store 8 bits (approximately 1 character).

Use fundamental data types in code

1   On the File menu, click the Open Project command.

The Open Project dialog box appears.

The Data program demonstrates fundamental data types in program code.

2   Open the Data project in the \Vb6Sbs\Less05 folder.

The Data project opens in the programming environment. Data is a complete Visual Basic program that demonstrates how several fundamental data types work. You'll run the program to see what the data types look like, and then you'll look at how the variables are declared and used in the program code.

Start button

3 Click the Start button on the toolbar.

The following application window appears:

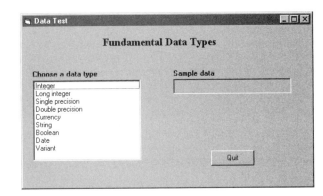

The Data program lets you experiment with nine data types, including integer, single-precision floating point, and date. The program displays an example of each type when you click its name in the list box.

4 Click the Integer type in the list box.

The number 37 appears in the Sample Data box.

5 Click the Date type in the list box.

The date Tuesday, November 19, 1963, appears in the Sample Data box.

6 Click each data type in the list box to see how Visual Basic displays it in the Sample Data box.

7 Click the Quit button to stop the program.

Now you'll examine how the fundamental data types are declared and used in the List1_Click event procedure.

8 If the form is not visible, highlight the form in the Project window, and then click the View Object button.

9 Double-click the list box object on the form, and enlarge the Code window to see more of the program code.

The List1_Click event procedure appears as shown in the figure on the following page.

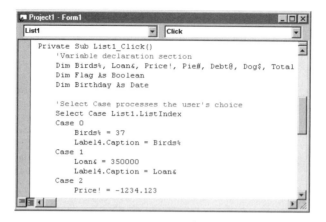

The first few lines of the procedure declare variables with specific data types in the procedure. These variables will be *local* to the procedure: they'll have no meaning in other event procedures in the program. Several of the variables are declared using special data type characters, such as %, #, and @. These symbols identify each variable as a specific fundamental data type in the program and mark the variables for the Visual Basic compiler and for people reading your program code.

The next section of the event procedure is called a Select Case decision structure. In the next lesson, we'll discuss how this group of program statements selects one choice from many. For now, notice how each section of the Select Case block assigns a sample value to one of the fundamental data type variables and then assigns the variable to the caption of the Label4 object on the form. You can use both of these techniques to manipulate fundamental data types in your own programs.

The Date data type is especially useful if you work with date and time values regularly. The date, surrounded by # characters, is assigned to the variable Birthday and is formatted with the Format function.

tip

Variables can also be *public*, or available in all form procedures and modules of a program. (*Modules* are special files that contain declarations and procedures not associated with a particular form.) For a variable to have this range, or scope, it needs to be declared in a standard module. For information about creating public variables in standard modules, see Lesson 10, "Using Modules and Procedures."

10 Scroll through the Code window and examine each of the variable assignments closely.

Try changing the data in a few of the variable assignment statements and running the program again to see what the data looks like.

11 When you've finished, close the Code window.

If you made any changes you want to save to disk, click the Save Project button on the toolbar.

User-Defined Data Types

Visual Basic also lets you create your own data types. This feature is most useful when you're dealing with a group of data items that naturally fit together but fall into different data categories. You create a *user-defined type* by using the Type statement, and you declare variables associated with the new type by using the Dim statement. (The Type statement must be located in the Declarations section of a standard module; to learn more about the Type statement, search for **module** in Visual Basic online Help.) For example, the following declaration creates a user-defined data type named Employee that can store the name, date of birth, and hire date associated with a worker:

```
Type Employee
    Name As String
    DateOfBirth As Date
    HireDate As Date
End Type
```

After you create a new data type, you can use it in the program code. The following statements use the new Employee type. The first statement creates a variable named ProductManager, of the Employee type, and the second statement assigns the name "Erick Cody" to the Name component of the variable:

```
Dim ProductManager As Employee
ProductManager.Name = "Erick Cody"
```

This looks a little like setting a property, doesn't it? Visual Basic uses the same notation for the relationship between objects and properties as it uses for the relationship between user-defined data types and component variables.

Constants: Variables That Don't Change

If a variable in your program contains a value that never changes (such as π, a fixed mathematical entity), you might consider storing the value as a constant instead of as a variable. A *constant* is a meaningful name that takes the place of a number or text string that doesn't change. Constants are useful because they increase the readability of program code, using them can save memory, and they make global changes easier to accomplish later. Constants operate a lot like variables, but you can't modify their values at runtime. They are declared with the Const keyword, as shown in the following example:

```
Const Pi = 3.14159265
```

The statement above creates a constant called Pi that can be used in place of the value of π in the program code. To make a constant available to all the objects and event procedures in your form, place the above statement in the Declaration section of your form (the top line in the Code window). To make the constant available to all the forms and modules in a program (not just Form1), create the constant in a standard module, with the Public keyword in front of it. For example:

```
Public Const Pi = 3.14159265
```

tip

For more information about standard modules, see Lesson 10, "Using Modules and Procedures."

The following exercise demonstrates how you can use a constant in an event procedure.

Use a constant in an event procedure

❶ On the File menu, click the Open Project command.

The Open Project dialog box appears.

❷ Open the Constant project in the \Vb6Sbs\Less05 folder.

The Constant program form appears on the screen. Constant is a skeleton program. The user interface is finished, but you need to type in the program code.

3 Double-click the Show Constant button on the form.

The Command1_Click event procedure appears in the Code window.

4 Type the following statements in the event procedure:

```
Const Pi = 3.14159265
Label1.Caption = Pi
```

Start button

5 Click the Start button to run the program.

6 Click the Show Constant button in the program.

The Pi constant appears in the label box, as shown here:

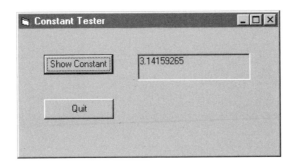

7 Click the Quit button to stop the program.

If you would like to keep a copy of the modified Constant program, save the form and project on your hard disk with the name **MyConstant**.

Constants are useful in program code, especially in involved mathematical formulas, such as Area = $2\pi r^2$. The next section describes how you can use operators and variables to write similar formulas.

Working with Visual Basic Operators

Visual Basic operators link the parts of a formula.

A *formula* is a statement that combines numbers, variables, operators, and keywords to create a new value. Visual Basic contains several language elements designed for use in formulas. In this section, you'll practice working with mathematical operators, the symbols used to tie together the parts of a formula. With a few exceptions, the mathematical symbols you'll use are the ones you use in everyday life, and their operations are fairly intuitive. You'll see each demonstrated in the following exercises.

Visual Basic provides the following operators:

Operator	Mathematical operation
+	Addition
–	Subtraction
*	Multiplication
/	Division
\	Integer (whole number) division
Mod	Remainder division
^	Exponentiation (raising to a power)
&	String concatenation (combination)

Basic Math: The +, –, *, and / Operators

The operators for addition, subtraction, multiplication, and division are pretty straightforward and can be used in any formula where numbers or numeric variables are used. The following exercise demonstrates how you can use them in a program.

Work with basic operators

❶ On the File menu, click the Open Project command.

❷ Open the BasicOp project in the \Vb6Sbs\Less05 folder.

The form for the program appears on the screen. The BasicOp program demonstrates how the addition, subtraction, multiplication, and division operators work with numbers you type in from the keyboard. It also demonstrates how you can use text box, option button, and command button objects to process user input in a program.

❸ Click the Start button on the toolbar.

A text box object is a useful tool for getting keyboard input from the user.

The BasicOp program runs in the programming environment. The program displays two text boxes in which you enter numeric values, a group of operator option buttons, a box that displays results, and two command buttons.

❹ Type **100** in the Variable 1 text box, and then press Tab.

The cursor moves to the second text box.

❺ Type **17** in the Variable 2 text box.

You can now apply any of the mathematical operators to the values in the text boxes.

❻ Click the Addition option button, and then click the Calculate command button.

The operator is applied to the two values, and the number 117 appears in the Result box, as shown in the illustration on the following page.

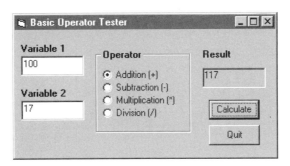

⑦ Practice using the subtraction, multiplication, and division operators with the two numbers in the variable boxes. (Click Calculate to calculate each formula.)

The results appear in the Result box. Feel free to experiment with different numbers in the variable text boxes. (Try a few numbers with decimal points if you like.)

⑧ When you've finished calculating, click the Quit button.

The program stops, and the programming environment returns.

Now take a look at the program code to see how the results were calculated. Basic Operators uses a few of the standard input controls you experimented with in Lesson 3 and an event procedure that uses variables and operators to calculate simple mathematical formulas. The procedure also uses the Val function to convert the string input received from the text boxes to numbers.

Examine the BasicOp program code

① Double-click the Calculate button on the form.

The Command1_Click event procedure appears in the Code window:

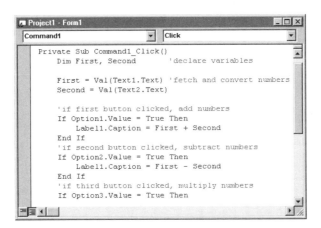

The first statement in the procedure declares two general-purpose variables of the variant type. The variants will hold the values typed in the two text boxes, and they are flexible enough to handle any numeric data type you want to use. The next two statements load the data from the text boxes into the variables and convert the text strings to numbers by using the Val function:

```
First = Val(Text1.Text) 'fetch and convert numbers
Second = Val(Text2.Text)
```

The Val function converts text values to numeric values.

The Val function is a special routine that converts a text argument to a numeric value. This conversion is necessary for the addition operation to work correctly in this program. The default data type returned by a text box object is text. This isn't a problem for three of the operators. The –, *, and / operators work only with numbers, so when the user selects one of these three operators in the program, Visual Basic automatically converts the values returned to the First and Second variables to numbers.

The + operator works with both text strings and numbers. Because the default data type returned by the text box object is text, Visual Basic would treat First's and Second's values as text when the + operator is used. Visual Basic would combine, or *concatenate,* the two values rather than add them mathematically. (For example, "100" + "17" would equal "10017.")

You'll learn more about string concatenation in the next exercise. For now, make a mental note that even though the variant data type can hold any fundamental data type, you need to watch closely how it is used in a program. It might default to something you don't expect.

important

It is critical to test each calculation in a program to verify that the whole program is working correctly. Testing one part of the program is not enough.

2 Scroll down the Code window, and examine the four formulas that use the basic mathematical operators.

The first formula in the procedure uses the addition operator (+) in an If...Then decision structure:

```
'if first button clicked, add numbers
If Option1.Value = True Then
    Label1.Caption = First + Second
End If
```

If the Value property of the first option button is set to True (if the button has been clicked), the two variables are added together with the + operator, and the result is assigned to the label. The three remaining formulas have a similar logic, each using an If...Then decision structure and the Caption property of the Label1 object. Decision structures such as If...Then are extremely useful in determining which option a user selects in your program when several options are available. You'll learn more about If...Then in the next lesson.

❸ Close the Code window.

You're done using the BasicOp program.

Visual Basic Mathematical Functions

Now and then you'll want to do a little extra number crunching in your programs. You may need to convert a value to a different type, calculate a complex mathematical expression, or introduce randomness to your programs. The following Visual Basic functions can help you work with numbers in your formulas. As with any function, the mathematical functions must be used in a program statement, and they will return a value to the program. In the following table, the argument n represents the number, variable, or expression you want the function to evaluate.

Function	Purpose
Abs(n)	Returns the absolute value of n.
Atn(n)	Returns the arctangent, in radians, of n.
Cos(n)	Returns the cosine of the angle n. The angle n is expressed in radians.
Exp(n)	Returns the constant e raised to the power n.
Rnd(n)	Generates a random number between 0 and 1.
Sgn(n)	Returns -1 if n is less than 0, 0 if n is 0, and $+1$ if n is greater than 0.
Sin(n)	Returns the sine of the angle n. The angle n is expressed in radians.
Sqr(n)	Returns the square root of n.
Str(n)	Converts a numeric value to a string.
Tan(n)	Returns the tangent of the angle n. The angle n is expressed in radians.
Val(n)	Converts a string value to a number.

Using Advanced Operators: \, Mod, ^, and &

In addition to the four basic mathematical operators, Visual Basic includes four advanced operators, which perform integer division (\), remainder division (Mod), exponentiation (^), and string concatenation (&). These operators are useful in special-purpose mathematical formulas and text processing applications. The following utility (a slight modification of the BasicOp program) shows how you can use each of these operators in a program.

Work with advanced operators

❶   On the File menu, click the Open Project command.

❷   Open the AdvOp project in the \Vb6Sbs\Less05 folder.

The form for the AdvOp program appears on the screen. The AdvOp program is identical to the BasicOp program, with the exception of the operators shown on the option buttons and the operators used in the program.

❸   Click the Start button on the toolbar.

The program displays two text boxes in which you enter numeric values, a group of operator option buttons, a box that displays results, and two command buttons.

❹   Type **9** in the Variable 1 text box, and then press Tab.

❺   Type **2** in the Variable 2 text box.

You can now apply any of the advanced operators to the values in the text boxes.

❻   Click the Integer Division option button, and then click the Calculate button.

The operator is applied to the two values, and the number 4 appears in the Result box, as shown here:

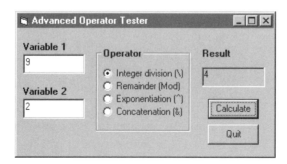

Integer division produces only the whole number result of the division operation. Although 9 divided by 2 equals 4.5, the integer division operation returns only the first part, an integer (the whole number 4). You might find this result useful if you're working with quantities that can't easily be divided into fractional components, such as the number of adults that can fit in a car.

7 Click the Remainder option button, and then click the Calculate button.

The number 1 appears in the Result box. Remainder division (modulus arithmetic) returns the remainder (the part left over that won't evenly divide) after two numbers are divided. Because 9 divided by 2 equals 4 with a remainder of 1 (2 × 4 + 1 = 9), the result produced by the Mod operator is 1. In addition to adding an early-seventies quality to your code, the Mod operator can help you track "leftovers" in your calculations, such as the amount of change left over after a financial transaction.

8 Click the Exponentiation option button, and then click the Calculate button.

The number 81 appears in the Result box. The exponentiation operator (^) raises a number to a power of itself. Because 9^2 equals 81, the result produced by the ^ operator is 81. In a Visual Basic formula, 9^2 is written 9 ^ 2.

9 Click the Concatenation option button, and then click the Calculate button.

The string "92" appears in the Result box. The string concatenation operator (&) combines two strings in a formula. The result ("92," in this case) is not a number; it is a combination of the "9" character and the "2" character. String concatenation can be performed only on text variables, strings delimited by quotation marks, and variant variables. Because the variables used in this program are variants, they were automatically converted to text for the operation. To see how this operator works with letters, type a few words in each variable box and then click the Calculate button again.

10 Click the Quit button to stop the program.

The program stops, and the programming environment returns.

Now take a look at the Command1_Click event procedure to see how the operators were used.

11 Double-click the Calculate button on the form.

The event procedure appears in the Code window, as shown in the illustration on the following page.

Variables and Operators

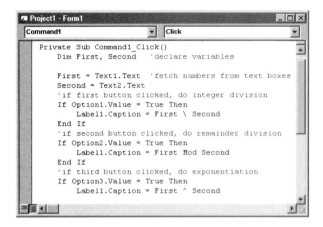

This Command1_Click procedure looks similar to the Command1_Click procedure in the BasicOp program. The code declares two variant variables, assigns data to the variables from the text boxes, and computes the selected formula with If…Then decision structures.

There is one important difference, however: this event procedure doesn't use the Val function to convert the data to a numeric type when it reads it from the text box objects. The conversion isn't necessary for the advanced operators because, unlike the + operator, each of the advanced operators works with only one type of data: \, Mod, and ^ work only with numbers; & works only with text. Because there's no type ambiguity, the variant variables can adequately convert the strings returned by the text boxes to numbers for the operations that require numbers.

12 Close the Code window.

You're finished working with the AdvOp program.

Operator Precedence

In the last two exercises, you experimented with seven mathematical operators and one string operator. Visual Basic lets you mix as many mathematical operators as you like in a formula, as long as each numeric variable and expression is separated from another by one operator. For example, this is an acceptable Visual Basic formula:

```
Total = 10 + 15 * 2 / 4 ^ 2
```

The formula processes several values and assigns the result to a variable named Total. But how is such an expression evaluated by Visual Basic? In other words, which mathematical operators does Visual Basic use first when solving the formula? You might not have noticed, but the order of evaluation matters a great deal in this example.

The operator order of evaluation is always important to keep in mind when you are building mathematical formulas.

Visual Basic solves this dilemma by establishing a specific *order of precedence* for mathematical operations. This list of rules tells Visual Basic which operators to use first when evaluating an expression that contains more than one operator. The following table lists the operators from first to last in the order in which they will be evaluated. (Operators on the same level in this table are evaluated from left to right as they appear in an expression.)

Operator(s)	Order of precedence
( )	Values within parentheses are always evaluated first.
^	Exponentiation (raising a number to a power) is second.
–	Negation (creating a negative number) is third.
* /	Multiplication and division are fourth.
\	Integer division is fifth.
Mod	Remainder division is sixth.
+ –	Addition and subtraction are last.

Given the order of precedence in the table above, the expression

```
Total = 10 + 15 * 2 / 4 ^ 2
```

would be evaluated by Visual Basic in the following steps. (Boldface type is used to show each step in the order of evaluation and its result.)

```
Total = 10 + 15 * 2 / 4 ^ 2
Total = 10 + 15 * 2 / 16
Total = 10 + 30 / 16
Total = 10 + 1.875
Total = 11.875
```

Variables and Operators

<table>
<tr><td>

One Step Further

</td><td>

Using Parentheses in a Formula

</td></tr>
</table>

Parentheses clarify and influence the order of evaluation.

You can use one or more pairs of parentheses in a formula to clarify the order of precedence. For example, Visual Basic would calculate the formula

```
Number = (8 - 5 * 3) ^ 2
```

by determining the value within the parentheses (–7) before doing the exponentiation—even though exponentiation is higher in order of precedence than subtraction and multiplication. You can further refine the calculation by placing nested parentheses in the formula. For example,

```
Number = ((8 - 5) * 3) ^ 2
```

directs Visual Basic to calculate the difference in the inner set of parentheses first, perform the operation in the outer parentheses next, and then determine the exponentiation. The result produced by the two formulas is different: the first formula evaluates to 49 and the second to 81. Parentheses can change the result of a mathematical operation, as well as make it easier to read.

If you want to continue to the next lesson

● Keep Visual Basic running, and turn to Lesson 6.

If you want to quit Visual Basic for now

● On the File menu, click Exit.

   If you see a Save dialog box, click Yes.

Upgrade Notes:
What's Different in Visual Basic .NET?

If you choose to upgrade to Visual Basic .NET in the future, you'll notice some new features related to the topics in this lesson, including the following:

■ To encourage better programming practices and cleaner program code, all Visual Basic .NET variables must be declared before they are used. The implicit declaration of variables (using variables without declaring them) is allowed only if you use the Option Explicit Off statement—a practice that is discouraged by Visual Basic .NET programmers.

■ Visual Basic .NET no longer supports the Variant data type. Visual Basic .NET programmers declare all variables using Dim and the keyword "As" to identify the type of data that they will hold.

■ There are several new fundamental data types in Visual Basic .NET, and some of the familiar Visual Basic 6.0 data types now support different ranges. For example, there is a 16-bit Short data type, a 32-bit Integer data type, and a 64-bit Long data type. The Visual Basic 6.0 Currency data type has been replaced with the Decimal data type.

■ Visual Basic .NET includes a new statement named Option Strict. When Option Strict is turned on, variables usually need to be the same type if they are added, compared, or combined. (Sometimes variables can be different types, as long as there won't be any data loss.) This means that type conversion is more important in Visual Basic .NET than in Visual Basic 6.0, and you'll need to become familiar with type conversion functions such as CInt, CLng, and CType to make different types of data compatible. As you upgrade your Visual Basic 6.0 applications, however, you can use the Option Strict Off statement to continue combining data types as you do in Visual Basic 6.0. This permits what is known as *automatic type coercion*, but the feature should be used sparingly and not relied on for future versions of Visual Basic .NET.

■ Visual Basic .NET now offers a few typing shortcuts for mathematical operations when arithmetic operators are used, such as addition (+), subtraction (−), and multiplication (*). These shortcuts allow you to write a formula such as X = X + 2 by using the syntax X += 2.

■ Visual Basic .NET no longer provides built-in keywords (such as Abs or Cos) for mathematical operations. Instead, you must use the methods in the System.Math class library of the .NET Framework for mathematical functions. The functionality of these methods is similar to the familiar Visual Basic 6.0 functions, although a few names have changed. (For example, Sqr is now Sqrt.) The .NET Framework is a very exciting repository for methods and functions, and in some ways it can be seen as a replacement for calling the Windows API. (See Lesson 18.)

Variables and Operators 5

Lesson 5 Quick Reference

To	Do this
Declare a variable	Type **Dim** followed by the variable name in the program code. For example: `Dim Storage         'Variant type`
Change the value of a variable	Assign a new value with the assignment operator (=). For example: `Country = "Japan"`
Get input with a dialog box	Use the InputBox function, and assign the result to a variable. For example: `UserName = InputBox("What is your name?")`

Display output in a dialog box	Use the MsgBox function. (The string to be displayed in the dialog box can be stored in a variable.) For example:
	`Forecast = "Rain, mainly on the plain."`
	`MsgBox(Forecast), , "Spain Weather Report"`

Declare a variable of a specific data type	Type **Dim** followed by the variable name and a type declaration character.
	or
	Type **Dim** followed by the variable name, the keyword **As**, and one of the eight fundamental data types. For example:
	`Dim MyBirthday As Date  'Date type`
	`Dim Price! 'single-precision floating point`

Create a constant	Type the **Const** keyword followed by the constant name, the assignment operator (=), and the fixed value. For example: `Const JackBennysAge = 39`
Create a formula	Link together numeric variables or values with one of the seven mathematical operators, and then assign the result to a variable or property. For example: `Result = 1 ^ 2 * 3 \ 4  'this equals 0`
Combine text strings	Use the string concatenation operator (&). For example: `Msg = "Hello" & "," & " world!"`
Convert text characters to number characters	Use the Val function. For example: `Pi = Val("3.1415926535897932")`

Lesson 5 Quick Reference

To	Do this
Use a mathematical function	Add the function and any necessary arguments to a formula. For example: `Hypotenuse = Sqr(x ^ 2 + y ^ 2)`

Control the evaluation order in a formula	Use parentheses in the formula. For example:
	`Result = 1 + 2 ^ 3 \ 4        'this equals 3`
	`Result = (1 + 2) ^ ( 3 \ 4)    'this equals 1`

6

Using Decision Structures

**ESTIMATED
TIME
45 min.**

In this lesson you will learn how to:

✔ *Write conditional expressions.*

✔ *Use an If...Then statement to branch to a set of program statements based on a varying condition.*

✔ *Use a Select Case statement to select one choice from many options in program code.*

✔ *Find and correct errors in your program code.*

In the last few lessons, you used several Microsoft Visual Basic tools to process user input. You used menus, objects, and dialog boxes to display choices for the user, and you processed input by using properties and variables. In this lesson, you'll learn how to branch conditionally to a specific program code section based on input you receive from the user. You'll also learn how to evaluate one or more properties or variables by using conditional expressions and then execute one or more program statements based on the results. Finally, you'll learn how to detect and fix programming mistakes in your code by using break mode.

Event-Driven Programming

The programs you have written so far in this book have displayed menus, objects, and dialog boxes on the screen, and these programs have encouraged users to manipulate the screen elements in whatever order they saw fit. The programs put the user in charge, waited patiently for a response, and then processed the input predictably. In programming circles, this methodology is known

Visual Basic programs are event-driven.

as *event-driven programming*. You build a program by creating a group of "intelligent" objects that know how to respond when the user interacts with them, and then you process the input by using event procedures associated with the objects. The following diagram shows how an event-driven program works in Visual Basic:

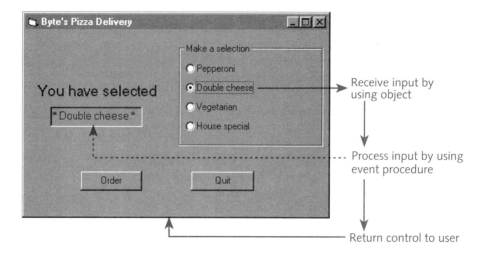

Program input can also come from the computer system itself. For example, your program might be notified when a piece of electronic mail arrives or when a certain period of time has elapsed on the system clock. These events are triggered by the computer, not by the user. Regardless of how an event is triggered, Visual Basic reacts by calling the event procedure associated with the object that recognized the event. So far, you've dealt primarily with the Click and Change events. However, Visual Basic objects also can respond to several other types of events.

The event-driven nature of Visual Basic means that most of the computing done in your programs will be accomplished by event procedures. These event-specific blocks of code process input, calculate new values, display output, and handle other tasks. In the previous lesson, you learned how to use variables, operators, and mathematical formulas to perform calculations in your event procedures. In this lesson, you'll learn how to use *decision structures* to compare variables, properties, and values, and you'll learn how to execute one or more statements based on the results. In the next lesson, you'll use *loops* to execute a group of statements over and over until a condition is met. Together, these powerful flow-control structures will help you build your procedures so that they can respond to almost any situation.

Events Supported by Visual Basic Objects

Each object in Visual Basic has a predefined set of events it can respond to. These events are listed for each object in the Proc (Procedure) drop-down list box in the Code window. You can write an event procedure for any of these events, and if that event occurs in the program, Visual Basic will execute the event procedure that is associated with it. For example, a list box object supports the Click, DblClick, DragDrop, DragOver, GotFocus, ItemCheck, KeyDown, KeyPress, KeyUp, LostFocus, Mouse-Down, Mouse-Move, MouseUp, OLECompleteDrag, OLEDragDrop, OLE-DragOver, OLE-GiveFeedback, OLESetData, OLEStartDrag, Scroll, and Validate events. You probably won't need to program for more than one or two of these events in your applications, but it's nice to know that you have so many choices when you create elements in your interface. The following illustration shows a partial listing of the events for a list box object in the Code window:

Using Conditional Expressions

Conditional expressions ask True-or-False questions.

One of the most useful tools for processing information in an event procedure is a conditional expression. A *conditional expression* is a part of a complete program statement that asks a True-or-False question about a property, a variable, or another piece of data in the program code. For example, the conditional expression

```
Price < 100
```

evaluates to True if the Price variable contains a value that is less than 100, and it evaluates to False if Price contains a value that is greater than or equal to 100. You can use the comparison operators shown below in a conditional expression.

Comparison operator	Meaning
=	Equal to
< >	Not equal to
>	Greater than
<	Less than
>=	Greater than or equal to
<=	Less than or equal to

tip
Expressions that can be evaluated as True or False are also known as *Boolean expressions*, and the True or False result can be assigned to a Boolean variable or property. You can assign Boolean values to certain object properties, variant variables, or Boolean variables that have been created by using the Dim statement and the As Boolean keywords.

The following table shows some conditional expressions and their results. In the next exercise, you'll work with the operators shown in the table.

Conditional expression	Result
10 < > 20	True (10 is not equal to 20)
Score < 20	True if Score is less than 20; otherwise, False
Score = Label1.Caption	True if the Caption property of the Label1 object contains the same value as the Score variable; otherwise, False
Text1.Text = "Bill"	True if the word *Bill* is in the first text box; otherwise, False

If...Then Decision Structures

If...Then decision structures let you add logic to your programs.

Conditional expressions used in a special block of statements called a *decision structure* control whether other statements in your program are executed and in what order they are executed. An If...Then decision structure lets you evaluate a condition in the program and take a course of action based on the result. In its simplest form, an If...Then decision structure is written on a single line:

```
If condition Then statement
```

where *condition* is a conditional expression and *statement* is a valid Visual Basic program statement. For example,

```
If Score >= 20 Then Label1.Caption = "You win!"
```

is an If...Then decision structure that uses the conditional expression

```
Score >= 20
```

to determine whether the program should set the Caption property of the Label1 object to "You win!" If the Score variable contains a value that is greater than or equal to 20, Visual Basic sets the Caption property; otherwise, it skips the assignment statement and executes the next line in the event procedure. This sort of comparison always results in a True or False value. A conditional expression never results in maybe.

Testing Several Conditions in an If...Then Decision Structure

ElseIf and Else clauses let you set several conditions in an If...Then structure.

Visual Basic also supports an If...Then decision structure that allows you to include several conditional expressions. This block of statements can be several lines long and contains the important keywords ElseIf, Else, and End If.

```
If condition1 Then
    statements executed if condition1 is True
ElseIf condition2 Then
    statements executed if condition2 is True
[Additional ElseIf clauses and statements can be placed here]
Else
    statements executed if none of the conditions is True
End If
```

In this structure, *condition1* is evaluated first. If this conditional expression is True, the block of statements below it is executed, one statement at a time. (You can include one or more program statements.) If the first condition is not True, the second conditional expression (*condition2*) is evaluated. If the second condition is True, the second block of statements is executed. (You can add additional ElseIf conditions and statements if you have more conditions to evaluate.) If none of the conditional expressions is True, the statements below the Else keyword are executed. Finally, the whole structure is closed by the End If keywords.

Multiline If...Then structures are perfect for calculating values that fall in different ranges, such as numbers in a tax return.

The following code shows how a multiline If...Then structure could be used to determine the amount of tax due in a hypothetical progressive tax return. (The income and percentage numbers are from the United States Internal Revenue Service 2001 Tax Rate Schedule for single filing status.)

```
Dim AdjustedIncome As Double, TaxDue As Double
AdjustedIncome = 32000    'set income to $32,000 to test
  If AdjustedIncome <= 27050 Then          '15% tax bracket
     TaxDue = AdjustedIncome * 0.15
ElseIf AdjustedIncome <= 65550 Then     '28% tax bracket
     TaxDue = 4057.5 + ((AdjustedIncome - 27050) * 0.28)
ElseIf AdjustedIncome <= 136750 Then     '31% tax bracket
     TaxDue = 14837.5 + ((AdjustedIncome - 65550) * 0.31)
ElseIf AdjustedIncome <= 297350 Then     '36% tax bracket
     TaxDue = 36909.5 + ((AdjustedIncome - 136750) * 0.36)
Else                                     '39.6% tax bracket
     TaxDue = 94725.5 + ((AdjustedIncome - 297350) * 0.396)
End If
```

important

The order of the conditional expressions in your If...Then and ElseIf clauses is critical. What if you reversed the order of the conditional expressions in the tax computation example and listed the rates in the structure from highest to lowest? Taxpayers in the 15 percent, 28 percent, and 31 percent tax brackets would all be placed in the 36 percent tax bracket because they all would have an income that is less than or equal to $297,350. (Visual Basic stops at the first conditional expression that is True, even if others are also True.) Because all the conditional expressions in this example test the same variable, they need to be listed in ascending order to get the taxpayers to fall out at the right spots. Moral: When you use more than one conditional expression, consider their order carefully.

This useful decision structure tests the double-precision variable AdjustedIncome at the first income level and subsequent income levels until one of the conditional expressions evaluates to True, and then determines the taxpayer's income tax accordingly. With some simple modifications, it could be used to compute the tax owed by any taxpayer in a progressive tax system such as the one in the United States. Provided that the tax rates are complete and up-to-date and that the value in the AdjustedIncome variable is correct, the program as written will give the correct tax for single U.S. taxpayers for 2001. If the tax rates change, it is a simple matter to update the conditional expressions. With an additional decision structure to determine taxpayers' filing status, the program readily extends itself to include all U.S. taxpayers.

In the next exercise, you'll use an If...Then decision structure to validate users as they log in to a program. You might use a similar program logic of user validation if you write a network application.

Validate users by using If...Then

❶ Start Visual Basic and open a new standard .exe project.

   If Visual Basic is already running, open a new project.

❷ Use the CommandButton control to create a command button in the upper-left corner of the form.

CommandButton control

❸ Set the Caption property of the command button to "Log In".

❹ Double-click the Log In button.

   The Command1_Click event procedure appears in the Code window.

By convention, statements below If...Then, ElseIf, and Else clauses are indented.

❺ Type the following program statements in the procedure:

```
UserName = InputBox("Enter your first name.")
If UserName = "Laura" Then
    MsgBox("Welcome, Laura!  Ready to start your PC?")
    Form1.Picture = _
        LoadPicture("c:\vb6sbs\less06\pcomputr.wmf")
ElseIf UserName = "Marc" Then
    MsgBox("Welcome, Marc!  Ready to display your Rolodex?")
    Form1.Picture = _
        LoadPicture("c:\vb6sbs\less06\rolodex.wmf")
Else
    MsgBox("Sorry, I don't recognize you.")
    End    'quit the program
End If
```

The line continuation characters (_) used after the Form1.Picture properties break two long program statements into four lines so that they can be printed in this book. If you choose, you can type each of these long statements on one line; the Code window will scroll to the right.

tip

Program lines can be 1023 characters long in the Visual Basic Code window, but it is usually easiest to work with lines of 80 or fewer characters. You can divide long program statements among multiple lines by using a line continuation character (_) at the end of each line in the statement except the last line. (You cannot use a line continuation character to break a string that is in quotation marks, however.)

When you've finished, your screen should look like the following:

The complete Login program is available on disk in the \Vb6Sbs\Less06 folder.

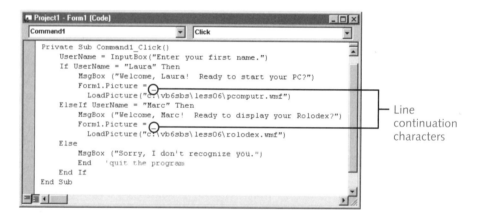

Line continuation characters

Start button

6 Click the Start button on the toolbar.

The program runs in the programming environment. A blank form appears on the screen, with a Log In button in the upper-left corner.

7 Click the Log In button.

The InputBox function in the Command1_Click event procedure displays a dialog box that asks you to enter your first name.

8 Type **Laura** and press Enter.

The If...Then decision structure compares the name you typed with the text "Laura" in the first conditional expression. If you typed *Laura*, the expression evaluates to True and the If…Then statement displays a welcome message by using the MsgBox function.

9 Click OK in the message box.

The message box closes, and a Windows metafile of a PC is loaded on the form, as shown in the following illustration:

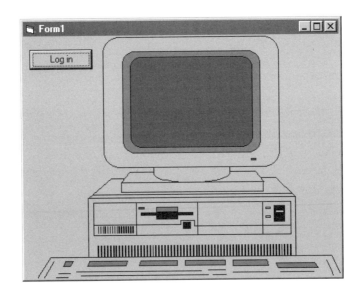

In this program, the Windows metafile is loaded directly on the form by using the Picture property. (Forms have Picture properties, just as image objects and picture box objects do.) When a graphic is loaded on a form, it appears in the background. Any control visible on the form appears on top of the graphic.

10 Click the Log In button, type **Marc**, and click OK.

This time the decision structure selects the ElseIf clause and admits Marc to the program. A welcome message is displayed on the screen again by the MsgBox function.

11 Click OK to display the Rolodex artwork.

The Rolodex Windows metafile is loaded on the form.

12 Click the Log In button, type **Frasier**, and click OK.

The Else clause in the decision structure is executed, and as shown in the illustration on the next page, a message appears in a MsgBox object.

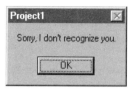

⓭ Click OK to close the message box.

The message box closes, and the program closes. An unauthorized user has been prohibited from using the program.

⓮ Save the form as **MyLogin.frm** and the project as **MyLogin.vbp**.

Using Logical Operators in Conditional Expressions

Logical operators let you add tests to your expressions.

Visual Basic lets you test more than one conditional expression in If…Then and ElseIf clauses if you want to include more than one selection criterion in your decision structure. The extra conditions are linked together by using one or more of the following logical operators:

Logical operator	Meaning
And	If both conditional expressions are True, then the result is True.
Or	If either conditional expression is True, then the result is True.
Not	If the conditional expression is False, then the result is True. If the conditional expression is True, then the result is False.
Xor	If one and only one of the conditional expressions is True, then the result is True. If both are True or both are False, then the result is False.

tip

When your program evaluates a complex expression that mixes different operator types, it evaluates mathematical operators first, comparison operators second, and logical operators third.

The table on the following page lists some examples of the logical operators at work. In the expressions, it is assumed that the variable Vehicle contains the value "Bike" and the variable Price contains the value 200.

Logical expression	Result
Vehicle = "Bike" And Price < 300	True (both conditions are True)
Vehicle = "Car" Or Price < 500	True (one condition is True)
Not Price < 100	True (condition is False)
Vehicle = "Bike" Xor Price < 300	False (both conditions are True)

In the following exercise, you will modify the MyLogin program to prompt the user for a password during the validation process. An input box gets the password from the user, and you modify the If...Then and ElseIf clauses in the decision structure so that they use the And operator to verify the password.

Add password protection by using the And operator

1 Double-click the Log In button to open the Command1_Click event procedure in the Code window.

2 Insert the following statement between the InputBox statement and the If...Then statement in the procedure (between the first and second lines):

```
Pass = InputBox("Enter your password.")
```

3 Modify the If...Then statement to the following:

```
If UserName = "Laura" And Pass = "May17" Then
```

The statement now includes the And logical operator, which verifies the user name and password before Laura is admitted to the program.

The complete Password application is available in the \Vb6Sbs\Less06 folder.

4 Modify the ElseIf statement to the following:

```
ElseIf UserName = "Marc" And Pass = "trek" Then
```

The And logical operator adds a check for the "trek" password in Marc's account.

5 Save the form as **MyPass.frm** and the project as **MyPass.vbp**.

Start button

6 Click the Start button on the toolbar.

The program runs in the programming environment.

7 Click the Log In button, type **Laura**, and then click OK.

The program prompts you for a password.

8 Type **May17** and click OK.

The And conditional expression evaluates to True, and Laura is welcomed to the program.

9 Click OK to close the message box.

End button

10 Click the End button on the toolbar to quit the program.

The program stops, and the programming environment returns.

Using Decision Structures

> **tip**
>
> If you are writing a full-featured version of the MyPass program, consider using a text box object to receive the password input in the program. Text box objects support the PasswordChar property, which lets you display a placeholder character, such as an asterisk (*), as the user types and the MaxLength property, which lets you limit the number of characters entered.

Select Case Decision Structures

Select Case decision structures base branching decisions on one key variable.

Visual Basic also lets you control the execution of statements in your programs by using Select Case decision structures. You used Select Case structures earlier in this book when you wrote event procedures to process list box, combo box, and menu item choices. A Select Case structure is similar to an If...Then...ElseIf structure, but it is more efficient when the branching depends on one key variable, or *test case*. You can also use Select Case structures to make your program code more readable.

The syntax for a Select Case structure looks like this:

```
Select Case variable
Case value1
    program statements executed if value1 matches variable
Case value2
    program statements executed if value2 matches variable
Case value3
    program statements executed if value3 matches variable
    .
    .
    .
End Select
```

A Select Case structure begins with the Select Case keywords and ends with the End Select keywords. You replace *variable* with the variable, property, or other expression that is to be the key value, or test case, for the structure. You replace *value1*, *value2*, and *value3* with numbers, strings, or other values related to the test case being considered. If one of the values matches the variable, the statements below its Case clause are executed and Visual Basic continues executing program code after the End Select statement. You can include any number of Case clauses in a Select Case structure, and you can include more than one value in a Case clause. If you list multiple values after a case, separate them with commas.

The example below shows how a Select Case structure could be used to print an appropriate message about a person's age in a program. If the Age variable matches one of the Case values, an appropriate message appears as a label.

```
Select Case Age
Case 16
    Label1.Caption = "You can drive now!"
Case 18
    Label1.Caption = "You can vote now!"
Case 21
    Label1.Caption = "You can drink wine with your meals."
Case 65
    Label1.Caption = "Time to retire and have fun!"
End Select
```

The organization of a Select Case structure can make it clearer than an equivalent If...Then structure.

A Select Case structure also supports a Case Else clause that you can use to display a message if none of the earlier cases matches. Here's how it works with the Age example:

```
Select Case Age
Case 16
    Label1.Caption = "You can drive now!"
Case 18
    Label1.Caption = "You can vote now!"
Case 21
    Label1.Caption = "You can drink wine with your meals."
Case 65
    Label1.Caption = "Time to retire and have fun!"
Case Else
    Label1.Caption = "You're a great age! Enjoy it!"
End Select
```

Using Comparison Operators with a Select Case Structure

A Select Case structure supports comparison operators just like an If...Then structure does.

Visual Basic lets you use comparison operators to include a range of test values in a Select Case structure. The Visual Basic comparison operators that can be used are =, < >, >, <, >=, and <=. To use the comparison operators, you need to include the Is keyword or the To keyword in the expression to identify the comparison you're making. The Is keyword instructs the compiler to compare the test variable to the expression listed after the Is keyword. The To keyword identifies a range of values. The following structure uses Is, To, and several comparison operators to test the Age variable and to display one of five messages:

```
Select Case Age
Case Is < 13
    Label1.Caption = "Enjoy your youth!"
Case 13 To 19
    Label1.Caption = "Enjoy your teens!"
Case 21
    Label1.Caption = "You can drink wine with your meals."
Case Is > 100
    Label1.Caption = "Looking good!"
Case Else
    Label1.Caption = "That's a nice age to be."
End Select
```

If the value of the Age variable is less than 13, the message "Enjoy your youth!" is displayed. For the ages 13 through 19, the message "Enjoy your teens!" is displayed, and so on.

A Select Case decision structure is usually much clearer than an If...Then structure and is more efficient when you're making three or more branching decisions based on one variable or property. However, when you're making two or fewer comparisons, or when you're working with several different values, you'll probably want to use an If...Then decision structure.

In the following exercise, you'll see how you can use a Select Case structure to process input from a list box. You'll use the List1.Text and List1.ListIndex properties to collect the input, and then you'll use a Select Case structure to display a greeting in one of four languages.

Use a Select Case structure to process a list box

1 On the File menu, click the New Project command and create a new standard application.

A blank form appears in the programming environment.

Label control

2 Click the Label control in the toolbox, and then create a large box in the top middle of the form to display a title for the program.

ListBox control

3 Click the ListBox control in the toolbox, and then create a list box below the title label.

CommandButton control

Properties Window button

④ Create a small label above the list box object, and then create two small labels below the list box to display program output.

⑤ Click the CommandButton control in the toolbox, and then create a small command button in the bottom of the form.

⑥ Click the Properties Window button on the toolbar, and then set the object properties as shown below the form.

Object	Property	Setting
Label1	Caption	"International Welcome Program"
	Font	Times New Roman, Bold, 14-point
Label2	Caption	"Choose a country"
Label3	Caption	(Empty)
Label4	Caption	(Empty)
	BorderStyle	1 – Fixed Single
	ForeColor	Dark red (&H00000080&)
Command1	Caption	"Quit"

When you've finished setting properties, your form should look similar to the following:

Now you'll enter the program code to initialize the list box.

⑦ Double-click the form.

The Form_Load event procedure appears in the Code window.

You load values in a list box by using the AddItem method.

8 Type the following program code to initialize the list box:

```
List1.AddItem "England"
List1.AddItem "Germany"
List1.AddItem "Spain"
List1.AddItem "Italy"
```

These lines use the AddItem method of the list box object to add entries to the list box on your form.

9 Open the Object drop-down list box, and then click the List1 object in the list box.

The List1_Click event procedure appears in the Code window.

10 Type the following lines to process the list box selection made by the user:

```
Label3.Caption = List1.Text
Select Case List1.ListIndex
Case 0
    Label4.Caption = "Hello, programmer"
Case 1
    Label4.Caption = "Hallo, programmierer"
Case 2
    Label4.Caption = "Hola, programador"
Case 3
    Label4.Caption = "Ciao, programmatori"
End Select
```

The ListIndex property contains the number of the list item selected.

The first line copies the name of the selected list box item to the caption of the third label on the form. The most important property used in the statement is List1.Text, which contains the exact text of the item selected in the list box. The remaining statements are part of the Select Case decision structure. The structure uses the property List1.ListIndex as a test case variable and compares it to several values. The ListIndex property always contains the number of the item selected in the list box; the item at the top is 0 (zero), the second item is 1, the next item is 2, and so on. Using ListIndex, the Select Case structure can quickly identify the user's choice and display the correct greeting on the form.

11 Open the Object drop-down list box, and then click the Command1 object in the list box.

The Command1_Click event procedure appears in the Code window.

12 Type **End** in the event procedure, and then close the Code window.

13 Save the form to disk under the name **MyCase.frm**, and then save the project to disk under the name **MyCase.vbp**.

Start button

14 Click the Start button on the toolbar to run the MyCase program.

15 Click each of the country names in the Choose A Country list box.

The program displays a greeting for each of the countries listed. The illustration below shows the greeting for Italy.

The complete Case project is located in the \Vb6Sbs\Less06 folder.

16 Click the Quit button to stop the program.

The program stops, and the programming environment returns.

You've finished working with Select Case structures in this lesson.

Finding and Correcting Errors

The process of finding and correcting errors in programs is called debugging.

The errors you have encountered in your programs so far have probably been simple typing mistakes or syntax errors. But what if you discover a nastier problem in your program—one you can't find and correct by a simple review of the objects, properties, and statements in your program? The Visual Basic programming environment contains several tools you can use to track down and fix errors, or *bugs*, in your programs. These tools won't stop you from making mistakes, but they'll often ease the pain when you encounter one.

Consider the following If...Then decision structure, which evaluates two conditional expressions and then displays one of two messages based on the result:

```
If Age > 13 AND Age < 20 Then
    Text2.Text = "You're a teenager."
Else
    Text2.Text = "You're not a teenager."
End If
```

Can you spot the problem with this decision structure? A teenager is a person who is between 13 and 19 years old, inclusive, yet the structure fails to identify the person who is exactly 13. (For this age, the structure erroneously displays the message "You're not a teenager.") This type of mistake is not a syntax error (the statements follow the rules of Visual Basic); it is a mental mistake, or *logic error*. The correct decision structure contains a greater than or equal to operator (>=) in the first comparison after the If...Then statement:

```
If Age >= 13 AND Age < 20 Then
```

Believe it or not, this type of mistake is the most common problem in a Visual Basic program. Code that works most of the time—but not all of the time—is the hardest to check out and fix.

Three Types of Errors

Three types of errors can occur in a Visual Basic program: syntax errors, runtime errors, and logic errors.

- A *syntax error* (or *compiler error*) is a programming mistake (such as a misspelled property or keyword) that violates the rules of Visual Basic. Visual Basic points out several types of syntax errors in your programs while you type program statements, and won't let you run a program until each syntax error is fixed.

- A *runtime error* is a mistake that causes a program to stop unexpectedly during execution. Runtime errors occur when an outside event or an undiscovered syntax error forces a program to stop while it is running. A misspelled filename in a LoadPicture function or an open floppy drive are conditions that can produce runtime errors.

- A *logic error* is a human error—a programming mistake that makes the program code produce the wrong results. Most debugging efforts are focused on tracking down logic errors introduced by the programmer.

Be sure to use the Visual Basic online Help resources when you encounter error messages produced by syntax errors or runtime errors. If a runtime error dialog box appears, click the Help button.

Using Break Mode

Break mode lets you see how your program executes.

One way to identify a logic error is to execute your program code one line at a time and examine the content of one or more variables or properties as it changes. To do this, you can enter *break mode* while your program is running and then view your code in the Code window. Break mode gives you a close-up look at your program while the Visual Basic compiler is executing it. It's kind of like pulling up a chair behind the pilot and copilot and watching them fly the airplane. But in this case, you can touch the controls.

While you are debugging your application, you might want to open the Debug toolbar, a special toolbar with buttons devoted entirely to tracking down errors. You might also want to open the Watches window, which can display the contents of critical variables you're interested in viewing. To enter program statements and see their immediate effect, use the Immediate window.

The following illustration shows the debugging toolbar, which you can open by pointing to the Toolbars command on the View menu and then clicking Debug.

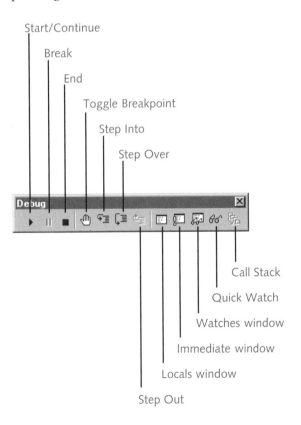

Start/Continue

Break

End

Toggle Breakpoint

Step Into

Step Over

Call Stack

Quick Watch

Watches window

Immediate window

Locals window

Step Out

Using Decision Structures

6

In the following exercise, you'll use break mode to find and correct the logic error you discovered earlier in the If...Then structure. (The error is part of an actual program.) To isolate the problem, you'll use the Step Into button on the Debug toolbar to execute program instructions one at a time, and you'll use the Quick Watch button on the Debug toolbar to watch the content of the Age variable change. Pay close attention to this debugging strategy. You can use it to correct many types of glitches in your own programs.

Debug the IfBug program

Open Project button

1 Click the Open Project button on the toolbar.

2 Open the project IfBug in the \Vb6Sbs\Less06 folder.

3 If the form isn't visible, highlight the IfBug form in the Project window, and then click the View Object button.

The form for the IfBug program appears. This program prompts the user for his or her age. When the user clicks the Test button, the program lets the user know whether he or she is a teenager. The program still has the problem with 13-year-olds that we identified earlier in the lesson. You'll open the Debug toolbar now, and use break mode to find the problem.

4 On the View menu, point to the Toolbars command and then click Debug if it is not already selected.

The Debug toolbar opens. (It might appear docked to the right of the Standard toolbar.)

5 Drag the Debug toolbar below the IfBug form so that you have it handy while you work.

Start button

6 Click the Start button on the Debug toolbar.

7 The program runs. Remove the 0 from the Age text box, type **14**, and then click the Test button.

The program displays the message "You're a teenager." So far, the program displays the correct result.

8 Type **13** in the Age text box, and then click the Test button.

The program displays the message "You're not a teenager.", as shown in the illustration on the following page.

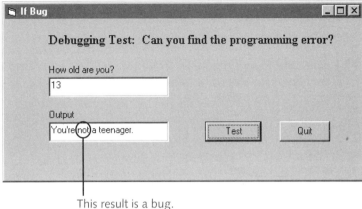

This result is a bug.

This answer is incorrect, and you need to look at the program code in order to fix the problem. Rather than quitting the program and searching the program code on your own, let Visual Basic help you out.

II

Break button

❾ Click the Break button on the Debug toolbar. (The Break button is just to the right of the Start button.)

The program pauses, and Visual Basic displays the Code window, which shows your code as Visual Basic runs it. Your screen should look like the following:

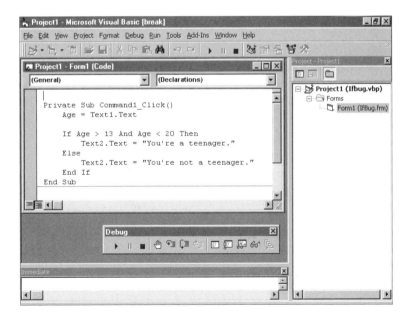

Step Into button

10 Click the Step Into button on the Debug toolbar to execute the next program statement.

Visual Basic returns control to the form in the program and waits for input.

11 Click the IfBug form on the Windows taskbar, verify that 13 is still in the text box, and then click the Test button.

Because Visual Basic is in break mode, something unusual happens. Visual Basic opens the Code window and displays the Command1_Click event procedure—the program code about to be executed by the compiler. The first statement in the procedure is highlighted with yellow. This gives you the opportunity to see how the logic in your program is evaluated.

12 Click the Step Into button to execute the first statement in the procedure.

The Sub statement is executed, and the statement containing the Age variable is highlighted. Age is the critical test variable in this program, so you'll place it in the Watches window now to see how it changes as the program executes.

tip

When your program is in break mode, you can check the value of a variable in the Code window by holding the mouse button over it.

Quick Watch button

13 Select the Age variable by using the mouse, and then click the Quick Watch button on the Debug toolbar.

A dialog box appears on the screen showing the context, name, and value of the Age variable in the program. You'll also see this dialog box if you click the Quick Watch command on the Debug menu.

The Watches window displays variables added by using the Quick Watch command.

14 Click Add in the Quick Watch dialog box. The Watches window appears docked at the bottom of the screen, as shown on the next page. (You might need to resize the window to see all of it.)

tip

To remove a watch variable from the Watches window, click the variable in the Watches window and press Del.

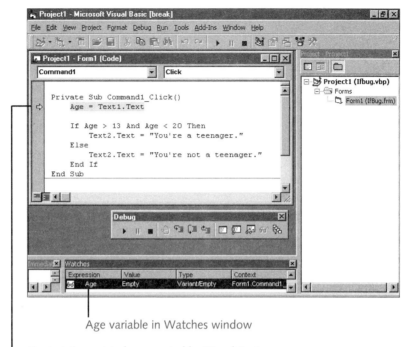

Age variable in Watches window

└─ Next statement to be executed by Visual Basic

The Age variable currently has no value because it hasn't been used yet in the event procedure. (Because the Age variable wasn't declared globally in the program, it is used as a local variable in the procedure and is reinitialized every time the procedure is called.)

When a decision structure branches incorrectly, look for the bug in the conditional expression and fix it if possible.

15 Click the Step Into button to execute the next instruction.

Visual Basic copies the number 13 from the text box to the Age variable, and the Age variable in the Watches window is updated. Visual Basic now highlights the first statement in the If...Then structure, the most important (and flawed) statement in the program. Because a 13-year-old is a teenager, Visual Basic should execute the Then clause after it evaluates this instruction.

16 Click the Step Into button again.

Visual Basic highlights the Else clause in the If...Then structure instead. The test fails on this value, and you need to find and fix the problem now if possible. (Visual Basic helped you find the problem, but you still have to recognize and fix it.) This time, you already know the answer. The first comparison needs the >= operator.

6

Using Decision Structures

17 Click after the > operator in the If...Then statement, and then type **=**. Your screen should look like the following:

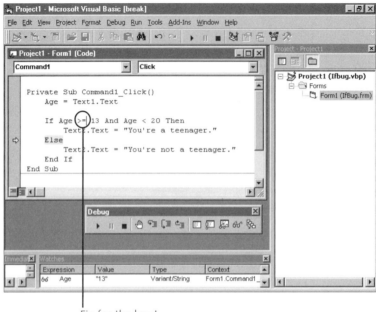

Fix for the bug!

Visual Basic lets you fix errors while in break mode, but if the changes you make are in statements that have already been executed, your corrections won't take effect until the next time the statements are run. To test your correction in this decision structure, you'll need to click the Test button again.

18 Click the Step Into button three times.

Visual Basic finishes executing the decision structure.

19 Click the Start button (now labeled Continue) on the Debug toolbar to resume full-speed execution of the program.

The IfBug form reappears.

20 Click the Test button to test your bug fix, verify the message "You're a teenager." in the Output box, and then click the Quit button to stop the program.

21 Click the Close button on the Debug toolbar and the Watches window (if it's still visible) to close them.

Congratulations! You've successfully used break mode to find and correct a logic error in a program. As you continue to work with Visual Basic, feel free to use break mode and the Debug toolbar to analyze your code.

| One Step Further | **Using a Stop Statement to Enter Break Mode** |

You can enter break mode by using a Stop statement.

If you know the exact place in the program code where you want to enter break mode and start debugging, you can place a Stop statement in your code at that place to pause the program and open the Code window. For example, as an alternative to clicking the Break button, you could have entered break mode in the previous exercise by inserting a Stop statement at the beginning of the Command1_Click event procedure, as shown below.

```
Private Sub Command1_Click()
    Stop     'enter break mode
    Age = Text1.Text
    If Age > 13 And Age < 20 Then
        Text2.Text = "You're a teenager."
    Else
        Text2.Text = "You're not a teenager."
    End If
End Sub
```

When you run a program that includes a Stop statement, Visual Basic enters break mode as soon as it hits the Stop statement. While in break mode, you can use the Code window and Debug toolbar just as you would if you had entered break mode manually. When you've finished debugging, remove the Stop statement.

If you want to continue to the next lesson

● Keep Visual Basic running, and turn to Lesson 7.

If you want to quit Visual Basic for now

● On the File menu, click Exit.

    If you see a Save dialog box, click Yes.

Using Decision Structures

Upgrade Notes:
What's Different in Visual Basic .NET?

If you choose to upgrade to Visual Basic .NET in the future, you'll notice some new features related to the topics in this lesson, including the following:

- Visual Basic .NET includes two new logical operators named AndAlso and OrElse. In a conditional statement that contains multiple conditions, such as an If...Then structure, it might not be necessary to always evaluate all the conditions. Passing over conditions is sometimes called "short-circuiting" and can be specified by using the AndAlso and OrElse operators.

- Visual Basic .NET includes several new tools for finding and correcting errors. Many of the familiar Visual Basic 6.0 debugging commands are still a part of Visual Studio (such as Start, Break, End, Next, Step Into, and Step Over), but some have been renamed. There are also new debugging tools and commands, including a revised Debug toolbar, menu commands that manage processes and exceptions, and tools that support the debugging of multilanguage solutions.

- Several new debugging windows have been added to the Visual Studio .NET user interface, including Autos, Command, Call Stack, Threads, Memory, Disassembly, and Registers. You won't use these tools for each debugging session, but you might find them useful in more-sophisticated applications.

Lesson 6 Quick Reference

To	Do this	Button
Write a conditional expression	Use a comparison operator between two values.	
Use a decision structure	Use an If…Then or Select Case statement and supporting expressions and keywords.	
Make two comparisons in a conditional expression	Use a logical operator between comparisons (And, Or, Not, or Xor).	
Display the Debug toolbar	From the View menu, point to the Toolbars submenu and click the Debug command.	
Enter break mode for debugging	Click the Break button on the Debug toolbar. *or* Place a Stop statement where you want to enter break mode.	❚❚
Execute one line of code in the Code window	Click the Step Into button on the Debug toolbar. *or* On the Debug menu, click the Step Into command.	
Examine a variable in the Code window	Highlight the variable you want to examine, and then click the Quick Watch button on the Debug toolbar. *or* Click the Quick Watch command on the Debug menu.	
Remove a watch expression	Click the expression in the Watches window, and then click Delete.	

Using Decision Structures

6

7

Using Loops and Timers

ESTIMATED TIME
50 min.

In this lesson you will learn how to:

✔ *Use a For...Next loop to execute statements a set number of times.*

✔ *Display output on a form by using the Print method.*

✔ *Use a Do loop to execute statements until a specific condition is met.*

✔ *Loop for a specific amount of time by using a timer object.*

✔ *Create your own digital clock and appointment alarm.*

In Lesson 6, you learned how to use the If...Then and Select Case decision structures to choose which statements to execute in a program. In this lesson, you'll learn how to execute a block of statements over and over again by using a *loop*. You'll use a For...Next loop to execute statements a set number of times, and you'll use a Do loop to execute statements until a conditional expression in the loop evaluates to True. You'll also learn how to use the Print method to display text and numbers on a form and how to use a timer object to execute code at specific intervals in your program.

Writing For...Next Loops

A For...Next loop lets you execute a specific group of program statements a set number of times in an event procedure. This approach can be useful if you are performing several related calculations, working with elements on the screen, or processing several pieces of user input. A For...Next loop is really just a shorthand way of writing out a long list of program statements. Because each group of statements in such a list would do essentially the same thing, Visual Basic lets you define just one group of statements and request that it be executed as many times as you want.

The syntax for a For...Next loop looks like this:

```
For variable = start To end
    statements to be repeated
Next variable
```

In a For...Next loop, start and end determine how long the loop runs.

In this syntax statement, For, To, and Next are required keywords and the equal to operator (=) also is required. You replace *variable* with the name of a numeric variable that keeps track of the current loop count, and you replace *start* and *end* with numeric values representing the starting and stopping points for the loop. The line or lines between the For and Next statements are the instructions that are repeated each time the loop is executed.

For example, the following For...Next loop sounds four beeps in rapid succession from the computer's speaker:

```
For i = 1 To 4
    Beep
Next i
```

This loop is the functional equivalent of writing the Beep statement four times in a procedure. It looks the same to the compiler as

```
Beep
Beep
Beep
Beep
```

The variable used in the loop is i, a single letter that, by convention, stands for the first integer counter in a For...Next loop. Each time the loop is executed, the counter variable is incremented by one. (The first time through the loop, the variable contains a value of 1, the value of *start*; the last time through, it contains a value of 4, the value of *end*.) As you'll see in the following examples, you can use this counter variable to great advantage in your loops.

Displaying a Counter Variable by Using the Print Method

The Print method sends output to a form or a printer. A counter variable is just like any other variable in an event procedure. It can be assigned to properties, used in calculations, or displayed in a program. One of the handiest techniques for displaying a counter variable is to use the Print method, a special statement that displays output on a form or prints output on an attached printer. The Print method has the following syntax:

```
Print expression
```

where *expression* is a variable, property, text value, or numeric value in the procedure. In the following exercise, you'll use the Print method to display the output of a For...Next loop on a form.

> **tip**
> If you plan to minimize a form that contains output from the Print method, set the form's AutoRedraw property to True so that Visual Basic will re-create your output automatically when you display the form again. Unlike other objects on a form, which redraw automatically, text displayed by the Print method reappears only if you set the AutoRedraw property to True.

Display information by using a For...Next loop

1 In Microsoft Visual Basic, open a new project.

2 Increase the length of the form with the sizing pointer to create some extra room to display your output.

CommandButton control

3 Use the CommandButton control to create a command button on the right side of the form.

4 Open the Properties window, and then set the Caption property of the command button to "Loop".

5 Open the object drop-down list box at the top of the Properties window, and then click the Form1 object name.

The properties for the form appear in the Properties window.

6 Change the Font property to Times New Roman.

The Font property controls how text is displayed on the form. You can use any font on your system with the form, but TrueType fonts work the best because they can be displayed in many sizes and they look the same on screen as they do in print.

7 Change the AutoRedraw property to True.

If your form is concealed, the AutoRedraw property will reprint any text displayed by the Print method.

8 Double-click the Loop button on the form.

The Command1_Click event procedure appears in the Code window.

9 Type the following program statements in the procedure:

```
For i = 1 To 10
    Print "Line"; i
Next i
```

This For...Next loop uses the Print method to display the word *Line*, followed by the loop counter, 10 times on the form. The semicolon (;) in the Print statement directs Visual Basic to display the counter variable next to the string "Line", with no additional spaces in between. (You will, however, see a space between "Line" and the counter variable when your program runs. When printing numeric values, the Print method reserves a space for a minus sign, even if the minus sign isn't needed.)

The complete ForLoop program is available in the \Vb6Sbs\Less07 folder.

tip

The Print method supports the semicolon (;) and the comma (,) symbols to separate elements in an expression list. The semicolon places the elements side by side, and the comma places the elements one tab field apart. You can use any combination of semicolon and comma symbols to separate expression list elements.

Now you're ready to run the program.

Start button

10 Click the Start button on the toolbar.

11 Click the Loop button.

The For...Next loop prints 10 lines on the form, as shown in the figure on the following page.

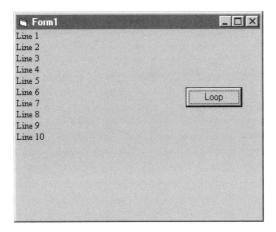

⑫ Click the Loop button again.

The For…Next loop prints another 10 lines on the form (or as many as will fit). Each time a line is printed, the invisible insertion point moves down one line, until it is below the edge of the form.

⑬ Click the End button on the toolbar to stop the program.

End button

Save Project button

⑭ Click the Save Project button on the toolbar. Save the form as **MyForLoop.frm**, and then save the project as **MyForLoop.vbp**.

Save the files in the \Vb6Sbs\Less07 folder.

Changing a property in a For…Next Loop

Use the FontSize property to change the point size of fonts on a form.

Visual Basic lets you change properties and update key variables in a loop. In the following exercise, you'll modify the MyForLoop program so that it changes the FontSize property in the For…Next loop. The FontSize property specifies the point size of the text on a form; you can use it as an alternative to changing the point size with the Font property.

Change the FontSize property

❶ Open the Command1_Click event procedure if it is not already open.

The For…Next loop appears in the Code window.

❷ Insert the following instruction directly below the For statement:

```
FontSize = 10 + i
```

This statement sets the FontSize property of the form to 10 points greater than the value of the loop counter. The first time through the loop, the font size will be set to 11 points, the next time to 12 points, and so on until the last loop, when the font will be enlarged to 20 points. When you've finished, your For…Next loop should look like the following:

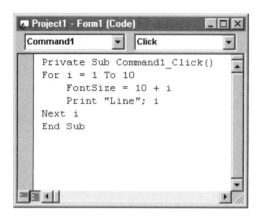

```
Private Sub Command1_Click()
For i = 1 To 10
    FontSize = 10 + i
    Print "Line"; i
Next i
End Sub
```

Start button

❸ Click the Start button on the toolbar to run the program.

❹ Click the Loop button.

The For…Next loop displays the following output on the form:

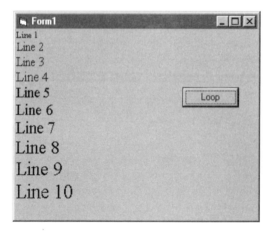

Each time the loop counter was incremented, it caused the point size on the form to grow.

End button

❺ Click the End button to stop the program.

The program stops, and the programming environment returns.

❻ On the File menu, click the Save MyForLoop.frm As command. Save the modified form as **MyGrowFont.frm**.

The complete GrowFont program is available in the \Vb6Sbs\Less07 folder.

❼   On the File menu, click the Save Project As command. Save the project as **MyGrowFont.vbp**.

important

A For...Next loop can save considerable space in a program. In the previous example, a For...Next loop four lines long processed the equivalent of 20 program statements.

Creating Complex For...Next Loops

You can create a different sequence of numbers for your For...Next counter variable by using the Step keyword.

The counter variable in a For...Next loop can be a powerful tool in your programs. With a little imagination, you can use it to create several useful sequences of numbers in your loops. To create a loop with a counter pattern other than 1, 2, 3, 4, and so on, you can specify a different value for *start* in the loop and then use the Step keyword to increment the counter at different intervals. For example, the loop

```
For i = 5 To 25 Step 5
    Print i
Next i
```

would print the following sequence of numbers on a form:

```
5
10
15
20
25
```

You can use the Step keyword with decimal values.

You can also specify decimal values in a loop. For example, the For...Next loop

```
For i = 1 To 2.5 Step 0.5
    Print i
Next i
```

would print the following numbers on a form:

```
1
1.5
2
2.5
```

In addition to displaying the counter variable, you can use the counter to set properties, calculate values, or process files. The following exercise shows how you can use the counter to open Visual Basic icons that are stored on your hard disk in files that have numbers in their names. The program also demonstrates how you can use a For...Next loop to work with several image objects as a group. To organize the image objects so that they can be processed efficiently, you'll place them in a container called a control array.

Open files by using a For...Next loop

Image control

❶ On the File menu, click the New Project command, and then click OK.

❷ Click the Image control in the toolbox, and then create a small, square image box near the upper-left corner of the form.

❸ On the Edit menu, click the Copy command.

A copy of the image box is placed on the Microsoft Windows Clipboard. You'll use this copy to create three additional image boxes on the form.

❹ On the Edit menu, click the Paste command.

You create a control array by copying and pasting objects.

Visual Basic displays a message asking whether you want to create a control array in your program. A *control array* is a collection of identical interface objects. Each object in the group shares the same object name, so the entire group can be selected and defined at once. However, the objects in a control array can also be referenced individually, giving you complete control over each item in your user interface.

❺ Click Yes to create a control array.

Visual Basic creates a control array of image boxes and pastes the second image box in the upper-left corner of the form. The new image box is selected.

❻ Drag the second image box to the right of the first image box.

tip
After you select an object, you can drag it to any location on the form.

❼ On the Edit menu, click the Paste command, and then drag the third image box to the right of the second image box.

❽ Click the Paste command again, and then place the fourth image box to the right of the third image box.

When you've finished pasting, your form should look like the following:

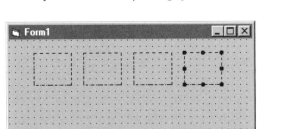

*CommandButton
control*

9 Click the CommandButton control in the toolbox, and then create a command button at the bottom of the form.

Now you'll set the properties of the objects on the form. First you'll set the properties of the image boxes in the control array as a group.

*You work with
all the objects
in a control
array by
selecting them
as a group.*

10 Click the first image box, hold down the Shift key, and then click the second, third, and fourth image boxes. Release the Shift key.

The image boxes in the control array appear selected on the form.

11 Open the Properties window and set the following properties. (After you set the image box properties, click the command button to set its property.)

Object	Property	Setting
Image1	BorderStyle	1 – Fixed Single
Control Array	Stretch	True
Command1	Caption	"Display icons"

12 Double-click the Display Icons button on the form to display the event procedure for the command button object.

The Command1_Click event procedure appears in the Code window.

13 Widen the Code window, and then type the following For…Next loop:

```
For i = 1 To 4
    Image1(i - 1).Picture = _
        LoadPicture("c:\vb6sbs\less07\misc0" & i & ".ico")
Next i
```

tip
The LoadPicture function in this event procedure is too long to fit on one line in this book, so I broke it into two lines by using the Visual Basic line continuation character (_). You can use this character anywhere in your program code except within a string expression.

The loop uses the LoadPicture function to load four icon files from the \Vb6Sbs\Less07 folder on your hard disk. The tricky part of the loop is the statement

```
Image1(i - 1).Picture = _
   LoadPicture("c:\vb6sbs\less07\misc0" & i & ".ico")
```

which loads the files from your hard disk. The first part of the statement,

```
Image1(i - 1).Picture
```

accesses the Picture property of each image box in the control array. Control array items are referenced by their index values, so you would refer to the individual image boxes in this example as Image1(0), Image1(1), Image1(2), and Image1(3). The number in parentheses is the index value in the array. In this example, the correct index value is calculated by subtracting 1 from the counter variable.

The filename is created by using the counter variable and the concatenation operator you learned about in the previous lesson. The code

```
LoadPicture("c:\vb6sbs\less07\misc0" & i & ".ico")
```

combines a pathname, a filename, and the .ico extension to create four valid filenames of icons on your hard disk. In this example, you're loading Misc01.ico, Misc02.ico, Misc03.ico, and Misc04.ico into the image boxes. This statement works because several files in the \Vb6Sbs\Less07 folder have the filename pattern Miscxx.ico. Recognizing the pattern lets you build a For...Next loop around the filenames.

Save Project button

14 Click the Save Project button on the toolbar.

Save the form to disk as **MyCtlArray.frm**, and then save the project to disk as **MyCtlArray.vbp**.

Start button

The complete CtlArray program is available in the \Vb6Sbs\Less07 folder.

15 Click the Start button on the toolbar to start the program, and then click the Display Icons button.

The For...Next loop loads the icons from your hard disk into the image boxes.

tip

If Visual Basic displays an error message, check your program code for typos and then verify that the icon files are in the path you specified in the program. If you installed the Step by Step practice files in a folder other than the default folder, or if you moved your icon files after installation, the pathname in the event procedure may not be correct.

The program displays the following output:

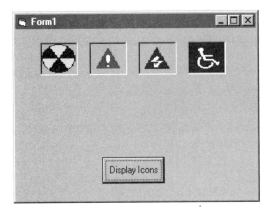

16 Click the Close button on the title bar to quit the program.

The program stops, and the programming environment returns.

Using the Step Keyword in the MyCtlArray Program

Imagine that the \Vb6Sbs\Less07 folder is full of files that have the filename pattern Misc*xx*.ico, and try using the Step keyword to display a few more icons in the image boxes. To load filenames that follow a different pattern, you simply need to change the numbers that appear after the For statement and touch up the code that creates the control array index and the icon filename. You also need to change the image box indexes to match the new counter values you'll be using.

Modify the MyCtlArray program

1 Click the first image box object on the form, and then open the Properties window.

The properties for the Image1(0) image box appear in the Properties window.

2 Change the Index property to 22.

The first item in a control array usually has an index value of 0, but you can change the index value to a different number if that makes the control array easier to use. In this exercise, the files you want to open are Misc22.ico, Misc24.ico, Misc26.ico, and Misc28.ico, so changing the object indexes to 22, 24, 26, and 28 will make the objects easier to reference.

3 Open the object drop-down list box in the Properties window, and then click the Image1(1) object name.

4 Change the Index property of the second image box to 24.

5 Open the object drop-down list box, and then click the Image1(2) object name.

6 Change the Index property of the third image box to 26.

7 Open the object drop-down list box, and then click the Image1(3) object name.

8 Change the Index property of the fourth image box to 28.

Now you'll change the code in the For...Next loop.

9 Double-click the Display Icons button on the form.

The Command1_Click event procedure appears in the Code window.

10 Change the For statement to the following:

```
For i = 22 To 28 Step 2
```

This code sets the counter variable to 22 in the first loop, 24 in the second loop, and 26 and 28 in subsequent loops.

Now you'll update the LoadPicture function in the loop.

11 Change the control array index from Image1(i − 1) to Image1(i).

Because the index now matches the loop and image object names exactly, no calculating is needed to determine the index.

⓬ Remove the second 0 (zero) from the pathname inside the LoadPicture function.

The Miscxx.ico filenames no longer contain zeros. When you've finished, your event procedure should look like the following:

```
Private Sub Command1_Click()
For i = 22 To 28 Step 2
    Image1(i).Picture = _
        LoadPicture("c:\vb6sbs\less07\misc" & i & ".ico")
Next i
End Sub
```

⓭ Click the Start button on the toolbar, and then click the Display Icons button.

The For...Next loop loads four new icons in the image boxes. Your screen should look like the following:

⓮ Click the Close button on the title bar.

The program stops, and the programming environment returns.

The complete StepLoop program is located on disk in the \Vb6Sbs\Less07 folder.

⓯ Save the revised form and project to your hard disk under the name **MyStepLoop**.

Exit For Statements

An Exit For statement allows you to exit a For...Next loop before the loop has finished executing. This lets you respond to a specific event that occurs before the loop runs the preset number of times. For example, in the following For...Next loop,

```
For i = 1 To 10
    InpName = InputBox("Enter your name or type Done to quit.")
    If InpName = "Done" Then Exit For
    Print InpName
Next i
```

the loop prompts the user for 10 names and prints them on the form, unless the word *Done* is entered (in which case, the program jumps to the statement immediately following the Next statement). Exit For statements are usually used with If statements. You'll find them useful for handling special cases that come up in a loop, such as stopping when a predefined limit has been reached.

Writing Do Loops

Do loops execute code until a specific condition is met.

As an alternative to a For...Next loop, you can write a Do loop that executes a group of statements until a certain condition is True in the loop. Do loops are valuable because often you can't know in advance how many times a loop should repeat. For example, you may want to let the user enter names in a database until the user types the word *Done* in an input box. In that case, you can use a Do loop to cycle indefinitely until the text string "Done" is entered.

A Do loop has several formats, depending on where and how the loop condition is evaluated. The most common syntax is

```
Do While condition
    block of statements to be executed
Loop
```

For example, the following Do loop will process input until the word *Done* is entered:

```
Do While InpName <> "Done"
    InpName = InputBox("Enter your name or type Done to quit.")
    If InpName <> "Done" Then Print InpName
Loop
```

The placement of the conditional test affects how a Do loop runs.

The conditional statement in this loop is InpName <> "Done", which the Visual Basic compiler translates to mean "loop as long as the InpName variable doesn't contain the word *Done*." This brings up an interesting fact about Do loops: if the condition at the top of the loop is not True when the Do statement is first evaluated, the Do loop is never executed. Here, if the InpName variable did contain the text string "Done" before the loop started (perhaps from an earlier assignment in the event procedure), Visual Basic would skip the loop altogether and continue with the line below the Loop keyword. Note that this type of loop requires an extra If...Then structure to prevent the exit value from being displayed when the user types it.

If you always want the loop to run at least once in a program, put the conditional test at the bottom of the loop. For example, the loop

```
Do
    InpName = InputBox("Enter your name or type Done to quit.")
    If InpName <> "Done" Then Print InpName
Loop While InpName <> "Done"
```

is essentially the same as the previous Do loop, but here the loop condition is tested after a name is received from the InputBox function. This has the advantage of updating the InpName variable before the conditional test in the loop, so a preexisting "Done" value won't cause the loop to be skipped. Testing the loop condition at the bottom ensures that your loop will be executed at least once, but often it will force you to add a few extra statements to process the data.

Avoiding an Endless Loop

Be sure that each loop has a legitimate exit condition.

Because of the relentless nature of Do loops, it is very important to design your test conditions so that each loop has a true exit point. If a loop test never evaluates to False, the loop will execute endlessly and your program will no longer respond to input. Consider the following example:

```
Do
    Number = InputBox("Enter a number to square. Type -1 to quit.")
    Number = Number * Number
    Print Number
Loop While Number >= 0
```

In this loop the user enters number after number, and the program squares each number and prints the result on the form. Unfortunately, when the user has had enough, he or she can't quit because the advertised exit condition doesn't work.

When the user enters –1, the program squares it and the Number variable is assigned the value 1. (The problem can be fixed by setting a different exit condition.) Watching for endless loops is essential when you're writing Do loops. Fortunately, they're pretty easy to spot if you test your programs thoroughly.

The following exercise shows how you can use a Do loop to convert Fahrenheit temperatures to Celsius temperatures. The simple program prompts the user for input by using the InputBox function, converts the temperature, and displays the output in a message box. The program also demonstrates how you can hide a form by setting its Visible property to False.

Convert temperatures by using a Do loop

1 On the File menu, click the New Project command and then click OK.

Visual Basic displays a new form in the programming environment.

You make a form invisible at runtime by setting its Visible property to False.

2 Open the Properties window, and set the form's Visible property to False.

When you set a form's Visible property to False, Visual Basic hides the form when you run the program. This essentially makes the entire user interface invisible at runtime—no objects can be displayed. You probably won't want to do this very often, but it's a useful technique when you want part or all of your program to work on a task in the background. Because this program only receives Fahrenheit temperatures and spits back Celsius temperatures, hiding its form is a good idea. You can handle the input by using the InputBox function and the output by using the MsgBox function.

3 Double-click the form.

The Form_Load event procedure is executed when a program starts running.

The Form_Load event procedure appears in the Code window. In this program, all the code goes here.

4 Type the following program statements:

```
Prompt = "Enter a Fahrenheit temperature."
Do
    FTemp = InputBox(Prompt, "Fahrenheit to Celsius")
    If FTemp <> "" Then
        Celsius = Int((FTemp + 40) * 5 / 9 - 40)
        MsgBox (Celsius), , "Temperature in Celsius"
    End If
Loop While FTemp <> ""
End
```

These nine lines handle the calculations for the utility. The first line assigns a text string to the Prompt variable, which is then used to display a message of instruction in the input box. The Do loop repeatedly prompts the user for a Fahrenheit temperature, converts the number to Celsius, and then displays it on the screen by using the MsgBox function. The loop executes until the user clicks the Cancel button, which returns an empty, or *null*, value to the Ftemp variable. Finally, the loop checks for the null value by using a While conditional test at the bottom of the loop. The program statement

```
Celsius = Int((FTemp + 40) * 5 / 9 - 40)
```

handles the conversion from Fahrenheit to Celsius in the program. This statement employs a standard conversion formula, but it uses the Int function to return to the Celsius variable a value that contains no decimal places. (Everything to the right of the decimal point is discarded.) This cutting sacrifices accuracy, but it helps you avoid long, unsightly numbers, such as 21.111111111111, the Celsius value for 70 degrees Fahrenheit.

Now try running the program.

Start button

5 Click the Start button on the toolbar.

The program starts, and the InputBox function prompts you for a Fahrenheit temperature. (The form is invisible.) Your screen should look like the following:

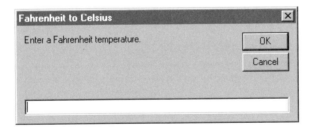

6 Type **32** and click OK.

The temperature 32 degrees Fahrenheit is converted to 0 degrees Celsius, as shown in the message box on the following page.

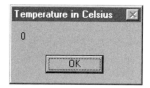

Using the Until Keyword in Do Loops

The Do loops you have worked with so far have used the While keyword to execute a group of statements as long as the loop condition remains True. Visual Basic also lets you use the Until keyword in Do loops to cycle *until* a certain condition is True. The Until keyword can be used at the top or bottom of a Do loop to test a condition, just like the While keyword. For example, the following Do loop uses the Until keyword to loop repeatedly until the user enters the word *Done* in an input box:

```
Do
    InpName = InputBox("Enter your name or type Done to quit.")
    If InpName <> "Done" Then Print InpName
Loop Until InpName = "Done"
```

As you can see, a loop that uses the Until keyword is very similar to a loop that uses the While keyword, except that the test condition usually contains the opposite operator—the = (equal to) operator versus the <> (not equal to) operator, in this case. If using the Until keyword makes sense to you, feel free to use it with test conditions in your Do loops.

❼ Click OK. Type **72** in the input box, and click OK.

The temperature 72 degrees Fahrenheit is converted to 22 degrees Celsius.

❽ Click OK, and then quit the program by clicking Cancel in the input box.

The program quits, and the programming environment returns.

Save Project button

❾ Click the Save Project button, and save the form and project to disk under the name **MyCelsius**.

Using Timer Objects

A timer object works like an invisible stopwatch in a program.

Visual Basic lets you execute a group of statements for a specified *period of time* by using a timer object. A *timer object* is an invisible stopwatch that gives you access to the system clock from your programs. It can be used like an egg timer to count down from a preset time, to cause a delay in a program, or to repeat an action at prescribed intervals.

A timer object is accurate to 1 millisecond, or 1/1000 of a second. Although timers aren't visible at runtime, each timer is associated with an event procedure that runs every time the timer's preset *interval* has elapsed. You set a timer's interval by using the Interval property, and you activate a timer by setting the timer's Enabled property to True. Once a timer is enabled, it runs constantly— executing its event procedure at the prescribed interval—until the user stops the program or the timer is disabled.

The Interval property sets the tick rate of a timer.

Creating a Digital Clock by Using a Timer Object

One of the most practical uses for a timer object is creating a digital clock. In the following exercise, you'll create a simple digital clock that keeps track of the current time down to the second. In the example, you'll set the Interval property for the timer to 1000, directing Visual Basic to update the clock time every 1000 milliseconds, or once a second. Because the Windows operating system is a multitasking environment and other programs will also require processing time, Visual Basic may not always get a chance to update the clock each second, but it will always catch up if it falls behind. To keep track of the time at other intervals (such as once every tenth of a second), simply adjust the number in the Interval property.

Create the DigClock program

1 On the File menu, click the New Project command and click OK.

2 Resize the form to a small window.

You don't want the clock to take up much room.

Timer control

3 Click the Timer control in the toolbox.

A timer object can be only one size.

4 Create a small timer object on the left side of the form.

After you create the timer, Visual Basic resizes it to its standard size.

Label control

5 Click the Label control in the toolbox.

6 In the center of the form, create a label that fills most of the form.

You'll use the label to display the time in the clock. Your form should look like the one shown on the following page.

The Caption property of a form controls the name displayed in the program's title bar.

7 Open the Properties window, and set the following properties in the program. To give the DigClock program a name that appears in its title bar, you'll set the Caption property of the Form1 object to "Digital Clock".

Object	Property	Setting
Label1	Caption	(Empty)
	Font	Times New Roman, Bold, 24-point
	Alignment	2 – Center
Timer1	Interval	1000
	Enabled	True
Form1	Caption	"Digital Clock"

tip

If you would like to put some artwork in the background of your clock, set the Picture property of the Form1 object to the pathname of a graphics file.

Now you'll write the program code for the timer.

The complete DigClock program is available in the \Vb6Sbs\Less07 folder.

8 Double-click the timer object on the form.

The Timer1_Timer event procedure appears in the Code window.

9 Type the following statement:

```
Label1.Caption = Time
```

This statement gets the current time from the system clock and assigns it to the caption property of the Label1 object. Only one statement is required in this program because you set the Interval property for the timer by using the Properties window. The timer object handles the rest.

Start button

10 Close the Code window, and then click the Start button on the toolbar to run the clock.

The clock appears, as shown here. (Your time may be different, of course.)

11 Watch the clock for a few moments.

Visual Basic updates the time every second.

12 Click the Close button in the title bar to stop the clock.

Clicking the Close button is an alternative to using the End button to stop the program. This is the method a user would use to close the clock if he or she were running it as a stand-alone program.

Save Project button

13 Click the Save Project button, and save the form and project to disk under the name **MyDigClock**.

The MyDigClock program is so handy that you may want to compile it into an executable file and use it now and then on your computer. Feel free to customize it by using your own artwork, text, and colors.

tip

See the section entitled "If You Want to Boost Your Productivity" near the end of this lesson for an alarm utility based on DigClock that will help you arrive on time for your appointments.

One Step Further   Using a Timer Object to Set a Time Limit

Another interesting use of a timer object is to set it to wait for a given period of time and then either to enable or prohibit an action. This is a little like setting an egg timer in your program—you set the Interval property with the delay you want, and then you start the clock ticking by setting the Enabled property to True.

The following exercise shows how you can use this approach to set a time limit for entering a password. (The password for this program is "secret".) The program uses a timer to close its own program if a valid password is not entered in

15 seconds. (Normally, a program like this would be part of a larger application.) You can also use this timer technique to display a welcome message or a copyright message on the screen, or to repeat an event at a set interval, such as saving a file to disk every 10 minutes.

Set a password time limit

❶ On the File menu, click the New Project command, and then click OK.

❷ Resize the form to a small rectangular window about the size of an input box.

TextBox control

❸ Click the TextBox control in the toolbox.

❹ Create a rectangular text box in the middle of the form.

❺ Click the Label control in the toolbox, and then create a long label above the text box.

Label control

❻ Click the CommandButton control in the toolbox, and then create a command button below the text box.

❼ Click the Timer control in the toolbox.

❽ Create a timer object in the lower-left corner of the form.

CommandButton control

❾ Set the properties in the table below for the program.

Timer control

Object	Property	Setting
Text1	Text	(Empty)
	PasswordChar	*
Label1	Caption	"Enter your password within 15 seconds."
Command1	Caption	"Try Password"
Timer1	Interval	15000
	Enabled	True
Form1	Caption	"Password"

The PasswordChar setting will display asterisk (*) characters in the text box as the user enters a password. Setting the timer Interval property to 15000 will give the user 15 seconds to enter a password and click the Try Password button. Setting the Enabled property to True (the default) will start the timer running when the program starts. (You could also disable this property and then enable it in an event procedure if your timer was not needed until later in the program.)

Your form should look like the following:

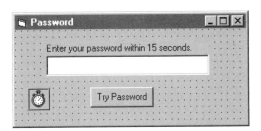

10 Double-click the timer object on the form, and then type the following statements.

```
MsgBox ("Sorry, your time is up.")
End
```

The first statement displays a message indicating that the time has expired, and the second statement stops the program. Visual Basic executes this event procedure if the timer interval reaches 15 seconds and a valid password has not been entered.

11 Click the Command1 object in the Code window drop-down list box, and then type the following statements in the Command1_Click event procedure:

```
If Text1.Text = "secret" Then
    Timer1.Enabled = False
    MsgBox ("Welcome to the system!")
    End
Else
    MsgBox ("Sorry, friend, I don't know you.")
End If
```

The complete TimePass program is available in the \Vb6Sbs\Less07 folder.

This program code tests whether the password entered in the text box is "secret." If it is, the timer is disabled, a welcome message is displayed, and the program ends. (A more useful program would continue working rather than ending here.) If the password entered is not a match, the user is notified with a message box and is given another chance to enter the password. But the user has only 15 seconds to do so!

Start button

12 Close the Code window, and then click the Start button to run the program.

The program starts, and the 15-second clock starts ticking.

13 Type **open** in the text box, and then click the Try Password button.

The dialog box shown on the following page appears on the screen, noting your incorrect response.

⓮ Click OK, and then wait patiently until the sign-on period expires.

The program displays the message shown in the figure on the following page.

⓯ Click OK to end the program.

The Visual Basic programming environment appears.

Save Project button

⓰ Click the Save Project button, and save the form and project to disk under the name **MyTimePass**.

If you want to boost your productivity

Take a few minutes to explore the Alarm utility (alarm.vbp) in the \Vb6Sbs \Extras folder on your hard disk. I wrote this program as an extension of the DigClock program to give you a little more practice with the Timer control and the time-keeping concepts introduced in this lesson. The application is a personal appointment reminder that sounds an alarm and displays a message when it is time for your next meeting or task. I find it a useful tool for keeping me on schedule when I'm working by my computer or in my office (it works better than those little yellow sticky notes, which seem to fall off). The Alarm program checks the current time stored in your computer's system clock, so before you use this program, open Control Panel and verify that the system time is correct. As you'll see, Alarm can be run in a window or minimized to the Windows taskbar, where it waits patiently until your appointment. You can customize the program yourself or simply use it as is for your daily work.

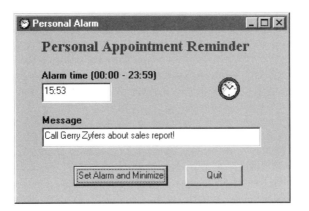

If you want to continue to the next lesson

● Keep Visual Basic running, and turn to Lesson 8.

If you want to quit Visual Basic for now

● On the File menu, click Exit.

If you see a Save dialog box, click Yes.

Upgrade Notes: What's Different in Visual Basic .NET?

If you choose to upgrade to Visual Basic .NET in the future, you'll notice some new features related to the topics in this lesson, including the following:

■ In Visual Basic 6.0, you can display text directly on your form (as I demonstrated above) using the Print method, a holdover from the Print statement in GW-BASIC and Microsoft QuickBasic. In Visual Basic .NET, the Print method can be used only to send data to a file on disk. As an alternative to displaying large amounts of text on a form, Visual Basic .NET programmers sometimes append text to a multiline text box object using the string concatenation operator (&).

■ In Visual Basic 6.0, a While loop is specified with the syntax While…Wend. In Visual Basic .NET, the closing statement has changed to While…End While to parallel similar structures.

■ The Visual Basic .NET Timer control is similar but not identical to the Visual Basic 6.0 Timer control you have used here. For example, the Timer1_Timer event procedure (which is executed at each pre-set timer interval) has been renamed Timer1_Tick in Visual Studio .NET. In addition, you can no longer disable a Timer by setting the Interval property to 0.

■ Visual Basic .NET no longer supports control arrays (collections of controls that share the same name and are processed as a group), and you cannot group controls by using the Windows Clipboard as I demonstrated in this lesson. However, in Visual Basic .NET, you can continue to store controls in an array if the array is declared in the object type.

Lesson 7 Quick Reference

To	Do This
Execute a group of program statements a set number of times	Insert the statements between For and Next statements in a loop. For example: ```For i = 1 To 10 MsgBox ("Press OK already!") Next i```
Display one or more lines of output on a form	Use the Print method. For example: ```For Cnt = 1 To 5 Print "The current count is"; Cnt Print "So far, so good." Next Cnt```
Use a specific sequence of numbers with statements	Insert the statements in a For...Next loop and use the To and Step keywords to define the sequence of numbers. For example: ```For i = 2 To 8 Step 2 Print i; "..."; Next i Print "Who do we appreciate?"```
Avoid an endless Do loop	Be sure the loop has a test condition that can evaluate to False.
Exit a For...Next loop prematurely	Use the Exit For statement. For example: ```For i = 1 To 10 InpName = InputBox("Name?") If InpName = "Trotsky" Then Exit For Print InpName Next i```

Lesson 7 Quick Reference

To	Do This
Execute a group of program statements until a specific condition is met	Insert the statements between Do and Loop statements. For example:

```
Do While Query <> "Yes"
    Query = InputBox("Trotsky?")
    If Query <> "Yes" Then Print Query
Loop
```

| Loop until a certain condition is True | Use a Do loop with the Until keyword. For example: |

```
Do
    GiveIn = InputBox("Say 'Uncle'")
Loop Until GiveIn = "Uncle"
```

| Loop for a specific period of time in your program | Use a Timer object. |
| Place a name in an application's title bar | Set the Caption property of the Form1 object to the name you want to use. |

PART 3

Creating the Perfect User Interface

LESSON

8

Working with Forms, Printers, and Error Handlers

**ESTIMATED
TIME
45 min.**

In this lesson you will learn how to:

✔ *Add new forms to a program.*

✔ *Send output to a printer.*

✔ *Process runtime errors by using error handlers.*

In Part 2, you learned how to use a variety of Microsoft Visual Basic statements, functions, and control structures to do useful work in your programs. In Part 3, you'll focus again on the user interface and you'll learn how to create impressive effects and bulletproof applications. In this lesson, you'll learn how to add more forms to an interface to handle input, output, or special messages. You'll also learn how to send the output of a program to an attached printer and how to use error handlers to process unexpected results.

Adding New Forms to a Program

Each new form has a unique name and its own set of objects, properties, and event procedures.

Each program you have written so far has used only one form for input and output. In many cases, one form will be sufficient for communication with the user. But if you need to offer more information to (or obtain more information from) the user, Visual Basic lets you add one or more extra forms to your program. Each new form is considered an object and maintains its own objects, properties, and event procedures. The first form in a program is named Form1. Subsequent forms are named Form2, Form3, and so on. The following table lists several practical uses for extra forms in your programs.

Form or forms	Description
Introductory screen	A screen that displays a welcome message, artwork, or copyright information when the program starts
Program instructions	A screen that displays information and tips about how the program works
Dialog boxes	Custom dialog boxes that accept input and display output in the program
Document contents files and artwork	A screen that displays the contents of one or more used in the program

Blank or Predesigned Forms

You can create a new form by clicking the Add Form command on the Project menu. A dialog box appears, prompting you for the type of form you want to create (each version of Visual Basic has a different collection of predesigned forms). You have the option of creating a new, blank form or a partially completed form designed for a particular task.

How Forms Are Used

Forms can be modal or nonmodal.

In Visual Basic, you have significant flexibility when using forms. You can make all of the forms in a program visible at the same time, or you can load and unload forms as the program needs them. If you display more than one form at once, you can allow the user to switch between the forms or you can control the order in which the forms are used. A form that must be used when it is displayed on the screen is a *modal* form—a form that retains the focus until the user clicks OK, clicks Cancel, or otherwise dispatches it.

A form that the user can switch away from is a *nonmodal,* or *modeless,* form. Most applications for Microsoft Windows use nonmodal forms when displaying information because they give the user more flexibility, so nonmodal is the default when you create a new form. You can also independently set any property on a form, including the form's caption, form size, border style, foreground and background colors, display font, and background picture.

Form Statements in Program Code

After you create a new form in the programming environment, you can load it into memory and access it by using specific statements in event procedures. The statement you use to load a new form has the syntax

```
Load formname
```

where *formname* is the name of the form you want to load. For example, the statement

The Load statement brings a new form into memory.

```
Load Form2
```

would load the second form in a program into memory when the statement was executed by Visual Basic. After you have loaded a form, you can use it from any event procedure in the program and you can access any property or method you want to use with it. For example, to set the Caption property of the second form in your program to "Sorting Results", you could type the following program statement in any event procedure:

```
Form2.Caption = "Sorting Results"
```

The Show method displays a loaded form.

When you are ready to display a loaded form, you call it by using the Show method and indicating whether it is modal or nonmodal. The syntax for the Show method is

```
formname.Show mode
```

The default for a new form is nonmodal.

where *formname* is the name of the form and *mode* is 0 for nonmodal (the default) or 1 for modal. For example, to display Form2 as a nonmodal form (the default), you could use the Show method without specifying a mode:

```
Form2.Show
```

To display Form2 as a modal form, you would type this statement:

```
Form2.Show 1
```

tip

If you use the Show method before using the Load statement, Visual Basic will load and display the specified form automatically. Visual Basic provides a separate Load statement to let programmers preload forms in memory so that the Show method works quickly and users don't notice any performance lag. It's a good idea to preload your forms, especially if they contain several objects or pieces of artwork.

Forms, Printers, and Errors

Hiding and Unloading Forms

The Hide method makes a form invisible.

You can hide forms by using the Hide method, and you can unload forms by using the Unload statement. These keywords are the opposites of Show and Load, respectively. Hiding a form makes the form invisible but keeps it in memory for use later in the program. (Hiding a form is identical to making it invisible by using the Visible property.) Unloading a form removes the form from memory. This frees up the RAM used to store the objects and graphics on the form, but it doesn't free up the space used by the form's event procedures. These are always in memory. You could use the Hide and Unload keywords to hide and unload Form2 in the following manner:

The Unload statement removes a form from memory.

```
Form2.Hide
Unload Form2
```

important

When you unload a form, its runtime values and properties are lost. If you reload the form later, it will contain the original values set in the program code.

Minimizing Forms

You can minimize a form (place it on the taskbar) or maximize a form (expand it to fill the screen) by using the WindowState property. For example, the following statement would minimize Form1 in a program:

```
Form1.WindowState = 1
```

To maximize Form1, you would use the statement:

```
Form1.WindowState = 2
```

To return Form1 to its normal, default view, you would use:

```
Form1.WindowState = 0
```

The Alarm program in the \Vb6Sbs\Extras folder demonstrates how the WindowState property works.

Adding Preexisting Forms to a Program

Visual Basic lets you reuse your forms in new programming projects. This is why you have been saving your forms as separate .frm files while using this book. To add a preexisting form to a programming project, click the Add Form command on the Visual Basic Project menu and then click the Existing tab. The Existing tab displays a dialog box that lists all the forms in the current folder (that is, the folder you used last in Visual Basic). To add an existing form, double-click the form filename in the dialog box. Visual Basic adds the specified form to the project, and you can view the form and modify its event procedures by clicking the View Object and View Code buttons in the Project window. You can specify the startup form in your program (the first form loaded) by clicking the Properties command on the Project menu, clicking the General tab, and choosing the appropriate form in the Startup Object drop-down list box. If you change a preexisting form in a new project, you should first save it with a different name. Otherwise, other projects using that form won't run correctly anymore.

Working with Multiple Forms: The Italian Program

The following exercises demonstrate how you can use a second form to display graphics and text in a foreign-language vocabulary program named Italian. Right now, the program uses a MsgBox function to display a definition for each word, but you'll modify the program so that it uses a second form to display the information.

Run the Italian program

❶   Start Visual Basic.

❷   Click the Existing tab in the New Project dialog box.

❸   Open the Italian project in the \Vb6Sbs\Less08 folder.

❹   If the Italian Step by Step form isn't open, click the Italian form in the Project window and then click the View Object button.

   The user interface for the program appears. You'll try running the utility now.

Start button

5 Click the Start button on the toolbar.

A list of Italian verbs appears in the list box on the form. To get the definition for a word, you double-click the word in the list box.

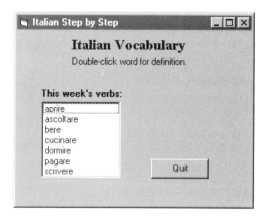

6 Double-click *dormire.*

A definition for the word *dormire* appears in a message box:

The output is displayed by the MsgBox function in a plain but effective dialog box.

7 Click OK to close the dialog box.

The dialog box closes, and the main form returns.

8 Click Quit to quit the program.

Now you'll remove the MsgBox function and replace it with an extra form used to display the information. You'll use the Form button on the toolbar to create the new form in the program.

Create a second form in the program

1 On the Project menu, click the Add Form command.

The Add Form dialog box appears, showing several predesigned forms in the New tab.

❷ Click Open to open a new, blank form in the project.

A blank form named Form2 appears in the programming environment.

❸ Resize the second form so that it's about the size and shape of a small, rectangular dialog box.

Make sure that you are resizing the Form2 window, not the Project1 window that contains the form!

Image control

❹ Click the Image control in the toolbox, and then create a medium-size image box on the left side of the form.

You'll use this image box to hold a bitmap of the Italian flag.

Label control

❺ Click the Label control, and then create a label in the top middle area of the form.

TextBox control

❻ Click the TextBox control, and then create a large text box below the label in the middle of the form.

Command-Button control

❼ Click the CommandButton control, and then create a command button on the right side of the form.

❽ Set the following properties for the objects on your new form:

Object	Property	Setting
Image1	Stretch	True
	Picture	"c:\vb6sbs\less08\flgitaly.ico"
Label1	Font	Times New Roman, Bold, 14-point
Text1	TabStop	False
Command1	Caption	"Close"
Form2	Caption	"Definition"

tip

Setting the TabStop property of the text box to False keeps the text box from getting the focus when the user presses the Tab key. If you don't set this property, the cursor will blink in the text box when the form appears.

When you've finished setting properties, your form should look similar to the following:

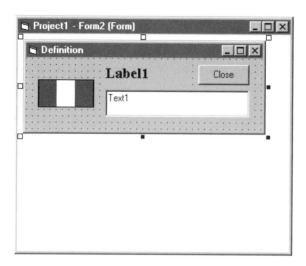

Now you'll save the new project and the new form. As you know, Visual Basic requires that each form be saved under its own filename. However, more than one project can share a form. Before you save Form2, be sure that it is the active, or selected, form in the programming environment (it should be now).

9 On the File menu, click the Save Form2 As command.

The Save File As dialog box appears.

10 Save Form2 to disk under the name **MyDef.frm**. Store the form in the \Vb6Sbs\Less08 folder.

The second form is saved to disk and is registered in the Project window. You can switch back and forth between forms by clicking a form or by highlighting a form name in the Project window and then clicking the View Object button.

11 Click Form1, and then click Save Italian.frm As on the File menu to save Form1. Type the name **MyWordList.frm** and press Enter.

Now changes you make to Form1 won't be reflected in the Italian project. (You've created another copy of the form under a new name.)

12 On the File menu, click the Save Project As command, and then save the project under the name **MyItalian2.vbp**.

Now you'll modify the Text1_DblClick event procedure to display the new form.

Access the second form in an event procedure

1   Click the first form (MyWordList), and then double-click the List1 object on the form.

The List1_DblClick event procedure appears in the Code window. In this event procedure, I placed a Select Case decision structure that uses a MsgBox function to display the definition of the selected Italian word. The decision structure determines the list box pick and then assigns the appropriate definition to the Def variable. Take some time to examine the decision structure if you like, and then continue.

2   Scroll to the bottom of the event procedure in the Code window.

The following MsgBox function appears:

```
MsgBox (Def), , List1.Text
```

3   Delete the MsgBox function, and then type the following program statements in its place:

The object name Form2 identifies the new form in the program.

```
Load Form2
Form2.Label1 = List1.Text
Form2.Text1 = Def
Form2.Show
```

The first statement loads Form2 into memory. (You could also preload the form by placing this statement in the Form_Load event procedure.) After bringing the form into memory, you can change the form's properties and get it ready for viewing. The second line puts a copy of the selected Italian word into the first label on Form2. The third line assigns the Def variable (containing the word's definition) to the text box on the new form. You're using a text box to support longer definitions in the program. If the definition fills the text box, scroll bars will appear to provide access to the whole string. Finally, the Show method displays the completed form on the screen.

Now you'll add a statement to the Close button on Form2 to close the form when the user is through with it.

4   Close the Code window, click Form2 (or display it by using the Project window), and then double-click the Close button.

Objects on different forms can have the same name.

The Command1_Click event procedure appears in the Code window. This event procedure is associated with the first button on Form2—not the first button on Form1. Objects on different forms can have the same name, and Visual Basic has no trouble keeping them separate. However, if similar or identical names make it hard for you to tell the objects apart, you can change their names by using the Properties window.

tip

To change an object's name, select the object on the form and then use the Properties window to change the object's Name property. The Name property holds the title that Visual Basic uses to identify the object, so if you change an object name, be sure to change it everywhere in your program code. An object name should be logical, so that you can easily remember what the object does. Object names, like variables, should also carry identifying prefixes. For example, a command button used to quit a program might be named cmdQuit.

⑤ Type the following program statement in the event procedure:

The Hide method makes your new form invisible when the user clicks Close.

```
Form2.Hide
```

This statement uses the Hide method to make Form2 invisible when the user clicks the Close button. Because Form2 was displayed in a nonmodal state, the user is free to switch between Form1 and Form2 while the program runs. The user can close Form2 by clicking the Close button.

⑥ Click the Save Project button to save your revised project to disk.

Save Project button

⑦ Click the Start button to run the program.

⑧ Double-click the verb *cucinare* in the list box.

The program displays the definition for the word on the second form, as shown in the following illustration:

Now you'll practice switching back and forth between the forms.

⑨ Click the first form, and then double-click the word *scrivere*.

The program displays the definition for *scrivere* (to write) on the second form. Because the forms are nonmodal, you can switch between them as you wish.

The Italian2 program is available in the \Vb6Sbs\Less08 folder.

⑩ Click Close on the second form.

The program hides the form.

⑪ Click Quit on the first form.

The program stops, and Visual Basic unloads both forms. The programming environment returns.

Sending Program Output to a Printer

The Printer object controls printing.

Visual Basic lets you send output to an installed printer by using the Print method. You learned about the Print method in Lesson 7 when you used it in a loop to display text on a form. To send output to an attached printer, you use the Print method with the Printer object. For example, the following line sends the text string "Mariners" to the Windows default printer:

```
Printer.Print "Mariners"
```

Before printing, you can also use the Printer object to adjust certain font characteristics. For example, the following code prints "Mariners" in 14-point type:

```
Printer.FontSize = 14
Printer.Print "Mariners"
```

The Printer object has several dozen properties and methods that you can use to control different aspects of printing. Many of these properties and methods are similar to keywords you've been using with forms and objects created by using toolbox controls. However, Printer properties differ in one crucial regard from the properties of forms and objects created by using controls in the toolbox: you can't set Printer properties by using the Properties window. Each Printer property must be set with program code at runtime.

tip

For a complete listing of Printer properties and methods, search for *Printer object* in the Visual Basic online Help. You can also use properties to determine the capabilities of your printer.

(The Form_Load event procedure is a good place to put standard Printer settings that you'll use every time your program runs.) The following tables list some of the more useful Printer methods and properties.

Method	Description
Print	Prints the specified text on the printer
NewPage	Starts a new page in the print job
EndDoc	Signals the end of a print job
KillDoc	Terminates the current print job

Forms, Printers, and Errors

8

MDI Forms: Windows That Have Parent-Child Relationships

In most of the programs you'll write, you will probably create a standard "home" form where the user does most of his or her work, and then you'll add special-purpose forms to handle the input and output of a program. However, Visual Basic also lets you set up a *hierarchy*, which is a special relationship among forms in a program that work best as a group. These special forms are called MDI (Multiple Document Interface) forms, and they are distinguished by their roles as *parent* and *child* forms. You create an MDI parent form by clicking the Add MDI Form command on the Project menu, and you create an MDI child form by clicking the Add Form command on the Project menu and then setting the form's MDIChild property to True. MDI forms perform like regular forms at runtime, with the following exceptions:

- All child forms are displayed within their parent form's window space.

- When a child form is minimized, it shrinks to a small title bar on the MDI form instead of appearing as a button on the taskbar.

- When the parent form is minimized, the parent and all its children appear as one button on the taskbar.

- All child menus are displayed on the parent form's menu bar. When a child form is maximized, its caption is displayed in the parent's title bar.

- You can display all the child forms of a parent form by setting the AutoShowChildren property of the parent form to True.

Parent and child forms are especially useful in so-called *document-centered applications*, in which many windows are used to display or edit a document. To learn more about MDI forms and their applications, search for *MDI applications, creating* in the Visual Basic online Help.

Property	Description
FontName	Sets the font name for the text
FontSize	Sets the font size for the text
FontBold	True sets the font style to bold
FontItalic	True sets the font style to italic
Page	Contains the number of the page that is being printed

In the following exercise, you'll add basic printing support to the MyItalian2 program you created earlier in this lesson. You'll use the FontName, FontSize, and FontBold properties to change the style of the text; the Print method to send definitions to the printer; and the EndDoc method to signal the end of the printing job.

Add printer support to the MyItalian2 program

To complete this exercise, open the MyItalian2 project in the \Vb6Sbs\Less08 folder.

1 Open the MyItalian2 project file if it is not already open.

If you didn't create MyItalian2.vbp, you can load Italian2.vbp from your hard disk.

2 Display the second form in the project (MyDef.frm, or Def.frm if you're using Italian2.vbp).

This form displays the definition for the Italian word that the user double-clicks in the list box. You'll add a Print button to this form to give the user the option of printing a copy of the definition.

CommandButton control

3 Click the CommandButton control in the toolbox, and then create a command button to the left of the Close button.

You may need to make room for the button by widening the form and moving the Close button to the right or by adjusting the size of the Label1 object. When you've finished, your revised form should look similar to the following illustration:

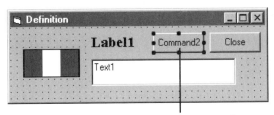

New Print button

④ Change the caption of the button to "Print" by using the Properties window.

⑤ Double-click the new Print button to edit its event procedure.

The Command2_Click event procedure appears in the Code window.

⑥ Type the following printing statements in the event procedure:

```
Printer.Print ""
Printer.FontName = "Arial"
Printer.FontSize = 18
Printer.FontBold = True
Printer.Print Label1.Caption
Printer.FontBold = False
Printer.Print Text1.Text
Printer.EndDoc
```

Here are some of the important elements in the print routine:

The first statement initializes the printer object to prepare it for output.

Using one of the TrueType fonts that was supplied with Windows will make your program compatible with most printers.

▓ The FontName property sets the printer font to Arial, a TrueType font.

▓ The FontSize property sets the font size to 18 point.

▓ Setting the FontBold property to True turns bold type on.

▓ The fifth and seventh lines use the Print method to print the Italian word and its definition.

▓ The last line ends the print job and sends it to the printer.

tip

If you want to allow the user to print several word definitions on one page, you might want to postpone using the EndDoc method until the user clicks Quit to end the program.

⑦ On the File menu, click the Save MyDef.frm As command, and then save the second form as **MyPrintFrm.frm**. This will preserve the original MyDef.frm form on disk.

The complete PrintFrm project is located on disk in the \Vb6Sbs\Less08 folder.

⑧ On the File menu, click the Save Project As command, and then save the new project as **MyPrintFrm.vbp**.

Because you didn't save MyWordList.frm under a new name, the MyPrintFrm.vbp project and the MyItalian2.vbp project will share its form and code. Whenever you make a change to the MyWordList.frm file (on the form or in the event procedures), the change will be reflected in both projects.

Run the MyPrintFrm program

Now you'll run the program if you have a printer attached to your system. Your application will use the default printer specified in the Windows Printers folder, so the device can be a local printer, a network printer, or a fax modem program. Verify that the printer is online and ready to go.

Start button

❶ Click the Start button on the toolbar.

The program runs in the programming environment.

❷ Double-click the Italian word *bere* in the list box.

The definition appears in the form below:

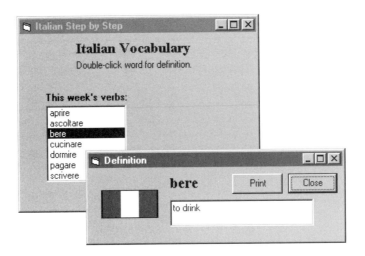

❸ Click the Print button on the form to print the definition on paper.

Visual Basic sends your document to the default printer.

important

If your printer is not ready to print, Windows may return an error to Visual Basic that your program is not ready to handle. This could result in a runtime error or program crash. You'll learn how to handle runtime errors associated with disk drives, printers, and other devices later in this lesson.

❹ Click Close to close the definition window, and then click Quit to end the program.

The program stops, and the programming environment returns.

Printing an Entire Form by Using the PrintForm Method

As an alternative to printing individual lines by using the Print method, you can send the entire contents of one or more forms to the printer by using the Print-Form method. This technique lets you arrange the text, graphics, and user interface elements you want on a form and then send the entire form to the printer. You can use the PrintForm keyword by itself to print the current form, or you can include a form name to print a specific form. For example, to print the contents of the second form in a program, you could enter the statement

```
Form2.PrintForm
```

in any event procedure in the program.

The following example shows how to use the PrintForm method to print a form containing both text and graphics. In most situations, PrintForm is the easiest way to send artwork to a printer.

> ## tip
> The PrintForm method prints your form at the current resolution of your display adapter, typically 96 dots per inch.

Use PrintForm to print text and graphics

Label control

CommandButton control

❶ On the File menu, click the New Project command, and then click OK to create a new, standard application.

❷ Click the Label control, and then create a medium-size label near the center of the form.

❸ Click the CommandButton control, and then create a button in the lower-right corner of the form.

❹ Set the following properties for the objects in the program:

Object	Property	Setting
Label1	Caption	"Quarterly Report"
	BackStyle	0 – Transparent
	Font	MS Sans Serif, Bold, 14-point
Command1	Caption	"Print this!"
Form1	Picture	"c:\vb6sbs\less08\prntout2.wmf"

⑤ Double-click the Print this! button to open its event procedure.

⑥ Type the following program statement:

```
Form1.PrintForm
```

Save Project button

⑦ Click the Save Project button on the toolbar to save the form and the project. Type **MyPrintWMF** for the form name and for the project name.

⑧ Click the Start button on the toolbar to run the program.

The program displays the following:

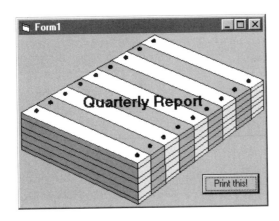

The complete PrintWMF project is located on disk in the \Vb6Sbs\Less08 folder.

⑨ Click the Print this! button to print the contents of the form.

Visual Basic sends the entire contents of the form (label, Windows metafile, and command button) to the printer. While the document prints, you might see the following Visual Basic dialog box:

In a few moments, the output of the program emerges from the printer.

⑩ Click the Close button on the form to end the program.

The PrintForm method prints all visible objects on a form.

important

The PrintForm method prints only the objects that are currently visible on the form. To remove unwanted objects from a printout (such as the Print this! button in the last example), set the Visible property of those objects to False before calling the PrintForm method. Then add a statement to make the objects visible again after you have sent the form to the printer.

Processing Errors by Using Error Handlers

Have you experienced a runtime error in a Visual Basic program yet? A *runtime error*, or *program crash*, is an unexpected problem that occurs in a Visual Basic program from which it can't recover. You may have experienced your first program crash in this lesson when you were trying to print, if something didn't work right. (Perhaps the printer was out of paper or was turned off and you received a printer error message from Visual Basic or Windows.) A runtime error happens anytime Visual Basic executes a statement that for some reason can't be completed "as dialed" while the program is running. It's not that Visual Basic isn't tough enough to handle the glitch; it's just that the compiler hasn't been told what to do when something goes wrong.

An error handler helps your program recover from runtime errors.

Fortunately, you don't have to live with occasional errors that cause your programs to crash. Visual Basic lets you write special routines, called *error handlers*, to respond to runtime errors. An error handler handles a runtime error by telling the program how to continue when one of its statements doesn't work. Error handlers are placed in the same event procedures where the potentially unstable statements are. As their name implies, error handlers handle, or *trap*, a problem by using a special error handling object named Err. The Err object has a Number property that identifies the error and lets your program respond to it. For example, if a floppy disk causes an error, your error handler might display a custom error message and then disable disk operations until the user fixes the problem.

When to Use Error Handlers

Most runtime errors are caused by external events.

You can use error handlers in any situation in which an unexpected action might result in a runtime error. Typically, error handlers are used to process external events that influence a program—for example, events caused by a failed network drive, an open floppy drive door, or a printer that is offline. The table on the following page lists potential problems that can be addressed by error handlers.

Problems	Description
Network problems	Network drives or resources that fail, or "go down," unexpectedly
Floppy disk problems	Unformatted or incorrectly formatted disks, open drive doors, or bad disk sectors
Printer problems	Printers that are offline, out of paper, or otherwise unavailable
Overflow errors	Too much printing or drawing information
Out-of-memory errors	Application or resource space is not available in Windows
Clipboard problems	Problems with data transfer or the Windows Clipboard
Logic errors	Syntax or logic errors undetected by the compiler and previous tests (such as an incorrectly spelled filename)

Setting the Trap: The On Error Statement

The On Error statement identifies the error handler.

The program statement used to detect a runtime error is On Error. You place On Error in an event procedure right before you use the statement you're worried about. The On Error statement sets, or *enables*, an event trap by telling Visual Basic where to branch if it encounters an error. The syntax for the On Error statement is

```
On Error GoTo label
```

where *label* is the name of your error handler.

Error handlers are typed near the bottom of an event procedure, following the On Error statement. Each error handler has its own label, which is followed by a colon (:) for identification purposes—ErrorHandler: or PrinterError:, for example. An error handler usually has two parts. The first part typically uses the Err.Number property in a decision structure (such as If...Then or Select Case) and then displays a message or sets a property based on the error. The second part is a Resume statement that sends control back to the program so that the program can continue.

Resume

Resume, Resume Next, and Resume label return control to the program.

In the Resume statement, you can use the Resume keyword alone, use the Resume Next keywords, or use the Resume keyword with a label you'd like to branch to, depending on which part of the program you want to continue next.

Forms, Printers, and Errors

8

The Resume keyword returns control to the statement that caused the error (in hopes that the error condition will be fixed or won't happen again). Using the Resume keyword is a good strategy if you're asking the user to fix the problem, for example, by closing the floppy drive door or by tending to the printer.

The Resume Next keywords return control to the statement *following* the one that caused the error. Using the Resume Next keywords is the strategy to take if you want to skip the problem command and continue working. You can also follow the Resume keyword with a label you'd like to branch to. This gives you the flexibility of moving to any place in the event procedure you want to go. A typical location to branch to is the last line of the procedure.

Floppy Drive Error Handler

The following example shows how you can create an error handler to recover from errors associated with floppy disk drives. You'll add the error handler to a program that attempts to load a Windows metafile from a disk in drive A. You can use the same technique to add error handling support to any Visual Basic program—just change the error numbers and messages.

tip

The following program uses an error number (from the Err.Number property) to diagnose a runtime error. To see a complete listing of error numbers, search for *errors, numbers* in the Visual Basic online Help.

Create a disk drive error handler

1   Open the DriveErr project file.

The DriveErr form appears in the Project window.

2   If the form is not visible, click the DriveErr form in the Project window, and then click the View Object button.

3   Double-click the Check Drive button on the form.

The event procedure for the Command1_Click object appears in the Code window. This event procedure loads a Windows metafile named Prntout2.wmf from the root folder of drive A, but it currently generates an error if the file does not exist or if the floppy drive door is open.

This error handler handles floppy drive problems

4   Type the following statement at the top of the event procedure:

```
On Error GoTo DiskError
```

This statement enables the error handler in the procedure and tells Visual Basic where to branch if a runtime error occurs. Now you'll add the DiskError error handler to the bottom of the event procedure.

5 Move one line below the LoadPicture statement, and then type the following program code:

```
Exit Sub  'exit procedure
DiskError:
    If Err.Number = 71 Then  'if DISK NOT READY
        MsgBox ("Please close the drive latch."), , _
           "Disk Not Ready"
        Resume
    Else
        MsgBox ("I can't find prntout2.wmf in A:\."), , _
           "File Not Found"
        Resume StopTrying
    End If
StopTrying:
```

The conditional expression in the error handler's If...Then statement tests the Err.Number property to see if it contains the number 71, the error code that is returned whenever a disk drive is not functioning. If a disk error has occurred, the program gives the user the opportunity to fix the problem (either by closing the drive latch or by inserting a new disk) and then continue with the loading operation. (The LoadPicture function is attempted again with the Resume keyword.)

If the error was not related to the disk drive, the program assumes that the disk is valid but that the file cannot be located in the root folder. Then the error handler branches to the StopTrying: label at the bottom of the procedure. In either case, the error handler prints a message for the user and stops the program from being prematurely terminated. You could add more ElseIf statements and error numbers to the error handler to give the user more specific and useful information about the disk problem.

You can use the Exit Sub statement to skip over an error handler in a procedure.

If the program encounters no disk problems or if the user fixes an initial problem, the program proceeds until the Exit Sub statement ends the event procedure. Exit Sub is a general-purpose statement that you can use to exit any Visual Basic procedure before the End Sub statement is executed. In this case, Exit Sub prevents the error handler from running after the program successfully loads the Windows metafile.

Forms, Printers, and Errors

8

6 On the File menu, click the Save DriveErr.frm As command, and then save the form as **MyFinalErr**.

7 On the File menu, click the Save Project As command, and then save the project as **MyFinalErr**.

8 Use Windows Explorer to copy the file Prntout2.wmf from the C:\Vb6Sbs\Less08 folder to a floppy disk in drive A. (You need a spare floppy disk to complete this step.)

Be sure to copy the file to the root folder on the disk (A:\).

9 Remove the floppy disk from drive A, or open the drive latch.

10 Click the Start button to run the program.

11 Click the Check Drive button on the form.

The complete FinalErr program is available in the \Vb6Sbs\Less08 folder.

Visual Basic generates a runtime error, and the error handler displays the error message shown in the illustration below:

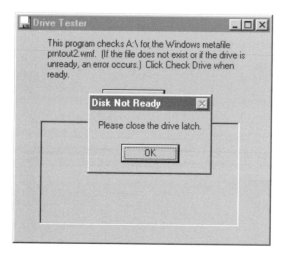

12 Insert the floppy disk that has the Windows metafile on it, or close the drive door.

13 Click OK to close the error handler and retry the loading operation.

After a few moments, the Prntout2.wmf Windows metafile is displayed on the form, as shown in the illustration on the following page.

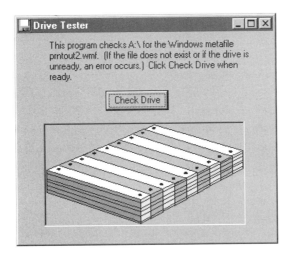

tip

If an error message still appears, you may have a different error in your program. Try stepping through your program code by using break mode. Errors are easy to spot by using Quick Watch expressions, and the process shows you graphically how error handlers work.

⑭   Click the Close button on the form to end the program.

One Step Further **More Techniques for Error Handlers**

The Err.Description property contains an explanation of a runtime error.

The Err object contains a few other properties that you might want to use to display additional information in your error handlers. The Err.Description property contains the error message returned to Visual Basic when a runtime error occurs. You can use this message as an additional source of information for the user, whether or not you plan to respond to the error programmatically. For example, the error handler code shown on the following page uses the Description property to display an error message if an error occurs when you are loading artwork from a floppy disk.

```
On Error GoTo DiskError
Image1.Picture = LoadPicture("a:\prntout2.wmf")
Exit Sub                   'exit procedure
DiskError:
MsgBox (Err.Description), , "Loading Error"
Resume                     'try LoadPicture function again
```

You can use this technique to trap floppy disk problems such as unformatted disks, missing files, or an open drive door. The error handler uses the Resume statement to try the loading operation again when the user fixes the problem and clicks OK in the message box. When the file eventually loads, the Exit Sub statement ends the event procedure.

tip
If you get stuck in an error loop and can't get out, press Ctrl+Break.

Specifying a Retry Period

Another strategy you can use in an error handler is to try an operation a few times and then jump over the problem if it isn't resolved. For example, the following error handler uses a counter variable named Retries to track the number of times an error message has been displayed, and then forces the program to skip the loading statement if it fails twice:

```
Retries = 0                'initialize counter variable
On Error GoTo DiskError
Image1.Picture = LoadPicture("a:\prntout2.wmf")
Exit Sub                   'exit the procedure
DiskError:
MsgBox (Err.Description), , "Loading Error"
Retries = Retries + 1      'increment counter on error
If Retries >= 2 Then
    Resume Next
Else
    Resume
End If
```

This is a useful technique if the error you're handling is a problem that can occasionally be fixed by the user. The important thing to remember here is that Resume retries the statement that caused the error and that Resume Next skips the statement and moves on to the next line in the event procedure. When you use Resume Next, be sure that the next statement really is the one you want to execute, and when you continue, make sure that you don't accidentally run the error handler again. A good way to skip over the error handler is to use the Exit Sub statement; or you can use Resume with a label that directs Visual Basic to continue executing below the error handler.

If you want to continue to the next lesson

●   Keep Visual Basic running, and turn to Lesson 9.

If you want to quit Visual Basic for now

●   On the File menu, click Exit.

     If you see a Save dialog box, click Yes.

Upgrade Notes:
What's Different in Visual Basic .NET?

If you choose to upgrade to Visual Basic .NET in the future, you'll notice some new features related to the topics in this lesson, including the following:

■   In Visual Basic .NET, you cannot set the properties of a second form in the project without having an instance variable of the form that you want to manipulate. In other words, the program syntax for manipulating forms is a bit different.

■   In Visual Basic 6.0, you can set a form's runtime position on the Windows desktop using the graphical Form Layout window. There is no Form Layout window in Visual Basic .NET, but you can use a new form property named DesktopBounds to set the size and location of a form at runtime.

■   In Visual Basic 6.0, you can add new controls to a form at runtime using program code. In Visual Basic .NET, you have a similar capability, but the syntax is slightly different.

■   In Visual Basic .NET, there is a new Anchor property for objects on a form that specifies which of the object's borders should remain fixed when the form is resized. A new Dock property also forces an object to remain attached to one edge of the form when the form is resized.

■ In Visual Basic 6.0, you can create MDI (multiple document interface) projects by using the Add MDI Form command on the Project menu. In Visual Basic .NET, MDI parent forms are regular forms that have their IsMdiContainer properties set to True. MDI child forms are regular forms that have their MdiParent properties set to the name of a parent form.

■ In Visual Basic .NET, you can inherit forms (pass the characteristics of one form on to a second form) by using the Inheritance Picker tool in the Visual Studio .NET development environment.

■ In Visual Basic 6.0, printing is accomplished using the methods and properties of the Printer object. For example, the Printer.Print method sends a string of text to the default system printer. In Visual Basic .NET, printing is accomplished using the new PrintDocument class, which provides more functionality than the Visual Basic 6.0 Printer.Print method but is also more complex.

■ In Visual Basic 6.0, you have access to one predefined dialog box for printing services—the Print dialog provided by the CommonDialog ActiveX control. In Visual Basic .NET, you have access to several predefined dialog box controls for printing, including PrintDialog, PrintPreviewDialog, and PageSetupDialog.

■ Visual Basic .NET has some impressive features that help to manage multipage print jobs. You begin by creating a PrintPage event handler that prints each page of your document one at a time. The objects in the StreamReader class of the System.IO namespace help you manage most of the remaining details.

■ The Try...Catch code block is the new mechanism in Visual Basic .NET for writing structured error handlers. Although you can still use Visual Basic 6.0 error-handling keywords, including On Error Goto, Resume, and Resume Next, the Try...Catch syntax avoids the potential complications of Goto constructions and offers a very efficient way to manage runtime errors.

■ The Catch When statement in Visual Basic .NET allows you to test specific program conditions and handle more than one runtime error in a Try...Catch code block.

■ The Exit Try statement offers a new way to exit structured error handlers in Visual Basic .NET.

■ Visual Basic .NET continues to provide the Err.Number and Err.Description properties to identify runtime errors. In addition, you can use the new Err.GetException method to return information about the underlying error condition, or *exception*, that halted program execution.

Lesson 8 Quick Reference

To	Do this
Add new forms to a program	Click the Add Form button on the toolbar, and then click Form. *or* On the Project menu, click Add Form, and then click Open.
Load a form into memory	Use the Load statement. For example: `Load Form2`
Display a loaded form	Use the Show method. For example: `Form2.Show`
Create a modal form	Include a 1 when displaying a form. For example: `Form2.Show 1`
Hide a form	Use the Hide method. For example: `Form2.Hide`
Remove a form from memory	Use the Unload statement. For example: `Unload Form2`
Change the name of an object	Change the Name property for the object in the Properties window.
Send a line of text to the printer	Use the Printer object and the Print method. For example: `Printer.Print "Mariners"`
Change printing options	Set properties of the Printer object at runtime.
End a printing job	Use the EndDoc method. For example: `Printer.EndDoc`
Print an entire form	Use the PrintForm method. For example: `Form2.PrintForm`
Detect runtime errors in your programs	Enable error handling by using the statement `On Error GoTo label` where *label* is the name of the error handler.
Process runtime errors	Create an error handling routine (usually consisting of If…Then or Select Case statements) beneath a label identifying the error handler. Typical error handlers set properties and use the MsgBox function to display messages to the user.
Continue after an error	Use Resume, Resume Next, or Resume *label*.
Exit a procedure before an End Sub statement	Use the Exit Sub statement.

8

Forms, Printers, and Errors

9

Adding Artwork and Special Effects

ESTIMATED TIME
55 min.

In this lesson you will learn how to:

- ✔ *Use the Line and Shape controls to add artwork to a form.*
- ✔ *Use the Image control to create graphical command buttons.*
- ✔ *Add drag-and-drop support to your programs.*
- ✔ *Change the shape of the mouse pointer.*
- ✔ *Create special effects with animation.*

For most developers, adding artwork and special effects to an application is the most exciting—and addicting—part of programming. Fortunately, creating impressive and useful graphical effects with Microsoft Visual Basic is both satisfying and easy. In this lesson, you'll learn how to add interesting "bells and whistles" to your programs. You'll learn how to create compelling artwork on a form, build graphical command buttons, and change the shape of the mouse pointer. You'll also learn how to add drag-and-drop support to your programs and how to create simple animation by using image and timer objects. When you've finished, you'll have the skills you need to create the ultimate user interface.

Adding Artwork by Using the Line and Shape Controls

The Line and Shape controls let you create geometric images.

You've already learned how to add bitmaps, icons, and Windows metafiles to a form by creating picture box and image objects. Adding ready-made artwork to your programs is easy in Visual Basic, and you've had practice doing it in almost every lesson. Now you'll learn how to create original artwork on your forms by using the Line and Shape controls. These handy tools are located in the toolbox, and you can use them to build a variety of images of different shapes, sizes, and colors. The objects you create by using these controls do have a few limitations— they can't receive the focus at runtime, and they can't appear on top of other objects—but they are powerful, fast, and easy to use.

The Line Control

Line control

You can use the Line control to create a straight line on a form. You can then set a variety of properties to change the appearance of the line object you create, just as you can for other objects. The most important line object properties are BorderWidth, BorderStyle, BorderColor, and Visible.

The BorderWidth property adjusts the thickness of the line on your form. This option is especially useful when you are creating an underline or a line that separates one object from another. The BorderStyle property lets you make the line solid, dotted, or dashed, and the BorderColor property lets you set the color of the line to any of Visual Basic's standard colors. Finally, the Visible property lets you hide the line or display it as it becomes necessary in your program.

You'll get a chance to work with the Line control after you learn a little about the Shape control.

The Shape Control

Shape control

You can use the Shape control to create rectangles, squares, ovals, and circles on your forms. You use the Shape control to draw the image you want, and then you use the Properties window to adjust the image characteristics. The Shape property controls the shape of the image; you can select a rectangle, rounded rectangle, square, rounded square, oval, or circle shape after you create the image. You can build complex images by drawing several shapes and lines.

Other important shape object properties include FillColor, which lets you specify the object's color; FillStyle, which lets you specify a pattern for the fill color; and BorderColor, which lets you specify a separate color for the shape's border. A shape object also has a Visible property, which lets you hide or display your artwork as necessary.

The following exercise gives you hands-on practice using the Line and Shape controls. You'll use the controls to create an introductory welcome screen used by a fictitious business named Northwest Window Screens. The welcome screen will look like this:

Use the Line and Shape controls

Label control

❶ Start Visual Basic and open a new, standard project.

If Visual Basic is already running, click the New Project command on the File menu, and open a new, standard project.

❷ Widen the form so that you have room for large type, shape objects, and command buttons.

❸ Click the Label control in the toolbox, and then create a long label across the top of the form.

❹ Open the Properties window, and then set the Caption property of the label to "Northwest Window Screens."

❺ Set the Font property of the label to Times New Roman, Bold, 26-point. Set the ForeColor property to Dark blue.

Your label should now take up most of the width of the screen. Adjust the label width and height, if necessary, so that the business name fits on one line.

Line control

❻ Click the Line control in the toolbox, and then create a line under the business name. Make the line stretch across most of the form, just as the label does.

The Line control places selection handles on either side of the line after you create it. You can use these handles to resize the line, if necessary.

*Properties
Window button*

7 Click the Properties Window button to display the Properties window, and then set the following properties for the line object:

Object	Property	Setting
Line1	BorderWidth	5
	BorderColor	Dark blue

The name of your new line object is Line1. The BorderWidth setting changes the width of the line to 5 twips. (A twip is 1/20 point, or 1/1440 inch.) The BorderColor setting changes the color of the line to dark blue.

Now you'll create two window screen images on the form.

Shape control

8 Click the Shape control in the toolbox, and then create a rectangle on the left side of the form.

This rectangle is the outline of the first window screen. You'll set the FillStyle property of this object a little later to make the rectangle look like a screen.

9 Click the Shape control again, and then create a second rectangle on the left side of the form, partially overlapping the first rectangle.

The Shape control works a lot like a general-purpose drawing tool in an art program. The control creates the basic shape, and then you set properties to refine that shape.

10 Click the Properties Window button, and then set the following properties for the two shapes:

Object	Property	Setting
Shape1	Shape	0 – Rectangle
	FillColor	Dark yellow
	FillStyle	6 – Cross
	BorderColor	Dark yellow
Shape2	Shape	4 – Rounded rectangle
	FillColor	Light blue
	FillStyle	6 – Cross
	BorderColor	Light blue

11 Create a label on the right side of the form. Create a fairly narrow label so that the label caption wraps over two lines. Then set the properties as shown in the table on the following page.

Object	Property	Setting
Label2	Caption	""Quality products for office and home.""
	Font	Times New Roman, Italic, 12-point
	Alignment	1 – Right Justify

CommandButton control

12 Click the CommandButton control in the toolbox, and then create a command button in the lower-right corner of the form. Create a second button to the left of the first command button.

13 Set the following properties for the command buttons:

Object	Property	Setting
Command1	Caption	"Quit"
Command2	Caption	"Continue"

14 Double-click the Quit command button, type **End** in the Command1_Click event procedure, and then close the Code window.

The welcome form you are creating is intended to be a gateway to the program, but if users want to quit without moving on in the program, the Quit button gives them a way out. Because the welcome screen is the only part of this program that exists now, you'll also use the Quit button to end the program.

15 Change the Caption property of the form to "Welcome," and then resize the objects and the form so that the screen looks well proportioned.

When you've finished, your form should look similar to the following:

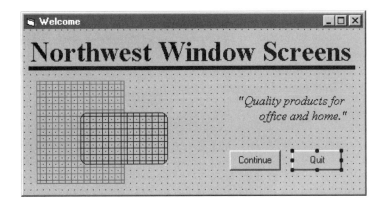

Using Graphics Methods to Create Shapes

Visual Basic supports several method keywords for adding artwork to your programs. You can use these graphics methods to create special visual effects. Graphics methods are commands you use in event procedures to create images on a form or send images to a printer.

The disadvantage of graphics methods is that they take considerable planning and programming to use. You need to learn the syntax of the commands, understand the coordinate system used on your form, and refresh the images if they become covered by another window. However, you can use graphics methods to create some visual effects that you can't create by using the Line control or the Shape control, such as arcs and individually painted pixels.

The most useful graphics methods are Line, which creates a line, rectangle, or solid box; Circle, which creates a circle, ellipse, or "pie slice"; and PSet, which sets the color of an individual pixel on the screen.

For example, the following Circle statement draws a circle with a radius of 750 twips at (x, y) coordinates (1500, 1500) on a form:

```
Circle (1500, 1500), 750
```

To learn more about available graphics methods, search for *line*, *circle*, or *pset* in the Visual Basic online Help.

You can use a welcome form like this for any program you write. Its purpose is to welcome users to the program gracefully and then let them continue or exit as they see fit. When users click the Continue button, the program should hide the welcome form and then display the main form of the application.

Run the StartFrm program

Start button

❶   Click the Start button on the toolbar.

The Welcome form appears, as shown in the illustration on the following page.

The complete StartFrm program is available in the \Vb6Sbs\Less09 folder.

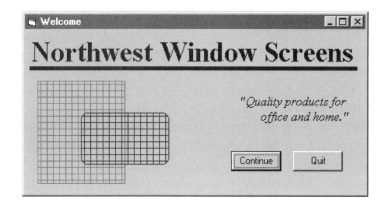

The line and shape objects appear immediately on the form and add to the general character of the welcome screen. Line and shape objects always appear faster than does artwork loaded from disk.

2 Click the Quit button to end the program.

3 Click the Save Project button on the toolbar, and then save your form in the Less09 folder as **MyStartFrm.frm**. Save the project file as **MyStartFrm.vbp**.

Save Project button

Creating Graphical Command Buttons

You've used command buttons throughout this book to give the user an intuitive method for issuing commands. As you've learned, you create a command button by using the CommandButton control, and then you set the caption property of the button to a word that describes the command the button executes.

You can use the Image control to create toolbar-style command buttons.

As an alternative to creating text-based buttons, Visual Basic lets you use the Image control to create graphical buttons in your programs. A *graphical button* contains artwork that is a visual representation of the command executed by the button. For example, a button containing a floppy disk icon could represent a command that saves information to your computer or to a disk drive. Graphical buttons can be placed individually in programs, or they can be grouped in collections called *toolbars*. The Visual Basic toolbar is an example of this type of button grouping. In this section, you'll learn how to create authentic graphical command buttons that "push in" and "pop out" when you click them, just like the buttons you've seen in other applications for Microsoft Windows.

Detecting a MouseDown Event

The Mouse-Down event detects the first half of a mouse button click.

To give your graphical buttons a realistic look and "feel," you'll want your program to respond as soon as the user places the mouse pointer over a graphical button and holds down the mouse button. So far, you've been using the Click event to take action in your programs, but in this case Click is not good enough. Your program needs to respond when the user first *presses* the button, not after the button is released. You can track mouse activity in Visual Basic by using the MouseDown event.

MouseDown is a special event that executes an event procedure whenever the user places the mouse pointer over an object on the form and then holds down the mouse button. If you write a special event procedure for the Mouse-Down event (such as Image1_MouseDown in the next section), your program can take action whenever the user holds down the mouse button while the mouse pointer is over the object. When you're creating graphical command buttons, you'll want your program to change the button when the user clicks, to give the button that "pushed in" look, and then execute the specified command in the program.

tip

In addition to recognizing MouseDown events, your programs can recognize MouseUp events (generated whenever the user releases the mouse button) and MouseMove events (generated whenever the user moves the mouse).

Swapping Out Buttons

So how do you make graphical command buttons look pushed in and popped out when they are clicked in a program? As you might suspect, the icon pictures aren't modified on the screen when the user clicks the icons. Instead, the icons are replaced by other icons, or *swapped out,* by a MouseDown event procedure. As the following illustration shows, each graphical command button has three states: up, down, and disabled.

Up   Down   Disabled

Up is the normal, or popped out, state—the appearance of the button when it is at rest, or in its default position. Down is the selected, or pushed in, state—the appearance of the button when it has been selected (clicked) or is active. Disabled is an optional state that is used when a button is not currently available for use in the program. Some graphical command buttons never use this state.

In a Visual Basic program, button states are controlled by swapping icons in and out of the image object used to hold the button. The MouseDown event procedure associated with the image object handles the swapping. For the event procedure to work correctly, it must read the current state of the button (up, down, or disabled), change to the requested state, and then execute the requested command (such as changing text to boldface). The button icons can be loaded at runtime by using the LoadPicture function, or they can be swapped on the form by using assignment statements. Some programmers put all three button states on the form to make the updating quicker.

You can update button states by using the MouseDown event procedure.

tip

You can create graphical buttons and toolbars on any Visual Basic form, but MDI forms have special built-in properties that make working with collections of buttons easier. In addition, the Toolbar ActiveX control, included with the Professional and Enterprise Editions of Visual Basic, helps you create and manage toolbars on your MDI forms.

In the following exercise, you'll create a program that uses three graphical command buttons (Bold, Italic, and Underline) to format text on a form. The program uses six icons from the Less09 folder to display the buttons on the form, and it uses three MouseDown event procedures to update the buttons and format the text. The illustration on the following page shows the form you'll build.

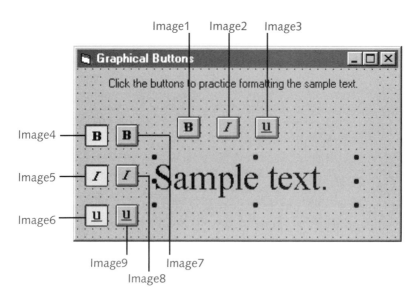

Create toolbar buttons

Label control

Image control

① On the File menu, click the New Project command, and then click OK to create a new, standard executable file.

② Resize the form so that it resembles a medium-size dialog box.

③ Click the Label control, and then create a long label along the top edge of the form.

④ Use the Image control to create three small image boxes centered below the label on the form.

These image boxes will hold the Bold, Italic, and Underline buttons you'll use in the program.

⑤ Create six image boxes on the left side of the form. See the illustration above for the suggested placement of these objects and try to create them like I did.

These image boxes will hold the six button states you'll be swapping in and out of the first three image boxes. (Alternatively, you could load these buttons from disk or store some of the states in global variables, but keeping them all on the form is fast and convenient for this example.)

Practice creating Bold, Italic, and Underline buttons.

⑥ Create a large label in the middle of the form to hold the sample text.

This is the label you'll format by using the toolbar buttons. You'll adjust the text by using the FontBold, FontItalic, and FontUnderline properties in the MouseDown event procedures.

The Tag property lets you place an identification note, or tag, in an object.

Now you'll set the properties for the objects on the form. First, you'll make the six swapping icons invisible on the form, and then you'll change and format the text in the labels. Next, you'll record the opening button states in a special image box property named *Tag*. You can use the Tag property to include descriptive notes in an object you're working with. Often, Tag is used to store the name of the object, but in this case you'll use it to store the button state: "Up" or "Down".

7 Set the following properties for the objects.

Object	Property	Setting
Label1	Caption	"Click the buttons to practice formatting the sample text."
Label2	Caption	"Sample text."
	Font	Times New Roman, 28-point
Form1	Caption	"Graphical Buttons"
Image1	Picture	"c:\vb6sbs\less09\bld-up.bmp"
	Tag	"Up"
Image2	Picture	"c:\vb6sbs\less09\itl-up.bmp"
	Tag	"Up"
Image3	Picture	"c:\vb6sbs\less09\ulin-up.bmp"
	Tag	"Up"
Image4	Picture	"c:\vb6sbs\less09\bld-dwn.bmp"
	Visible	False
Image5	Picture	"c:\vb6sbs\less09\itl-dwn.bmp"
	Visible	False
Image6	Picture	"c:\vb6sbs\less09\ulin-dwn.bmp"
	Visible	False
Image7	Picture	"c:\vb6sbs\less09\bld-up.bmp"
	Visible	False
Image8	Picture	"c:\vb6sbs\less09\itl-up.bmp"
	Visible	False
Image9	Picture	"c:\vb6sbs\less09\ulin-up.bmp"
	Visible	False

tip

When you set the Picture property, the image boxes adjust to the size of the toolbar icon.

When you've finished, your form should look similar to the following:

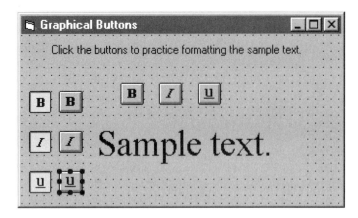

Now you'll enter the code for the three MouseDown event procedures.

8 Double-click the Image1 object (the Bold button above the sample text) on the form.

The Image1_Click event procedure appears in the Code window. This time you'll write code for the MouseDown event rather than for the Click event. To open a different event procedure for an object, you click the event in the Procedure drop-down list box.

9 Open the Procedure drop-down list box in the Code window.

The drop-down list box displays the events that can be recognized by the image object.

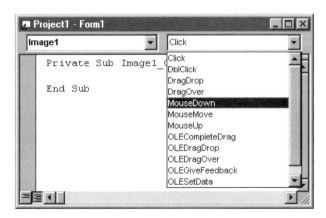

The Mouse-Down event procedure supplies four variables you can use in your programs.

⑩ Click the MouseDown event in the list box.

The Image1_MouseDown event procedure appears in the Code window. This event procedure receives four pieces of information about the MouseDown event: the mouse button pressed; the combination of Alt, Ctrl, and Shift keys being held down (if any); the *x* (horizontal) screen coordinate of the mouse pointer; and the *y* (vertical) screen coordinate of the mouse pointer. These values are returned, or *passed,* to the event procedures in variables that you can use in your code. Although you won't use event procedure variables, or *parameters,* in this program, they can be useful tools, and many event procedures provide them. You'll learn a little about using parameters in the DragDrop program later in this lesson.

⑪ Type the following program statements in the Image1_MouseDown event procedure:

The FontBold property controls boldface formatting.

```
If Image1.Tag = "Up" Then
    Image1.Picture = Image4.Picture
    Label2.FontBold = True
    Image1.Tag = "Down"
Else
    Image1.Picture = Image7.Picture
    Label2.FontBold = False
    Image1.Tag = "Up"
End If
```

This simple If decision structure processes the two types of Bold button clicks the user can perform in the program. If the Bold button is initially in the up state, the procedure replaces the Bld-up.bmp icon with the Bld-dwn.bmp icon, changes the text to boldface, and sets the image box tag to "Down". If the button is initially in the down state, the procedure replaces the Bld-dwn.bmp icon with the Bld-up.bmp icon, cancels the boldface setting, and sets the image box tag to "Up". Whichever state the button is in, the decision structure changes it to the opposite state.

⑫ Open the Object drop-down list box in the Code window, and then select the Image2 object. Open the Procedure drop-down list box, and then select the MouseDown event.

The Image2_MouseDown event procedure appears.

13 Type the following program statements:

The Tag property is used to determine the current button state.

```
If Image2.Tag = "Up" Then
    Image2.Picture = Image5.Picture
    Label2.FontItalic = True
    Image2.Tag = "Down"
Else
    Image2.Picture = Image8.Picture
    Label2.FontItalic = False
    Image2.Tag = "Up"
End If
```

This decision structure controls the operation of the Italic button in the program. The code is almost identical to the Image1_MouseDown procedure. The only differences are the names of the image boxes and the use of the FontItalic property instead of the FontBold property.

14 Open the Object drop-down list box, and then select the Image3 object. Open the Procedure drop-down list box, and then select the MouseDown event. When the Image3_MouseDown event procedure appears, type the following program statements:

The Picture property is used to switch the buttons.

```
If Image3.Tag = "Up" Then
    Image3.Picture = Image6.Picture
    Label2.FontUnderline = True
    Image3.Tag = "Down"
Else
    Image3.Picture = Image9.Picture
    Label2.FontUnderline = False
    Image3.Tag = "Up"
End If
```

This decision structure controls the operation of the Underline button. It is nearly identical to the two previous procedures. You've finished building the program, so now you'll save it to disk.

Save Project button

15 Click the Save Project button on the toolbar. Specify the \Vb6Sbs\Less09 folder, and then save your form as **MyButtons.frm**. Save your project as **MyButtons.vbp** in the same folder.

Now you'll run the program.

Run the program and test the buttons

Start button

The complete Buttons program is available in the \Vb6Sbs\Less09 folder.

① Click the Start button on the toolbar.

The MyButtons program runs, as shown in the following illustration:

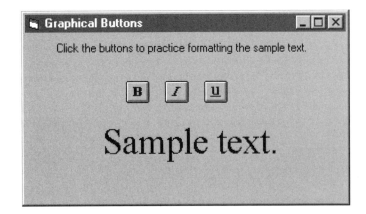

The instructions, toolbar buttons, and sample text appear on the form. You can use the three buttons in any order and as many times as you like.

② Click the Italic button.

As soon as you press the mouse button, the Italic button "pushes in" and the sample text is italicized.

③ Click the Underline button.

tip

If you wanted to wait until the mouse button was released to format the text, you could still handle the icon swap in the MouseDown procedure but you could use a MouseUp event to change the font. As the programmer, you have complete control over how the buttons affect the text.

Your screen should look like this:

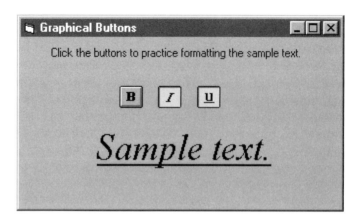

❹   Click the Italic and Underline buttons again.

The buttons "pop out," and the text returns to normal.

❺   Experiment with the Bold button to see how it works. Try using different buttons in different combinations.

❻   When you've finished testing the buttons, click the End button on the toolbar.

End button

The program stops, and the programming environment returns.

Adding Drag-and-Drop Support to Your Programs

Drag-and-drop support can make your user interface more intuitive and easier to use.

In applications for Windows, users execute many commands by clicking menus and buttons with the mouse. Visual Basic lets you provide another way to perform some actions in your programs—you can allow users to *drag and drop*. To drag and drop, the user holds down the mouse button, drags an object from one location to another, and then releases the mouse button to relocate the object or to issue a command. One application of drag and drop is to move text from one location to another in a word processing program. Another is to drag unwanted items to a "recycle bin" to remove them from the screen.

The DragDrop event procedure recognizes when an object has been dropped.

You can use several properties and two event procedures to control drag-and-drop operations. You can set an object's DragMode property to 1 to allow the user to drag the object. You can also use the DragIcon property to specify that the mouse pointer appears as a picture of the dragged object while the object is being dragged. When the user drops an object on the form or on another object, Visual Basic responds to the event by executing the DragDrop event procedure for the object on which the icon was dropped. When one object is dragged over another object on the form, Visual Basic executes the DragOver event procedure for the object over which the object is being dragged.

Drag and Drop Step by Step

To add drag-and-drop support to a program, you need to follow three steps:

❶ Enable drag and drop for the object. Visual Basic requires that you enable objects on your form for drag and drop individually. To add drag-and-drop support to an object, you set its DragMode property to 1 by using program code or the Properties window.

❷ Select a drag icon. Visual Basic uses a rectangle to represent an object being dragged, but you can substitute a different drag icon if you want to. To specify a different icon, set the DragIcon property of the object to the bitmap or icon you want by using program code or the Properties window.

❸ Write a DragDrop or DragOver event procedure for the target object. Write an event procedure for the object that is the target, or *destination*, object of the dragging motion. Visual Basic executes the event procedure for the object onto which the dragged object is dragged or dropped. The event procedure should perform some appropriate action, such as relocating or hiding the dragged object, executing a command, or changing the destination object in some way. You open the event procedure by clicking the destination object on the form, opening the Code window, and then clicking the DragDrop or DragOver event in the Procedure drop-down list box.

The following illustration shows the three programming steps visually:

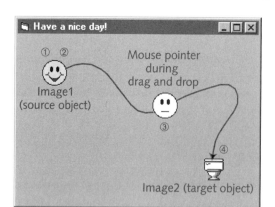

Form_Load
① Image1.Picture = LoadPicture("c:\Vb6Sbs\less09\face03.ico")
② Image1.DragMode = 1
③ Image1.DragIcon = LoadPicture("c:\Vb6Sbs\less09\face01.ico")

Image2_DragDrop
④ Image1.Visible = False

The DragDrop Program

The burn barrel in the DragDrop program gives users a place to toss unwanted items.

The following program shows you how to add drag-and-drop functionality to your applications. The program lets the user drag three items to a burn barrel on the form and then drop in a match and torch the items. The burn barrel is similar in some ways to the Microsoft Windows Recycle Bin or a Macintosh-style trash can. You can use the burn barrel in your programs to let users dispose of a variety of objects, including unwanted documents, files, artwork, electronic mail, network connections, screen elements, and so on. The program uses image boxes for the screen elements, and it hides objects by setting their Visible properties to False.

Use drag and drop to create a burn barrel

1 On the File menu, click the New Project command, and then click OK to create a new, standard executable file.

2 Resize the form so that it resembles a medium-size dialog box.

Label control

3 Click the Label control in the toolbox, and then create a long label across the top of the form.

This label will contain the program instructions for the user.

4 Use the Image control to create the six image boxes shown in the following illustration. Be sure to create the image boxes in the order indicated. (Create Image1 first, Image2 second, and so on.) When you set the image box properties in the next step, this will ensure that the correct icon will be placed in each image box.

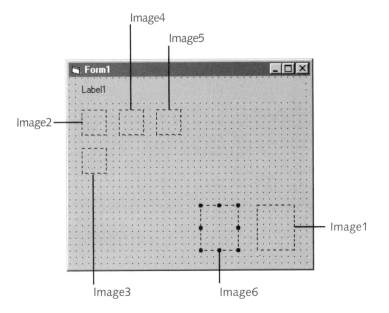

The "Fire" tag will help you identify the match icon.

5 Set the properties shown in the table on the following page for the objects in the program. As you do this, note the "Fire" setting for the Image3 Tag property. You'll use this tag to identify the match when the user drops it in the burn barrel.

tip
You must set the Stretch property before the Picture property for the icons to size correctly.

Object	Property	Setting
Label1	Caption	"Throw everything away, and then drop in the match."
	Font	Times New Roman, Bold, 10-point
Form1	Caption	"Burn Barrel"
Image1	Stretch	True
	Picture	"c:\vb6sbs\less09\trash02a.ico"
Image2	Picture	"c:\vb6sbs\less09\cdrom02.ico"
	DragIcon	"c:\vb6sbs\less09\cdrom02.ico"
	DragMode	1 – Automatic
Image3	Picture	"c:\vb6sbs\less09\fire.ico"
	DragIcon	"c:\vb6sbs\less09\fire.ico"
	DragMode	1 – Automatic
	Tag	"Fire"
Image4	Picture	"c:\vb6sbs\less09\gaspump.ico"
	DragIcon	"c:\vb6sbs\less09\gaspump.ico"
	DragMode	1 – Automatic
Image5	Picture	"c:\vb6sbs\less09\point11.ico"
	DragIcon	"c:\vb6sbs\less09\point11.ico"
	DragMode	1 – Automatic
Image6	Stretch	True
	Picture	"c:\vb6sbs\less09\trash02b.ico"
	Visible	False

When you've finished setting the properties, your form should look similar to the figure on the following page.

6 Double-click the Image1 object (the empty burn barrel) on the form.

The Image1_Click event procedure appears in the Code window.

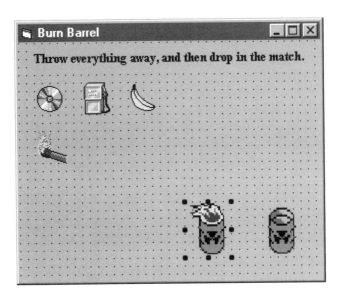

7 Open the Procedure drop-down list box in the Code window, and then click the DragDrop event in the list box.

The DragDrop event procedure returns three parameters that you can use in your program: Source, X, and Y.

The Image1_DragDrop event procedure appears. The Sub statement of the procedure lists three parameters that are returned when an object is dropped: Source, X, and Y. The Source parameter identifies the source object that was dragged in the program. You'll use this parameter to hide the source object on the form to make it look as if the object has been thrown away. You won't use the X and Y parameters in this procedure.

8 Type the following program statements in the event procedure:

```
Source.Visible = False
If Source.Tag = "Fire" Then
    Image1.Picture = Image6.Picture
End If
```

The Source variable identifies the object dropped in the burn barrel.

These are the only program statements in the program. The first line uses the Source variable and the Visible property to hide the object that was dragged and dropped. This makes the item appear to have been thrown into the burn barrel. The remaining lines check whether the object thrown away was the match icon.

Remember that when you set the properties for this program, you set the Tag property of the Image3 object to "Fire" to identify it as the match that would light the burn barrel. The If...Then decision structure uses Tag now to check whether the match is being thrown into the barrel. If it is, the decision structure "lights the fire" by copying the burning barrel icon over the empty barrel icon.

Save Project button

9 Click the Save Project button on the toolbar. Specify the \Vb6Sbs\Less09 folder, and then save your form as **MyDragDrop.frm**. Save your project as **MyDragDrop.vbp** in the same folder.

Run the MyDragDrop program

Start button

The complete DragDrop program is available in the \Vb6Sbs\Less09 folder.

1 Click the Start button on the toolbar.

The MyDragDrop program appears, as shown in the illustration below.

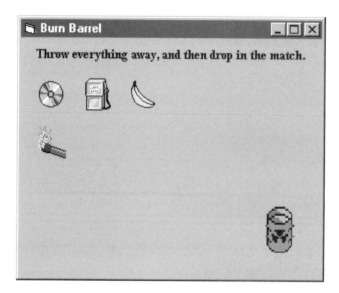

2 Drag the CD-ROM icon into the burn barrel, and then release the mouse button.

Drag icons appear as you drag objects.

As you drag the icon, the mouse pointer changes to the original CD-ROM icon (the DragIcon property at work). When you release the mouse button over the burn barrel, the mouse pointer changes back to its original shape and the original CD-ROM icon disappears.

3 Drag and drop the gas pump icon and the banana icon into the burn barrel.

The mouse pointer changes to the appropriate drag icons as you drag the elements. (The gas pump will really get the fire going.)

Changing the Mouse Pointer

In the DragDrop program, you learned how to use the DragIcon property to change the mouse pointer during a drag-and-drop operation. You can also change the mouse pointer to one of 12 predefined pointers by using the MousePointer property, or you can load a custom pointer by using the MouseIcon property.

Predefined mouse pointers let the user know graphically how the mouse should be used. If you set the MousePointer property for an object on the form, the mouse pointer will change to the specified shape when the user moves the mouse pointer over that object. If you set the MousePointer property for the form itself, the mouse pointer will change to the shape you specify unless it is over another object that already has a predefined shape or custom pointer.

The table below lists a few of the pointer shapes you can select by using the MousePointer property. (You can check the Properties window for a complete list.) If you specify shape 99 (Custom), Visual Basic uses the MouseIcon property to set the pointer shape.

Pointer	MousePointer setting	Description
+	2	Crosshairs pointer for drawing
⌶	3	Insertion pointer for text-based applications
✥	5	Sizing pointer (pointers whose arrows point in other directions are available)
⌛	11	Hourglass pointer, which indicates that the user needs to wait
⊘	12	No-drop pointer, which indicates that the action the user is attempting to perform can't be performed

❹   Now drop in the match.

As soon as you release the mouse button, the burn barrel starts burning, as shown in the following illustration:

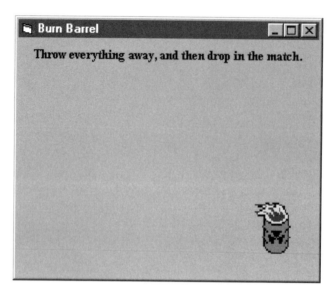

❺   Click the Close button to stop the program.

tip

This general drag-and-drop technique has several applications. Consider using it whenever you want to give users visual feedback when the program is processing or deleting an object. For example, you could change the barrel icon to another shape and use drag and drop to process artwork, print files, send faxes and electronic mail, work with databases, or organize resources on a network.

Adding Animation to Your Programs

Animation makes objects "come alive" in a program.

Switching icons and dragging objects adds visual interest to a program, but for programmers, the king of graphical effects has always been animation. *Animation* is the simulation of movement produced by rapidly displaying a series of related images on the screen. In a way, drag and drop is a "poor man's animation" because it lets you move images from one place to another on a form.

Real animation involves moving objects programmatically, and it often involves changing the size or shape of the images along the way.

In this section, you'll learn how to add simple animation to your programs. You'll learn how to use the Move method, update a picture box's Top and Left properties, and control the rate of animation by using a timer object.

Using a Form's Coordinate System

A common trait of animation routines is that they move images in relation to a predefined coordinate system on the screen. In Visual Basic, each form has its own coordinate system. The coordinate system's starting point, or *origin*, is in the upper-left corner of a form. The default coordinate system is made up of rows and columns of device-independent twips. (Recall that a twip is 1/20 point, or 1/1440 inch.)

The Visual Basic coordinate system is a grid of rows and columns on the form.

In the Visual Basic coordinate system, rows of twips are aligned to the *x*-axis (horizontal axis) and columns of twips are aligned to the *y*-axis (vertical axis). You define locations in the coordinate system by identifying the intersection of a row and column with the notation (*x*, *y*). Although you can change the coordinate system to a scale other than twips, the (*x*, *y*) coordinates of the upper-left corner of a form are always (0, 0). The following illustration shows how an object's location is described in the Visual Basic coordinate system.

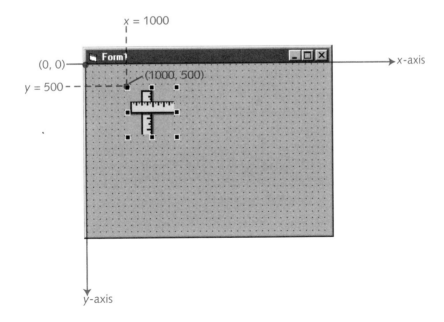

Moving Objects in the Coordinate System

The Move method lets you move objects.

Visual Basic includes a special method named Move that lets you move objects in the coordinate system. The basic syntax for the Move method is

```
.Move        ,
```

where *object* is the name of the object on the form that you want to move, and *left* and *top* are the screen coordinates of the new location for the object, measured in twips. The *left* measurement is the distance between the left edge of the form and the object, and the *top* measurement is the distance between the top edge of the form and the object. (The Move method also lets you adjust the height and width of an object. See "Expanding and Shrinking Objects While a Program Is Running" later in this lesson for an example.)

The Visual Basic statement

```
Picture1.Move 1440, 1440
```

moves the Picture1 object to the location (1440, 1440) on the screen, or exactly 1 inch from the top edge of the form and 1 inch from the left edge of the form.

Relative movements are specified with the Left and Top properties of the object.

You can also use the Move method to specify a relative movement. A relative movement is the distance the object should move from its *current location*. When specifying relative movements, you use the Left and Top properties of the object (values that maintain its *x*-axis and *y*-axis location) and a + (plus) or – (minus) operator. For example, the statement

```
Picture1.Move Picture1.Left - 50, Picture1.Top - 75
```

moves the Picture1 object from its current position on the form to a location 50 twips closer to the left edge and 75 twips closer to the top edge.

tip

A picture box object is usually used with the Move method because it creates less flicker on the screen than an image box object.

Creating Animation by Using the Move Method and a Timer Object

A timer object sets the pace of movement in a program.

The trick to creating animation in a program is placing one or more Move methods in a timer event procedure so that at set intervals the timer will cause one or more objects to drift across the screen. In Lesson 7, you learned to use a timer object to update a simple clock utility every second so that it displayed the correct time. When you create animation, you set the Interval property of the timer to a much faster rate—1/5 second (200 milliseconds), 1/10 second (100 milliseconds), or less. The exact rate you choose depends on how fast you want the animation to run.

Another trick is to use the Top and Left properties to "sense" the top edge and the left edge of the form. Using these values in an event procedure will let you stop the animation (disable the timer) when an object reaches the edge of the form. You can also use the Top property or the Left property, or both, in an If…Then or Select Case decision structure to make an object appear to bounce off one or more edges of the form.

Adding a Smoke Cloud to the DragDrop Program

You can create animation by using the Move method.

The following exercise demonstrates how you can animate a picture box in a program by using the Move method and a timer object. In this exercise, you'll add a smoke cloud to the DragDrop program. The smoke cloud is made visible when the user drops the match in the burn barrel. Using the Move method and a timer object, the program makes the smoke cloud appear to drift gently in the wind until it flies off the form.

Create smoke animation

❶ On the File menu, click the Save MyDragDrop.frm As command, and then save the DragDrop form as **MySmoke.frm**.

❷ On the File menu, click the Save Project As command, and then save the DragDrop project as **MySmoke.vbp**.

  Saving the form and project in new files will preserve the original DragDrop program on your disk.

PictureBox control

❸ Click the PictureBox control in the toolbox, and then draw a small rectangle above the empty burn barrel on the form.

  You'll place a cloud icon in this picture box when you set properties.

Timer control

4 Click the Timer control in the toolbox, and then draw a timer object in the lower-left corner of the form.

The timer object (Timer1) resizes itself on the form.

5 Set the following properties for the picture box and timer:

Object	Property	Setting
Picture1	Appearance	3D
	BackColor	Light gray
	BorderStyle	0 – None
	Picture	"c:\vb6sbs\less09\cloud.ico"
	Visible	False
Timer1	Enabled	False
	Interval	65

After you set these properties, your form will look similar to the following:

6 Double-click the empty burn barrel (the Image1 object) to edit its event procedure.

The Image1_DragDrop event procedure appears in the Code window.

❼ Update the event procedure so that it looks like the one below. (The fourth and fifth lines are new.)

```
Source.Visible = False
If Source.Tag = "Fire" Then
    Image1.Picture = Image6.Picture
    Picture1.Visible = True
    Timer1.Enabled = True
End If
```

The new statements make the cloud icon visible when the barrel lights, and they start the timer running to get the cloud moving. Because you've already set the timer interval to 65 milliseconds, the timer is ready to go. You only need to add the Move method.

❽ Open the Object drop-down list box in the Code window, and then click the Timer1 object.

The Timer1_Timer event procedure appears in the Code window.

❾ Type the following program statements:

```
If Picture1.Top > 0 Then
    Picture1.Move Picture1.Left - 50, Picture1.Top - 75
Else
    Picture1.Visible = False
    Timer1.Enabled = False
End If
```

To make the cloud drift to the right or down, use a positive operator with the Move method.

As long as the timer is enabled, this If...Then decision structure is executed every 65 milliseconds. The first line in the procedure checks whether the smoke cloud has reached the top of the form. If it hasn't (if its Top property is still positive), the procedure uses a relative Move method to move the cloud 50 twips closer to the left edge of the form and 75 twips closer to the top edge of the form.

As you'll see when you run the program, this movement gives the cloud animation a gentle drift quality. To make the cloud drift to the right, you would simply add a positive value to the Left property. To make the cloud move down, you would add a positive value to the Top property. When the cloud reaches the top of the form, the Else clause in the Timer1_Timer procedure makes the picture invisible and disables the timer. Disabling the timer ends the animation.

Artwork and Special Effects

9

Save Project button

The complete Smoke program is available on disk in the \Vb6Sbs\Less09 folder.

10 Close the Code window, and then click the Save Project button to save your changes.

Now you'll run the program.

11 Click the Start button on the toolbar to run the program.

The MySmoke program runs in the programming environment.

12 Drag and drop the CD-ROM, gas pump, and banana into the burn barrel, and then drop in the match.

The burn barrel lights, and the smoke cloud starts moving, as shown in the following illustration:

The animation stops when the cloud reaches the top of the form.

After a few moments, the cloud drifts off the edge of the screen and the animation stops.

13 Click the End button to stop the program.

tip

For another example of animation with the Move method, load and run the StepUp program in the \Vb6Sbs\Less01 folder. The StepUp program bounces a stick of dynamite down a few steps and then displays a smoke cloud when the dynamite explodes. (The animation code is in the timer event procedures.) You might remember StepUp as the welcome program you ran in the first lesson. You've certainly come a long way since then!

Congratulations! You've added animation—and a number of other useful programming skills—to your graphics repertoire. Feel free to continue to experiment on your own with Visual Basic graphics. You'll learn a lot about programming in the process, and your users will appreciate the results.

Expanding and Shrinking Objects While a Program Is Running

The Height and Width properties let you expand and shrink an object.

Interested in one last special effect? In addition to maintaining a Top property and a Left property, Visual Basic maintains a Height property and a Width property for most objects on a form. You can use these properties in clever ways to expand and shrink objects while a program is running. The following exercise shows you how to do it.

Expand a picture box at runtime

① On the File menu, click the New Project command, and then click OK to open a new, standard application.

Image control

② Click the Image control in the toolbox, and then draw a small image box near the upper-left corner of the form.

③ Set the following properties for the image box and the form. When you set the properties for the image box, note the current values in the Height and Width properties. (You can set these at design time, too.)

Object	Property	Setting
Image1	Stretch	True
	Picture	"c:\vb6sbs\less09\earth.ico"
Form1	Caption	"Approaching Earth"

④ Double-click the Image1 object on the form.

The Image1_Click event procedure appears in the Code window.

⑤ Type the following program code in the event procedure:

Increasing the Height and the Width properties of the Earth icon makes the Earth icon grow larger.

```
Image1.Height = Image1.Height + 200
Image1.Width = Image1.Width + 200
```

These two lines increase the height and width of the Earth icon by 200 twips each time the user clicks the picture box. If you let your imagination run a little, watching the effect makes you feel like you're approaching the Earth in a spaceship.

6 Close the Code window, and then click the Start button to run the program.

The Earth icon appears alone on the form, as shown here:

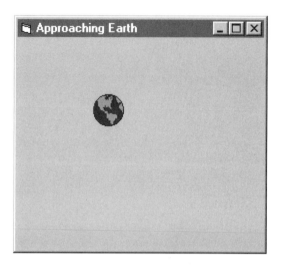

The complete Zoom program is available on disk in the \Vb6Sbs\Less09 folder.

7 Click the Earth icon several times to expand it on the screen.

After 10 or 11 clicks, your screen should look similar to the following:

"Standard orbit, Mr. Sulu."

⑧ When you get close enough to establish a standard orbit, click the Close button to quit the program.

The program stops, and the programming environment returns.

⑨ Click the Save Project button, and then save the form as **MyZoom.frm**. Save the project as **MyZoom.vbp**.

One Step Further **Naming Objects in a Program**

Naming interface objects helps you identify them in the program code.

Earlier in this lesson, you created the MyButtons program, which demonstrated how graphical command buttons are created and processed in a Visual Basic program. The program contains nine image box objects (Image1 through Image9) and three event procedures that display and process the buttons. In addition to showing how graphical buttons are used in a program, the exercise demonstrates the inadequacy of using the default object names to manage objects of the same type in a program. If you (or another programmer) revisit the MyButtons program in a few weeks, it will probably take you some time to figure out which object is doing what in the program code.

You can assign intuitive, easy-to-remember object names by using the Name property.

The solution to the problem of object name ambiguity is to assign each object a unique name by using the Name property. Each object name (like any variable name) should clearly identify the purpose of the object in the program and the control that created the object. The name you give an object must begin with a letter, and it can be no longer than 40 characters. Unique and intuitive object names will help you identify objects on the form and in the program code. Because object names are included in event procedure names and property settings in the program code, you should set an object's Name property immediately after creating the object.

The illustration on the following page shows the MyButtons program with its original object names and a set that I think are more intuitive and easier to use. I began each object name with the img prefix (an abbreviation for the Image control) and described the function of each button in the name.

Artwork and Special Effects

9

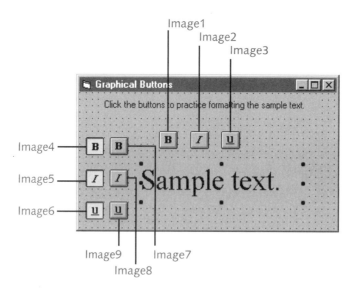

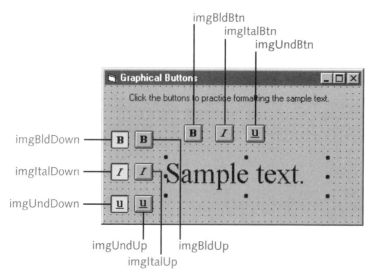

Object Naming Conventions

The Visual Basic community has agreed on a set of three-character prefixes that everyone can use in their object names. Using these standard prefixes helps programmers identify which control created an object. You can use

By convention, Visual Basic programmers use three-character prefixes to identify objects.

these naming conventions for the objects you create to make your program code more descriptive and more easily understood by other Visual Basic developers. Learning the naming conventions will also help you understand the sample programs that are included with Visual Basic. In addition, the naming conventions cause objects to be listed alphabetically in groups in the Object list box in the Code window.

The following table lists the object naming conventions and includes an example of each. You'll get a chance to practice using the conventions in the next exercise.

Object	Prefix	Example
combo box	cbo	cboEnglish
check box	chk	chkReadOnly
command button	cmd	cmdCancel
common dialog	dlg	dlgOpen
Data	dat	datBiblio
data-bound combo box	dbc	dbcEnglish
data-bound list box	dbl	dblPolicyCode
directory list box	dir	dirSource
drive list box	drv	drvTarget
file list box	fil	filSource
Frame	fra	fraLanguage
Form	frm	frmPrintForm
horizontal scroll bar	hsb	hsbVolume
Image	img	imgEmptyBarrel
Label	lbl	lblInstructions
Line	lin	linUnderline
list box	lst	lstPeripherals
Menu	mnu	mnuFileOpen
OLE	ole	oleObject1
option button	opt	optFrench
picture box	pic	picSmokeCloud
Shape	shp	shpWireScreen
text box	txt	txtGetName
Timer	tmr	tmrRunAnimation
vertical scroll bar	vsb	vsbTemperature

Artwork and Special Effects

9

tip

Some Visual Basic programmers also use naming conventions to describe the variable types they are using or the source of external objects and constants, such as third-party ActiveX controls or Microsoft Office applications. For example, the variable name strFileName contains a str prefix that by convention identifies the variable type as String, and the constant name wdPaperLegal contains a wd prefix that by convention identifies the value as a constant supplied by Microsoft Word. Feel free to use these naming conventions in your programs as well.

Use the Name property to change object names

Label control

Properties
Window
button

❶ On the File menu, click the New Project command, and then click OK.

❷ Use the Label control to create two label objects in the center of the form, one near the top edge of the form and one in the middle.

❸ Click the Properties Window button on the toolbar, and then set the following properties for the label and form objects. Use the naming conventions, as indicated.

Object	Property	Setting
Label1	Caption	"Welcome to the program!"
	Name	lblWelcome
Label2	Caption	"To exit the program, click Quit."
	Name	lblInstructions
Form1	Caption	"Naming Conventions"
	Name	frmMainForm

When you set the Name properties, the names of the objects change both in the Properties window and internally in the program. The *lbl* or *frm* prefix identifies each object as a label or a form, and the rest of each object name identifies the object's purpose in the program.

CommandButton
control

❹ Use the CommandButton control to create a command button below the lblInstructions object.

5 Click the Properties Window button on the toolbar, and then set the properties for the command button:

Object	Property	Setting
Command1	Caption	"Quit"
	Name	cmdQuit

The *cmd* prefix identifies the object as a command button, and *Quit* describes the purpose of the button in the program.

6 Double-click the cmdQuit button to open the object's event procedure.

The event procedure cmdQuit_Click appears in the Code window. Visual Basic is using the name you entered as the official name of the object.

7 Open the Object drop-down list box in the Code window.

The list of object names appears in the list box, as shown below.

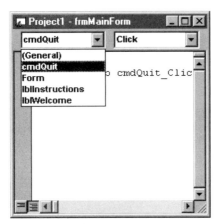

Here, the value of the object naming you've done becomes immediately apparent. It's easy to recognize which object does what in the program. Other programmers will benefit from your new names, too.

8 Press Esc to close the Object list box, and then type **End** in the cmdQuit_Click event procedure.

Start button

9 Close the Code window, and then click the Start button on the toolbar to run the program.

Your screen should look similar to the following:

The complete NameConv program is available in the \Vb6Sbs\Less09 folder.

10 Click the Quit button to stop the program.

The program stops, and the programming environment returns.

Save Project button

11 Click the Save Project button on the toolbar, and then save the form as **MyNameConv.frm** in the \Vb6Sbs\Less09 folder. Save the project file as **MyNameConv.vbp**.

important

Assigning intuitive names to objects will really pay off when you start to write longer programs or work in a group with other programmers. In general, it's a good idea to use the naming conventions if you have more than two objects of the same type on a form.

If you want to boost your productivity

Take a few minutes to explore the Browser utility (browser.vbp) in the \Vb6Sbs\Extras folder on your hard disk. I wrote this program as an extension of the Magnify program to give you a little more practice with the printing, form, and drag-and-drop concepts in Lessons 8 and 9. The application is a bitmap browser that lets you evaluate up to three bitmaps at a time on your system and print them. I find it a useful tool for evaluating the dozens of bitmap (.bmp) files I routinely use in my programming projects for toolbars and other artwork. (Look in your \Windows folder for a few good examples.) If you like, you can try to expand the program yourself or simply use it as is for your daily work.

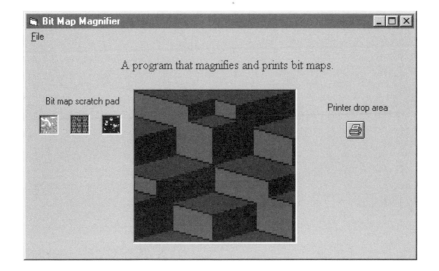

If you want to continue to the next lesson

● Keep Visual Basic running, and turn to Lesson 10.

If you want to quit Visual Basic for now

● On the File menu, click Exit.

Artwork and Special Effects

Upgrade Notes:
What's Different in Visual Basic .NET?

If you choose to upgrade to Visual Basic .NET in the future, you'll notice some new features related to the topics in this lesson, including the following:

■   In Visual Basic 6.0, you can use the Line and Shape Toolbox controls to create simple lines, rectangles, and circles on your forms. In Visual Basic .NET, no drawing controls are provided in the Toolbox. Instead, you are encouraged to use the GDI+ graphics services directly from a library called the System.Drawing namespace.

■   The Visual Basic 6.0 keywords Circle, Line, and PSet have been replaced by two methods—DrawEllipse and DrawLine—and the Point structure, in the System.Drawing.Graphics class.

■   The default coordinate system in Visual Basic .NET is pixels rather than twips.

■   In Visual Basic 6.0, many controls can be relocated, or "animated," on the form by rapidly changing the control's Move method. Visual Basic .NET controls don't have the Move method, but they can still be relocated quickly if you update the control's Left, Top, or Location property or if you use the SetBounds method.

■   Visual Basic .NET controls continue to support drag-and-drop effects, but they handle them in a different way. For example, although Visual Basic .NET continues support for the DragDrop event, the DragIcon and DragMode properties are no longer available.

■   Visual Studio .NET can work with more image formats than Visual Basic 6.0. In particular, the System.Drawing.Imaging namespace contains functions to work with the following image formats: BMP, EMF, EXIF, GIF, Icon, JPEG, MemoryBMP, PNG, TIFF, and WMF.

Lesson 9 Quick Reference

To	Do this	Button
Create straight lines on a form	Use the Line control in the toolbox.	
Create rectangles, squares, ovals, and circles on a form	Use the Shape control in the toolbox. Set the Shape property of the object to set the shape type and characteristics.	
Create graphical command buttons	Place one or more image boxes on a form, and load bitmapped icons into them. Put any code that processes mouse clicks in the MouseDown or MouseUp event procedures associated with the image boxes.	
Support drag and drop in a program	Enable an object for drag and drop by setting its DragMode property to 1. You can select a drag icon for the object if you want to. Write a DragDrop or DragOver event procedure for the object on which the source object will be dragged or dropped.	
Change the mouse pointer to a predefined shape	Set the MousePointer property of the form and of any related objects to one of the 16 pointer styles.	
Specify a custom mouse pointer	Set the MousePointer property to 99, and then specify the custom pointer by using the MouseIcon property.	
Move an object on a form	Relocate the object by using the Move method. For example: `Picture1.Move 1440, 1440`	
Animate an object	Place one or more Move methods in a timer event procedure. Animation speed is controlled by the timer's Interval property.	
Expand or shrink an object at runtime	Change the object's Height property or Width property.	
Name an object	Specify a unique name in the Name property. Use the appropriate naming conventions so that the object can be identified.	

9

Artwork and Special Effects

PART 4
Managing Corporate Data

Using Modules and Procedures

ESTIMATED
TIME
55 min.

✔ *Create standard modules.*
✔ *Create your own public variables and procedures.*
✔ *Call public variables and procedures from event procedures.*

After studying the programs and completing the exercises in Lessons 1 through 9, you can safely call yourself an intermediate Visual Basic programmer. You've learned the basics of programming in Microsoft Visual Basic, and you have the skills necessary to create a variety of useful utilities. In Part 4, you'll learn what it takes to write more complex programs in Visual Basic. You'll start by learning how to create standard modules.

A standard module is a separate container in a program that contains global, or *public,* variables and Function and Sub procedures. In this lesson, you'll learn how to create your own public variables and procedures and how to call them from event procedures. The skills you'll learn will be especially applicable to larger programming projects and team development efforts.

Working with Standard Modules

As you write longer programs, you're likely to have several forms and event procedures that use some of the same variables and routines. By default, variables are *local* to an event procedure, meaning that they can be read or changed only in the event procedure in which they were created. Likewise, event procedures are local to the form in which they were created—you can't, for example, call the cmdQuit_Click event procedure from Form2 if the event procedure is associated with Form1.

Standard modules let you share variables and procedures throughout a program.

To share variables and procedures among all the forms and event procedures in a project, you need to declare them in one or more *standard modules* for that project. A standard module, or code module, is a special file that has the filename extension *.bas* and contains variables and procedures that can be used anywhere in the program. Just like forms, standard modules are listed separately in the Project window, and a standard module can be saved to disk by using the Save Module1 As command on the File menu. Unlike forms, however, standard modules contain no objects or property settings—only code that can be displayed and edited in the Code window.

The following illustration shows how a public variable declared in a standard module can be used in other event procedures in a Visual Basic project.

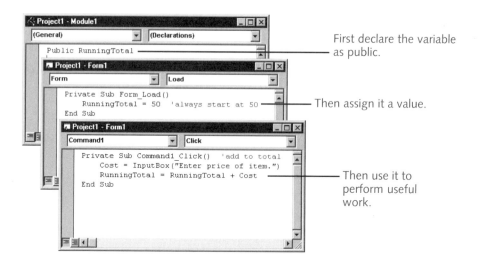

10

Modules and Procedures

tip

By contrast to those in standard modules, the objects and event procedures associated with a form are stored in a *form module,* and a new object is created in a *class module.*

Creating a Standard Module

To create a new standard module in a program, you click the Down Arrow on the Add Form button on the toolbar and click Module, or you click the Add Module command on the Project menu. When you create a new standard module, it appears immediately in the Code window. The first standard module in a program is named Module1 by default, but you can change the name when you save the module to disk. Try creating an empty standard module in your project now.

Create and save a standard module

1. Start Visual Basic and open a new standard project, and then click the Add Module command on the Project menu and click Open.

   Visual Basic adds a standard module named Module1 to your project. The module appears in the Code window, as shown here:

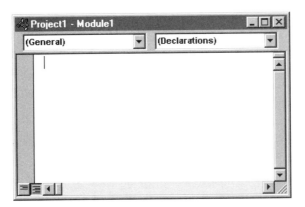

   The Object and Procedure list boxes indicate that the general declarations section of the standard module is open. Variables and procedures declared here will be available to the entire program. (You'll try declaring variables and procedures later.)

2 Double-click the Project window title bar to see the entire Project window.

The Project window appears, as shown here:

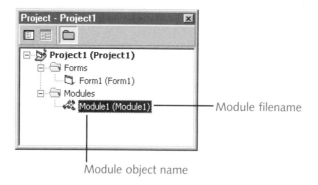

Module object name

The Project window lists the standard module you added to the program in a new folder. The name Module1 in parentheses shows the default filename of the module. The Module object name (the name of the module in the program) appears to the left of the parentheses. You'll change both settings in the next steps.

3 On the File menu, click the Save Module1 As command to save the empty standard module to disk.

Standard modules have the filename extension .bas.

4 Select the \Vb6Sbs\Less10 folder if it is not already selected. Type **MyTestMod.bas** and press Enter.

The standard module is saved to disk as a .bas file, and the module filename in the Project window is updated.

tip

You can also load this file by name in a different project by using the Add File command on the Project menu.

5 Double-click the Properties window title bar.

The Properties window appears full size, as shown in the illustration on the following page.

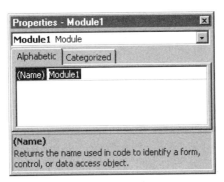

Because a standard module has no objects, its only property is Name. The Name property lets you specify an object name for the module, which you can use to distinguish one module from another if you create more than one. By convention, module names are given the prefix *mod*.

The Name property lets you set the object name of the module.

6 Change the Name property to **modVariables**, and press Enter.

The object name of the standard module is updated in the Properties window, the Project window, and the Code window.

As you can see, working with standard modules in a project is a lot like working with forms. In the next exercise, you'll add a public variable to the standard module you've created.

tip

To remove a standard module from a project, click the module in the Project window, and then click the Remove command on the Project menu. Remove does not delete the module from your hard disk, but it does remove the link between the specified module and the current project.

Working with Public Variables

Declaring a global, or public, variable in a standard module is simple—you type the keyword *Public* followed by the variable name. After you declare the variable, you can read it, change it, or display it in any procedure in your program. For example, the program statement

```
Public RunningTotal
```

declares a public variable named RunningTotal in a standard module.

Modules and Procedures

10

Public variables can be used by all the procedures in a program.

By default, public variables are declared as variant types in modules, but you can specify a fundamental type name by using the *As* keyword and indicating the type. For example, the statement

```
Public LastName As String
```

declares a public string variable named LastName in your program.

Lucky Seven is the slot machine program from Lesson 2.

The following exercises demonstrate how you can use a public variable named Wins in a standard module. You'll revisit Lucky Seven, the first program you wrote in this book, and you'll use the Wins variable to record how many spins you win as the slot machine runs.

Revisit the Lucky Seven project

❶ Click the Open Project button on the toolbar, click No to discard your changes, and then open the project Lucky.vbp in the \Vb6Sbs\Less02 folder.

❷ If the Lucky form is not visible, select Lucky.frm in the Project window and click the View Object button. (Resize the form window, if necessary.)

You'll see the following user interface:

❸ Click the Start button on the toolbar to run the program.

Start button

4 Click the Spin button six or seven times, and then click the End button.

You win the first five spins (a seven appears each time), and then your luck goes sour. As you might recall, the program uses the Rnd function to generate three random numbers each time you click the Spin button. If one of the numbers is a seven, the event procedure for the Spin button (Command1_Click) displays a stack of coins and sounds a beep.

In your revision to the program, you'll add a new label to the form and you'll add a public variable that tracks the number of times you win.

5 On the File menu, click the Save Lucky.frm As command. Specify the \Vb6Sbs\Less10 folder, and then save the form to disk with the name **MyWins.frm**.

6 On the File menu, click the Save Project As command. Specify the \Vb6Sbs\Less10 folder, and then save the project to disk with the name **MyWins.vbp**.

Now you'll edit the Wins form, and add a standard module to create a new program.

Add a standard module

1 Resize the Lucky Seven label so that it takes up less space on the form. The object currently extends far below the label text.

Label control

2 Click the Label control, and then create a new rectangular label below the Lucky Seven label.

3 Set the properties shown in the following table for the new label and the form. To help identify the new label in the program code, you'll change the new label object's name to lblWins.

Object	Property	Setting
Label5	Alignment	2 – Center
	Caption	"Wins: 0"
	Font	Arial, Bold Italic, 12-point
	ForeColor	Green
	Name	lblWins
Form1	Caption	"Lucky Seven"

When you've finished, your form should look similar to the following:

New lblWins
label

Now you'll add a new standard module to the project.

④ Click the Add Module command on the Project menu, and then click Open.

A module named Module1 appears in the Code window.

⑤ Type **Public Wins** in the standard module, and then press Enter.

This program statement declares a public variable of the variant type in your program. When your program runs, each event procedure in the program will have access to this variable. Your standard module should look like the following:

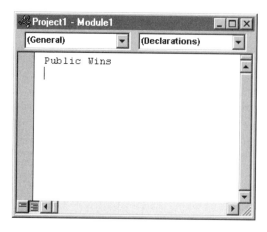

6 On the File menu, click the Save Module1 As command, type **MyWins.bas**, and then press Enter to save the module to disk.

7 In the Project window, click Form1 (MyWins.frm), click the View Object button, and then double-click the Spin button.

The Command1_Click event procedure for the Spin button appears in the Code window.

8 Type the following statements below the Beep statement in the event procedure:

```
Wins = Wins + 1
lblWins.Caption = "Wins: " & Wins
```

The public variable Wins is updated in an event procedure.

This is the part of the program code that increments the Wins public variable if a seven appears in a spin. The second statement uses the concatenation (&) operator to assign a string to the lblWins object in the format *Wins: X*, where *X* is the number of wins. The completed event procedure should look like this:

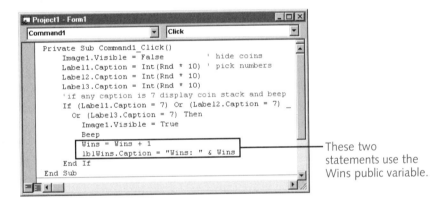

These two statements use the Wins public variable.

9 Close the Code window, and then click the Save Project button to save the project to disk.

10 Click the Start button to run the program.

11 Click the Spin button 10 times.

The Wins variable keeps a running total of your jackpots.

The Wins label keeps track of your jackpots. Each time you win, it increments the total by 1. After 10 spins, you'll have won 6 times, as shown in the illustration on the following page.

Modules and Procedures 10

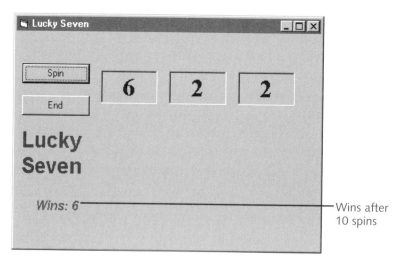

Wins after
10 spins

⓬   Click End to quit the program.

The public variable Wins was useful here because it maintained its value through 10 calls to the Command1_Click event procedure. If you had declared Wins locally in the Command1_Click event procedure, the variable would have reset each time, just as the trip odometer in your car does when you reset it. Using a public variable in a standard module lets you avoid "hitting the reset." Public variables have more in common with the main odometer in your car.

Creating General-Purpose Procedures

In addition to containing public variables, standard modules can contain general-purpose procedures that can be called from anywhere in the program. A general-purpose procedure is not like an event procedure because it is not associated with a runtime event or with an object you created by using a toolbox control. General-purpose procedures are similar to built-in Visual Basic statements and functions—they're called by name, they can receive arguments, and each performs a specific task.

For example, imagine a program that has three mechanisms for printing a bitmap: a menu command named Print, a Print toolbar button, and a drag-and-drop printer icon. You could place the same printing routine in each of the three event procedures, or you could handle printing requests from all three sources by using one procedure in a standard module. General-purpose procedures save you typing time, reduce the possibility of errors, make programs smaller and easier to handle, and make event procedures easier to read.

You can create three types of general-purpose procedures in a standard module:

Function and Sub procedures in a standard module let you create general-purpose routines.

- **Function procedures.** Function procedures are called by name from event procedures or other procedures. They can receive arguments, and they always return a value in the function name. They are typically used for calculations.

- **Sub procedures.** Sub procedures are called by name from event procedures or other procedures. They can receive arguments, and they also can be used to perform tasks in the procedure and to return values. Unlike functions, however, Subs do not return values associated with their particular Sub names (although they can return values through variable names). Sub procedures are typically used to receive or process input, display output, or set properties.

- **Property procedures.** Property procedures are used to create and manipulate user-defined properties in a program. This is a useful, if somewhat advanced, feature that lets you customize existing Visual Basic controls and extend the Visual Basic language by creating new objects, properties, and methods. For more information about Property procedures, type **property procedures** in the Index tab of the MSDN Library online Help.

Advantages of General-Purpose Procedures

General-purpose procedures allow you to associate an often-used routine with a familiar name in a standard module. General-purpose procedures provide the following benefits:

- Eliminate repeated lines. You can define a procedure once and have your program execute it any number of times.

- Make programs easier to read. A program divided into a collection of small parts is easier to take apart and understand than is a program made up of one large part.

- Simplify program development. Programs separated into logical units are easier to design, write, and debug. Plus, if you're writing a program in a group setting, you can exchange procedures and modules instead of entire programs.

- Can be reused in other programs. You can easily incorporate standard-module procedures into other programming projects.

- Extend the Visual Basic language. Procedures often can perform tasks that can't be accomplished by individual Visual Basic keywords.

Modules and Procedures

10

Writing Function Procedures

A function performs a service, such as a calculation, and returns a value.

A *Function procedure* is a group of statements located between a Function statement and an End Function statement in a standard module. The statements in the function do the meaningful work—typically processing text, handling input, or calculating a numeric value. You execute, or *call*, a function in a program by placing the function name in a program statement along with any required arguments. (*Arguments* are the data used to make functions work.) In other words, using a Function procedure is exactly like using a built-in function such as Time, Int, or Str.

> ## tip
> Functions declared in standard modules are public by default; they can be used in any event procedure.

Function Syntax

Functions can have a type.

The basic syntax of a function is as follows:

```
Function FunctionName([arguments]) [As Type]
    function statements
End Function
```

The following syntax items are important:

- *FunctionName* is the name of the function you are creating in the standard module.

- *arguments* is a list of optional arguments (separated by commas) to be used in the function.

- As *Type* is an option that specifies the function return type (the default is Variant).

- *function statements* is a block of statements that accomplish the work of the function.

Brackets ([]) enclose optional syntax items. Syntax items not enclosed by brackets are required by Visual Basic.

Functions always return a value to the calling procedure in the function's name (*FunctionName*). For this reason, the last statement in a function is often an assignment statement that places the final calculation of the function in *FunctionName*. For example, the Function procedure TotalTax shown below computes the state and city taxes for an item and then assigns the result to the TotalTax name:

TotalTax is a sample function with one argument.

```
Function TotalTax(Cost)
    StateTax = Cost * 0.05   'State tax is 5%
    CityTax = Cost * 0.015   'City tax is 1.5%
    TotalTax = StateTax + CityTax
End Function
```

important

I recommend that you assign a value to the function's name each time you write a function. That way, you'll always be sure of the result you're returning to the program.

Calling a Function Procedure

To call the TotalTax function in an event procedure, you would use a statement similar to the following:

Functions are typically assigned to variables or properties.

```
lblTaxes.Caption = TotalTax(500)
```

This statement computes the total taxes required for a $500 item and then assigns the result to the Caption property of the lblTaxes object. The TotalTax function can also take a variable as an argument, as shown in the following statement:

```
TotalCost = SalesPrice + TotalTax(SalesPrice)
```

This line uses the TotalTax function to determine the taxes for the number in the SalesPrice variable and then adds them to SalesPrice to get the total cost of an item. See how much clearer the code is when a function is used?

Using a Function to Perform a Calculation

In the following exercise, you'll add a function to the Lucky Seven program to calculate the win rate in the game (the percentage of spins in which one or more sevens appear). To do this, you'll add a function named Rate and a public variable named Spins to the standard module. Then you'll call the Rate function every time the Spin button is clicked. You'll display the results in a new label you'll create on the form.

Create a win rate function

1 Open the Project window.

The components of the MyWins.vbp project appear in the Project window. You'll save the components of the project as MyRate to preserve the MyWins program.

2 Click the MyWins.frm form. On the File menu, click the Save MyWins.frm As command. Save the form to disk as **MyRate.frm** in the \Vb6Sbs\Less10 folder.

3 Click the MyWins.bas standard module in the Project window. On the File menu, click the Save MyWins.bas As command. Save the module to disk as **MyRate.bas**.

4 On the File menu, click the Save Project As command. Save the project as **MyRate.vbp**.

View Object button

5 If the form is not visible, click the MyRate.frm form in the Project window and then click the View Object button.

The user interface for the Lucky Seven program appears.

6 Move the Wins label closer to the Lucky Seven label to make room for a new label. You might need to resize one or both labels to make enough room.

Label control

7 Use the Label control to create a new label below the Wins label. Set the following properties for the label:

Object	Property	Setting
Label5	Alignment	2 – Center
	Caption	"0.0%"
	Font	Arial, Bold Italic, 12-point
	ForeColor	Red
	Name	lblRate

Your form should look similar to the figure on the following page.

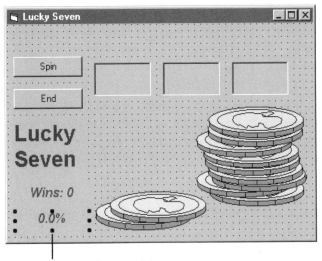

New label named lblRate

8 In the Project window, click the MyRate.bas module, and then click the View Code button in the Project window.

The Module1 standard module appears in the Code window.

9 Type the following public variable declaration below the Public Wins statement:

```
Public Spins
```

The standard module now includes two public variables (Wins and Spins) that will be available to all the procedures in the program. You'll use Spins as a counter to keep track of the number of spins you make.

10 Now type the following function declaration:

```
Function Rate(Hits, Attempts) As String
    Percent = Hits / Attempts
    Rate = Format(Percent, "0.0%")
End Function
```

The Rate function goes in the Module1 standard module.

After you type the first line of the function code, Visual Basic opens a new procedure in the standard module to hold the function declaration. After you type the remainder of the function's code, your screen should look identical to the figure on the following page.

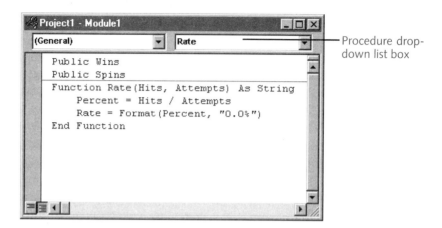

Procedure drop-down list box

The Rate function determines the percentage of wins by dividing the Hits argument by the Attempts argument and then adjusting the appearance of the result by using the Format function. The Rate function is declared as a string because the Format function returns a string. The Hits argument and Attempts argument are placeholders for the two variables that will be passed to the function during the function call. The Rate function is general-purpose enough to be used with any numbers or variables, not only with Wins and Spins.

⓫ Close the Code window, and then double-click the Spin button on the Lucky Seven form to bring up the Command1_Click event procedure.

⓬ Below the fourth line of the event procedure (the third statement containing the Rnd function), type the following statement:

```
Spins = Spins + 1
```

This statement increments the Spins variable each time the user clicks Spin and new numbers are placed in the spin windows.

⓭ Scroll down in the Code window, and then type the following statement as the last line in the Command1_Click event procedure, between the End If and the End Sub statements:

This function call includes two variables.

```
lblRate.Caption = Rate(Wins, Spins)
```

As you type the Rate function, notice how Visual Basic automatically displays the names of the arguments for the Rate function you just built (a nice touch).

The purpose of this statement is to call the Rate function, using the Wins and Spins variables as arguments. The result returned is a percentage in string format, and this value is assigned to the Caption property of the lblRate label on the form after each spin. That's all there is to it!

Save Project button

14 Close the Code window, and then click the Save Project button to update your project files.

Now you'll run the program.

Run the MyRate program

Start button

1 Click the Start button to run the program.

2 Click the Spin button 10 times.

The first 5 times you click Spin, the win rate stays at 100.0%. You're hitting the jackpot every time. As you continue to click, however, the win rate adjusts to 83.3%, 71.4%, 75.0% (another win), 66.7%, and 60.0% (a total of 6 for 10). After 10 spins, your screen looks like the following:

The complete Rate.vbp program is available on disk in the \Vb6Sbs\Less10 folder.

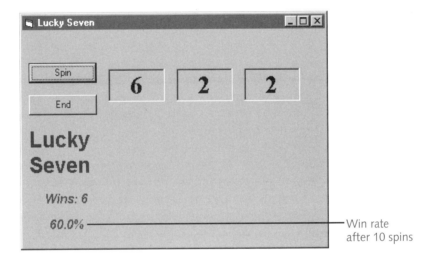

Win rate
after 10 spins

The actual win rate for Lucky Seven is about 28%.

If you continue to spin, you'll notice that the win rate drops to about 28%. The Rate function shows you that you were really pretty lucky when you started spinning, but after a while reality set in.

3 When you're finished with the program, click the End button.

The program stops, and the programming environment returns.

tip

To revise this program so that it displays a random series of spins each time you run the program, put a Randomize statement in the Form_Load event procedure. For instructions, see the section in Lesson 2 entitled "One Step Further: Adding to a Program."

Writing Sub Procedures

Sub procedures process information.

A *Sub procedure* is similar to a Function procedure, except that a Sub doesn't return a value associated with its name. Subs are typically used to get input from the user, display or print information, or manipulate several properties associated with a condition. Subs are also used to process and return several variables during a procedure call. Most functions can return only one value, but Sub procedures can return many.

Sub Procedure Syntax

The basic syntax for a Sub procedure is

```
Sub ProcedureName([arguments])
    procedure statements
End Sub
```

The following syntax items are important:

- *ProcedureName* is the name of the Sub procedure you're creating.
- *arguments* is a list of optional arguments (separated by commas, if there's more than one) to be used in the Sub.
- *procedure statements* is a block of statements that accomplish the work of the procedure.

The arguments in a procedure call must match the arguments in the Sub declaration.

In the procedure call, the number and type of arguments sent to the Sub procedure must match the number and type of arguments in the Sub declaration. If variables passed to a Sub are modified during the procedure, the updated variables are returned to the program. By default, Sub procedures declared in a standard module are public, so they can be called by any event procedure.

important

Passing a variable to a procedure is called passing an argument *by reference*, because a variable can be modified by a procedure and returned to the program. Passing a literal value (such as a string in quotation marks) to a procedure is called passing an argument *by value*, because a value cannot be modified by a procedure. You can pass variables by value if you use a special notation. You'll learn how to do this in the section entitled "Passing a Variable by Value" later in this lesson.

You can use the Sub procedure below to add names to a list box on a form at runtime. The procedure receives one string variable passed by reference.

If this Sub procedure is declared in a standard module, it can be called from any event procedure in the program.

```
Sub AddNameToListBox(person$)
    If person$ <> "" Then
        Form1.List1.AddItem person$
        Msg$ = person$ & " added to list box."
    Else
        Msg$ = "Name not specified."
    End If
    MsgBox (Msg$), , "Add Name"
End Sub
```

This Sub procedure receives the person$ argument.

The AddNameToListBox procedure receives the name to be added by using the person$ argument, a string variable received by reference during the procedure call. If the value of person$ is not empty, or *null*, the specified name is added to the List1 list box object by using the AddItem method, and a confirming message is displayed by the MsgBox function. If the argument is null, the procedure skips the AddItem method and displays the message "Name not specified."

tip

When you set properties from a procedure in a standard module, you need to prefix each object name with the form name and a period (Form1., in this example). This lets Visual Basic know which form you're referencing.

Calling a Sub Procedure

Arguments passed by value use literal values.

To call a Sub procedure in a program, you specify the name of the procedure and then list the arguments required by the Sub. For example, to call the AddNameToListBox procedure by using a literal string (to call it *by value*), you could type the following statement:

```
AddNameToListBox "Kimberly"
```

Arguments passed by reference use variables.

Similarly, you could call the procedure by using a variable (call it *by reference*) by typing this statement:

```
AddNameToListBox NewName$
```

In both cases, the AddNameToListBox procedure would add the specified name to the list box. In this Sub procedure, calls by value and calls by reference produce similar results because the argument is not modified in the procedure.

10

Modules and Procedures

The space-saving advantages of a Sub procedure become clear when you call the procedure many times, as shown in the example below.

```
AddNameToListBox "Kimberly"  'always add two names
AddNameToListBox "Rachel"
Do                              'then let user add extra names
    NewName$ = InputBox("Enter a list box name.", "Add Name")
    AddNameToListBox NewName$
Loop Until NewName$ = ""
```

Here the user is allowed to enter as many names to the list box as he or she likes. The next exercise gives you a chance to practice using a Sub procedure to handle another type of input in a program.

Using a Sub Procedure to Manage Input

Sub procedures are often used to handle input in a program when information comes from two or more sources and needs to be in the same format. In the following exercise, you'll create a Sub procedure named AddName that prompts the user for input and formats the text so that it can be displayed on multiple lines in a text box. The procedure will save you programming time because you'll use it in two event procedures, each associated with a different text box. Because the procedure will be declared in a standard module, you need to type it in only one place.

Create a text box Sub procedure

❶   On the File menu, click the New Project command, and then click OK to open a new, standard application.

A new, empty form appears.

TextBox control

❷   Use the TextBox control to create two text boxes, side by side, in the middle of the form.

You'll use these text boxes to hold the names of employees you'll be assigning to two departments. You get to make your own personnel decisions today.

Label control

❸   Use the Label control to create two labels above the text boxes.

These labels will hold the names of the departments.

CommandButton control

❹   Use the CommandButton control to create a command button under each text box and a separate command button at the bottom of the form.

You'll use the first two command buttons to add employees to their departments. You'll use the last command button to quit the program.

These are typical settings for a text box used to display several lines of text.

5 Set the properties shown in the table for the objects in the program.

Because the text boxes will contain more than one line, you'll set their MultiLine properties to True and their ScrollBars properties to Vertical. You'll also set their TabStop properties to False and their Locked properties to True so that the information can't be modified. These settings are typically used when multiple lines are displayed in text boxes.

Object	Property	Setting
Text1	Text	(Empty)
	MultiLine	True
	ScrollBars	2 – Vertical
	TabStop	False
	Locked	True
	Name	txtSales
Text2	Text	(Empty)
	MultiLine	True
	ScrollBars	2 – Vertical
	TabStop	False
	Locked	True
	Name	txtMkt
Label1	Caption	"Sales"
	Font	Bold
	Name	lblSales
Label2	Caption	"Marketing"
	Font	Bold
	Name	lblMkt
Command1	Caption	"Add Name"
	Name	cmdSales
Command2	Caption	"Add Name"
	Name	cmdMkt
Command3	Caption	"Quit"
	Name	cmdQuit
Form1	Caption	"Assign Department Teams"

Modules and Procedures

10

When you've finished, your form should look similar to the following:

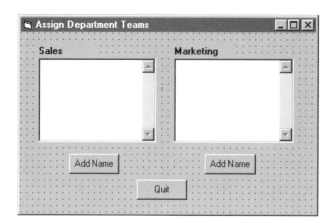

Now you'll add a standard module and create the general-purpose AddName Sub procedure.

6 On the Project menu, click the Add Module command, and then click Open.

A new standard module appears in the Code window.

7 Type the AddName procedure into the standard module:

Use Chr(13) and Chr(10) to create a new line in a text box.

```
Sub AddName(Team$, ReturnString$)
    Prompt$ = "Enter a " & Team$ & " employee."
    Nm$ = InputBox(Prompt$, "Input Box")
    WrapCharacter$ = Chr(13) + Chr(10)
    ReturnString$ = Nm$ & WrapCharacter$
End Sub
```

This general-purpose Sub procedure uses the InputBox function to prompt the user for an employee name. It receives two arguments during the procedure call: Team$, a string containing the department name; and ReturnString$, an empty string variable that will return the formatted employee name to the calling event procedure.

Before the employee name is returned, carriage return and linefeed characters are appended to the string so that each name in the text box will appear on its own line. This is a general technique that you can use in any text box.

Your Code window should look like the following:

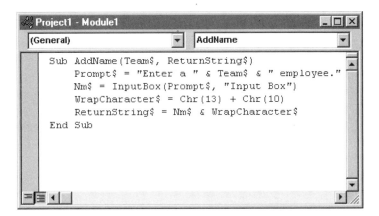

```
Project1 - Module1

(General)                          AddName

    Sub AddName(Team$, ReturnString$)
        Prompt$ = "Enter a " & Team$ & " employee."
        Nm$ = InputBox(Prompt$, "Input Box")
        WrapCharacter$ = Chr(13) + Chr(10)
        ReturnString$ = Nm$ & WrapCharacter$
    End Sub
```

8 Close the Code window, and then double-click the first Add Name button on the form (the button below the Sales text box). Type the following statements in the cmdSales_Click event procedure:

```
AddName "Sales", SalesPosition$
txtSales.Text = txtSales.Text & SalesPosition$
```

The call to the AddName Sub procedure includes one argument passed by value ("Sales") and one argument passed by reference (SalesPosition$). The second line uses the argument passed by reference to add text to the txtSales text box. The concatenation operator (&) adds the new name to the end of the text in the text box.

9 Open the Object drop-down list box in the Code window and click the cmdMkt object. Type the following statements in the cmdMkt_Click event procedure:

```
AddName "Marketing", MktPosition$
txtMkt.Text = txtMkt.Text & MktPosition$
```

This event procedure is identical to cmdSales_Click, except that it sends "Marketing" to the AddName procedure and updates the txtMkt text box. The name of the local return variable was changed to make it more intuitive.

10 Open the Object drop-down list box and click the cmdQuit object. Type **End** in the cmdQuit_Click event procedure, and then close the Code window.

Save Project button

> ⓫ Click the Save Project button on the toolbar. Specify the \Vb6Sbs\Less10 folder, and then save the standard module as **MyTeams.bas**. Save your form as **MyTeams.frm**, and then save the project as **MyTeams.vbp**.

That's it! Now you'll run the MyTeams program.

Run the MyTeams program

Start button

> ❶ Click the Start button on the toolbar to run the program.
>
> ❷ Click the Add Name button under the Sales text box, and then type **Maria Palermo** in the Input Box.
>
> Your input box should look like the following:

The complete Teams.vbp program is available on disk in the \Vb6Sbs\Less10 folder.

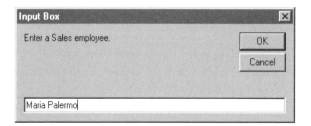

> ❸ Click the OK button to add the name to the Sales text box.
>
> The name appears in the text box.
>
> ❹ Click the Add Name button under the Marketing text box, type **Henry James** in the Marketing Input Box, and then press Enter.
>
> The name appears in the Marketing text box. Your screen should look like the following:

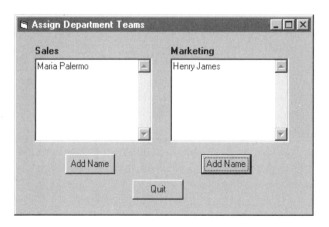

⑤ Enter four or five more names in each of the text boxes. This is your chance to create your own dream departments.

Each name should appear on its own line in the text boxes. The text boxes don't scroll automatically, so you won't see every name you've entered if you enter more names than can fit in a text box. You can use the scroll bars to access names that are not visible.

⑥ When you've finished, click the Quit button to stop the program.

One Step Further **Passing Arguments by Value**

In the discussion of Sub procedures, you learned that arguments are passed to procedures by reference or by value. When a variable is passed by reference (the default), any changes made to the variable are passed back to the calling procedure. You took advantage of this feature in the MyTeams program when you used a variable passed by reference to add names to a text box. Passing by reference can have significant advantages, as long as you're careful not to change a variable unintentionally in a procedure. For example, consider the following Sub procedure declaration and call:

```
Sub CostPlusInterest(Cost, Total)
    Cost = Cost * 1.05  'add 5% to cost...
    Total = Int(Cost)    'then make integer and return
End Sub
.
.
.

Price = 100
Total = 0
CostPlusInterest Price, Total
Print Price; "at 5% interest is"; Total
```

Beware the pitfalls of passing variables by reference.

In this example, the programmer passes two variables by reference to the CostPlusInterest procedure: Price and Total. The programmer plans to use the updated Total variable in the subsequent Print method but has unfortunately forgotten that the Price variable was also updated in an intermediate step in the procedure. (Because Price was passed by reference, changes to Cost automatically result in the same changes to Price.) This produces the following erroneous result when the program is run:

```
105 at 5% interest is 105
```

The ByVal Keyword

An obvious way to avoid the preceding problem is never to modify a variable passed in a procedure. But this solution can add program code and can prove unreliable if you're working as part of a group of several programmers. A better method is to use the ByVal keyword in the argument list when you declare a procedure. This tells Visual Basic to keep a copy of the original argument and to return it unchanged when the procedure ends—even if the variable was modified in the procedure. ByVal is used in an argument list in the following manner:

```
Sub CostPlusInterest(ByVal Cost, Total)
```

When the Cost argument is declared by using ByVal, the program produces the correct output:

```
100 at 5% interest is 105
```

Passing a Variable by Value

You can pass a variable by value by putting the variable in parentheses.

If you don't want to rely on the ByVal keyword, you can use an alternative method to prevent a passed variable from being modified: you can convert it to a literal value by enclosing it in parentheses. This seldom-used trick always works in Visual Basic, and it makes your procedure calls more intuitive. If you specifically pass the variable by value, everyone will know what you mean. It's also an efficient way to pass a variable by value *sometimes*. The syntax for calling the CostPlusInterest procedure and passing the Price variable by value is

```
CostPlusInterest (Price), Total
```

If the example program is called in this way, the correct result is produced:

```
100 at 5% interest is 105
```

In this lesson, you've learned to use public variables, functions, and Sub procedures to manage information in a program. Do take advantage of these constructions as your programs get larger. You'll find that they save you considerable time and that they can be used again in future projects.

If you want to continue to the next lesson

● Keep Visual Basic running, and turn to Lesson 11.

If you want to quit Visual Basic for now

● From the File menu, choose Exit.

If you see a Save dialog box, click Yes.

Upgrade Notes:
What's Different in Visual Basic .NET?

If you choose to upgrade to Visual Basic .NET in the future, you'll notice some new features related to the topics in this lesson, including the following:

■ Standard modules are still supported in Visual Basic .NET, but there are now Module and End Module keywords that enclose the module content within the Code window. Public variables are declared in standard modules as they are in Visual Basic 6.0.

■ Visual Basic .NET continues to support the Function and Sub keywords, allowing you to create your own functions and subprograms. However, the syntax for declaring and calling functions and subprograms has changed a little.

■ If you are using the default Option Explicit setting to control variable declaration in Visual Basic .NET, a specific type declaration is also required for functions when you declare them. It is also recommended that you specifically declare all types in your Visual Basic .NET function and subprogram parameter lists. If you don't assign a type using the As keyword, Visual Basic .NET will use the default Object type for the parameter, a data type that is often less efficient than a specific data type.

■ Visual Basic .NET has changed the way that arguments are passed to and from procedures. In Visual Basic 6.0, the default mechanism for passing arguments was by reference (ByRef), meaning that changes to arguments in the procedure were passed back to the calling routine. In Visual Basic .NET, the default way to pass arguments is by value (ByVal), meaning that changes to arguments within a procedure aren't passed back to the calling routine. You can explicitly specify the argument passing behavior by using the ByRef and ByVal keyword in your argument declarations. If necessary, you can specify ByRef to achieve the same functionality we have used in Visual Basic 6.0.

■ When you call functions and subprograms in Visual Basic .NET, parentheses are now required around all argument lists. The Visual Studio .NET development environment will add these for you—even if your procedures don't require any arguments.

■ Visual Basic .NET programmers now have the option of using the Return statement to send the result of a function calculation back to the calling routine. The standard Visual Basic 6.0 method—assigning a value to the function name—is also supported.

Lesson 10 Quick Reference

To	Do this
Name an object	Specify a unique name in the Name property. Use the appropriate naming conventions so that the object can be identified.
Create a new module	Click the Down Arrow on the Add Form button, and then click Module in the drop-down list. *or* Click the Add Module command on the Project menu.
Save a new module	Select the module in the Project window, and then click the Save Module1 As command on the File menu.
Remove a module from a program	Select the module in the Project window, and then click the Remove command on the Project menu.
Add an existing module to a program	On the Project menu, click the Add File command.
Create a public variable	Declare the variable by using the Public keyword in a standard module. For example: `Public TotalSales As Integer`

Create a public function	Place the function statements between the Function keyword and the End Function keyword in a standard module. Functions are public by default.
	For example:
	`Function Rate(Hits, Attempts) As String`
	`    Percent = Hits / Attempts`
	`    Rate = Format(Percent, "0.0%")`
	`End Function`

Call a user-defined function	Type the function name and any necessary arguments in an event procedure program statement. For example: `lblRate.Caption = Rate(NumHits, NumTrys)`

Create a Sub procedure	Place the procedure statements between the Sub keyword and the End Sub keyword in a standard module. Sub procedures are public by default.
	For example:
	`Sub CostPlusInterest(Cost, Total)`
	`    Cost = Cost * 1.05`
	`    Total = Int(Cost)`
	`End Sub`

Lesson 10 Quick Reference

To	Do this
Call a Sub procedure	Type the procedure name and any necessary arguments in an event procedure program statement. For example: `CostPlusInterest PriceTag, TotalPrice`
Set or use an object property in a general-purpose procedure	Specify the form name and a period (.) before the object name. For example: `Form1.Label1.Caption = "Trip to Germany!"`

Pass arguments by value	Specify a variable with parentheses around it or use a literal value as a procedure argument. For example:
	
	`CalculateInterest (Price)`
	or
	`CalculateInterest 500`

Pass an argument by reference	Specify a variable as a procedure argument: `CalculateInterest 500`

Working with Collections and Arrays

ESTIMATED TIME
45 min.

In this lesson you will learn how to:

✔ *Work with collections.*

✔ *Process collections by using a For Each...Next loop.*

✔ *Organize variables into arrays.*

In this lesson, you will learn about groups of objects called *collections* in a Microsoft Visual Basic program, and you'll see how you can process collections by using a special loop called For Each...Next. You'll also learn how to organize variables into containers called *arrays*. Arrays make data management in a program easy, and they provide a good introduction to the database programming techniques you'll use in Lesson 13.

Working with Object Collections

A collection is a group of related objects.

You already know that objects on a form are stored together in the same file. But did you also know that Visual Basic considers the objects to be members of the same group? In Visual Basic terminology, the entire set of objects on a form is called the *Controls collection*. The Controls collection is created automatically when you open a new form and expands when you add objects to the form. In fact, Visual Basic maintains several standard collections of objects that you can use when you write your programs. In the first section of this lesson, you will learn the basic skills you need to work with any collection you encounter.

Collection Notation

Each collection in a program has its own name so that you can reference it as a distinct unit in the program code. For example, as you just learned, the collection containing all the objects on a form is called the Controls collection. However, because you can have more than one form in a program (and therefore more than one Controls collection), you need to include the form name when you use the Controls collection in a program that contains more than one form. For example, to refer to the Controls collection on Form1, you would use the following name in your code:

```
Form1.Controls
```

Each form has a Controls collection.

The period between the Form1 object name and the Controls keyword makes Controls look like a property in this notation, but Visual Basic programmers describe the Controls collection as an object *contained by* the Form1 object. The relationship, or *hierarchy,* between objects is a little like that between folders in a pathname; you'll see this notation again when you start working with application objects in Lesson 14.

In addition to letting you work with objects and collections in your own programs, Visual Basic lets you browse your system for other application objects and use them in your programs. We'll pick up this topic again in Lesson 14 when you learn how to use the Visual Basic Object Browser.

Referencing Objects in a Collection

You can reference the objects in a collection, or the individual members of the collection, in several ways. The first way is to specify the objects by using their names directly in an assignment statement. For example, the statement

```
Form1.Controls!Label1.Caption = "Employees"
```

singles out the Label1 object in the Controls collection and sets its Caption property to "Employees". An exclamation point (!) is used to link the Label1 object to the Controls collection. Although this statement might seem like a mouthful for the compiler, it gives a precise description of the hierarchy within the collection.

You can reference the objects in a collection individually or in groups.

The second way to address an object in a collection is to specify the *index position* of the object in the group. Visual Basic stores collection objects in the reverse order of that in which they were created, so you can use an object's "birth order" to reference the object individually, or you can use a loop to step through several objects. For example, to identify the last object created on a form, you would specify the 0 (zero) index, as shown in this example:

```
Form1.Controls(0).Caption = "Business"
```

This statement sets the Caption property of the last object on the form to "Business". (The second to the last object created has an index of 1, the third to the last object created has an index of 2, and so on.)

Writing For Each...Next Loops

Although you can reference individual members of a collection, the most useful way to work with objects in a collection is to process them as a group. In fact, the reason collections exist is so that you can process groups of objects efficiently. For example, you might want to display, move, sort, rename, or resize an entire collection of objects at once.

For Each...Next loops are designed to process collections.

To handle one of these tasks, you can use a special loop called For Each...Next to cycle through objects in a collection one at a time. A For Each...Next loop is similar to a For...Next loop, which you learned about in Lesson 7. When a For Each...Next loop is used with the Controls collection, it looks like this:

```
For Each Control in FormName.Controls
    process object
Next Control
```

The Control variable represents the current object in a For Each...Next loop.

Control is a special variable representing the current object in the collection, and *FormName* is the name of the form. The body of the loop is used to process the individual objects of the collection. For example, you might want to change the Enabled, Left, Top, Caption, or Visible properties of the objects in the collection, or you might want to list the name of each object in a list box.

Moving a Collection of Objects

In the following exercise, you'll use the Controls collection to move a group of objects from left to right across the form at the same time. The program uses a For Each...Next loop to move the objects every time the user clicks a command button named Move Objects. Sometimes certain objects in a collection require special treatment, so in the exercise that follows this one you'll learn how to modify the program so that it moves every object except the command button.

Use a For Each...Next loop
to process the Controls collection

① Start Visual Basic.

The New Project dialog box appears.

② Click on the Existing tab, and open the project Move.vbp in the
\Vb6Sbs\Less11 folder.

③ If the Working with Collections form does not appear, select Move.frm in
the Project window, and then click the View Object button.

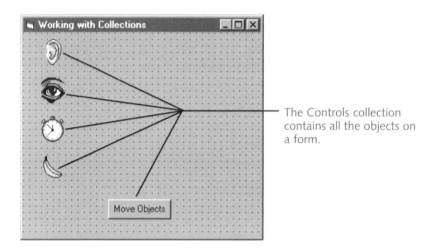

The Controls collection
contains all the objects on
a form.

This form contains five objects that are part of the Controls collection. The
Picture, Name, and Caption properties for the objects have been set, but
you need to add the code to move the collection across the screen.

④ Double-click the Move Objects button on the form.

The cmdButton_Click event procedure appears in the Code window.

⑤ Type the following program statements:

*Using a For
Each...Next
loop to adjust
the Left prop-
erty of each
object makes
the objects
move as a
group.*

```
For Each Ctrl In Controls
    Ctrl.Left = Ctrl.Left + 200
Next Ctrl
```

Each time the user clicks the Move Objects button, this For Each...Next loop
steps through the objects in the Controls collection one by one and moves
them 200 twips to the right. (To move objects 200 twips to the left, you would
subtract 200 instead.) The Ctrl variable is a "stand-in" for the current object
in the collection and contains the same property settings as the object it
represents. In this loop, you're adjusting the Left property, which determines an object's position relative to the left side of the form.

6 On the File menu, click the Save Move.frm As command. Save the form as **MyMove.frm**.

7 On the File menu, click the Save Project As command. Save the project as **MyMove.vbp**.

Start button

8 Close the Code window, and then click the Start button on the toolbar.

The program runs, and four icons appear on the left side of the form. A command button appears at the bottom of the form.

The Move Objects button also moves as you click it.

9 Click the Move Objects button several times.

Each time you click the button, the objects on the form move to the right. The Move Objects button marches right along with the images because it is part of the Controls collection.

10 Click the End button on the toolbar to stop the program.

End button

Moving all the objects together is not a requirement. Visual Basic allows you to process collection members individually if you want to. In the next exercise, you'll learn how to keep the Move Objects button in one place while the image objects move to the right.

Using the Tag Property in a For Each...Next Loop

If you want to process one or more members of a collection differently than you want to process the other members, you can use the Tag property. You set the Tag property of objects that you want to process differently. Your program reads each object's Tag property while it's processing the items in a For Each...Next loop; based on the value of the Tag property, the program either processes the object as usual or gives it special treatment.

The Tag property lets you identify objects that need special treatment in a loop.

For example, let's say you placed the word *Slow* in the Tag property of the imgBanana object in the MyMove program. You could use an If...Then statement to spot the Slow tag when the loop evaluated the imgBanana object, and then you could move the banana a shorter distance than the other objects.

> ## tip
> If you plan to give several objects special treatment in a For Each...Next loop, you can use ElseIf statements with the If...Then statement, or you can use a Select Case decision structure.

In the following exercise, you'll set the cmdButton Tag property to "Button" to stop the For Each...Next loop from moving the command button to the right.

Use a tag to give a collection object special treatment

❶ On the File menu, click the Save MyMove.frm As command. Save the form as **MyTag.frm**.

Before you make changes to the program, you save it under a new name to preserve the original MyMove project.

❷ On the File menu, click the Save Project As command. Save the project as **MyTag.vbp**.

❸ Click the Move Objects button on the form, and then open the Properties window.

❹ Set the Tag property of the cmdButton object to "Button".

❺ Double-click the Move Objects button on the form.

The cmdButton_Click event procedure appears in the Code window, as shown in the following illustration:

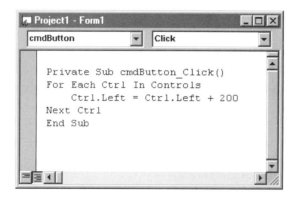

❻ Modify your event procedure so that it looks like the following. (The third and fifth lines are new, and the fourth line has been further indented.)

```
Private Sub cmdButton_Click()
For Each Ctrl In Controls
    If Ctrl.Tag <> "Button" Then
        Ctrl.Left = Ctrl.Left + 200
    End If
Next Ctrl
End Sub
```

The If...Then statement checks for the "Button" tag.

The new feature of this For Each...Next loop is the If...Then statement that checks each collection member to see if it has a Tag property containing

"Button". If the loop encounters this marker, it passes over the object without moving it. The tag "Button" has no special meaning to Visual Basic—it's simply a word I decided to use to identify the command button object in the program. I could just as easily have used a tag such as "Don't Move" or "Leave It".

Start button

7 Close the Code window, and then click the Start button on the toolbar.

The program runs, and the five interface objects appear on the form.

8 Click the Move Objects button seven or eight times.

As you click the button, the icons on the form move across the screen. The Move Objects button stays in the same place, however:

The Tag.vbp program is available in the \Vb6Sbs\Less11 folder.

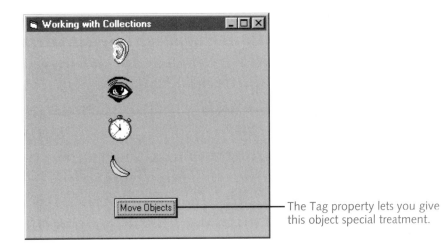

The Tag property lets you give this object special treatment.

Giving one object in a collection special treatment can be very useful. In this case, using a tag in the For Each…Next loop improved the usability of the user interface. As you use other types of collections in Visual Basic, be sure to keep the Tag property in mind.

End button

9 Click the End button on the toolbar to stop the program.

10 Click the Save Project button on the toolbar to save your changes to MyTag.vbp.

Useful Visual Basic Collections

Visual Basic provides built-in support for the following collections in your programs, in addition to the Controls collection. To learn more about these collections, search for *collections* in the Visual Basic online Help.

Collections and Arrays

Collection	Description
Forms collection	A collection of all the loaded forms in a program. By using a For Each...Next loop, you can set the characteristics of one or more of these forms or one or more of the objects contained in them.
Printers collection	A collection of all the available printers on your system. By using a For Each...Next loop and the AddItem method, you can display the names of all the available printers in a list box and then let the user pick the printer to use for output.
Database collections	A variety of collections related to data access and database management. Especially useful database collections include Columns, Containers, Indexes, and Databases. You'll learn more about databases in the next lesson.

Visual Basic for Applications Collections

If you decide to write Visual Basic macros for Microsoft Office applications in the future, you'll find that collections play a big role in the object models of Microsoft Word, Microsoft Excel, Microsoft Access, Microsoft PowerPoint, and several other applications that support the Visual Basic for Applications programming language. In Microsoft Word, for example, all the open documents in the word processor are stored in the Documents collection, and each paragraph in the current document is stored in the Paragraphs collection. You can manipulate these collections with the For...Each loop just as you did in the preceding exercise.

For example, the following sample code comes from a Word 97 macro that uses a For...Each loop to check each open document in the Documents collection for a file named MyLetter.doc. If the file is found in the collection, the macro makes MyLetter the active document in Word with the Activate method. If the file is not found in the collection, the macro loads the file from the Samples folder on drive C.

```
Dim aDoc, docFound, docLocation
docLocation = "c:\samples\myletter.doc"
For Each aDoc In Documents
    If InStr(1, aDoc.Name, "myletter.doc", 1) Then
        aDoc.Activate
        Exit For
    Else
        docFound = False
    End If
Next aDoc
If docFound = False Then Documents.Open FileName:=docLocation
```

tip
I've included this sample Word macro to show you how you can use collections in Visual Basic for Applications, but the source code is designed for Microsoft Word, not the Visual Basic compiler. To try it you'll need to open up Microsoft Word and enter the code in Word's special macro editor. (If you're not in Word, the Documents collection won't have any meaning to the compiler.)

The macro begins by declaring three variables, all of type Variant. The aDoc variable will represent the current collection element in the For... Each loop. The variable docFound will be assigned a Boolean value of False if the document is not found in the Documents collection. The variable docLocation will contain the pathname of the MyLetter.doc file on disk. (This routine assumes that the MyLetter.doc file is in a hypothetical folder named Samples on drive C.)

The For...Each loop cycles through each document in the Documents collection searching for the MyLetter file. If the file is detected by the InStr function (which detects one string in another), the file is made the active document. If the file is not found, the macro opens it by using the Open method of the Documents object.

Also note the Exit For statement, which I use to exit the For...Each loop when the MyLetter file has been found and activated. Exit For is a special program statement you can use to exit a For...Next loop or For...Each loop when continuing will cause unwanted results. In our example, if the MyLetter.doc file has been located in the collection, continuing the search would be fruitless. Here, the Exit For statement affords a graceful way to stop the loop as soon as its task is completed.

Working with Arrays of Variables

In Lesson 7, you used cut-and-paste techniques to create a control array to store more than one picture box under the same object name. In the control array you used, each object in the group shared the same object name, so you were able to process the entire set of picture boxes by using one For...Next loop.

An array is a collection of values stored under a single name.

In this section, you'll learn how to use similar techniques to store variables in an array. Just like control arrays and collections, variable arrays (simply called *arrays*) allow you to refer to an entire group of values by using one name and then to process the values individually or as a group by using a For...Next or Do loop.

Collections and Arrays

11

Arrays are useful because they help you track large amounts of data in ways that would be impractical using traditional variables. For example, imagine creating a nine-inning baseball scoreboard in a program. To save the scores for each inning of the game, you might be tempted to create two groups of 9 variables (a total of 18 variables) in the program. You'd probably name them something like Inning1HomeTeam, Inning1AwayTeam, and so on, to keep them straight. Working with the variables individually would take considerable time and real estate in your program. Fortunately, Visual Basic lets you organize groups of variables like these in an array that has one common name and an easy-to-use index. For example, you could create a two-dimensional (2-by-9) array named Scoreboard to contain the scores for the baseball game. Let's see how this works.

Creating an Array

Before you can use an array, you must declare it.

You create, or *declare*, arrays in program code just as you declare variables. However, the place in which you declare the array determines where it can be used, or its *scope*, in the program. If an array is declared locally, it can be used only in the procedure in which it is declared. If an array is declared publicly in a standard module, it can be used anywhere in the program. When you declare an array, you need to include the following information in your declaration statement.

Information in an array declaration statement	Description
Array name	The name you will use to represent your array in the program. In general, array names follow the same rules as variable names. (See Lesson 5 for more information on variables.)
Data type	The type of data you will store in the array. In most cases, all the variables in an array will be of the same type. You can specify one of the fundamental data types, or, if you're not yet sure which type of data will be stored in the array or whether you will store more than one type, you can specify the Variant type.
Number of dimensions	The number of dimensions your array will contain. Most arrays are one-dimensional (a list of values) or two-dimensional (a table of values), but you can add dimensions if you're working with a complex mathematical model such as a three-dimensional shape.
Number of elements	The number of elements your array will contain. The elements in your array correspond directly to the array index. By default, the first array index is 0 (zero), as it is with control arrays.

> **tip**
>
> Arrays that contain a set number of elements are called *fixed-size* arrays. Arrays that contain a variable number of elements (arrays that can expand during the execution of the program) are called *dynamic* arrays.

Declaring a Fixed-Size Array

The basic syntax for a public fixed-size array is

```
Public ArrayName(Dim1Elements, Dim2Elements, ...) As DataType
```

The following arguments are important:

The Public keyword creates a public, or global, array.

- Public is the keyword that creates a global array.
- *ArrayName* is the variable name of the array.
- *Dim1Elements* is used to specify the number of elements in the first dimension of the array.
- *Dim2Elements* is used to specify the number of elements in the second dimension of the array (additional dimensions can be included).
- *DataType* is a keyword corresponding to the type of data that will be included in the array.

Because the array is public, you need to place the declaration in a standard module in the project (along with other public, or global, variables).

> **tip**
>
> To declare arrays locally in an event procedure, replace the Public keyword with the Static keyword and place the declaration inside an event procedure. Local arrays can be used only inside the procedure in which they are declared.

For example, to declare a public one-dimensional string array named Employees that has room for 10 employee names, you would type the following in a standard module:

```
Public Employees(9) As String
```

By default, the first element in an array has an array index of 0.

When you create the array, Visual Basic sets aside room for it in memory. The illustration on the following page shows conceptually how the array is organized. The 10 array elements are numbered 0 through 9 rather than 1 through 10, because

11

Collections and Arrays

array indexes start with 0 unless you use the Option Base statement. (See "The Option Base Statement" sidebar later in this lesson for more information.)

Employees

```
0 ┌─────────────────────┐
  ├─────────────────────┤
1 │                     │
  ├─────────────────────┤
2 │                     │
  ├─────────────────────┤
3 │                     │
  ├─────────────────────┤
4 │                     │
  ├─────────────────────┤
5 │                     │
  ├─────────────────────┤
6 │                     │
  ├─────────────────────┤
7 │                     │
  ├─────────────────────┤
8 │                     │
  ├─────────────────────┤
9 │                     │
  └─────────────────────┘
```

To declare a public two-dimensional array named Scoreboard that has room for two rows and nine columns of variant data, you would type the following statement in a standard module. (This array would be suitable for the baseball scoreboard discussed earlier in this lesson and will be used in an exercise later in this lesson.)

```
Public Scoreboard(1, 8) As Variant
```

Two-dimensional arrays require two indexes.

When you declare a two-dimensional array, Visual Basic sets aside room for it in memory. You can then use the array in your program as if it were a table of values, as shown in the illustration below. (In this case, the array elements are numbered 0 through 1 and 0 through 8.)

Scoreboard

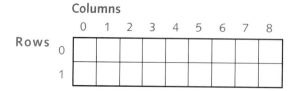

Working with Array Elements

After you've declared an array by using the Static or Public keyword, you're ready to use the array in the program. To refer to an element of an array, you use the array name and an array index enclosed in parentheses. The index must be an integer value; for example, it can be a simple number or an integer variable. (The counter variable of a For...Next loop is often used.) The following statement would assign the value "Leslie" to element 5 in the Employees array example in the previous section:

```
Employees(5) = "Leslie"
```

Arrays are maintained in system memory, or RAM, while the program is running.

This would produce the result shown in the following illustration in our Employees array.

Employees

0	
1	
2	
3	
4	
5	Leslie
6	
7	
8	
9	

The Option Base Statement

If you think your program would be clearer conceptually if the index of the first element in each array were 1 instead of 0, you can place the following Option Base statement in a standard module:

```
Option Base 1
```

This statement associates the first element—or base—of all the arrays in a program with the number 1. The program you'll create in the following section will use Option Base in this way.

Similarly, the following statement would assign the number 4 to row 0, column 2 (the top of the third inning) in the Scoreboard array example in the previous section:

```
Scoreboard(0, 2) = 4
```

This would produce the following result in our Scoreboard array:

Scoreboard

You can use these indexing techniques to assign or retrieve any array element.

Creating a Fixed-Size Array to Hold Temperatures

The FixArray program uses an array to hold a week's worth of temperatures.

The following exercise uses a one-dimensional public array named Temperatures to record the daily high temperatures for a seven-day week. The program demonstrates how you can use an array to store and process a collection of related values in a program. Temperatures are assigned to the array by using an InputBox function and a For…Next loop. The loop counter in the loop is used to reference each element in the array. The array contents are then displayed on the form by using a For…Next loop and the Print method, and the average high temperature is calculated and displayed.

Use a fixed-size array

1. On the File menu, click the New Project command, and click OK.

2. Use the CommandButton control to create three command buttons at the bottom of the form.

3. Set the following properties for the command button and form objects:

Object	Property	Setting
Command1	Caption	"Enter Temperatures"
	Name	cmdEnterTemps
Command2	Caption	"Display Temperatures"
	Name	cmdDisplayTemps
Command3	Caption	"Quit"
	Name	cmdQuit
Form1	Caption	"Temperatures"
	AutoRedraw	True

important

Always set a form's AutoRedraw property to True when you're using the Print method to display information on the form. This will cause Visual Basic to redraw the screen if the form gets covered by another window.

④ Your form should look like the following:

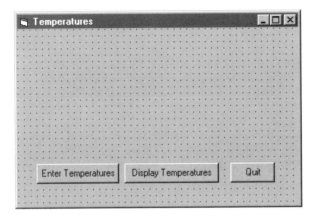

⑤ On the Project menu, click the Add Module command, and then click Open to create a standard module for the array declaration.

A standard module appears in the Code window.

⑥ Type the following statements in the standard module:

```
Option Base 1
Public Temperatures(7) As Variant
```

Option Base sets the array index to 1.

The Option Base statement changes the index of the first array element from 0 to 1 for all arrays in the program. The second statement creates a public array named Temperatures (of the type *Variant*) that has seven elements. Because the array has been declared publicly, it will be available throughout the program.

⑦ Close the standard module Code window, and then double-click the Enter Temperatures button.

The cmdEnterTemps_Click event procedure appears in the Code window.

8 Type the following program statements to prompt the user for temperatures and to load the input into the array:

```
Cls
Prompt$ = "Enter the high temperature."
For i% = 1 To 7
    Title$ = "Day " & i%
    Temperatures(i%) = InputBox(Prompt$, Title$)
Next i%
```

tip

The Cls method at the top of the event procedure clears any previous Print statements from the form so that you can enter more than one set of temperatures.

The counter variable i% is used as an array index.

The For...Next loop uses the counter variable i% as an array index to load temperatures into array elements 1 through 7. The input is received by the InputBox function, which uses the Prompt$ and Title$ variables as arguments.

9 Open the Object drop-down list box in the Code window, and then click the cmdDisplayTemps object. Type the following statements in the cmdDisplayTemps_Click event procedure:

```
Print "High temperatures for the week:"
Print
For i% = 1 To 7
    Print "Day "; i%, Temperatures(i%)
    Total! = Total! + Temperatures(i%)
Next i%
Print
Print "Average high temperature:   "; Total! / 7
```

This event procedure uses the Print method to display the information stored in the Temperatures array on the form. It uses a For...Next loop to cycle through the elements in the array, and it calculates the total of all the temperatures by using the statement

```
Total! = Total! + Temperatures(i%)
```

The complete FixArray.vbp project can be found in the \Vb6Sbs\Less11 folder.

The last line in the event procedure displays the average high temperature of the week, the result of dividing the temperature total by the number of days.

⏺ Open the Object drop-down list box in the Code window, and then click the cmdQuit object. Type the following statement in the cmdQuit_Click event procedure:

End

⏹ Click the Save Project button on the toolbar to save the standard module, the form, and the project to disk. Select the \Vb6Sbs\Less11 folder, and save each file using the name **MyFixArray**.

⏺ Click the Start button to run the program.

⏺ Click the Enter Temperatures button, and then enter seven different temperatures as you are prompted to by the InputBox function. (How about the temperatures during your last vacation?)

The InputBox function dialog box should look similar to the following illustration:

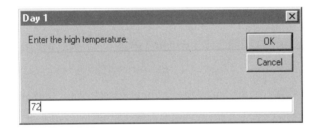

⏺ After you've entered the temperatures, click the Display Temperatures button.

Visual Basic uses the Print method to display each of the temperatures on the form and prints an average at the bottom. Your screen should look similar to the following:

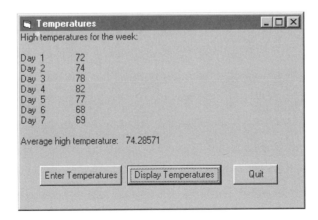

⏺ Click the Quit button to end the program.

Creating a Dynamic Array

As you can see, arrays are quite handy for working with lists of numbers, especially if you process them by using For...Next loops. But what if you're not sure how much array space you'll need before you run your program? For example, what if you want to let the user choose how many temperatures are entered into the MyFixArray program?

Dynamic arrays are dimensioned at runtime.

Visual Basic handles this problem efficiently with a special elastic container called a *dynamic array*. Dynamic arrays are dimensioned at runtime, either when the user specifies the size of the array or when logic you add to the program determines an array size based on specific conditions. Dimensioning a dynamic array takes several steps because although the size of the array isn't specified until the program is running, you need to make "reservations" for the array at design time. To create a dynamic array, you follow these basic steps:

- Specify the name and type of the array in the program at design time, omitting the number of elements in the array. For example, to create a public dynamic array named Temperatures, you type

  ```
  Public Temperatures() as Variant
  ```

- Add code to determine the number of elements that should be in the array at runtime. You can prompt the user by using an InputBox function, or you can calculate the storage needs of the program by using properties or other logic. For example, the following statement gets the array size from the user and assigns it to the Days variable:

  ```
  Days = InputBox("How many days?", "Create Array")
  ```

- Use the variable in a ReDim statement to dimension the array. For example, the following statement sets the size of the Temperatures array at runtime by using the Days variable:

  ```
  ReDim Temperatures(Days)
  ```

- Use the number as the upper bound in a For...Next loop to process the array element, if necessary. For example, the following For...Next loop uses the Days variable as the upper bound of the loop:

  ```
  For i% = 1 to Days
      Temperatures(i%) = InputBox(Prompt$, Title$)
  Next i%
  ```

In the following exercise, you'll use these four steps to revise the MyFixArray program so that it can process any number of temperatures by using a dynamic array.

Use a dynamic array to hold temperatures

1 Open the Project window, and click MyFixArray.frm. You'll save each of the files in the MyFixArray project under a new name to preserve the originals.

2 On the File menu, click the Save MyFixArray.frm As command. Type **MyDynArray.frm** in the Save File As dialog box, and then click Save.

3 Click the MyFixArray.bas module in the Project window. Then, on the File menu, click the Save MyFixArray.bas As command. Next type **MyDynArray.bas** in the Save File As dialog box, and then click Save.

4 On the File menu, click the Save Project As command, and then type **MyDynArray.vbp**. Click Save when you're finished.

View Code button

5 Click Module1 in the Project window, and then click the View Code button to open it in the Code window.

6 Remove the number 7 from the array declaration statement to make Temperatures a dynamic array.

The statement should look like the following:

```
Public Temperatures() As Variant
```

7 Add the following public variable declaration to the standard module as the third line:

```
Public Days As Integer
```

The public integer variable Days will be used to receive input from the user and to dimension the dynamic array at runtime.

View Object button

8 Close the standard module. Click Form1 in the Project window, click the View Object button, and then double-click the Enter Temperatures button. Modify the cmdEnterTemps_Click event procedure so that it looks like the following. (The changed or added elements appear in boldface text.)

```
Cls
Days = InputBox("How many days?", "Create Array")
If Days > 0 Then ReDim Temperatures(Days)
Prompt$ = "Enter the high temperature."
For i% = 1 To Days
    Title$ = "Day " & i%
    Temperatures(i%) = InputBox(Prompt$, Title$)
Next i%
```

The second and third lines prompt the user for the number of temperatures he or she wants to save, and then they use the input to dimension a dynamic array. The If...Then statement is used to verify that the number of days is greater than 0. (Dimensioning an array with the number 0 or a number less than 0 will cause a runtime error.) The Days variable is also used as the upper bound of the For...Next loop.

9 Open the Object drop-down list box, and then click the cmdDisplayTemps object. Modify the cmdDisplayTemps_Click event procedure so that it looks like the following code. (The changed elements appear in boldface.)

```
Print "High temperatures:"
Print
For i% = 1 To Days
    Print "Day "; i%, Temperatures(i%)
    Total! = Total! + Temperatures(i%)
Next i%
Print
Print "Average high temperature:   "; Total! / Days
```

The variable Days replaces the number 7 twice in the event procedure.

Save Project button

10 Close the Code window, and then click the Save Project button to save your changes to disk.

11 Click the Start button on the toolbar to run the program.

Start button

12 Click the Enter Temperatures button, and type **5** when you are prompted for the number of days you want to record.

13 Enter five temperatures as you are prompted to do so.

14 When you've finished entering temperatures, click the Display Temperatures button.

The complete DynArray.vbp program is available on disk in the \Vb6Sbs\Less11 folder.

The program displays the five temperatures on the form along with their average. Your screen should look similar to the following:

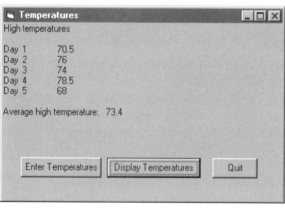

15 Click the End button on the toolbar to end the program.

End button

Congratulations! You've learned to store an unlimited number of values by using an array, and you've learned how to process them by using a For...Next loop. These skills will be useful whenever you need to store large amounts of information in memory while a program runs. In the next two lessons, you'll learn how to store this type of information in text files and databases.

One Step Further Using Multidimensional Arrays

Multidimensional arrays handle one or more tables of information.

In addition to one-dimensional arrays, which handle lists of information, Visual Basic lets you create *multidimensional arrays,* which handle one or more tables of information. Working with multidimensional arrays can be difficult until you get the hang of it, and many of the applications are beyond the scope of this book, but the results can save you considerable time and energy if you're working with large tables of data.

In the following exercise, you'll use a two-dimensional array called Scoreboard to record the runs in an imaginary baseball game between the Seattle Mariners and the New York Yankees. The array you'll use will be a 2-by-9 array similar to the one you dimensioned earlier. After you master two-dimensional arrays, you might wish to experiment with three-dimensional or four-dimensional arrays to push your brain to its conceptual limits. (These sophisticated arrays are often used for computer graphics or scientific applications.)

Create a baseball scoreboard by using a two-dimensional array

Open Project button

View Object button

1 Click the Open Project button on the toolbar.

2 Open the Baseball.vbp project in the \Vb6Sbs\Less11 folder.

The program loads, and the project files appear in the Project window.

3 If the Baseball.frm form does not appear, click it and then click the View Object button.

The Scoreboard form appears, as shown here:

Scoreboard

Baseball Scoreboard
Yankees vs. Mariners

Yankees
Mariners

Inning 1 Scores

Yankees:

Mariners: Next Inning   Quit

The Scoreboard form uses two text boxes and two command buttons to display the runs scored in a nine-inning baseball game. The Mariners are listed as the home team on the scoreboard, and the Yankees are listed as the away team, but you can change these names to those of your own favorite teams. The information is displayed on the scoreboard by using the Print method and is stored in the program by using a two-dimensional public array named Scoreboard.

Start button

4 Click the Start button on the toolbar to run the program.

The program starts, and the cursor blinks in the Yankees text box at the bottom of the form.

The label above the text box indicates that the program is ready to record the first inning of the game. You get to create your own dream game.

5 Type **0** and then press Tab.

The cursor moves to the Mariners text box.

6 Type **0**, and then click the Next Inning button.

A 0–0 tie is recorded in the scoreboard on the form.

7 Continue to enter baseball scores inning by inning until you finish with the ninth inning.

If you want, you can click the Next Inning button more than once to record the same score for multiple innings.

When you've finished, your screen should look similar to the one below. I've chosen my scoreboard to replay Game 1 of the 1995 American League Division Series, in which New York beat Seattle (the Mariners had trouble with relief pitching).

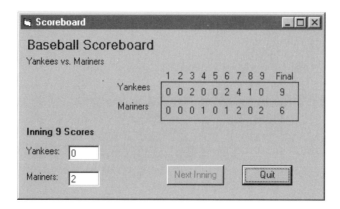

8 Click the Quit button to end the program.

Now you'll look at the program code to see how the Scoreboard array was created and used.

View Code button

9 Click the Baseball.bas standard module in the Project window, and then click the View Code button.

The Code window appears, containing the declarations section of the standard module and the first part of the AddUpScores procedure, as shown below.

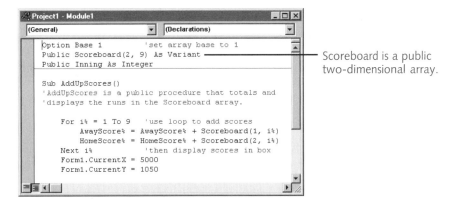

Scoreboard is a public two-dimensional array.

A standard module can contain public arrays, variables, and procedures.

There are four critical components here: an Option Base statement, the declaration statement for a public two-dimensional (2-by-9) array named Scoreboard, the declaration for a public variable named Inning, and a general-purpose public procedure named AddUpScores. The Scoreboard array is declared as a table of values in memory, with rows representing the two teams and columns representing the nine innings. The organization is similar to that of a basic spreadsheet. The Inning variable is used to reference the column (or inning) values in the array.

10 Spend a few moments examining the code in the AddUpScores procedure.

AddUpScores is used to sum the scores in the array and to display them. Because this public procedure is declared in a standard module, it is available throughout the program.

11 Now close the standard module, and then double-click the Next Inning button on the Baseball.frm form.

The CurrentX and CurrentY properties position the cursor on the scoreboard.

The event procedure associated with this button handles the task of moving baseball scores from the team text boxes to the Scoreboard array and finally to the scoreboard on the form. Each Scoreboard array assignment requires two index values, one for the row and one for the column. Considerable care was taken to place the cursor in the correct *x, y* location on the scoreboard to display the information. CurrentX and CurrentY are properties that determine the coordinates of the cursor on the form, and they require values in twips, an effective measurement system to use when you get the hang of it. Because there are 1440 twips in an inch, the coordinate system is granular enough to place the cursor anywhere you want on the form.

Collections and Arrays

11

⑫ Scroll down to the Form_Load event procedure in the Code window.

The Show method is required for Print output while a form is loading.

The Form_Load event procedure initializes the Inning variable to 1 and displays the header on the scoreboard. The Show method is required in this procedure before the Print method is used. Normally, the Print method displays information without help, but because the form is still loading, the Show method is required to print while the Form_Load event is in progress.

⑬ Continue to explore the Baseball program for ideas you can use in your own programs, and run it again if you like.

If you want to continue to the next lesson

● Keep Visual Basic running, and turn to Lesson 12.

If you want to quit Visual Basic for now

● On the File menu, click Exit.

If you see a Save dialog box, click No.

Upgrade Notes:
What's Different in Visual Basic .NET?

If you choose to upgrade to Visual Basic .NET in the future, you'll notice some new features related to the topics in this lesson, including the following:

■ Visual Basic .NET no longer has a single Collection data type. Instead, the functionality for collections is provided through the System.Collections namespace of the .NET Framework class library. Using System.Collections, you can access several useful collection types such as Stack, Queue, Dictionary, and Hashtable.

■ Visual Basic .NET no longer supports control arrays (collections of controls that share the same name and are processed as a group), and you cannot group controls by using the Windows Clipboard as you can in Visual Basic 6.0. However, you can continue to store controls in an array if the array is declared in the object type.

■ Arrays in Visual Basic .NET are now always zero-based, meaning that the lowest array element is always 0. In Visual Basic 6.0, the Option Base statement allows programmers to set the base of arrays to either 0 or 1. Option Base is no longer supported.

■   Because Visual Basic .NET arrays are now always zero-based, arrays can no longer be declared using the "To" keyword with specific lower and upper bounds. Another side effect of zero-bound arrays is that the LBound statement always returns a value of 0, because the lower bound for an array is always 0. (The UBound statement, however, continues to return the highest index in an array, which is the number of elements minus 1.)

■   Visual Basic .NET arrays can now be declared and assigned data using the same program statement. For example, the syntax to declare an array named myList() and add four elements to it is

Dim myList() As Integer = {5, 10, 15, 20}.

■   The ReDim statement is still valid in Visual Basic .NET, although it cannot be used to change the number of dimensions in an existing array. Also, you can't use the ReDim statement in your initial array declaration in Visual Basic .NET.

Lesson 11 Quick Reference

To	Do this

Process objects in a collection	Write a For Each...Next loop that addresses each member of the collection individually. For example:
	`For Each Ctrl In Controls`
	`     Ctrl.Visible = False`
	`Next Ctrl`

Move objects in the Controls collection from left to right across the screen	Modify the Control.Left property of each collection object in a For Each...Next loop. For example:
	`For Each Ctrl In Controls`
	`     Ctrl.Left = Ctrl.Left + 200`
	`Next Ctrl`

Give special treatment to an object in a collection	Set the Tag property of the object to a recognizable value, and then use a For Each...Next loop to test for that value. For example:
	`For Each Ctrl In Controls`
	`     If Ctrl.Tag <> "Button" Then`
	`         Ctrl.Left = Ctrl.Left + 200`
	`     End If`
	`Next Ctrl`

Create a public array	Dimension the array by using the Public keyword in a standard module. For example: `Public Employees(9) As String`

11

Collections and Arrays

Lesson 11 Quick Reference

To	Do this
Create a local array	Dimension the array by using the Static keyword in an event procedure. For example: `Static Employees(9) As String`
Assign a value to an array	Specify the array name, the index of the array element, and the value. For example: `Employees(5) = "Leslie"`
Set the base of all arrays in a program to 1	Place the Option Base statement in a standard module. For example: `Option Base 1`
Clear Print statements from a form	Use the Cls method.
Create a dynamic array	Specify the name and type of the array at design time, but omit the number of elements. While your program is running, specify the size of the array by using the ReDim statement. For example: `ReDim Temperatures(Days)`

Process the elements in an array	Write a For...Next loop that uses the loop counter variable to address each element in the array. For example:
	`For i% = 1 To 7`
	`        Total! = Total! + Temperatures(i%)`
	`Next i%`

Position the cursor on the form (for use with Print and other methods)	Set the CurrentX and CurrentY properties of the form. CurrentX and CurrentY represent the x, y coordinates of the cursor in twips.

12

Exploring Text Files and String Processing

ESTIMATED TIME
40 min.

> **In this lesson you will learn how to:**
>
> ✔ *Display a text file by using a text box object.*
> ✔ *Save notes in a text file.*
> ✔ *Use string processing techniques to sort and encrypt text files.*

In this lesson, you'll learn how to work with information stored in text files on your system. You'll learn how to open a text file and display its contents by using a text box object, and you'll learn how to create a new text file on disk. You'll also learn how to manage textual elements called *strings* in your programs and to use strings to combine, sort, encrypt, and display words, paragraphs, and entire text files.

Displaying Text Files by Using a Text Box Object

The simplest way to display a text file in a program is to use a text box object. You can create text box objects in a variety of sizes. If the contents of the text file don't fit neatly in the text box, you can also add scroll bars to the text box so that the user can examine the entire file. To load the contents of a text file into a text box, you need to use three statements and one function. Their corresponding keywords are described in the following table and will be demonstrated in the first exercise in this lesson.

Keyword	Description
Open	Opens a text file for input or output
Line Input	Reads a line of input from the text file
EOF	Checks for the end of the text file
Close	Closes the text file

Opening a Text File for Input

Text files contain recognizable characters.

A *text file* consists of one or more lines of numbers, words, or characters. Text files are distinct from *document files,* which contain formatting codes, and from *executable files,* which contain instructions for the operating system. Typical text files on your system will be identified by Microsoft Windows Explorer as "Text Documents" or will have the extension .txt, .ini, .log, .inf, .dat, or .bat. Because text files contain only ordinary, recognizable characters, you can display them easily by using text box objects.

A common dialog object displays the Open common dialog box.

You can let the user decide which text file to open in a program by using a common dialog object to prompt the user for the file's pathname. Common dialog objects support the ShowOpen method, which displays the Open common dialog box on the screen. After the user selects the file in the dialog box, its pathname is returned to the program in the FileName property, and you can use this name to open the file. The common dialog object doesn't open the file; it just gets the pathname.

The Open Statement

After you get the pathname from the user, you open the file in the program by using the Open statement. The syntax for the Open statement is

```
Open pathname For mode As #filenumber
```

The following arguments are important:

- *pathname* is a valid Microsoft Windows pathname.
- *mode* is a keyword indicating how the file will be used. (You'll use the Input and Output modes in this lesson.)
- *filenumber* is an integer from 1 through 255.

The file number will be associated with the file when it is opened. You then use this file number in your code whenever you need to refer to the open file. Aside from this association, there's nothing special about file numbers; Microsoft Visual Basic simply uses them to keep track of the different files you open in your program.

A typical Open statement using a common dialog object looks like this:

```
Open CommonDialog1.FileName For Input As #1
```

Here the CommonDialog1.FileName property represents the pathname, Input is the mode, and 1 is the file number.

tip

Text files that are opened by using this syntax are called *sequential files*, because their contents must be worked with in sequential order. By contrast, you can access the information in a database file in any order. (You'll learn more about databases in Lesson 13.)

The following exercise demonstrates how you can use a common dialog object and the Open statement to open a text file. The exercise also demonstrates how you can use the Line Input and EOF keywords to display the contents of a text file in a text box and how you can use the Close keyword to close a file.

Run the Text Browser program

① Start Visual Basic if it is not already running.

Open Project button

② Click the Existing tab in the New Project dialog box, or click the Open Project button on the toolbar.

The ShowText program is located in the \Vb6Sbs\Less12 folder.

③ Select the \Vb6Sbs\Less12 folder, and then double-click the filename ShowText.

The ShowText program loads into the programming environment.

④ If the form is not already visible, select the ShowText form in the Project window, and then click the View Object button.

The ShowText form appears, as shown in the illustration on the following page.

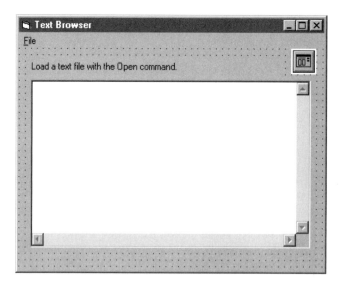

The form contains a large text box object that has scroll bars. It also contains a common dialog object, a label that provides operating instructions for the program, and a File menu containing Open, Close, and Exit commands. I also created the property settings shown in the following table. (Note especially the text box settings.)

Object	Property	Setting
txtFile	Enabled	False
	Multiline	True
	Name	txtFile
	ScrollBars	3 – Both
	Text	(Empty)
mnuItemClose	Enabled	False
	Name	mnuItemClose
lblFile	Caption	"Load a text file with the Open command."
	Name	lblFile
Form1	Caption	"Text Browser"

Start button

5 Click the Start button on the toolbar.

The Text Browser program starts to run.

6 On the Text Browser's File menu, click the Open command.

The Open dialog box appears, as shown in the illustration on the next page.

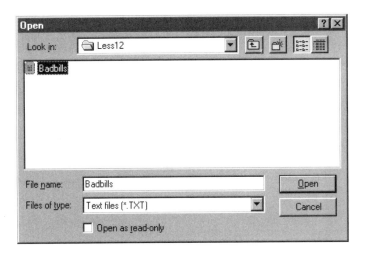

❼ Select the \Vb6Sbs\Less12 folder, and then double-click the filename Badbills.txt in the Open dialog box.

Badbills, a text file containing an article written in 1951 about the dangers of counterfeit money, appears in the text box:

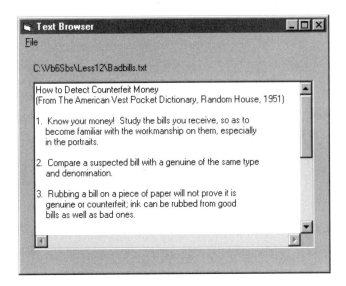

❽ Use the scroll bars to view the entire document. Memorize number 5.

❾ When you've finished, click the Close command on the File menu to close the file, and then click the Exit command to quit the program.

The program stops, and the programming environment returns. Now you'll take a look at two important event procedures in the program.

Text Files and Strings

12

Examine the ShowText program code

❶ On the Text Browser form's File menu, click the Open command.

The mnuItemOpen_Click event procedure appears in the Code window.

❷ Resize the Code window to see more of the program code.

Your screen should look similar to the following illustration:

A partial listing of the ShowText program.

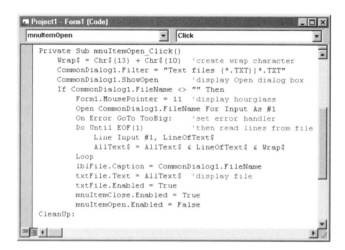

```
Private Sub mnuItemOpen_Click()
    Wrap$ = Chr$(13) + Chr$(10)    'create wrap character
    CommonDialog1.Filter = "Text files (*.TXT)|*.TXT"
    CommonDialog1.ShowOpen          'display Open dialog box
    If CommonDialog1.FileName <> "" Then
        Form1.MousePointer = 11  'display hourglass
        Open CommonDialog1.FileName For Input As #1
        On Error GoTo TooBig:      'set error handler
        Do Until EOF(1)            'then read lines from file
            Line Input #1, LineOfText$
            AllText$ = AllText$ & LineOfText$ & Wrap$
        Loop
        lblFile.Caption = CommonDialog1.FileName
        txtFile.Text = AllText$  'display file
        txtFile.Enabled = True
        mnuItemClose.Enabled = True
        mnuItemOpen.Enabled = False
CleanUp:
```

This event procedure performs the following actions. The Visual Basic statements used are shown in parentheses.

- Prompts the user for a pathname by using a common dialog object.
- Opens the specified file for input (Open...For Input).
- Copies the file one line at a time into a string named AllText$ (Line Input).
- Copies lines until the end of the file is reached (EOF) or until there is no more room in the string. The AllText$ string has room for 64 KB of characters.
- Displays the AllText$ string in the text box and enables the scroll bars.
- Handles any errors that occur (On Error GoTo).
- Updates the File menu commands and the mouse pointer and closes the file (Close).

❸ Take a moment to see how the statements in the mnuItemOpen_Click event procedure work—especially the Open, Line Input, EOF, and Close keywords. For more information about these statements and functions, highlight the keyword you're interested in and press F1 to see a discussion of it in the Visual Basic online help.

The TooBig: error handler in the procedure displays a message and aborts the loading process if the user selects a file bigger than 64 KB. This error handler is necessary because of the 64 KB string size limitation of the text box object. (For files bigger than 64 KB in size, you'll want to use the Rich TextBox control.)

If you select a file that is several pages long, Visual Basic will take a few moments to load it. For this reason, I use the MousePointer property to change the pointer to an hourglass shape until the file is displayed on the screen. It's always a good idea to give users some visual feedback if they have to wait for more than a second or so for an action to occur.

❹ Open the Object drop-down list box, and then click mnuItemClose to display the mnuItemClose_Click event procedure.

This procedure runs when the Close menu command is executed. The procedure clears the text box, disables the Close command, enables the Open command, and disables the text box.

❺ When you've finished looking at the ShowText program code, close the Code window.

Now you can use this simple program as a template for more advanced utilities that process text files. In the next exercise, you'll learn how to type your own text into a text box and how to save the text and text box to disk in a file.

Creating a New Text File on Disk

You use the keywords For Output in the Open statement when you want to create a new file on disk.

To create a new text file on disk by using Visual Basic, you'll use many of the objects and keywords you used in the last example. Creating new files on disk and saving data to them will be useful if you plan to generate custom reports or logs, save important calculations or values, or create a special-purpose word processor or text editor. Here's an overview of the steps you'll need to follow in the program:

❶ Get input from the user or perform mathematical calculations, or do both.

❷ Assign the results of your processing to one or more variables. For example, you could assign the contents of a text box to a variable named InputForFile$.

❸ Prompt the user for a pathname by using a Save As common dialog box. You use the ShowSave method of a common dialog object to display the dialog box.

*The Print #
statement
sends output to
the specified
file.*

④ Use the pathname received in the dialog box to open the file for output (Open...For Output).

⑤ Use the Print # statement to save one or more values to the open file (Print #).

⑥ Close the file when you've finished (Close).

The following exercise demonstrates how you can use text box and common dialog objects and the Open, Print #, and Close statements to create a simple note-taking utility. You can use this tool to take notes at home or at work and then to stamp them with the current date.

Run the QNote program

*Open Project
button*

① Click the Open Project button on the toolbar.

② Select the \Vb6Sbs\Less12 folder, and then double-click the project QNote.

The QNote program loads into the programming environment.

③ If the form is not visible, click the QNote form in the Project window, and then click the View Object button.

The QNote form appears, as shown in the following illustration:

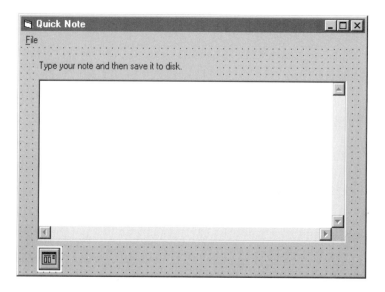

The form contains a large text box object that has scroll bars. It also contains a common dialog object, a label that provides operating instructions for the program, and a File menu containing Save As, Insert Date, and Exit commands. I set the properties as shown in the table on the following page.

Object	Property	Setting
txtNote	Multiline	True
	Name	txtNote
	ScrollBars	3 – Both
	Text	(Empty)
Label1	Caption	"Type your note and then save it to disk."
Form1	Caption	"Quick Note"

Start button

④ Click the Start button on the toolbar.

⑤ Type the following text, or some text of your own, in the text box:

How to Detect Counterfeit Coins

1. **Drop coins on a hard surface. Genuine coins have a bell-like ring; most counterfeit coins sound dull.**

2. **Feel all coins. Most counterfeit coins feel greasy.**

3. **Cut edges of questionable coins. Genuine coins are not easily cut.**

When you've finished, your screen should look similar to the following:

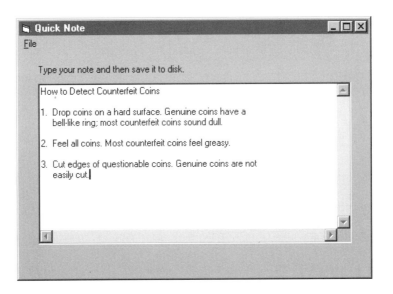

tip
To copy text from the Windows Clipboard into the text box, press Shift+Ins. To copy text from the text box to the Windows Clipboard, select the text by using the mouse and then press Ctrl+C.

Text Files and Strings

12

Now try using the commands on the File menu.

6 On the File menu, click the Insert Date command.

The current date appears as the first line in the text box:

Current date

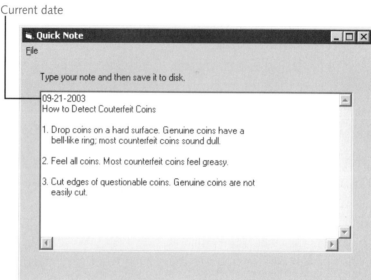

The Insert Date command provides a handy way to include the current date in a file. This is useful if you're creating a diary or a log book.

7 On the File menu, click the Save As command.

8 In the Save As dialog box, select the \Vb6Sbs\Less12 folder if it is not already selected. Then type **Badcoins.txt** in the File Name text box and click Save.

The text of your document is saved in the new text file Badcoins.txt.

9 On the File menu, click the Exit command.

The program stops, and the programming environment returns.

Now you'll take a look at the event procedures in the program.

Examine the QNote program code

1 On the QNote form File menu, click the Insert Date command.

The mnuItemDate_Click event procedure appears in the Code window, as shown in the illustration on the following page.

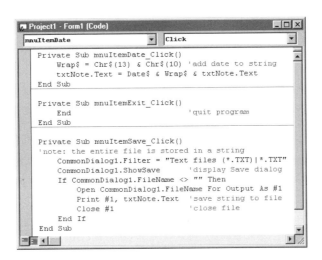

```
Project1 - Form1 (Code)                                    _ □ ×
mnuItemDate              ▼   Click                          ▼
    Private Sub mnuItemDate_Click()
        Wrap$ = Chr$(13) & Chr$(10) 'add date to string
        txtNote.Text = Date$ & Wrap$ & txtNote.Text
    End Sub

    Private Sub mnuItemExit_Click()
        End                          'quit program
    End Sub

    Private Sub mnuItemSave_Click()
    'note: the entire file is stored in a string
        CommonDialog1.Filter = "Text files (*.TXT)|*.TXT"
        CommonDialog1.ShowSave      'display Save dialog
        If CommonDialog1.FileName <> "" Then
            Open CommonDialog1.FileName For Output As #1
            Print #1, txtNote.Text  'save string to file
            Close #1                'close file
        End If
    End Sub
```

The Date$ function retrieves the current date.

This event procedure adds the current date to the text box by linking together, or *concatenating,* the current date (generated by the Date$ function), a carriage return, and the Text property. You could use a similar technique to add the current time or any other information to the text in the text box.

② Take a moment to see how the concatenation statements work, and then examine the mnuItemSave_Click event procedure in the Code window.

This block of statements uses a common dialog object to display a Save As common dialog box, opens the file for output as file number 1, writes the value in the txtNote.Text property to disk by using the Print # statement, and then closes the text file. Note especially the statement

The Print # statement takes a file number as its first argument.

```
Print #1, txtNote.Text
```

which assigns the entire contents of the text box to the open file. Print # is similar to the Print method, except that it directs the output to the specified file rather than to the screen or the printer. The important thing to note here is that the entire file is stored in the txtNote.Text string.

③ Review the Open, Print #, and Close statements, and then close the Code window.

You've finished with the QNote program.

Processing Text Strings with Program Code

As you learned in the preceding exercises, you can quickly open, edit, and save text files to disk with the TextBox control and a handful of well-chosen program statements. Visual Basic also provides a number of powerful statements and functions specifically designed for processing the textual elements in your programs. In this section, you'll learn how to extract useful information from a text string, copy a group of strings into a string array, sort a text box by comparing string expressions, and protect sensitive information by encrypting strings.

Sorting Text

An extremely useful skill to develop when working with textual elements is the ability to sort a list of strings. The basic concepts in sorting are simple. You draw up a list of items to sort, and then compare the items one by one until the list is sorted in ascending or descending alphabetical or numeric order. In Visual Basic, you compare one item to another using the same relational operators that you use to compare numeric values. The tricky part (which sometimes provokes long-winded discussion among computer scientists) is the specific sorting algorithm you use to compare elements in a list. We won't get into the advantages and disadvantages of different sorting algorithms in this lesson. (The bone of contention is usually speed, which only makes a difference when several thousand items are sorted.) Instead, we'll explore how the basic string comparisons are made in a sort. Along the way, you'll learn the skills necessary to sort your own text boxes, list boxes, files, and databases.

Processing Strings with Statements and Functions

The most common task you'll do with strings is concatenating them by using the & (concatenation) operator. For example, the following program statement concatenates three literal string expressions and assigns the result (*Bring on the circus!*) to the string variable slogan$:

```
slogan$ = "Bring" & " on the " & "circus!"
```

You can also modify string expressions by using several special statements, functions, and operators in your program code. The following table lists the most useful keywords; I'll introduce several in subsequent exercises.

Keyword	Description	Example
Ucase	Changes a string's letters to uppercase	`Ucase("Kim")` *returns* `KIM`
Lcase	Changes a string's letters to lowercase	`Lcase("Kim")` *returns* `kim`
Len	Determines the length (in characters) of a string	`Len("Mississippi")` *returns* 11
Right	Returns a fixed number of characters from the right side of a string	`Right("Budapest", 4)` *returns* `pest`
Left	Returns a fixed number of characters from the left side of a string	`Left("Budapest", 4)` *returns* `Buda`
Mid	Returns a fixed number of characters in the middle of a string from a given starting point	`Mid("Sommers", 4, 3)` *returns* `mer`
InStr	Finds starting point of one string within a larger string	`start% = InStr("bobby", "bob")` *returns* 1 to start% variable
String	Repeats a string of characters	`String(8,"*")` *returns* `********`
Asc	Returns the ASCII code of the specified letter	`Asc("A")` *returns* 65
Chr	Returns the character for the specified ASCII code	`Chr$(65)` *returns* `A`
Xor	Performs an "exclusive or" operation on two numbers, returning a value that can be used to encrypt and decrypt text	`65 Xor 50` *returns* 115 `115 Xor 50` *returns* 65

12

Text Files and Strings

What Is ASCII?

To see a table of the codes in the ASCII character set, search for ASCII in the Visual Basic online Help.

Before Visual Basic can compare one character to another in a sort, it must convert each character into a number by using a translation table called the *ASCII character set* (also called the ANSI character set). ASCII is an acronym standing for American Standard Code (for) Information Interchange. Every symbol that you can display on your computer has a different ASCII code. The ASCII character set includes the basic set of "typewriter" characters (codes 32 through 127); special "control" characters, such as tab, linefeed, and carriage return (codes 0 through 31); and the foreign-language and drawing characters in the *IBM extended character set* (codes 128 through 255). For example, the lowercase letter "a" corresponds to the ASCII code 97, and the uppercase letter "A" corresponds to the ASCII code 65. (This fact explains why Visual Basic treats these two characters quite differently when sorting or performing other comparisons.)

tip

In older versions of the BASIC language, string processing functions that returned string values typically had a $ symbol at the end of their name. Thus Chr was named Chr$ and Mid was named Mid$. You can still use these older names in Visual Basic if you like. Both forms call the same function. (Now and then you'll see me use them interchangeably.)

To determine the ASCII code of a particular letter, you can use the Asc function. For example, the following program statement assigns the number 122 (the ASCII code for the lowercase letter "z") to the AscCode% integer variable:

```
AscCode% = Asc("z")
```

Conversely, you can convert an ASCII code to a letter with the Chr function. For example, this program statement assigns the letter "z" to the letter$ string variable:

```
letter$ = Chr(122)
```

The same result could also be achieved if you used the AscCode% variable, defined above:

```
letter$ = Chr(AscCode%)
```

How can you compare one text string or ASCII code with another? You simply use one of the six relational operators Visual Basic supplies for working with textual and numeric elements. These relational operators are shown in the table on the following page.

Operator	Meaning
<>	Not equal
=	Equal
<	Less than
>	Greater than
<=	Less than or equal to
>=	Greater than or equal to

A character is "greater than" another character if its ASCII code is higher. For example, the ASCII value of the letter "B" is greater than the ASCII value of the letter "A", so the expression

```
"A" < "B"
```

is true, and the expression

```
"A" > "B"
```

is false.

When comparing two strings that each contain more than one character, Visual Basic begins by comparing the first character in the first string to the first character in the second string and then proceeds through the strings character by character until it finds a difference. For example, the strings Mike and Michael are the same up to the third characters ("k" and "c"). Because the ASCII value of "k" is greater than that of "c", the expression

```
"Mike" > "Michael"
```

is true.

If no differences are found between the strings, they are equal. If two strings are equal through several characters but one of the strings continues and the other one ends, the longer string is greater than the shorter string. For example, the expression

```
"AAAAA" > "AAA"
```

is true.

Sorting Strings in a Text Box

The following exercise demonstrates how you can use relational operators and several string functions to sort lines of text in a Visual Basic text box. The program is a revision of the QNote utility and features an Open command that allows you to open an existing file. There is also a Sort Text command on the File menu that lets you sort the text currently displayed in the text box.

Because the entire contents of a Visual Basic text box are stored in one string, the program must first break that long string into smaller individual strings. These strings can then be sorted by using the *ShellSort subprogram,* a sorting routine based on an algorithm created by Donald Shell in 1959. To simplify these tasks, I created a standard module that defines a dynamic string array to hold each of the lines in the text box. I also placed the ShellSort subprogram in the standard module so that I could call it from any event procedure in the project. (For more about standard modules, see Lesson 11.)

One interesting part of this program is the routine that determines the number of lines in the text box object. No existing Visual Basic function computes this value automatically. I wanted the program to be able to sort a text box of any size line by line. To accomplish this, I created the code shown below. It uses the Chr function to detect the carriage return character at the end of each line.

```
'determine number of lines in text box object (txtNote)
lineCount% = 0   'this variable holds the total number of lines
charsInFile% = Len(txtNote.Text)   'get total characters in box
For i% = 1 To charsInFile%   'move one char at a time through box
        letter$ = Mid(txtNote.Text, i%, 1) 'put next char in letter$
        If letter$ = Chr(13) Then 'if carriage ret found (end of line!)
            lineCount% = lineCount% + 1 'go to next line (add to count)
            i% = i% + 1    'skip linefeed char (which always follows cr)
        End If
Next i%
```

This routine returns the number of lines in the text box to the lineCount% variable. I can use this value to dimension a dynamic array in the program to hold each individual text string. The resulting array of strings then gets passed to the ShellSort subprogram for sorting, and ShellSort returns the string array in alphabetical order. Once the string array is sorted, I can simply copy it back to the text box by using a For loop.

Run the SortDemo program

1 Click the Open Project button on the toolbar and open the SortDemo project in the \Vb6Sbs\Less12 folder.

2 Click the Start button on the toolbar to run the program.

Start button

3 Type the following text, or some text of your own, in the text box:

Zebra

Gorilla

Moon

Banana

Apple
Turtle

Be sure to press Enter after "Turtle" when you enter text in the text box, so that Visual Basic will calculate the number of lines correctly.

④ On the File menu, click the Sort Text command.

The text you typed is sorted and redisplayed in the text box as follows:

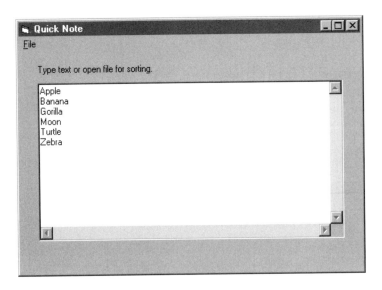

⑤ On the File menu, click the Open command and open the file abc.txt in the \Vb6Sbs\Less12 folder.

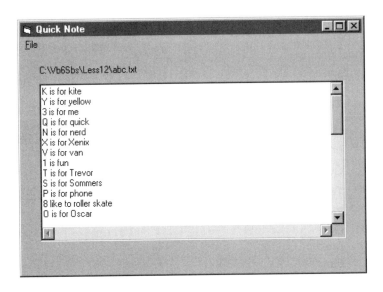

The abc.txt file contains 36 lines of text. Each line begins with either a letter or a number (1–10).

6 On the File menu, click the Sort Text command to sort the contents of the abc.txt file.

The SortDemo program sorts the file in ascending order and displays the sorted list of lines in the text box.

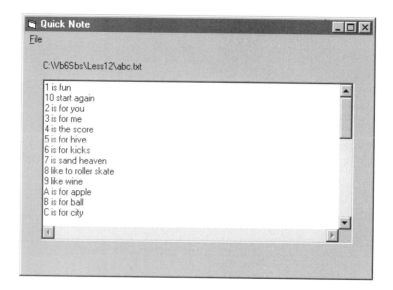

7 Scroll through the file to see the results of the alphabetical sort.

Notice that although the alphabetical portion of the sort ran perfectly, the sort did produce a strange result for one of the numeric entries—the line beginning with the number 10 appears second in the list rather than tenth. What's happening here is that Visual Basic is reading the 1 and the 0 in the number 10 as two independent characters, not as a number. Because we're comparing the ASCII codes of these strings from left to right, the program produces a purely alphabetical sort. If you want to sort numbers with this program, you'll need to store the numbers in numeric variables and compare them without using string functions.

Examine the SortDemo program code

1 On the SortDemo program's File menu, click the Exit command to stop the program.

2 Open the Code window (if it is not already open), and display the code for the mnuItemSortText event procedure.

We've already discussed the first routine in this event procedure, which counts the number of lines in the text box by using the Mid function to search for carriage return codes. The remainder of the event procedure dimensions a string array, copies each line of text into the array, calls a sub-program to sort the array, and displays the reordered list in the text box.

3 Scroll down to the second routine in the event procedure.

Your screen should look similar to the following:

```
Project1 - Form1 (Code)
mnuItemSortText                          Click

  'build an array to hold the text in the text box
  ReDim strArray$(lineCount%) 'create array of proper size
  curline% = 1
  ln$ = ""  'use ln$ to build lines one character at a time
  For i% = 1 To charsInFile%          'loop through text again
      letter$ = Mid(txtNote.Text, i%, 1)
      If letter$ = Chr$(13) Then 'if carriage return found
          curline% = curline% + 1      'increment line count
          i% = i% + 1              'skip linefeed char
          ln$ = ""                 'clear line and go to next
      Else
          ln$ = ln$ & letter$      'add letter to line
          strArray$(curline%) = ln$  'and put in array
      End If
  Next i%

  'sort array
  ShellSort strArray$(), lineCount%
```

The array strArray$ was declared in a standard module (SortDemo.bas) that is also part of this program. By using the Redim statement, I am dimensioning strArray$ as a dynamic array with the lineCount% variable. This statement creates an array that has the same number of elements as the text box has lines of text (a requirement for the ShellSort subprogram). Using a For loop and the ln$ variable, I scan through the text box again, looking for carriage return characters and copying each complete line found to strArray$. After the array is full of text, I call the ShellSort subprogram I created previously in the SortDemo.bas standard module.

The ShellSort subprogram uses the <= relational operator to compare array elements and swap any that are out of order. The subprogram looks like this:

```
Sub ShellSort(sort$(), numOfElements%)
'The ShellSort subprogram sorts the elements of sort$()
'array in descending order and returns it to the calling
'procedure.
span% = numOfElements% \ 2
```

(continued)

Text Files and Strings

12

continued

```
Do While span% > 0
    For i% = span% To numOfElements% - 1
        j% = i% - span% + 1
        For j% = (i% - span% + 1) To 1 Step -span%
            If sort$(j%) <= sort$(j% + span%) Then Exit For
            'swap array elements that are out of order
            temp$ = sort$(j%)
            sort$(j%) = sort$(j% + span%)
            sort$(j% + span%) = temp$
        Next j%
    Next i%
    span% = span% \ 2
Loop
End Sub
```

The method of the sort is to continually divide the main list of elements into sublists that are smaller by half. The sort then compares the tops and the bottoms of the sublists to see if the elements are out of order. If the top and bottom are out of order, they are exchanged. The end result is an array (sort$) that is sorted alphabetically in descending order. To change the direction of the sort, simply reverse the relational operator (change <= to >=).

Protecting Text with Encryption

Now that you've had some experience with ASCII codes, you can begin to write simple encryption routines that shift the ASCII codes in your documents and "scramble" the text to hide it from intruding eyes. This process, known as *encryption*, mathematically alters the characters in a file, making them unreadable to the casual observer. Of course, to use encryption successfully you also need to be able to reverse the process—otherwise, you'll simply be "trashing" your files rather than protecting them. The following exercises show you how to encrypt and decrypt text strings safely. You'll run the Encrypt program now to see a simple encryption scheme in action.

Encrypt text by changing ASCII codes

❶ Click the Open Project button on the toolbar and open the Encrypt project in the \Vb6Sbs\Less12 folder.

❷ Click the Start button on the toolbar to run the program.

3 Type the following text, or some text of your own, in the text box:

**Here at last, my friend, you have the little book long since
expected and promised, a little book on vast matter,
namely, "On my own ignorance and that of many others."**

Francesco Petrarca, c. 1368

4 On the File menu, click the Save Encrypted File command and save the file in the \Vb6Sbs\Less12 folder with the name **padua.txt**.

As you save the text file, the program scrambles the ASCII code and displays the results in the text box shown below.

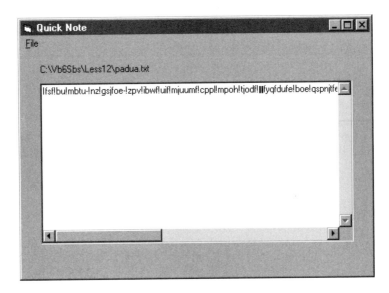

If you open this file in Microsoft Word or another text editor, you'll see the same result—the characters in the file have been encrypted to prevent unauthorized reading.

5 To restore the file to its original form, choose the Open Encrypted File command on the File menu, and open the padua.txt file in the \Vb6Sbs\Less12 folder.

The file appears again in its original form, as shown in the figure on the following page.

12

Text Files and Strings

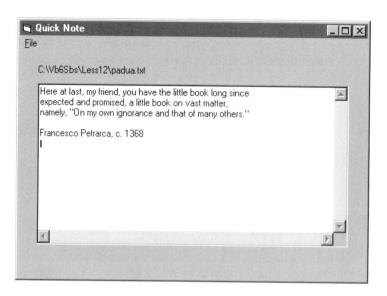

⑥ On the File menu, click the Exit command to end the program.

Examine the Encrypt program code

❶ Open the mnuItemSave event procedure in the Code window to see the program code that produces the encryption you observed when you ran the program.

Although the effect you saw might have looked mysterious, it was a very straightforward encryption scheme. Using the Asc and Chr functions and a For loop, I simply added one number to the ASCII code for each character in the text box, and then saved the encrypted string to the specified text file.

```
'save text with encryption scheme (ASCII code + 1)
encrypt$ = ""    'initialize encryption string
charsInFile% = Len(txtNote.Text) 'find string length
For i% = 1 To charsInFile%    'for each character in file
    letter$ = Mid(txtNote.Text, i%, 1) 'read next char
    'determine ASCII code of char and add one to it
    encrypt$ = encrypt$ & Chr(Asc(letter$) + 1)
Next i%
Open CommonDialog1.FileName For Output As #1 'open file
Print #1, encrypt$              'save encrypted text to file
txtNote.Text = encrypt$         'display encrypted text
```

The crucial statement is

```
encrypt$ = encrypt$ & Chr(Asc(letter$) + 1)
```

This statement determines the ASCII code of the current letter, adds 1 to it, converts the ASCII code back to a letter, and adds it to the encrypt$ string. In the last two statements of this routine, the encrypt$ string is used to pass the encrypted text to a file and display it in the text box.

② Now open the mnuOpenItem event procedure in the Code window to see how the program reverses the encryption.

This program code is nearly identical to that of the Save command, but rather than adding 1 to the ASCII code for each letter, it subtracts 1:

```
'now, decrypt string by subtracting 1 from ASCII code
decrypt$ = ""      'initialize string for decryption
charsInFile = Len(AllText$)   'get length of string
For i% = 1 To charsInFile     'loop once for each char
    letter$ = Mid(AllText$, i%, 1)  'get char with Mid
    decrypt$ = decrypt$ & Chr(Asc(letter) - 1) 'subtract 1
Next i%                        'and build new string
txtNote.Text = decrypt$        'then display converted string
```

This type of simple encryption may be all you need to conceal the information in your text files. However, files encrypted in this way can easily be decoded. By searching for possible equivalents of common characters such as the space character, determining the ASCII shift required to restore the common character, and running the conversion for the entire text file, a person experienced in encryption could readily decipher the file's content. Also, this sort of encryption doesn't prevent a malicious user from physically tampering with the file—for example, simply by deleting it if it is unprotected on your system, or by modifying it in significant ways. But if you're just looking to hide information quickly, this simple encryption scheme could do the trick.

One Step Further ## Using the Xor Operator

The encryption scheme demonstrated above is quite "safe" for text files, because it only shifts the ASCII character code value up by one. However, you'll want to be careful about shifting ASCII codes more than a few characters if you store the result as text in a text file. Keep in mind that dramatic shifts in ASCII codes (such as adding 500 to each character code) will not produce actual ASCII characters that can be decrypted later. For example, adding 500 to the ASCII code for the letter "A" (65) would give a result of 565. This value could not be translated into a character by the Chr function. Instead, Chr would return a Null value, which you could not decrypt later. In other words, you could not recover the encrypted text—it would be lost forever.

A safe way around this problem is to convert the letters in your file to numbers when you encrypt the file, so that you can reverse the encryption no matter how large (or small) the numbers get. If you followed this line of thought, you could then apply mathematical functions—multiplication, logarithms, and so on—to the numbers as long as you knew how to reverse the results.

One of the best tools for encrypting numeric values is already built into Visual Basic. This tool is the *Xor operator,* which performs the "exclusive or" operation, a function carried out on the bits that make up the number itself. The Xor operator can be best observed by using the Immediate window tool, which executes program code immediately when it is entered. You can open the Immediate Window in Visual Basic by choosing the Immediate Window command from the View menu. If you type

```
print asc("A") Xor 50
```

in the Immediate window and press Enter, Visual Basic displays a numeric result of 115 directly below the program statement. If you type

```
print 115 Xor 50
```

in the Immediate window, Visual Basic displays a result of 65, the ASCII code for the letter A (our original value). In other words, the Xor operator produces a result that can be reversed—if the original Xor code is used again on the result of the first operation. This interesting behavior of the Xor function is used in many popular encryption algorithms. It can make your secret files much more difficult to decode.

Encrypt text with the Xor operator

Run the Encrypt2 program now to see how the Xor operator works.

1 Click the Open Project button on the toolbar and open the Encrypt2 project in the \Vb6Sbs\Less12 folder.

2 Click the Start button on the toolbar to run the program.

3 Type the following text (or some of your own) for the encrypted text file:

Rothair's Edict (Lombard Italy, c. 643)

296. On Stealing Grapes. He who takes more than three grapes from another man's vine shall pay six soldi as compensation. He who takes less than three shall bear no guilt.

4 On the File menu, click the Save Encrypted File command, and save the file in the \Vb6Sbs\Less 12 folder with the name **oldlaws.txt**.

The program prompts you for a secret encryption code that will be used to encrypt the file and decrypt it later. (Take note—you'll need to remember this code to decode the file.)

⑤ Type **500**, or another numeric code, and press Enter.

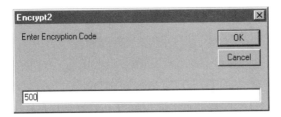

Visual Basic encrypts the text by using the Xor operator and stores it on disk as a series of numbers. You won't see any change on your screen, but rest assured that the program created an encrypted file on disk. (You can verify this with a word processor or text editor.)

⑥ Delete the text in the text box by selecting it with the mouse and pressing the Del key.

Now you'll restore the encrypted file.

⑦ On the File menu, click the Open Encrypted File command.

⑧ Double-click the oldlaws.txt file, type **500** in the encryption code dialog box when it appears, and click OK. (If you specified a different encryption code, enter that instead.)

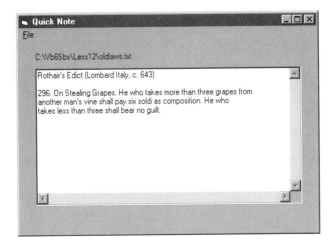

The program opens the file and restores the text by using the Xor operator and the encryption code you specified.

⑨ On the File menu, click the Exit command to end the program.

Examining the Encryption Code

The Xor operator is used in both the mnuOpenItem and the mnuItemSave event procedures. By now, these generic menu processing routines will be quite familiar to you. Specifically, this mnuItemSave event procedure uses the following statements to prompt the user for an encryption code and to encrypt the file based on that code:

```
code = InputBox("Enter Encryption Code", , 1)
If code = "" Then Exit Sub   'if Cancel chosen, exit sub
Form1.MousePointer = 11       'display hourglass
charsInFile% = Len(txtNote.Text) 'find string length
Open CommonDialog1.FileName For Output As #1 'open file
For i% = 1 To charsInFile%  'for each character in file
    letter$ = Mid(txtNote.Text, i%, 1) 'read next char
    'convert to number w/ Asc, then use Xor to encrypt
    Print #1, Asc(letter$) Xor code; 'and save in file
Next i%
Close #1                      'close file when finished
```

In the Print #1 statement, the Xor operator is used to convert each letter in the open text box to a numeric code, which is then saved to disk. (To see how this process is reversed, you can open and review the code for the mnuOpenItem event procedure.) As I mentioned earlier, the look of these encrypted files is no longer textual, but numeric—guaranteed to bewilder even the nosiest snooper. For example, the following illustration shows the encrypted file produced by the preceding encryption routine, displayed in Windows Notepad. (I've enabled Word Wrap so that you can see all of the codes.) Although the file's contents might look like gibberish, you now have the skills to decrypt codes like these. Just be sure not to lose your encryption key!

If you want to continue to the next lesson

●   Keep Visual Basic running, and turn to Lesson 13.

If you want to quit Visual Basic for now

●   On the File menu, click Exit.

    If you see a Save dialog box, click Yes.

Upgrade Notes:
What's Different in Visual Basic .NET?

If you choose to upgrade to Visual Basic .NET in the future, you'll notice some new features related to the topics in this lesson, including the following:

■   In Visual Basic 6.0, you can open and manipulate text files using the Open, Line Input #, Print #, EOF, and Close keywords. In Visual Basic .NET, there is a new set of functions that manage text file operations. These functions are provided by the Microsoft.VisualBasic.FileSystem namespace, and include FileOpen, LineInput, PrintLine, and FileClose.

■   In addition to the built-in Visual Basic .NET functions mentioned above, you can also use the objects in the System.IO namespace to open and manipulate files, browse drives and folders, copy and delete files, process text streams, and complete other file-management tasks. The objects in the System.IO namespace aren't a replacement for the built-in Visual Basic .NET functions listed above, but they do complement them.

■   In terms of string-processing, several of the "classic" Visual Basic 6.0 text functions have been supplemented by new methods in the .NET Framework String class. For example, the new SubString method provides functionality similar to the Visual Basic Mid function, and the ToUpper method is similar to the Visual Basic UCase function. You can use either method to manipulate text strings, but the newer .NET Framework methods are recommended.

12

Text Files and Strings

Lesson 12 Quick Reference

To	Do This
Open a text file	Use the Open...For Input statement. For example: `Open CmnDialog1.FileName For Input As #1`
Get a line of input from a text file	Use the Line Input statement. For example: `Line Input #1, LineOfText$`

Check for the end of a file	Use the EOF function. For example:
	<pre>Do Until EOF(1)
	    Line Input #1, LineOfText$
	    Text$ = Text$ & LineOfText$ & Wrap$
	Loop</pre>

Close an open file	Use the Close statement. For example: `Close #1`

Display a text file	Use the Line Input statement to copy text from an open file to a string variable, and then assign the string variable to a text box object. For example:
	<pre>Do Until EOF(1)
	    Line Input #1, LineOfText$
	    Text$ = Text$ & LineOfText$ & Wrap$
	Loop
	txtDisplay.Text = Text$</pre>

Display an Open dialog box	Use the ShowOpen method of the common dialog object. For example: `CmnDialog1.ShowOpen`
Create a new text file	Use the Open...For Output statement. For example: `Open CmnDialog1.FileName For Output As #1`
Display a Save As dialog box	Use the ShowSave method of the common dialog object. For example: `CmnDialog1.ShowSave`

Lesson 12 Quick Reference

To	Do This
Save text to a file	Use the Print # statement. For example: ```\nPrint #1, txtNote.Text\n```
Convert text characters to ASCII codes	Use the Asc function. For example: ```\ncode% = Asc("A") 'code% equals 65\n```
Convert ASCII codes to text characters	Use the Chr function. For example: ```\nletter$ = Chr(65) 'letter$ equals A\n```
Extract characters from the middle of a string	Use the Mid function. For example: ```\nname$ = "Henry Halvorson"\nstart% = 7\nlength% = 9\nlastName$ = Mid(name$, start%, length%)\n```
Encrypt text	Use the Xor operator and a user-defined encryption code. For example, this code block uses Xor and a user code to encrypt the text in the txtNote text box and to save it in the encrypt.txt file as a series of numbers: ```\ncode = InputBox("Enter Encryption Code", , 1)\nOpen "encrypt.txt" For Output As #1\ncharsInFile% = Len(txtNote.Text)\nFor i% = 1 To charsInFile%\n letter$ = Mid(txtNote.Text, i%, 1)\n Print #1, Asc(letter$) Xor code;\nNext i%\n```
Decrypt text	Request the code the user chose to encrypt the text, and use Xor to decrypt the text. For example, this code block uses Xor and a user code to reverse the encryption created in the preceding example: ```\ncode = InputBox("Enter encryption code", , 1)\nOpen "encrypt.txt" For Input As #1\ndecrypt$ = ""\nDo Until EOF(1)\n Input #1, Number&\n e$ = Chr(Number& Xor code)\n decrypt$ = decrypt$ & e$\nLoop\ntxtNote.Text = decrypt$\n```

13

Managing Access Databases

**ESTIMATED
TIME
40 min.**

In this lesson you will learn how to:

✔ *Create a database viewer by using the Data control.*

✔ *Search for information in a database.*

✔ *Add and delete database records.*

✔ *Back up files by using the FileCopy statement.*

In this lesson you'll learn how to work with information stored in Microsoft Access databases on your system. You'll learn how to open existing databases by using a data object, how to search for specific items, and how to add and delete database records. Microsoft Visual Basic was specifically designed to create custom interfaces, or *front ends,* for existing databases, so if you'd like to customize or dress up data that you've already created with another application, such as Access, you can get started immediately.

Working with Databases in Visual Basic

As you learned in Lesson 3, a database is an organized collection of information stored electronically in a file. You can create powerful databases by using a variety of database products, including Microsoft Access, Microsoft FoxPro, Btrieve, Paradox, and dBASE. You can also use Open Database Connectivity (ODBC) client-server databases, such as Microsoft SQL Server.

Visual Basic can read from and write to a variety of database formats.

If you regularly work with databases—especially the databases listed above— you should consider using Visual Basic as a powerful tool to enhance and display your data. Because Visual Basic implements the same database technology that is included with Microsoft Access (a database engine called Microsoft Jet), you can create basic custom database applications with just a few dozen lines of program code.

In this section, you'll learn how to use a Visual Basic data object to manage a database named Students.mdb that I created in Microsoft Access. Students.mdb contains various tables of academic information that would be useful for a teacher who is tracking student coursework or a school administrator who is scheduling rooms, assigning classes, or building a time schedule. You'll learn how to display several fields of information from this database, and how to write program code that performs useful tasks, such as searching for records, adding new records, deleting unwanted records, and backing up files. When you've finished, you'll be able to put these skills to work in your own database projects.

Creating Customized Database Applications

Customized database applications present personalized lists of database fields and records.

A *customized database application* is a program that takes the fields and records of a database and displays them in a way that is meaningful to a specific group of users. For example, a public library might create a customized version of its card catalog for a group of scientific researchers. Customized database applications typically present a variety of commands to their users. The commands allow users to use viewing filters; to search for, print, add, and delete records; and to make backup copies of the database. Because of the peculiarities of their design or subsequent evolution, some databases are organized in a way that makes them difficult to use in their original form or database environment. With Visual Basic, you can build a custom database application that displays just the information that your users want, and you can supply just the commands they need to process the data.

Using Bound Controls to Display Database Information

Bound controls process database information automatically.

Most objects you create by using the Visual Basic toolbox controls have the built-in ability to display database information. In database terminology, these objects are called *bound controls*. An object is bound to a database when its DataSource property is set to a valid database name and its DataField property is set to a valid table in the database. A *table* is a group of fields and records that you or someone else defined when the database was created. As you learned in Lesson 3, you can link your Visual Basic program to a database by using a data object. After the connection has been established, you can display database information by using objects created with any of the standard controls shown in the following table:

Control	Description
☑	CheckBox
	ComboBox
	Image
A	Label
	ListBox
	PictureBox
abl	TextBox

Using Text Box Objects to Display Data

The following program uses one data object and four text box objects to display four database fields from the Students.mdb database. This program demonstrates how you can create a custom database application to view only the information you want. In this application, the ReadOnly property of the data object is set to True, so the information in the database can be viewed but not changed. To allow users to make changes to the Students.mdb database, you set the ReadOnly property to False by using the Properties window.

13

Access Databases

tip
To keep the original Students.mdb database unchanged, use Microsoft Windows Explorer to make a backup copy of it before you complete the following exercises.

Run the Courses program

1 Start Visual Basic, and open the Courses.vbp project in the \Vb6Sbs\Less13 folder.

The Courses program loads into the programming environment.

View Object button

2 If the form is not visible, click the Courses form in the Project window, and then click the View Object button.

The Courses form appears, as shown in the following illustration:

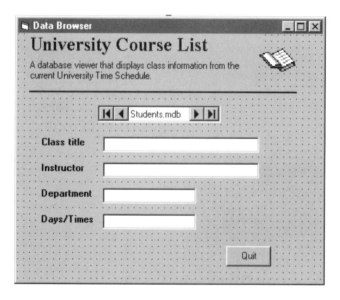

The form contains information about the program, artwork, a data object, several labels and text boxes, and a command button. The property settings on the next page have been made for the data object and the text box objects, which are the objects involved with data transfer. To examine the property settings for the other objects, use the Properties window.

Object	Property	Setting
datStudent	Caption	"Students.mdb"
	Connect	Access
	DatabaseName	"c:\vb6sbs\less03\students.mdb"
	Name	datStudent
	ReadOnly	True
	RecordsetType	0 – Table
	RecordSource	Classes
txtTitle	DataField	ClassName
	DataSource	datStudent
	Name	txtTitle
	Text	(Empty)
txtProf	DataField	Prof
	DataSource	datStudent
	Name	txtProf
	Text	(Empty)
txtDept	DataField	Department
	DataSource	datStudent
	Name	txtDept
	Text	(Empty)
txtTime	DataField	DaysAndTimes
	DataSource	datStudent
	Name	txtTime
	Text	(Empty)

The data object has its RecordSource property set to Classes and its DatabaseName property set to "c:\vb6Sbs\less03\students.mdb". The four text boxes have the same DataSource property (datStudent), but different field settings for the DataField property. These settings establish the basic link between the school database on disk, the data object in the program, and the individual text fields on the form. The other properties fine-tune these basic settings.

tip

The DatabaseName property points to the same Students.mdb file you first used in Lesson 3.

Access Databases

Start button

3 Click the Start button on the toolbar.

The Courses program starts, and the first record of the Classes table in the Students.mdb database appears on the form.

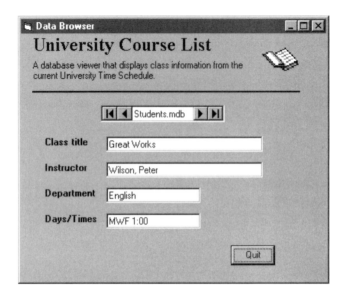

4 Click the inside right arrow on the data control to view the second record in the Classes table.

The record for the course *Relational Database Design* appears on the form. Each time you scroll in the database, all four text boxes are updated.

5 Click the outside right arrow to view the last record in the Classes table.

The record for the psychology course *Deviant Behavior* appears.

6 Click the Quit button to stop the program.

The Courses program ends.

This program contains only one line of program code (the End statement), but it still gives you quite a bit of information. The nice thing about it is that it displays only the database fields *you* want to see. By using a data object and several data-bound text boxes, you can create an effective window into your data.

Using a Recordset Object

A Recordset object represents the data you're working with in the program.

In the Courses program, you used a data property named RecordsetType to identify your database information as a table. In Visual Basic, a *Recordset* is an object representing the part of the database you're working with in the program.

The Recordset object includes special properties and methods that let you search for, sort, add, and delete records. In the following exercise, you'll use a Recordset object to search for course titles in the Students.mdb database and display them.

Search for data in Students.mdb

Before you modify the program, you'll save it under a new name to protect the original.

① On the File menu, click the Save Courses.frm As command. Save the Courses form in the \Vb6Sbs\Less13 folder as **MyFindRec.frm**.

② On the File menu, click the Save Project As command. Save the project as **MyFindRec.vbp**.

CommandButton control

③ Click the CommandButton control, and then create a command button object on the lower-left side of the form.

④ Set the following properties for the command button object:

Object	Property	Setting
Command1	Caption	"Find"
	Name	cmdFind

⑤ Double-click the Find command button to open the cmdFind_Click event procedure in the Code window.

⑥ Type the following program statements in the event procedure:

```
prompt$ = "Enter the full (complete) course title."
'get string to be used in the ClassName field search
SearchStr$ = InputBox(prompt$, "Course Search")
datStudent.Recordset.Index = "ClassName"    'use ClassName
datStudent.Recordset.Seek "=", SearchStr$   'and search
If datStudent.Recordset.NoMatch Then          'if no match
    datStudent.Recordset.MoveFirst           'go to first record
End If
```

The Seek method searches for a matching record.

This event procedure displays a search dialog box to get a course name (SearchStr$) from the user. Next it uses the Seek method to search the database ClassName field from beginning to end until it finds a match or reaches the end of the list. If no match is found, Visual Basic displays a message, and the first record in the Recordset appears in the first text box. The Recordset properties and methods shown on the next page are used in the event procedure.

Access Databases

Recordset property or method	Description
Index	A property used to define the database field that will be used for the search and future sorting.
Seek	A method used to search for the record. In addition to =, the relational operators >=, >, <=, and < can be used to compare the search string to text in the database.
NoMatch	A property set to True if no match is found in the search.
MoveFirst	A method that makes the first record in the Recordset the current record.

Save Project button

7 Close the Code window, and click the Save Project button to save your changes to disk.

Now you'll run the program.

Run the MyFindRec program

Start button

The complete FindRec program is available in the \Vb6Sbs\Less13 folder.

1 Click the Start button on the toolbar.

Information from the Classes table in the Students.mdb database appears in the text boxes, as before.

2 Click the Find button.

The Course Search dialog box appears, as shown in the following illustration.

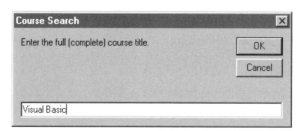

3 Type **Visual Basic** in the dialog box, and then press Enter.

The cmdFind_Click event procedure searches the ClassName field of the database and stops on the record shown in the illustration on the following page.

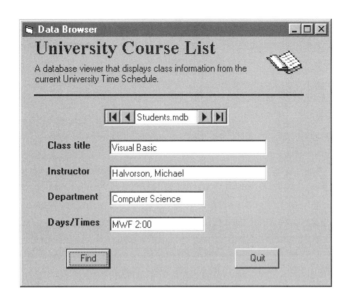

❹ Click the Find button again, type **Norwegian 101**, and press Enter.

The event procedure doesn't find a course named *Norwegian 101,* so the following dialog box appears:

❺ Click OK to close the dialog box.

The program uses the MoveFirst method to display the first record in the table. However, take a close look at this record—does it look like the one you saw when the program first ran? Actually, it's not. A side effect of setting the Index property as shown for the search operation is that it changes the field to be sorted in the table. Originally, this program used the default CourseID field to sort records in the table. CourseID is an internal field in the Students database that tracks the order in which records were created. However, by changing the Index field to ClassName, we directed the Data object to use the ClassName field as the key for the alphabetical sort.

In this demonstration program, the particular order in which records are listed is not significant. However, if you find that a consistent sorting order is important to you, be sure to use the Index property consistently in your code.

⑥ Click the Quit button to end the program.

The program stops, and the programming environment returns.

Adding Records to the Students.mdb Database

To add a new record to a database, you set the data object's ReadOnly property to False in design mode, and then you use the AddNew method in an event procedure to open a new record in the database. When the blank record appears on the form, the user fills in the necessary fields and, when finished, moves to a different record in the database. The easiest way for the user to move to a different record is to click one of the buttons on the data object. When the user moves to a different record, the new record is inserted into the database in alphabetical order.

The following exercise demonstrates how the ReadOnly property and the AddNew method can be used to insert new records in a database. An InputBox function gives the user some visual feedback during the process.

Let users add records to the database

Before you modify the program, you'll save it under a new name to protect the original.

① On the File menu, click the Save MyFindRec.frm As command. Save the MyFindRec form as **MyAddRec.frm**. Use the Save Project As command to save the project as **MyAddRec.vbp**.

② Click the datStudent object (the data object) on the form, and then open the Properties window.

③ Set the datStudent object's ReadOnly property to False.

The ReadOnly property determines how the Students.mdb database will be opened. Setting this property to False lets the user make changes to the database and insert new records.

CommandButton control

④ Click the CommandButton control, and then create a command button object to the right of the Find button on the form.

⑤ Set the following properties for the command button object:

Object	Property	Setting
Command1	Caption	"Add"
	Name	cmdAdd

Your form should look similar to the following illustration:

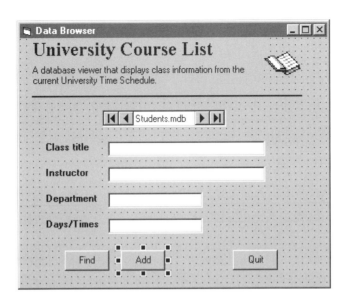

⑥ Double-click the Add button to open the cmdAdd_Click event procedure in the Code window.

⑦ Type the following program statements in the event procedure:

```
prompt$ = "Enter new record, then click the left arrow."
reply = MsgBox(prompt$, vbOKCancel, "Add Record")
If reply = vbOK Then              'if the user clicks OK
    txtTitle.SetFocus             'move cursor to Title box
    datStudent.Recordset.AddNew   'and get new record
End If
```

The AddNew method adds a new record to the database.

The procedure first displays a dialog box containing data entry instructions for the user. The MsgBox function uses the vbOKCancel argument (a numeric constant defined by Visual Basic) to display a dialog box that has OK and Cancel buttons. If the user clicks OK, the AddNew method creates a new record. If the user clicks Cancel, the operation is skipped. The event procedure also uses the SetFocus method to place the cursor in the Title text box. The SetFocus method can be used to activate any object that can receive the focus.

Save Project button

⑧ Close the Code window, and then click the Save Project button on the toolbar to save your changes.

Now you'll use the Add button to add a record to the database.

Run the MyAddRec program

Start button

The complete AddRec program is available in the \Vb6Sbs\Less13 folder.

① Click the Start button on the toolbar.

Information from the Titles table in the Students.mdb database appears in the text boxes.

② Click the Add button.

The Add Record dialog box appears, as shown in the following illustration:

③ Click the OK button.

A new, blank record appears on the form. Enter the information shown in the following illustration for the new record; press Tab to move between fields:

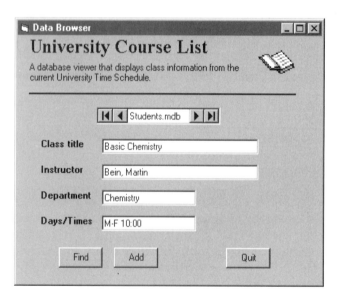

④ When you've finished entering the fictitious record, click the outside-left arrow button on the data object.

The record for a new Basic Chemistry course is inserted in the database as the last record. The program then displays the first record in the database (if you clicked the outside-left arrow on the data object).

⑤ Click the Find button, type **Basic Chemistry**, and press Enter.

The record for Basic Chemistry appears on the form. After the search, the record is first in the alphabetically sorted course list.

⑥ Click the Quit button to end the program.

The program stops, and the programming environment returns. You can use the Add button to add any number of records to the Students.mdb database.

Deleting Records from the Students.mdb Database

To delete a record from a database, you display the record you want to delete and then use the Delete method with the Recordset object to remove the record. Before you open the database in the program, you must set the data object's ReadOnly property to False. (You did this earlier when you used the AddNew method to add a record.) After deleting the record, your code should display another record in the database, because the data object doesn't do this automatically. Usually, the best technique is to use the MoveNext method to display the next record in the database.

The following exercise shows how you can use Visual Basic to delete records from the Students.mdb database. Pay particular attention to the use of the MsgBox function in the program. Because the data object doesn't provide an "undo" feature, it is important that the program verify the user's intentions before it permanently deletes a record from the database.

important

The Delete method permanently deletes a record from the database. Don't give your users access to this method unless you want them to be able to delete records.

Let users delete records from the database

Before you modify the MyAddRec program, you'll save it under a new name to protect the original.

① On the File menu, click the Save MyAddRec.frm As command. Save the MyAddRec form as **MyDelRec.frm**. Use the Save Project As command to save the project as **MyDelRec.vbp**.

2 Click the datStudent object (the data object) on the form, and then open the Properties window.

3 Verify that the datStudent object's ReadOnly property is set to False.

CommandButton control

4 Click the CommandButton control, and then create a command button object to the right of the Add button on the form.

5 Set the following properties for the command button object:

Object	Property	Setting
Command1	Caption	"Delete"
	Name	cmdDelete

Your form should look like the following illustration:

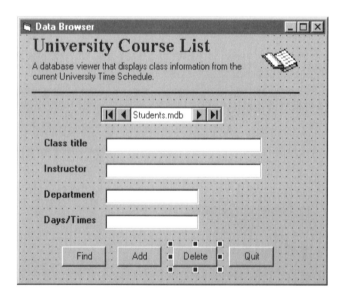

6 Double-click the Delete command button to open the cmdDelete_Click event procedure in the Code window.

7 Type the following program statements in the event procedure:

The Delete method deletes a record from the database.

```
prompt$ = "Do you really want to delete this course?"
reply = MsgBox(prompt$, vbOKCancel, "Delete Record")
If reply = vbOK Then              'if the user clicks OK
    datStudent.Recordset.Delete   'delete current record
    datStudent.Recordset.MoveNext 'move to next record
End If
```

This procedure first displays a dialog box asking whether the user wants to delete the current record. Again, the MsgBox function is used with the vbOKCancel argument to let the user back out of the delete operation if he or she decides not to go through with it. If the user clicks OK, the Delete method deletes the current record, and the MoveNext method displays the next record. If the user clicks Cancel, the delete operation is skipped.

Save Project button

8 Close the Code window, and then click the Save Project button to save your changes.

Now you'll use the Delete button to delete the record for the new Chemistry course from the database.

Run the MyDelRec program

Start button

The complete DelRec program is available in the \Vb6Sbs\Less13 folder.

1 Click the Start button on the toolbar.

Information from the Classes table in the Students.mdb database appears in the text boxes.

2 Use the Find button to display the record for the course entitled Basic Chemistry.

The record you added in the last exercise appears on the form.

important

The following steps will delete this record permanently from the Students.mdb database.

3 Click the Delete button on the form.

The Delete Record dialog box appears, as shown in the following illustration:

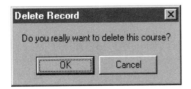

4 Click the OK button to delete the record.

The record for Basic Chemistry is deleted from the database.

13

Access Databases

⑤   Click the Quit button to end the program.

You've finished working with the data object in this lesson. To learn more about writing database applications, type **Recordset property** in the Index tab of the MSDN Library online Help, and review the sample applications included with your Visual Basic software. I'll also discuss more advanced database programming concepts later in the book.

**One
Step
Further   Making a Backup Copy of a File**

*The FileCopy
statement
makes a
backup copy
of a file.*

If you're like most people, the information you keep in databases is very important, and you'd be in a bind if something happened to it. For this reason, you should always make a backup copy of each database you use before making changes to it. If anything goes wrong when you're working with the copy, you can simply replace the copy with the original database. Your backup routine might include using a commercial backup program, Windows Explorer, or a special backup feature of your own in your database program. As an additional safeguard, you can create a backup copy of one or more files from within a Visual Basic program by using the FileCopy statement. FileCopy makes a separate copy of the file (as Windows Explorer's Edit Copy command does) when you use the statement with the following syntax:

```
FileCopy sourcepath destinationpath
```

where *sourcepath* is the pathname of the file you want to copy and *destinationpath* is the pathname of the file you want to create.

tip
FileCopy does not work if the file specified by *sourcepath* is currently open.

In the following exercise, you'll add a backup feature to the MyDelRec program by placing a FileCopy statement in the Form_Load event procedure.

Use FileCopy to make a backup of Students.mdb

First you'll save the MyDelRec program under a new name to protect the original. If MyDelRec isn't open, load DelRec.vbp from disk and display its form.

1 On the File menu, click the Save MyDelRec.frm As command. Save the MyDelRec form as **MyBackup.frm**. Use the Save Project As command to save the project as **MyBackup.vbp**.

2 If the form is not already visible, select the form in the Project window, and click the View Object button.

3 Double-click the form (not an object) to open the Form_Load event procedure in the Code window.

Placing the FileCopy statement in the startup procedure gets the user to back up the database before making any changes to it.

4 Type these program statements in the Form_Load event procedure:

```
prompt$ = _
    "Would you like to create a backup copy of the database?"
reply = MsgBox(prompt$, vbOKCancel, datStudent.DatabaseName)
If reply = vbOK Then  'copy the database if the user clicks OK
    FileNm$ = InputBox$ _
        ("Enter the pathname for the backup copy.")
    If FileNm$ <> "" Then _
        FileCopy datStudent.DatabaseName, FileNm$
End If
```

The FileCopy statement makes a copy of the database.

This routine displays a message box when the program starts, asking the user if he or she would like to make a backup copy of the database. The MsgBox function is used with the vbOKCancel argument to give the user a chance to cancel. This time the DatabaseName property is also used in the MsgBox function to display the name of the database in the dialog box title bar. If the user clicks OK, another message box gets the pathname of the backup file from the user. When the user clicks OK again, the FileCopy statement copies the file.

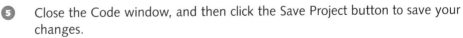

5 Close the Code window, and then click the Save Project button to save your changes.

Save Project button

Now you'll run the program to see how the backup feature works.

Run the MyBackup program

Start button

❶ Click the Start button on the toolbar.

The following dialog box appears on the screen, asking whether you want to make a backup copy of the database:

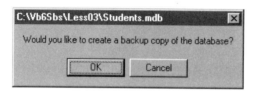

The complete Backup program is available in the \Vb6Sbs\Less13 folder.

❷ Click OK to make a backup copy.

A dialog box appears asking for the pathname of your backup file.

❸ Type **c:\vb6Sbs\less13\mystudents.mdb**, and then click OK.

Visual Basic copies the Students.mdb database to the Lesson 13 folder and gives it the name MyStudents.mdb. Now, if you make any mistakes in the Students.mdb file, you have a backup.

❹ Click the Quit button to end the program.

If you want to boost your productivity

● Take a few minutes to explore the BookInfo utility (bookinfo.vbp) in the \Vb6Sbs\Extras folder on your hard disk. I wrote this program to give you a little more practice with the database concepts in this lesson. The application is an interface for the Biblio.mdb database supplied with most versions of Visual Basic and Microsoft Access. Biblio.mdb contains useful information about database programming books and techniques available from a variety of publishers—I sometimes use it to find a special book I need on new terms and concepts, or to practice my database programming. (The database contains over 10,000 records.) The utility displays a selection of fields and records from the database; you can use the program now to search for your favorite books, or expand it to practice working with databases.

If you want to continue to the next lesson

● Keep Visual Basic running, and turn to Lesson 14.

If you want to quit Visual Basic for now

● On the File menu, click Exit.

If you see a Save dialog box, click Yes.

Upgrade Notes:
What's Different in Visual Basic .NET?

If you choose to upgrade to Visual Basic .NET in the future, you'll notice some new features related to the topics in this lesson, including the following:

- In Visual Basic .NET, the Remote Data Objects (RDO) and ActiveX Data Objects (ADO) data access models have been replaced by the ADO.NET data access model. ADO.NET is based on a recent Microsoft data access technology known as ADO+, and offers a wider range of data access possibilities than its predecessors.

- The introduction of ADO.NET means that the familiar Data control and ADO Data control are no longer available in the Visual Basic .NET Toolbox. To display data on a form in Visual Basic .NET, you typically create a data adapter and a dataset, and then add bound controls to your form that can display the data and allow users to navigate from one record to the next.

- In Visual Basic 6.0, database information is represented in a program by the recordset object, as you have learned in this lesson. In Visual Basic .NET, database information is represented by the Dataset object, a disconnected image of the database table you are accessing. This means that the syntax for data access is a little different in Visual Basic .NET.

- The internal data format of ADO.NET is XML, making it easier to use existing XML data sources, and to use ADO.NET in programs designed for the Web. However, database information is still accessed using the familiar concepts of tables, fields, and records.

13

Access Databases

Lesson 13 Quick Reference

To	Do this
Open a database	Use the Data control to create a data object on a form, and then set its DatabaseName property to the name of the database. Specify the database type by using the Connect property, and specify the record type by using the RecordsetType property.
Open a database in read-only mode	Set the ReadOnly property of the data object to True.
Display a data field in a text box object	Set the DataField and DataSource properties in the text box.
Search for data in a database	Prompt the user for a search string, and then use the Index, Seek, NoMatch, and MoveFirst properties of the Recordset object in an event procedure. For example:

```
Prompt$ = "Enter the full course title."
SearchStr$ = InputBox(Prompt$, "Course Search")
datStudent.Recordset.Index = "ClassName"
datStudent.Recordset.Seek "=", SearchStr$
If datStudent.Recordset.NoMatch Then
MsgBox ("Course not found.")
End If
```

To	Do this
Add a record to a database	Use the AddNew method of the Recordset object. For example:

```
datStudent.Recordset.AddNew
```

| Delete a record from a database | Use the Delete method of the Recordset object. For example: |

```
datStudent.Recordset.Delete
```

| Display the first record of a database | Use the MoveFirst method of the Recordset object. For example: |

```
datStudent.Recordset.MoveFirst
```

| Copy a file | Use the FileCopy statement. For example: |

```
FileCopy datStudent.DatabaseName, FileNm$
```

| Give an object the focus | Use the object's SetFocus method. For example: |

```
txtTitle.SetFocus
```

14

Connecting to Microsoft Office

ESTIMATED TIME
35 min.

In this lesson you will learn how to:

✓ *Use the Object Browser to examine application objects.*

✓ *Use Automation to control the Microsoft Excel 2002 application.*

In this lesson, you'll learn how to control Microsoft Office XP applications from Visual Basic. You'll use the Object Browser to examine the exposed objects in Windows-based programs, and you'll learn how to incorporate the functionality of Office XP applications on your system into Visual Basic programs. In particular, you'll use Microsoft Excel 2002 to create two Automation solutions—you'll build a mortgage payment calculator that uses Excel's Pmt function, and you'll open a worksheet in Excel and perform worksheet-manipulation commands.

Programming Application Objects by Using Automation

Automation is a technology based on the Component Object Model (COM) interoperability standard, an important guideline for designing applications and components that can be used together—even without an understanding of how the underlying components work. The goal of Automation is to use one application's features from within another application. Windows-based applications that fully support Automation make available, or *expose,* their application features as a collection of objects with associated properties and methods. The

Windows-based applications that expose their objects are called *object*, or *server*, applications, and the programs that use the objects are called *controlling*, or *client*, applications. Currently, the following Microsoft applications can be used as either object or controlling applications:

- Microsoft Visual Basic 6, Microsoft Visual Studio .NET
- Microsoft Word 2002, Microsoft Word 2000, Microsoft Word 97
- Microsoft Excel 2002, Microsoft Excel 2000, Microsoft Excel 97, Microsoft Excel 95, Microsoft Excel 5.0
- Microsoft PowerPoint 2002, Microsoft PowerPoint 2000, Microsoft PowerPoint 97
- Microsoft Project 2000, Microsoft Project 97, Microsoft Project 95
- Microsoft Outlook 2002, Microsoft Outlook 2000, Microsoft Outlook 97/98

tip

Microsoft is currently licensing the Visual Basic for Applications programming language, so you'll soon find other applications for Windows that support object Automation and Visual Basic programming techniques.

Using Automation in Visual Basic

In Visual Basic 6, you can create both object and controlling applications that support Automation. Creating object applications that expose their functionality requires that you have Visual Basic Professional or Enterprise Edition and is beyond the scope of this lesson. Creating controlling applications that use the features of object applications is a straightforward process in all editions of Visual Basic.

tip

The applications in Microsoft Office XP (Excel, Word, Access, PowerPoint, and Outlook) are all capable of exposing their functionality through Automation. Because the features and objects provided by each of these applications are unique, you'll need to review the product documentation or online Help for each program before you move beyond the examples I show you here. If you have Microsoft Office installed on your system now, the Visual Basic Object Browser will let you explore the objects, properties, and methods available to you.

In the next few sections, you will learn how to write Visual Basic programs that work with Microsoft Excel 2002, the most commonly-automated Office application. As you work through the exercises, note that the objects, properties, and methods exposed by the Excel application correspond with some regularity to the menu commands and dialog box options provided by Excel. As a general rule, the more you know about the object application, the easier it is to use its Automation features.

The Visual Basic Object Browser

The Visual Basic Object Browser is a viewing utility that has two uses. First, it can display the objects, properties, and methods used by the program you're working on in the Visual Basic programming environment. In addition, the Object Browser can display the objects, properties, and methods available to you from object applications installed on your system. In the following exercise, you'll use the Object Browser to view the Automation objects exposed by Excel.

> **tip**
>
> The illustrations show the Excel 10.0 Object Library included in Excel 2002. If you don't have Excel, use the Object Browser to examine other application objects on your system.

Use the Object Browser to view Excel objects

❶ Start Visual Basic and open a new standard project.

If Visual Basic is already running, click New Project on the File menu.

The Object Browser lets you view objects on your system.

❷ On the Project menu, click the References command.

The References dialog box appears. In the References dialog box, you can include in your project references to any object libraries that are available on your system. Adding references to your project won't make your compiled program any bigger. However, the more references you have, the longer it will take Visual Basic to compile the program. Therefore, Visual Basic adds references to Automation object libraries only if you ask it to.

The References dialog box lets you add references to object libraries to your project.

❸ Select the check box next to the reference titled Microsoft Excel 10.0 Object Library.

You might have to scroll through the list to find the library. (The references are listed in alphabetical order.) Your screen should look like the following:

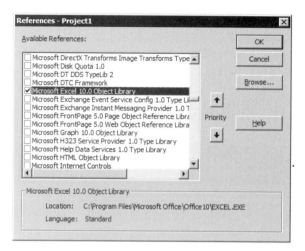

4 Click and add the reference to your project.

Now you're ready to use the Object Browser.

5 On the View menu, click the Object Browser command.

The Object Browser appears, as shown in the following illustration:

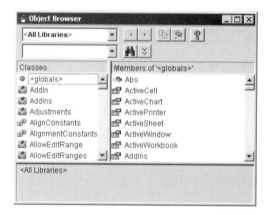

The Object Browser contains a Project/Library drop-down list box, which you can use to display the object libraries included in your project. It also contains a Search Text drop-down list box for creating keyword searches, and a Classes list box that you can use to select a particular object to examine. When you select an object in the Classes list box, the methods, properties, and events featured in the object are listed in the Members list box.

6 Click the down arrow to open the Project/Library drop-down list box, and then click the Excel object library.

A list of the Automation objects exposed by Excel fills the Classes list box.

The object library Help system describes the properties and methods exposed by an object application.

7 Scroll down the list in the Classes list box, and then click the Application object.

A list of the methods and properties associated with the Application object appears in the Members list box. These are the commands Excel provides for manipulating information in worksheets.

8 Click the Quit method in the Members list box.

The syntax for the Quit method appears at the bottom of the Object Browser. This method closes the Excel application when you are done using it. It is a standard feature of most Office Automation sessions. The method syntax shows you the basic arguments for the method (none in this case), and the parent objects for the method (Excel.Application). Your screen should look like the illustration on the following page.

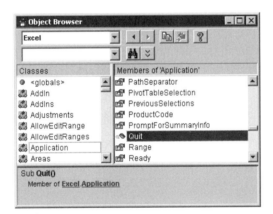

9 Click the question mark button at the top of the Object Browser.

If you installed the Visual Basic for Applications Help file when you ran the Office XP Setup program, a Help file for the Quit method will open in the programming environment, as shown in the illustration on the next page.

This Help file gives you detailed information about how to use the properties and methods in the Excel object library. (If the file doesn't appear, you can run the Office Setup program again to copy it to your system.) Many object applications provide this information along with their object libraries so that Automation programmers can take full advantage of the programmable features of the application. Using the object library Help system is a great way to learn more about Automation programming.

10 Review the article on the Quit method, and then close the Help file.

11 Click the Close button in the Object Browser.

You've finished exploring Automation objects for the time being. Now it's time to put a few Excel Automation commands to work.

Automating Excel from Visual Basic

To use Excel commands in a Visual Basic program, you need to complete the following programming steps. Because these steps apply to other applications too, you can use these guidelines to incorporate into your own programs the functionality of most applications that support Automation.

Step 1 Add references to the necessary object libraries to your project by using the References command.

Step 2 Write your Visual Basic program. In the event procedure in which you plan to use Automation, create an object variable by using the Dim statement, and then load an Automation object into the object variable by using the CreateObject function:

```
Dim xlApp As Object
Set xlApp = CreateObject("Excel.Application")
```

Step 3 Use the methods and properties of the Automation object in the event procedure, consulting the Help files in the Object Browser or the object application documentation for the proper syntax:

```
Dim LoanPayment As Single
LoanPayment = xlApp.WorksheetFunction.Pmt _
    (txtInterest.Text / 12, txtMonths.Text, txtPrincipal.Text)
MsgBox "The monthly payment is " & _
    Format(Abs(LoanPayment), "$#.##"), , "Mortgage"
```

Step 4 When you've finished using the object application, quit the application and release the object variable to conserve memory:

```
xlApp.Quit
Set xlApp = Nothing
```

In the following exercise, you'll create an application that uses the Excel Pmt method to compute loan payments for a mortgage. The arguments for Pmt will be drawn from three text box objects on your form. The program will be built entirely in Visual Basic, using the functionality of Excel through Automation.

tip

The following steps require that you have Excel 2002 (or Office XP, which includes Excel 2002) installed on your system. You may be able to adapt this program code if you have a different version of Excel, but in my experience this is a nontrivial process. For this reason, I don't recommend Automation for programs that will be widely distributed—especially among users with different versions of Office.

Build a mortgage payment calculator

❶ On the Project menu, click the References command. Verify that the reference Microsoft Excel 10.0 Object Library has a check mark next to it, and then click OK.

The Microsoft Excel 10.0 Object Library gives you access to the objects, methods, and properties exposed by the Excel object application. This is the object library reference you added earlier in this lesson.

tip
Object library references must be added to each new project by using the References command.

Now you'll create the form for mortgage payment analyzer and add the program code.

② Resize the form until it appears as a medium-size window that is nearly square.

Label control

③ Use the Label control to create a long label across the top of the form.

④ Below the label, use the TextBox control to draw three text box objects on the right side of the form.

The text box objects will allow you to enter arguments for the Pmt function.

TextBox control

⑤ Using the Label control, draw a label object next to each of the text box objects.

The labels you've created will identify the Pmt function arguments, to help you type them in the right place.

CommandButton control

⑥ Use the CommandButton control to draw a button object at the bottom of the form.

⑦ Set the following properties for the objects on your form:

Object	Property	Setting
Form1	Caption	"Mortgage"
Label1	Alignment	2-Center
	Caption	"Calculate Payments Using Excel"
	Font	MS Sans Serif, Bold, 12-point
Label2	Caption	"Interest"
Label3	Caption	"Months"
Label4	Caption	"Principal"
Text1	Name	txtInterest
	Text	(Empty)
Text2	Name	txtMonths
	Text	(Empty)
Text3	Name	txtPrincipal
	Text	(Empty)
Command1	Caption	"Calculate"

After you set the properties, your form should look like this:

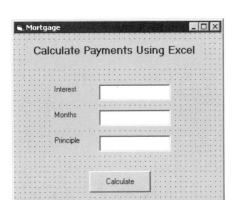

8 Double-click the Calculate command button to open the Command1_Click event procedure. Type the following program code to issue Excel commands via Automation and calculate the home mortgage payment:

```
Dim xlApp As Object
Set xlApp = CreateObject("Excel.Application")
Dim LoanPayment As Single
LoanPayment = xlApp.WorksheetFunction.Pmt _
   (txtInterest.Text / 12, txtMonths.Text, txtPrincipal.Text)
MsgBox "The monthly payment is " & _
   Format(Abs(LoanPayment), "$#.##"), , "Mortgage"
xlApp.Quit
Set xlApp = Nothing
```

These statements create an object variable named xlApp and assign it the Excel.Application object. Then the routine calls the Pmt function through Excel's WorksheetFunction object and converts the mortgage payment returned to a positive number with the Abs (absolute value) function. In Excel, loan payments are typically displayed as negative numbers (debits), but on a Visual Basic form, payments usually look best as positive values.

If one of the required arguments for the Pmt function is missing, the Excel application will generate a runtime error that will cause the Visual Basic application to crash. (My goal here is to demonstrate Excel Automation quickly, not to create a bullet-proof application.) Should you choose to use and expand this program logic, I recommend that you test or *validate* the contents of the text boxes before you call the Excel Pmt function by employing a suitable If...Then...Else decision structure or another test condition.

Finally, the routine displays the mortgage payment using a message box, and closes the Excel application using the Quit method. In this example, the Excel application is never displayed, so the user won't even know it has been loaded.

9 Use the Save Form1 As command to save the form to disk under the name **MyUseExcel.frm**. Use the Save Project As command to save the project to disk under the name **MyUseExcel.vbp**. (Use the \Vb6Sbs\Less14 folder for both files.)

Now you'll run the program to see how Automation works.

Run the MyUseExcel program

Start button

1 Click the Start button on the toolbar.

The program runs in the programming environment.

2 Type **0.09** in the Interest text box.

3 Type **360** in the Months text box.

4 Type **100000** in the Principal text box.

Your form should look like this:

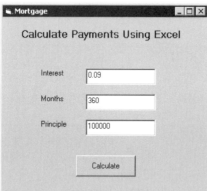

The complete UseExcel program is located on disk in the \Vb6Sbs\Less14 folder.

5 Click the Calculate button.

The program uses Excel to calculate the mortgage payment for a $100,000 loan at 9% interest over 360 months (30 years). As shown in the illustration on the following page, a result of $804.62 appears in a message box on the screen. (Remember that if this were a home mortgage payment, this amount would represent principal and interest only, not taxes, insurance, or other items that are typically included!)

6 Click the OK button, and then make a few more mortgage payment calculations using different values.

7 When you're finished, click the Close button on the form's title bar.

Now let's try an Excel Automation exercise that makes more detailed use of a visible Excel worksheet. G16x05.eps

Manipulate Excel worksheets

1 On the File menu, click the New Project command, and then click OK to open a new, standard application.

In this exercise, you'll issue Excel Automation commands that insert numbers and labels in worksheet cells, apply character formatting, insert a Sum function, and save the worksheet to disk. Using these basic skills, you can generate extensive Excel worksheets from within your Visual Basic applications.

2 On the Project menu, click the References command.

The References dialog box appears.

3 Select the check box next to the reference entitled Microsoft Excel 10.0 Object Library, and click OK.

4 Using the CommandButton control, add a large button object to the form.

5 Use the Properties window to set the Caption property of the command button object to **Create Worksheet**, and then set the Caption property of the form to **Excel Worksheet Builder**.

These are the only properties you'll set for this demonstration program—most of the work will be accomplished in Microsoft Excel.

6 Double-click the Create Worksheet button to open the button's Click event procedure in the Code window.

7 Type the following program statements:

```
'Declare Excel object variables and assign types
Dim xlApp As Excel.Application
Dim xlBook As Excel.Workbook
Dim xlSheet As Excel.Worksheet
Set xlApp = CreateObject("Excel.Application")
Set xlBook = xlApp.Workbooks.Add
Set xlSheet = xlBook.Worksheets(1)
```

Connecting to Office

14

```
' Activate sheet and insert data
xlSheet.Activate
xlSheet.Cells(1, 2) = 5000
xlSheet.Cells(2, 2) = 75
xlSheet.Cells(3, 1) = "Total"
' Insert a Sum formula in cell B3
xlSheet.Range("B3").Formula = "=Sum(R1C2:R2C2)"
' Format cell B3 with bold
xlSheet.Range("B3").Font.Bold = True
' Display the sheet.
xlSheet.Application.Visible = True
' Save the sheet to c:\vb6sbs\less14 folder.
xlSheet.SaveAs ("c:\vb6sbs\less14\myexcelsheet.xls")
' Leave Excel running and sheet open
```

The program code for this event procedure is a little longer than the last Excel Automation sample—it could be much longer still if you choose to add numerous values and formatting options to the worksheet. Of particular interest are the first three variable declarations and the Set statements. Because I'm actually manipulating an Excel worksheet, not just running Excel commands, I need to create three Excel variables and assign them the proper types from the Microsoft Excel 10.0 object library. The first variable declaration references the Excel.Application type, the second variable declaration references the Excel.Workbook type (which relies on Excel.Application), and the third variable declaration references the Excel.Worksheet type (which relies on Excel.Workbook). Take note of these important variable and type declarations for your future work with Excel.

The remainder of the event procedure activates the worksheet and loads values into Excel cells. (Note the difference between how numeric and string values are entered.) A formula is then entered in cell B3 that uses a Sum function to total cells B1 and B2, and the result is formatted with Bold type. At this point, the event procedure displays the active worksheet, and the worksheet is saved to disk in the c:\vb6sbs\less14 folder. (If the file already exists, a dialog box will appear asking you if you want to overwrite the file, which you may do.) At this point the event procedure ends, and the Excel application remains open and visible, inviting the user to complete additional Excel tasks. (Note that the Visual Basic program, too, continues running.) We could also have closed the program using the Quit method, as we did in the first Excel Automation sample.

8   Use the Save Form1 As command to save the form to disk under the name **MyExcelTasks.frm**. Use the Save Project As command to save the project to disk under the name **MyExcelTasks.vbp**. (Use the \Vb6Sbs\Less14 folder for both files.)

Run the Excel Sheet Tasks program

1   Click the Start button on the toolbar.

The simple form for your project appears, as shown here:

2   Click the Create Worksheet button.

Visual Basic starts Excel and quickly performs the Automation tasks you requested. After the Visible property is set to True, an Excel worksheet appears on your screen, as shown here:

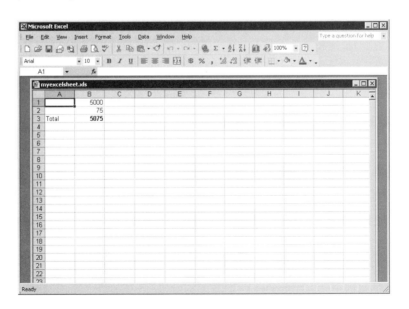

Note the position and content of the cells in columns A and B—the Automation commands have completed their work, and the Sum function produced the correct result in cell B3 (5000 + 75 = 5075). The current filename also appears on the Excel title bar (myexcelsheet.xls).

The complete ExcelTasks program is located in the c:\Vb6Sbs\Less14 folder.

❸ Continue to manipulate the Excel worksheet if you like, and then close the application. Note that the program you have written will work whether the Excel application is open or not.

❹ Click the Close button on your Visual Basic program to stop it, too.

That's it! You've learned the essential skills to automate a useful application in the Microsoft Office XP software suite. The Object Browser will teach you more about the details of the application objects if you choose to explore Automation on your own. And, more importantly, you've mastered all the fundamental concepts in introductory Visual Basic programming. You are now ready to move on to more advanced topics. Congratulations on a job well done!

If you want to quit Visual Basic for now

● On the File menu, click Exit.

If you see a Save dialog box, click Yes.

Upgrade Notes:
What's Different in Visual Basic .NET?

If you choose to upgrade to Visual Basic .NET in the future, you'll notice some new features related to the topics in this lesson, including the following:

■ In Visual Basic .NET, the built-in Toolbox controls are no longer designed to COM specifications, and Visual Basic .NET programmers must follow specific steps to add older ActiveX controls (including those from Visual Basic 6 and Microsoft Office) to their toolboxes. To integrate older controls in Visual Basic .NET, you click the Add Reference command on the View menu, then add a reference to the component using the COM tab in the Add Reference dialog box. When you select a COM component, Visual Basic .NET automatically generates a "wrapper" with the necessary types and classes, and you can use it as you did in Visual Basic 6.

- Microsoft Office XP applications and components (which continue to conform to COM specifications) can still be used in Visual Basic .NET applications through the Automation techniques you have learned in this lesson. The syntax is slightly different. For example, the Set keyword is no longer used and the CType keyword is typically utilized during the assignment of an application object. In addition, application objects can no longer be assigned at runtime, but rather they must be assigned at compile time. (In other words, Visual Basic .NET programs should be designed to perform *early* rather than *late* binding when Automation is used.)

- In Visual Basic 6, you can use the OLE control to add application objects to your Visual Basic forms. (You experimented with this feature in Lesson 3.) However, the OLE control is no longer included in the Visual Basic .NET Toolbox, so you shouldn't rely on the OLE object if you plan to upgrade programs to Visual Basic .NET.

- In Visual Basic 6, some programmers use the Shell function to start Windows applications from within a Visual Basic program, as an alternative to the more sophisticated Automation techniques I introduced in this lesson. In Visual Basic .NET, the ad-hoc starting and stopping of applications is more easily handled by the new Process component, which is located on the Components tab of the Visual Basic .NET Toolbox.

Lesson 14 Quick Reference

To	Do this
Select an application library	On the Project menu, click the References command. Select the check box next to the desired application or applications.
View application objects that support Automation	On the View menu, click the Object Browser command. Select the objects you want to examine in the Project/Library drop-down list box.

Create an object variable in a program	Use the Dim and Set statements. For example:
	`Dim xlApp As Object`
	`Set xlApp = CreateObject`
	`("Excel.Application")`

Lesson 14 Quick Reference

To	Do this

Access application features by using Automation	Create an object variable, and then reference the methods or properties of the object. For example:
	
	`xlSheet.Activate`
	
	`xlSheet.Cells(1, 2) = 5000`

Release the memory used by an object variable	Use the Set statement and the keyword Nothing with the variable name. For example: `Set xlApp = Nothing`

PART 5

Professional
Edition Tools
and Techniques

15

Word Processing with the Rich Textbox Control

ESTIMATED TIME
40 min.

In this lesson you will learn how to:

✔ *Install and use the ActiveX controls in Visual Basic Professional Edition.*

✔ *Integrate word-processing functionality with the Rich Textbox control.*

✔ *Use the Windows clipboard for cut-and-paste operations.*

✔ *Open, save, and print RTF files with menu commands.*

✔ *Track unsaved changes in a document with the Change event.*

In Parts 1 through 4, you learned the fundamental programming skills that are applicable to each edition in the Microsoft Visual Basic 6 family of products (Visual Basic 6 Learning Edition, Visual Basic 6 Professional Edition, and Visual Basic 6 Enterprise Edition). In Parts 5, 6, and 7 you will explore the specific advanced features included in Visual Basic 6 Professional Edition. I have divided these useful "professional" software development tools into three basic categories: Professional ActiveX controls, Internet and Dynamic HTML applications, and advanced database management features. You'll learn how to create powerful Visual Basic applications that exploit each of these vital technologies.

In Lesson 15, you'll learn how to install and use the impressive collection of ActiveX controls included in Visual Basic 6 Professional Edition. (These controls are also included in Visual Basic 6 Enterprise Edition, so if you decide to upgrade to the high-end product someday, you'll be on familiar ground.) After an introduction to this potent family of ActiveX controls, you'll get down to business with the

Rich Textbox control—a powerful tool that helps you add word-processing support to your application. Rich Textbox, a more sophisticated version of the standard Textbox control in the Visual Basic toolbox, allows you to include advanced formatting information with your text, streamlines file operations and searches, and stores its information in a sophisticated document format known as RTF (Rich Text Format). As you'll see in the RTFEdit utility I've created, you can quickly build a program with Rich Textbox that looks and operates just like WordPad, the RTF text editor included with Windows.

Installing Professional Edition ActiveX Controls

When you installed the Visual Basic Professional Edition software, part of the setup process included copying a large collection of .ocx files called *ActiveX controls* to your \Windows\System folder or System32 folder. The setup process also involved registering these controls in your system registry, so that Visual Basic and other applications would know how to load the controls when you needed them. Most of the .ocx files that were installed represent individual ActiveX controls that you can add to the Visual Basic toolbox. However, a few .ocx files represent collections of controls that are organized around a particular theme. For example, the Windows Common Control (mscomctl.ocx) contains nine toolbox controls that you can use to add professional-looking interface options, such as toolbars, progress bars, and status windows to your application.

The following table lists all the ActiveX controls that are included in the Professional Edition of Visual Basic 6. Each of these controls is documented fully in the Visual Basic online Help. In the following lessons, I will use several of these controls to create interesting and useful utilities.

ActiveX control	Filename	Description
ADO data	msadodc.ocx	Provides access to database information through the ActiveX Data Object (ADO) format.
Animation	mscomct2.ocx	Creates animation effects by playing .avi files (sound not supported). (In Windows Common Control-2.)
Chart	mschart.ocx	Allows you to chart the data stored in spreadsheets and databases.
Communications	mscomm32.ocx	Provides serial communications for your application through the serial port.

ActiveX control	Filename	Description
Cool bar	comct332.ocx	A container control that can be used to create user-configurable toolbars similar to those in Microsoft Internet Explorer. (In Windows Common Control-3.)
Data repeater	msdatrep.ocx	Displays several instances of an ActiveX control in handy rows (especially useful for displaying different instances of a database).
DTPicker	mscomct2.ocx	Provides a drop-down calendar for quick entry of dates and times. (In Windows Common Control-2.)
Flat scrollbar	mscomct2.ocx	Standard scroll bar functionality with a slick "flat" look. (In Windows Common Control-2.)
Flex grid	msflxgrd.ocx	Adds spreadsheet functionality to your application. Especially useful for displaying database information.
Hierarchical flex grid	mshflxgd.ocx	Enhanced version of the Flex grid control that can display hierarchical recordsets (recordsets created from several different tables).
Image combo	mscomctl.ocx	Similar to the standard combo box control, but with support for images. (In Windows Common Control.)
Image list	mscomctl.ocx	Holds a collection of images that can be used by other controls. (In Windows Common Control.)
Internet transfer	msinet.ocx	Allows you to connect to the Internet and download via the HTTP and FTP protocols.
List view	mscomctl.ocx	Displays data in "Windows Explorer" format using icons, small icons, list, or report views. (In Windows Common Control.)
MAPI	msmapi32.ocx	Provides access to the MAPI messages and MAPI session controls, which establish and process mail-related tasks through the Messaging Application Program Interface (MAPI).
Masked edit	msmask32.ocx	A text box that places constraints on the data input by the user.

15

The Rich Textbox Control

ActiveX control	Filename	Description
MonthView	mscomct2.ocx	Allows the end user to pick dates and contiguous ranges of dates from a graphic representation of a calendar. (In Microsoft Common Control-2.)
Multimedia MCI	mci32.ocx	Manages the recording and playback of MCI multimedia devices.
Picture clip	picclp32.ocx	Displays one part of a bitmap.
Progress bar	mscomctl.ocx	Uses blocks to display the progress of an operation graphically. (In Windows Common Control.)
Rich textbox	richtx32.ocx	Allows the user to type, edit, and format text in Rich Text Format (RTF).
Slider	mscomctl.ocx	Provides both an input device with "tick marks" and a method for displaying the progress of an operation. (In Windows Common Control.)
Status bar	mscomctl.ocx	Displays a status bar window with up to 16 panels for program information. (In Windows Common Control.)
Sys info	sysinfo.ocx	Monitors various parameters of the Windows operating system.
Tab strip	mscomctl.ocx	Similar to the Tabbed dialog control. (In Windows Common Control.)
Tabbed dialog	tabctl32.ocx	Presents dialog box information through a series of "tabbed" windows.
Toolbar	mscomctl.ocx	Creates a toolbar with individual buttons. (In Windows Common Control.)
Tree view	mscomctl.ocx	Displays hierarchical information in nested "trees." (In Windows Common Control.)
UpDown	mscomct2.ocx	Displays a pair of arrow buttons that lets the user scroll through a list or set the value of an associated "buddy" control. (In Windows Common Control-2.)
Windowless	mswless.ocx	Special, memory-conserving versions of the nine standard toolbox controls. Use windowless controls when you don't need to use memory addresses called "handles" in your code—they will save your system resources.

ActiveX control	Filename	Description
Winsock	mswinsck.ocx	Provides access to TCP (transfer control protocol) and UDP (user datagram protocol) network services.

Adding Professional Edition ActiveX Controls to the Toolbox

To add a Professional Edition ActiveX control to the toolbox, you follow a three-step process.

1 On the Project menu, click the Components command, and then click the Controls tab.

When you issue the Components command, Visual Basic will check the system registry and display all the ActiveX controls that are available on your system (not just the controls installed by Visual Basic).

2 Select the check box to the left of the control name you want to add to the toolbox.

3 Click OK to close the Components dialog box and add the ActiveX control.

Visual Basic displays the control you specified in the toolbox.

Introducing the Rich Textbox Control

One of the most useful ActiveX controls in Visual Basic Professional Edition is the Rich Textbox control, which allows you to add advanced word processing features to your application. Unlike the simple Textbox control included in the standard toolbox, the Rich Textbox control lets you format text by using a popular encoding standard called RTF. Like HTML (Hypertext Markup Language), RTF adds special formatting codes to your text to convey font information, point size, type style, paragraph style, alignment, and other common formatting options.

Add the Rich Textbox control to the toolbox

Before you work with the Rich Textbox control, you must add it to the toolbox.

1 On the Project menu, click the Components command, and then click the Controls tab.

Visual Basic displays the ActiveX controls installed in your system.

2 Scroll down the list of controls until you see the name Microsoft Rich Textbox Control 6.0.

❸   Click the check box next to the control name, and then click OK.

Visual Basic adds the Rich Textbox control to your toolbox. Your toolbox will now look something like this:

Creating a text box with the Rich Textbox control is similar to creating a text box with the standard Textbox control. You simply click the Rich Textbox control in the toolbox, and then drag on your form to create a text box of the appropriate size for your application. However, the differences between the controls become obvious when you start manipulating the Rich Textbox control's properties and methods. The following demonstration program highlights the important differences.

Run the RTFEdit program

To explore the powerful capabilities of the Rich Textbox control, try running the RTFEdit program, a utility I created in Visual Basic that mimics much of the functionality of the Windows WordPad program.

❶   Open the RTFEdit.vbp project, located in the C:\Vb6Sbs\Less15 folder.

If you are prompted to save the changes in your empty project (which contains a reference to the Rich Textbox control), click No.

Start button

❷   Click the Start button on the toolbar to run the program.

The RTFEdit program appears on the screen, as shown in the illustration on the following page.

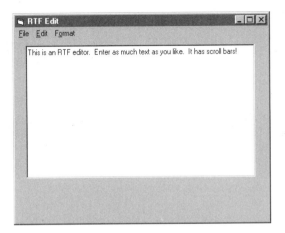

Use the Format menu commands

First you'll experiment with the text formatting capabilities of the program.

①   Select the first sentence displayed in the text box (*This is an RTF editor.*), and then click the Format menu.

The formatting commands provided by the RTF editor appear on the menu:

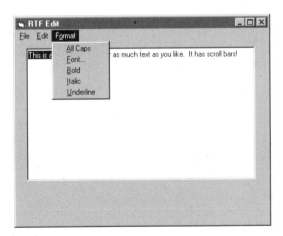

I created each menu command in the Menu Editor, and wrote an event procedure for each command in the Code window.

②   Click the All Caps command on the Format menu.

The RTF editor changes the selected text to all capital letters.

③   Reselect the first sentence and click the Font command on the Format menu.

The Font dialog box opens as shown in the illustration on the following page.

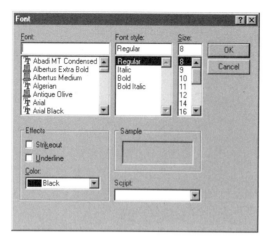

④ Specify a new font, the strikeout style, a larger point size, and a new color, and then click OK.

The RTF editor formats the text as you requested.

⑤ Now practice using the Bold, Italic, and Underline commands on the Format menu.

These commands are toggles—you can repeat them to reverse your formatting choice for the selected text. Just like WordPad, the RTF editor gives you full RTF formatting capabilities!

Use the Edit menu commands

Now you'll try the four commands on the Edit menu.

① Select the last sentence in the text box (*It has scroll bars!*).

② On the Edit menu, click the Cut command.

The text is copied to the Windows clipboard and removed from the text box.

③ Move the insertion point to the end of the paragraph, press Enter, and then click the Paste command on the Edit menu.

The text is pasted from the clipboard into the text box.

④ Select the first sentence again (*This is an RTF editor.*), and then choose the Copy command from the Edit menu.

The RTF editor copies the text with all of its formatting to the clipboard.

⑤ Press the Home key, and then click the Paste command on the Edit menu to paste the text into the text box.

Now you'll try searching for text.

6 On the Edit menu, click the Find command.

7 Type the acronym **RTF** in the input box and click OK.

The RTF editor highlights the first occurrence of the acronym in the text box.

tip
If you select text in the text box before choosing the Find command, the RTF editor searches for the first occurrence of the word in the selection.

Use the File menu commands

Now you'll try using the file-oriented commands in the RTF editor.

1 On the File menu, click the Save As command.

The RTF editor displays a Save As dialog box prompting you for the name of the file.

2 Type **sample.rtf** and click Save. (You may also specify a different folder if you wish.)

The program saves the file in RTF format in the location you specified.

important
Be sure to type the .rtf extension or click the Rich Text Format type in the Save As Type list box to register the file as an RTF file in Windows Explorer. If you don't, the file won't appear as an RTF file in the Open dialog box.

3 On the File menu, click the Close command.

The RTF editor clears the text box. (If you have unsaved changes, you'll be prompted to save them.)

4 On the File menu, click the Open command.

The RTF editor displays an Open dialog box, and lists the RTF files in the current folder.

5 Double-click the sample.rtf file to display it again.

6 If you have a printer attached to your system, turn it on, and then click the Print command on the File menu.

The RTF editor sends a copy of the document to the printer.

7 On the File menu, click the Exit command.

The program closes. If you have unsaved changes, the RTF editor will prompt you to save them.

Event Procedures that Handle RTF Formatting

In most respects, the RTFEdit program is a fully functional word-processing application. If you need this kind of functionality in your Visual Basic programs, you can add it quickly with the Rich Textbox and Common Dialog controls. Let's take a look at the source code that produced these results, beginning with the menu commands on the Format menu. (Open each event procedure in the Code window as I discuss it in the text.)

The All Caps Command

In the Rich Textbox control, the SelText property represents the text that is currently selected in the text box. One of the simplest formatting activities is to use one of Visual Basic's built-in functions to modify this text, such as UCase, which converts lowercase characters to uppercase. (If the text is already in uppercase, the function has no effect.) When the user clicks the All Caps command on the Format menu, Visual Basic executes the following event procedure to convert the text:

```
Private Sub mnuAllcapsItem_Click()
    RichTextBox1.SelText = UCase(RichTextBox1.SelText)
End Sub
```

To convert the text to lowercase, simply substitute the LCase command for the UCase command.

The Font Command

The Font command uses the ShowFont method of the Common Dialog control to open a standard Font dialog box and return the selected information to the RTFEdit program. You learned how to use the Open, Save As, and Color standard dialog boxes provided by the Common Dialog control earlier in this book; opening the Font dialog box is a similar process. In the source code, notice that the properties returned by the CommonDialog1 object are immediately assigned to similar properties in the RichTextBox1 object (the text box in your program). The Rich Textbox control can produce any formatting style offered by the Font dialog box. The source code is shown on the following page.

```
Private Sub mnuFontItem_Click()
    'Force an error if the user clicks Cancel
    CommonDialog1.CancelError = True
    On Error GoTo Errhandler:
    'Set flags for special effects and all available fonts
    CommonDialog1.Flags = cdlCFEffects Or cdlCFBoth
    'Display font dialog box
    CommonDialog1.ShowFont
    'Set formatting properties with user selections:
    RichTextBox1.SelFontName = CommonDialog1.FontName
    RichTextBox1.SelFontSize = CommonDialog1.FontSize
    RichTextBox1.SelColor = CommonDialog1.Color
    RichTextBox1.SelBold = CommonDialog1.FontBold
    RichTextBox1.SelItalic = CommonDialog1.FontItalic
    RichTextBox1.SelUnderline = CommonDialog1.FontUnderline
    RichTextBox1.SelStrikeThru = CommonDialog1.FontStrikethru
Errhandler:
    'exit procedure if the user clicks Cancel
End Sub
```

The Bold, Italic, and Underline Commands

The Bold, Italic, and Underline commands on the Format menu are quite easy to manage in the Rich Textbox control. The only trick is to make sure that each command works as a *toggle*, a command that switches the current formatting state to the opposite state. For example, the Bold command should change bold text to regular text and regular text to bold text. This behavior is easily accomplished by using the Not logical operator in your program statements, which reverses the Boolean value stored in the SelBold, SelItalic, and SelUnderline properties. Use the following code:

```
Private Sub mnuBoldItem_Click()
    RichTextBox1.SelBold = Not RichTextBox1.SelBold
End Sub
```

```
Private Sub mnuItalicItem_Click()
    RichTextBox1.SelItalic = Not RichTextBox1.SelItalic
End Sub
```

```
Private Sub mnuUnderlineItem_Click()
    RichTextBox1.SelUnderline = Not RichTextBox1.SelUnderline
End Sub
```

Editing Text with the Windows Clipboard

When you create a full-featured word-processing application, you'll need to give the user access to the standard text editing commands, such as Cut, Copy, and Paste, on the Edit menu. The most convenient way to accomplish this is to use the SetText and GetText methods of the Clipboard object, which connect your program to the data on the Windows clipboard. In this section, you'll examine the source code I used to cut, copy, and paste text with the Clipboard object. You'll also explore how to search for text with the Find method. (I recommend that you examine each event procedure in the Code window as you read this text.)

The Cut, Copy, and Paste Commands

The Edit menu in the RTFEdit program contains four commands: Cut, Copy, Paste, and Find. The first three operations are facilitated by the SetText and GetText methods of the Clipboard object and the SelRTF property of the rich text box object. At runtime, the rich text box object's SelRTF property contains the complete text and formatting information stored in the text box. When you're working with the Windows clipboard, this is the property that holds your data during cut, copy, and paste operations. In addition, the Clipboard object's SetText and GetText methods are used to copy text to and from the clipboard, respectively. The only real difference between the Copy and Cut commands is that the Cut command deletes the selected text from the text box after the copy operation, and the Copy command does not. Here is the code you need to use:

```
Private Sub mnuCopyItem_Click()
    Clipboard.SetText RichTextBox1.SelRTF
End Sub

Private Sub mnuCutItem_Click()
    Clipboard.SetText RichTextBox1.SelRTF
    RichTextBox1.SelRTF = ""
End Sub

Private Sub mnuPasteItem_Click()
    RichTextBox1.SelRTF = Clipboard.GetText
End Sub
```

The Find Command

Most word-processing applications provide basic text-searching functionality, and the RTFEdit program is no exception. The Find command is facilitated by the Find method of the rich text box object, which searches for a specified text string in the text box. The exact specifications of the search are controlled by the following options:

```
RichTextBox1.Find(string, start, end, options)
```

The *string* argument specifies the text that you want to find in the text box. The *start* argument is the starting position of the search (an integer from 1 to the number of characters in the document). The *end* argument is the ending position of the search. In the *options* argument is one of the following constants: rtfWholeWord (whole word search), rtfMatchCase (case-sensitive search), rtfNoHighlight (highlight found string in document).

The following event procedure demonstrates how you can search for the first matching word in a text box by prompting the user with an InputBox function. The Span method selects the word that is found.

```
Private Sub mnuFindItem_Click()
    Dim SearchStr As String   'text used for search
    Dim FoundPos As Integer   'location of found text
    SearchStr = InputBox("Enter search word", "Find")
    If SearchStr <> "" Then   'if search string not empty
        'find the first occurrence of the whole word
        FoundPos = RichTextBox1.Find(SearchStr, , , _
            rtfWholeWord)
        'if the word is found (if not -1)
        If FoundPos <> -1 Then
        'use Span method to select word (forward direction)
            RichTextBox1.Span " ", True, True
        Else
            MsgBox "Search string not found", , "Find"
        End If
    End If
End Sub
```

Managing File Operations with the Rich Textbox Control

Finally, you'll probably want to add basic file management features to your RTF application. I accomplished this in my program by adding a File menu with Open, Close, Save As, Print, and Exit commands. Examine the following source code now in the Code window to see how the essential File management tasks are handled with the rich text box object. You'll find that the process is a little different from the procedure I recommended for managing text files with the Textbox control in Lesson 12.

The Open Command

Opening files in a rich text box object is made easy by using the object's LoadFile method, which opens the specified file in the text box. Be sure to set the ScrollBars property to rtfVertical in the Properties window if you want to view documents longer than one page.

When you load a file in a text box, you should specify whether the file is in RTF or text format. This distinction is controlled by the rtfRTF and rtfText options in the LoadFile method. When a document is stored in RTF, it contains a number of formatting codes that instruct the loading application how to display the file's formatting information. If you load an RTF file as "text," the codes themselves are displayed in the text box. (For an example of this, see the exercise in "One Step Further" at the end of this lesson.)

The Open command in the RTFEdit program sets the CancelError property of the common dialog object to True. If the user clicks the Cancel button in the Open dialog box, the event procedure will therefore skip the loading operation. The ShowOpen method displays the Open dialog box to allow the user to specify which file to load. The LoadFile method opens the file returned by the common dialog object. I also specified the rtfRTF argument so that the rich text box object will convert any RTF codes it sees to the proper formatting.

```
Private Sub mnuOpenItem_Click()
    CommonDialog1.CancelError = True
    On Error GoTo Errhandler:
    CommonDialog1.Flags = cdlOFNFileMustExist
    CommonDialog1.ShowOpen
    RichTextBox1.LoadFile CommonDialog1.FileName, rtfRTF
Errhandler:
    'if Cancel clicked, then exit procedure
End Sub
```

The Close Command

The purpose of the Close command on the File menu is simply to close the open RTF file by clearing the contents of the text box with the Text method and an empty string argument (""). However, I also decided to add several lines of code to handle an important closing condition: determining if there are currently any unsaved changes in the document, and if so, prompting the user to save them. To handle this condition, I created a public variable named UnsavedChanges of type Boolean in the Declarations section:

```
Dim UnsavedChanges As Boolean
```

The variable is of type Boolean because I want it to maintain a True or False value to reflect the current state (saved or unsaved) of any changes to the document. UnsavedChanges will be set to True if there are unsaved changes in the document and False if there are not. The program manages this editorial state by using a handy Rich Textbox event called Change. Whenever the text is changed or the formatting is modified in the text box, the rich text box object triggers the Change event and executes the code in the RichTextBox1_Change event procedure. By placing a statement that sets the value of UnsavedChanges to True in this procedure, I am able to check for unsaved changes—the problem I want to catch—when the user clicks the Close and Exit commands. (I could also check this variable in the Form_Unload procedure, to stop the user from closing the form without saving its contents.) The code for the RichTextBox1_Change event procedure is the following:

```
Private Sub RichTextBox1_Change()
    'Set public variable UnsavedChanges to True each time
    'the text in the Rich textbox is modified.
    UnsavedChanges = True
End Sub
```

In the event procedure for the Close menu command, I check the value of the UnsavedChanges variable. If it evaluates to True (if there are unsaved changes), I prompt the user to save those changes via a message box. If the user decides to save the changes, the Save As dialog box requests a filename. The file is then saved with the SaveFile method:

```
Private Sub mnuCloseItem_Click()
    Dim Prompt As String
    Dim Reply As Integer
    'jump to error handler if the Cancel button is clicked
    CommonDialog1.CancelError = True
    On Error GoTo Errhandler:
    If UnsavedChanges = True Then
        Prompt = "Would you like to save your changes?"
        Reply = MsgBox(Prompt, vbYesNo)
        If Reply = vbYes Then
            CommonDialog1.ShowSave
            RichTextBox1.SaveFile CommonDialog1.FileName, _
                rtfRTF
        End If
    End If
```

```
        RichTextBox1.Text = ""   'clear text box
        UnsavedChanges = False
    Errhandler:
        'Cancel button clicked.
        Exit Sub
    End Sub
```

The Save As Command

To save the RTF file that is currently loaded in a rich text box object, you call the SaveFile method with the name of the file and the argument rtfRTF. (Although I don't do it in this program, you could also save the file in plain text format by specifying the rtfText argument.) You'll typically want to specify the pathname for the saved file by using the FileName property of the common dialog object. In my program, I also allow the user to abort the save operation by clicking the Cancel button in the Save As dialog box.

```
Private Sub mnuSaveAsItem_Click()
    CommonDialog1.CancelError = True
    On Error GoTo Errhandler:
    CommonDialog1.ShowSave
    'save specified file in RTF format
    RichTextBox1.SaveFile CommonDialog1.FileName, rtfRTF
    UnsavedChanges = False
Errhandler:
    'Cancel button clicked
End Sub
```

The Print Command

Printing is quite simple in a rich text box. You simply use the SelPrint method and specify the internal address or *device handle* of the printer that you want to use. In this program, printing is accomplished by using the Printer object and the hDC property, which contains the current device handle of the system printer:

```
Private Sub mnuPrintItem_Click()
    'Prints the current document using the device
    'handle of the current printer
    RichTextBox1.SelPrint (Printer.hDC)
End Sub
```

The Exit Command

The basic purpose of the Exit command is to terminate the program via the End statement. However, as in the Close command above, I have included program code that first checks to see if there are any unsaved changes in the document before I allow the program to exit and discard the user's data permanently. Again, I test for the current save state by using the public variable UnsavedChanges, and give the user an opportunity to save any unsaved changes. Notice that, like the Close command, the Exit command also sets the value of UnsavedChanges to False after it saves the file to disk.

```
Private Sub mnuExitItem_Click ()
Dim Prompt As String
    Dim Reply As Integer
    CommonDialog1.CancelError = True
    On Error GoTo Errhandler:
    If UnsavedChanges = True Then
        Prompt = "Would you like to save your changes?"
        Reply = MsgBox(Prompt, vbYesNo)
        If Reply = vbYes Then
            CommonDialog1.ShowSave
            RichTextBox1.SaveFile CommonDialog1.FileName, _
                rtfRTF
            UnsavedChanges = False
        End If
    End If
    End 'after file has been saved, quit program
Errhandler:
    'Cancel button clicked (return to program)
End Sub
```

One Step Further

Displaying the RTF Codes in a Document

As you've just learned, the Rich Textbox control lets you create advanced effects in your document by adding special codes to your file in a formatting scheme known as RTF. Because the Rich Textbox control also has the ability to display straight text files, you can examine the document's formatting codes up close if you want more information about RTF. To modify the RTFEdit program so that it opens files in *text mode* and displays the RTF formatting, follow these steps.

View your RTF code

① Open the Code window and select the mnuOpenItem event procedure in the Object drop-down list box.

② Change the program statement that loads the RTF file in the event procedure to the following:

```
RichTextBox1.LoadFile CommonDialog1.FileName, rtfText
```

Note that the final argument in the statement has been changed from rtfRTF to rtfText.

Start button

③ Click the Start button on the toolbar, and then click the Open command on the File menu.

④ Open the sample.rtf file that you created earlier in this lesson.

You may open a different RTF file, if you like. Your form will look similar to the following:

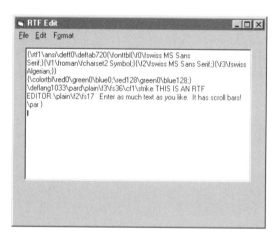

⑤ Take a few minutes to examine the RTF codes in the document.

You'll see information about the font, color, text style, alignment, and so on. Somewhere in the middle, you'll also see your text. (So this explains why word-processing files get so big!)

⑥ On the File menu, choose the Exit command to close the program. Click No when you are asked to save your changes.

⑦ In the mnuOpenItem_Click event procedure, change the rtfText argument back to rtfRTF.

Congratulations! You're now ready to create your own RTF documents and (if you like) a full-featured word-processing application.

If you want to continue to the next lesson

● Keep Visual Basic running, and turn to Lesson 16.

If you want to quit Visual Basic for now

● On the File menu, click Exit.

 If you see a Save dialog box, click Yes. Save any edits you have made to the RTF Editor as MyRTFEditor.

Upgrade Notes: What's Different in Visual Basic .NET?

If you choose to upgrade to Visual Basic .NET in the future, you'll notice some new features related to the topics in this lesson, including the following:

■ Visual Studio .NET Professional Edition offers several new Toolbox controls, and several familiar controls that are functionally equivalent to the ActiveX controls that you have been using in this book. Occasionally you will see that a .NET control has a different name than its Visual Basic 6.0 equivalent (the Visual Basic 6.0 Slider control is now called TrackBar, for example), and more often the .NET controls will have some new methods and properties to learn. The reason for these changes is that .NET controls have been designed and coded from scratch for Visual Studio .NET, and the controls are now shared across the entire Visual Studio programming suite—Visual Basic .NET programmers use them along with Visual C++ .NET and Visual C# programmers.

■ In addition to the new user interface controls being offered with Visual Studio .NET (LinkLabel, Splitter, DomainUpDown, HelpProvider, NotifyIcon, ToolTip, ContextMenu, various printing dialog boxes, and so on), you'll find several new tabs in the .NET Toolbox with supplementary controls for database management, process control, and system services.

■ Visual Basic .NET includes an entire class of controls that are designed specifically to be used with Web Forms; they appear on the Web Forms tab in the Toolbox when the Visual Studio .NET development environment has been configured for Internet development.

■ A few of the familiar Visual Basic 6.0 Professional Edition controls have been dropped from the Visual Studio .NET product, although you can continue to use them efficiently via the COM interface that Visual Studio .NET provides. The dropped controls include Multimedia MCI, Internet Transfer, and Communications.

■ Visual Studio .NET also includes a Rich textbox control, and it is similar in many ways to the Visual Basic 6.0 control you have been using in this lesson. Several properties and methods are different, however, as is the technique for selecting and formatting text.

■ If you migrate a Visual Basic 6.0 application that uses the Rich textbox control to Visual Basic .NET, you can either continue using the Visual Basic 6.0 control through the COM interface, or modify your existing code. The choice is up to you!

Lesson 15 Quick Reference

To	Do this
Install Professional Edition ActiveX controls	Click the Components command on the Project menu, click the Controls tab, and then click the check box next to the ActiveX control that you want to install.

Change selected text to all caps in a rich text box object	Use the UCase function. For example:
	`RichTextBox1.SelText = _`
	`    Ucase(RichTextBox1.SelText)`

Display the Font dialog box	Use the ShowFont method of the common dialog object. For example: `CommonDialog1.ShowFont`
Change formatting of selected text to bold	Use the SelBold property. For example: `RichTextBox1.SelBold = Not RichTextBox1.SelBold`

Change formatting of selected text to italic	Use the SelItalic property. For example:
	`RichTextBox1.SelItalic = _`
	`    Not RichTextBox1.SelItalic`

Change formatting of selected text to underline	Use the SelUnderline property. For example:
	`RichTextBox1.SelUnderline = _`
	`    Not RichTextBox1.SelUnderline`

Copy selected text to the Windows clipboard	Use the Clipboard object and the SetText method. For example: `Clipboard.SetText RichTextBox1.SelRTF`

Lesson 15 Quick Reference

To	Do This
| Cut selected text | Use the Clipboard object and the SetText method, and then clear the text. For example:<br><br>```
Clipboard.SetText RichTextBox1.SelRTF
RichTextBox1.SelRTF = ""
``` |
| Paste text at the insertion point | Use the Clipboard object and the GetText method. For example:<br><br>```
RichTextBox1.SelRTF = Clipboard.GetText
``` |
| Find text in a rich text box object | Use the Find method. For example, to find the first occurrence of the word Monday in the text box:<br><br>```
RichTextBox1.Find("Monday", , , rtfWholeWord)
``` |
| Load an RTF file | Use the LoadFile method. For example:<br><br>```
CommonDialog1.ShowOpen
RichTextBox1.LoadFile CommonDialog1.FileName, _
    rtfRTF
``` |
| Close an RTF file | Clear the contents of the text box with the Text property. For example:<br><br>```
RichTextBox1.Text = ""
``` |
| Save an RTF file | Use the SaveFile method. For example:<br><br>```
CommonDialog1.ShowSave
RichTextBox1.SaveFile CommonDialog1.FileName, _
    rtfRTF
``` |
| Print an RTF file | Use the SelPrint method. For example:<br><br>```
RichTextBox1.SelPrint (Printer.hDC)
``` |
| Exit the program | Use the End statement. |
```

16

Displaying Progress and Status Information

ESTIMATED TIME 40 min.

In this lesson you will learn how to:

✔ *Graphically display the progress of an operation with the Progress Bar control.*

✔ *Create a horizontal bar for user input with the Slider control.*

✔ *Display a status window at the bottom of your application with the Status Bar control.*

In Lesson 15, you learned how to add word-processing features to your application with the Rich Textbox control. In this lesson, you'll continue your work with Microsoft Visual Basic Professional Edition ActiveX controls by integrating the Progress Bar, Slider, and Status Bar controls into your application. The Progress Bar is designed to give the user some visual feedback during lengthy operations, such as complex sorting or saving a file. The Slider provides a mechanism both for receiving input and for displaying output: you can either drag the slider tab across a horizontal bar with tick marks, or you can have your program move the slider tab to show the progress of a task. Finally, the Status Bar control displays useful information about your program and keyboard states in up to 16 panes at the bottom of your application. These boxes are typically used to display the time and date, font information, spreadsheet data, facts about the operating system, and the status of toggle keys on your keyboard. As a group, these three ActiveX controls allow you to create handsome and effective graphical user interfaces.

Displaying Task Progress with the Progress Bar Control

In this age of the World Wide Web, most software professionals spend a little time each day downloading files or other information from the Internet. As a result, one of the regular players in our computing experience is the *progress bar*, a horizontal status indicator that shows us graphically how long a particular operation is taking. A typical progress bar in Microsoft Internet Explorer looks like this:

A progress bar doesn't always indicate how many minutes or seconds it will take the computer to perform a given task, but it does provide the visual feedback necessary to convince the user that his or her transaction hasn't ground to a halt or locked up the computer. In psychological terms, a progress bar eases the tension associated with waiting for the results of complex calculations and provides a tangible measure of the progress of a particular computing task.

In this section, you'll learn how to add a progress bar to your application's user interface. I use a progress bar whenever the task my application is tackling causes a delay of five or more seconds for the user of a typical computer. The following list shows a few activities that can cause this type of delay:

- Downloading files from the Internet
- Opening and saving files
- Sorting long lists
- Playing songs or other media on a multimedia device
- Tracking time-intensive computations, such as complex financial calculations
- Copying disks or setting up software

Installing the Progress Bar Control

Before you can use the Progress Bar control, you must add it to your toolbox. The Progress Bar ActiveX control and all the other ActiveX controls you'll use in this lesson are stored in a master file called the Microsoft Windows Common Control (mscomctl.ocx). When you add the Windows Common Control to your toolbox, you get a set of nine ActiveX controls that you can use to customize your program's user interface.

tip

For more information about the ActiveX controls included with Visual Basic Professional Edition, see "Installing Professional Edition ActiveX Controls" in Lesson 15, "Word Processing with the Rich Textbox Control."

Add the Windows Common Control to your toolbox

The sample project you'll use in this lesson already has the Windows Common Control included in the toolbox. When you create your own projects in the future, however, you'll need to add it manually. The following steps show you how. (You can either practice them now, or keep them handy for future reference.)

1. On the Project menu, click the Components command, and then click the Controls tab.

   Visual Basic displays the ActiveX controls installed in your system.

2. Scroll through the list of controls until you see the name Microsoft Windows Common Controls 6.0.

3. Click the check box next to the control name, and then click OK.

   Don't pick Microsoft Windows Common Controls-2 or Microsoft Windows Common Controls-3. These master files contain other useful ActiveX controls, including Month View, Date and Time Picker, and Flat Scroll Bar (see Lesson 15 for the details).

   After you click OK, Visual Basic adds nine Windows user interface controls to your toolbox. Your toolbox will look something like the figure on the following page.

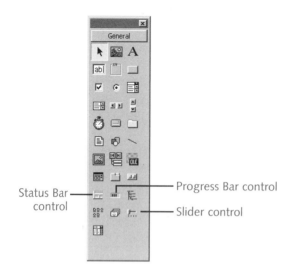

Status Bar control —— Progress Bar control

Slider control

The Progress Program

I created the Progress program in the \Vb6Sbs\Less16 folder to demonstrate how you can use a progress bar to provide appropriate feedback during lengthy computations. The Progress program is a revision of the SortDemo program in Lesson 12, which uses the Shell sort algorithm to sort a text box. Because the sort takes several seconds to reorganize a lengthy list, I thought it might be nice to give the user something to look at while the sort algorithm runs through its paces. You'll run the Progress program now to see how it works.

Run the Progress program

① Open the Progress.vbp project in the \Vb6Sbs\Less16 folder.

If you are prompted to save your changes (the Windows Common Control you practiced adding above), click No.

Start button

② Click the Start button on the toolbar to run the program.

Visual Basic displays the user interface of the Progress program.

③ On the File menu of the Progress program, click the Open command, and then open the sorttest.txt file in the \Vb6Sbs\Less16 folder.

Visual Basic displays the contents of the text file in the text box. (The file contains five copies of an ABCs text—a total of 180 lines.)

④ On the File menu, click the Sort Text command to sort the text box alphabetically.

Visual Basic begins the sort, and as shown in the figure on the following page, displays a progress bar at the bottom of the form to track the progress of the calculation.

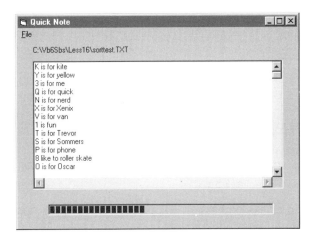

Watch closely: you'll see the progress bar fill two times. The first pass is a measure of the data prep process, in which the file is scanned to determine the number of lines; the second pass tracks the progress of the actual sort. I like showing a lengthy computation like this in individual phases; it makes the user feel more involved.

After a moment, the program displays the sorted list in the text box, and the progress bar disappears.

5 On the File menu, click the Exit command to quit the program.

Examine the Progress program code

The program code that manipulates the progress bar is located in the mnuItemSortText_Click event procedure, a routine that runs each time the user clicks the Sort Text command on the File menu. You'll take a look at the code now.

● Display the Code window, and open the mnuItemSortText_Click event procedure.

You've seen this source code before—in Lesson 12 you used it to sort the contents of a text box with the Shell sort algorithm. The actual contents of the Shell sort are located in the progress.bas code module of this project. The event procedure handles several important tasks before and after the sort is calculated. These include determining the number of lines in the text box, loading each line into a string array named strArray, calling the ShellSort procedure, and displaying the results in the text box. In this lesson, I'll focus exclusively on the program code that controls the progress bar.

In design mode, I set the progress bar's Visible property to False, so that it wouldn't appear on the screen until I needed it. Accordingly, my first task in the mnuItemSortText_Click event procedure is to make the progress bar visible and set its Max property to the number of characters in the file. I also set its Min property to 1 and its Value property to 1 (the starting square in the progress bar):

```
charsInFile% = Len(txtNote.Text)

...
ProgressBar1.Visible = True
ProgressBar1.Min = 1
ProgressBar1.Max = charsInFile%     'set max for progress bar
ProgressBar1.Value = 1              'set initial value
```

Next, I scan the contents of the text box character by character to determine the number of lines in the document, a value I need when I call the ShellSort procedure later in the routine. As I process each line, I update the progress bar's Value property with the current character, represented by the counter variable i% (shown in bold below):

```
'determine number of lines in the text box
For i% = 1 To charsInFile%
    letter$ = Mid(txtNote.Text, i%, 1)
    ProgressBar1.Value = i%     'move progress bar
    If letter$ = Chr$(13) Then 'if carriage ret found
        lineCount% = lineCount% + 1   'increment line count
        i% = i% + 1                    'skip linefeed char
    End If
Next i%
```

After the first pass through the progress bar, I reset the Value property to the first square, and set the Max property to the number of lines in the document (this amount is currently held in the lineCount% variable):

```
'reset progress bar for next phase of sort
ProgressBar1.Value = 1
ProgressBar1.Max = lineCount%
```

As I add each line to the strArray in preparation for the sort, I update the progress bar with the value of the current line (curline%) (shown in bold on the following page). As the Value property grows in size, it again causes dark squares to fill the progress bar:

```
'build an array to hold the text in the text box
ReDim strArray$(lineCount%) 'create array of proper size
curline% = 1
ln$ = ""    'use ln$ to build lines one character at a time
```

```
For i% = 1 To charsInFile%      'loop through text again
    letter$ = Mid(txtNote.Text, i%, 1)
    If letter$ = Chr$(13) Then 'if carriage return found
        ProgressBar1.Value = curline%  'show progress
        curline% = curline% + 1     'increment line count
        i% = i% + 1                 'skip linefeed char
        ln$ = ""                    'clear line and go to next
    Else
        ln$ = ln$ & letter$      'add letter to line
        strArray$(curline%) = ln$  'and put in array
    End If
Next i%
```

Finally, after the sort is complete, I hide the progress bar:

```
ProgressBar1.Visible = False
```

As you can see, the progress bar is a handy tool to have on your form when you're processing lengthy computations in a program. If you set the Min and Max properties to the appropriate range beforehand, you can easily control the progress bar within a For...Next statement or other looping structure.

Managing Input Graphically with the Slider Control

If you like the look of pictorial bars in your application, you can also use an ActiveX control called the Slider to receive input and display the progress of a task. The Slider control is a user interface component containing a slider peg and optional tick marks. You can move the slider peg within the slider window by dragging the peg, clicking tick marks, or using the direction keys on the keyboard. I find the Slider control a useful input device for setting document margins in a word processor, controlling multimedia applications, scrolling in a window, and other tasks that require relative movements. You may also find the Slider control useful for entering numeric values or color settings.

Run the RTFEdit2 program

To practice using the Slider control, you'll load and run the RTFEdit2 program, an enhanced version of the RTF Editor you created in Lesson 15.

❶   Open the RTFEdit2.vbp project located in your \Vb6Sbs\Less16 folder and run it.

❷   On the program's File menu, click the Open command and open the file named picnic.rtf in the \Vb6Sbs\Less16 folder.

Your form should look like this:

The RTFEdit2 program contains two new features: a Slider control at the top of the form and a Status Bar control at the bottom of the form. This slider gives you a handy way to adjust the left margin of the text that is currently selected or contains the insertion point. In addition, you'll see a status bar with four panels that display the name of the open file, the selected font, the current time, and the current date.

3 Click the second line of text in the picnic.rtf file.

The slider moves in one tab stop, reflecting the left margin of the current line.

4 Drag the slider to the right to increase the left margin.

As you drag the slider, the text margin expands automatically. In addition, a tooltip (or pop-up text window) appears and indicates the size of the margin in twips, the default measurement scale for a Visual Basic form and its controls. (A twip is 1/1440 of an inch.) You can adjust the measurement unit by modifying the ScaleMode property for the form.

5 Practice setting margins with the slider until you get the hang of it.

If you wish, you can select several lines and adjust the margin settings for the entire group in one action. Notice that each time you click a new line, the slider snaps to display the correct margin measurement.

6 When you're finished, click the Exit command on the RTFEdit2 File menu.

7 Click No when you are asked to save changes.

Examine the Slider control source code

Now that you've had a chance to see what the Slider control can do, take a minute to see how it is controlled by three event procedures.

❶ Double-click the form to display the Form_Load event procedure. You'll see the following program code:

```
Private Sub Form_Load()
    'Set initial values for Slider control
    Slider1.Left = RichTextBox1.Left  'align to text box
    Slider1.Width = RichTextBox1.Width
    'note: all slider measurements in twips (form default)
    Slider1.Max = RichTextBox1.Width
    Slider1.TickFrequency = Slider1.Max * 0.1
    Slider1.LargeChange = Slider1.Max * 0.1
    Slider1.SmallChange = Slider1.Max * 0.01
End Sub
```

The Form_Load event procedure is the typical place to put statements that configure the slider for use. The first two statements use the Left and Width properties of the rich text box object to align the slider object with the text box. Although I aligned the control approximately when I created it above the rich text box, the Left and Width properties allow me to do this precisely, using the same settings as those of the rich text box.

Next, I set the slider's Max property to the width of the rich text box. You can also set the Max property with the Properties windows at design time, but I found it convenient to precisely link the maximum range of the slider object to the size of the word processing window. (If the window changes size, so will the slider.) The setting for the Min property, the initial setting for the slider, is zero.

Finally, I've configured the TickFrequency, LargeChange, and SmallChange properties in the Form_Load event procedure. TickFrequency sets the frequency of tick marks on the slider in relation to its range (in other words, the difference between the Min and Max value). For example, if the range were 1000, and the TickFrequency property were set to 100, there would be 10 tick marks. The LargeChange property sets the number of ticks the slider will move when you click to the left or right of the slider, or press Page Up or Page Down, respectively. The SmallChange property sets the number of ticks the slider will move when you press the Right or Left arrow key.

❷ Use the Object list box in the Code window to display the Slider1_Scroll event procedure.

The Slider1_Scroll event procedure links the activity in the slider object to the margin formatting in the rich text box. Each time the user scrolls with the slider, Visual Basic calls this event procedure. Using the Value property of the slider object, this routine copies the value of the current slider position to the SelIndent property of the rich text box object, which sets the left margin of the selected text.

```
Private Sub Slider1_Scroll()
    RichTextBox1.SelIndent = Slider1.Value
End Sub
```

This statement works because I set the Max property of the slider object to the width of the rich text box object when I started the program. If the two objects were sized differently, the measurement scales in the slider's Value property would not match the dimensions of the rich text box.

3 Use the Object list box in the Code window to display the RichTextBox1_SelChange event procedure.

Visual Basic executes this event procedure when the current selection is changed in a rich text box object or when the insertion point has moved. Because I want the slider to move appropriately when different paragraphs are selected in the document, I've added program code to the event procedure that updates the slider position based on the margin formatting of the current selection:

```
Private Sub RichTextBox1_SelChange()
    . . .
    'if there is one indent style in the selection, display
    'it on the slider bar (multiple styles return Null)
    If Not IsNull(RichTextBox1.SelIndent) Then
        Slider1.Value = RichTextBox1.SelIndent
    End If
End Sub
```

Note the IsNull function in this procedure, which checks to see if the SelIndent property of the rich text box object contains a Null (or empty) value. SelIndent returns Null when the current selection contains two different margin styles, which results in a runtime error when assigned to the Value property of the slider object. To stop this from happening, I verify that the measurement held in SelIndent is not Null before I assign it to the slider. Your applications should also include this basic bulletproofing.

You've just learned how to use the Slider control to indent the margins in an RTF document. Before you move on, however, take a look at the data displayed by the Status Bar control in the RTFEdit2 application.

16

Progress Information

Displaying Application Information with the Status Bar Control

A *status bar* is a collection of rectangular boxes or *panels* along the bottom of a Windows application. A typical example is the status bar in Microsoft Word, which displays the current page and section number, the position of the cursor, the status of several toggle switches, an auto correct feature, and several other useful items.

The status bar in Microsoft Word.

You can add a status bar to your Visual Basic application by using the Status Bar ActiveX control, which is part of the Windows Common Control (mscomctl.ocx). When you place a status bar object on your form, it immediately snaps to the bottom of the form. You can then configure the general characteristics of the object with the Properties window, and you can add and remove panels in the status bar by right-clicking the status bar object, clicking the Properties command, and specifying settings in the Panels tab of the Property Pages dialog box. You can include up to 16 panels of information in each status bar.

The Panels tab of the Property Pages dialog box lets you add panels to the status bar.

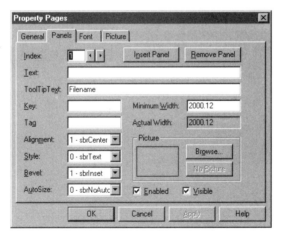

Run the RTFEdit2 program

Run the RTFEdit2 program again to see how the status bar works in the RTF editor.

Start button

❶ Click the Start button on the toolbar to run the RTFEdit2 program again.

If you closed the program or just started the lesson in this section, load the RTFEdit2 program from the \Vb6Sbs\Less16 folder now and run it.

Notice that the current time and date appear on the status bar at the bottom of the screen. Point to the time and date with the mouse, and a tooltip will appear that describes what each box does.

② Open the picnic.rtf file in the \Vb6Sbs\Less16 folder.

The name picnic.rtf appears in the leftmost status box.

③ Click the last line in the document.

MS Sans Serif, the name of the current font, appears in the second status box.

Your form should look like this:

④ Select the third line, and then click the Font command on the Format menu.

⑤ When the Font dialog box appears, change the font to Times New Roman or another font in your system. Click OK.

The font changes in your document, and the font name in the status bar changes to match.

⑥ On the File menu, click the Exit command to quit that program.

Now you'll take a look at the property pages that create the status bar.

Examine the status bar property pages

A property page is a group of settings that work collectively to configure an aspect of a control's behavior. In Visual Basic, you can use property pages to customize several ActiveX controls. Follow these steps to see how I used property pages to create the panels on the RTFEdit2 status bar.

① Click the status bar on the form with the right mouse button.

② Click the Properties command on the pop-up menu.

The Property Pages dialog box for the status box object appears.

❸ Click the Panels tab.

The Panels tab contains several settings for each panel in the status bar. To add a new panel to the status bar, click the Insert Panel button. To remove a panel, click the Remove Panel button. As a group, the panels that you create in the status bar are called the *Panels collection.* You can reference each panel individually by using the Panels collection and the index of a particular panel. For example, to place the filename *myfile.txt* in the first panel in the status bar, you would use the following program code:

```
StatusBar1.Panels(1).Text = "myfile.txt"
```

Likewise, you could assign the value held in another object to the status bar. For example, this program code places the filename (without path) stored in the common dialog object's FileTitle property into the first panel in the status bar:

```
StatusBar1.Panels(1).Text = CommonDialog1.FileTitle
```

❹ Click the Alignment drop-down list box in the Panels tab.

You'll see a list of text alignment choices in the list box, including left, center, and right. This setting controls how the text is displayed in the panel you are configuring.

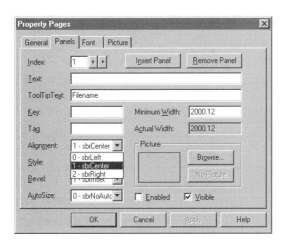

❺ Click the Style drop-down list box in the Panels tab.

You'll see a list of formatting entries in the list box, which controls the type of information that is displayed by the status bar panel. The sbrText entry (the default) means that you will enter the contents of the panel manually with the Text property, either through the Text text box in the Panel tab, or through the Text property in your program code (see step 3 above). The remaining style entries are automatic settings—if you choose one, Visual Basic automatically displays the value that you have selected when it displays the status bar. The style entries have the following meanings:

Style	Displays the following information
SbrText	User-defined text in Text property
sbrCaps	Status of Caps Lock key
sbrNum	Status of Num Lock key
sbrIns	Status of Insert key
sbrScrl	Status of Scroll Lock key
sbrTime	Current time from the system clock
sbrDate	Current date from the system clock
sbrKana	Status of Kana Lock key (Japanese operating systems only)

6 Click the right Panel Index arrow in the Panel tab twice to advance to the third panel in the status bar (Time).

I configured this panel so that it would display the current time on the status bar. (Note the sbrTime value in the Style setting.)

7 Click the right Panel Index arrow again to advance to the fourth panel in the status bar (Date).

This panel uses the sbrDate setting to display the current date on the status bar.

I've also manually set two other settings for each panel with property pages: ToolTip Text, which contains the tooltip text displayed when the user holds the mouse over the panel, and Minimum Width, which sets the starting width of the panel in twips. A minimum setting lets you align your panels on the form in design mode, while still allowing for growth if the user chooses to enlarge the form. Alternatively, I could have picked the sbrContents option in the AutoSize drop-down list box, which would
have resized the panels dynamically based on their content.

8 Take a moment to explore the remaining settings and tabs in the Property Pages dialog box, and then click Cancel.

Now you're ready to look at the event procedures that control the status bar at runtime.

Examine the status bar program code

Unlike many ActiveX controls, the status bar doesn't usually require much supporting code. Your task is typically to display one or two pieces of information on the status bar with the Text property. Let's see how this works in the RTFEdit2 program, where a status bar displays the current filename, font, time, and date.

❶ Open the mnuSaveAsItem_Click event procedure.

As you may recall from Lesson 15, this event procedure saves the current document as an RTF file by using a Save As dialog box and the SaveFile method of the rich text box object. To display the new filename in the first panel of the status bar object, I added the following line of code below the SaveFile method:

```
StatusBar1.Panels(1).Text = CommonDialog1.FileTitle
```

This statement copies the name in the FileTitle property (a filename without the path) to the Text property of the first panel in the status bar. To specify a different panel, you would simply change the numeric index.

tip

To handle the two other mechanisms for saving files in this program, I also added the preceding line of code to the mnuCloseItem and mnuExitItem event procedures.

❷ Open the RichTextBox1_SelChange event procedure.

As I noted earlier in this chapter, the RichTextBox1_SelChange event procedure runs when the current selection is changed in the rich text box object or when the user has moved the insertion point. Because the second panel in my status bar needs to display the font used in the current selection, I've added an If...Then...Else decision structure to this event procedure to check for a new font name and copy it to the second panel:

```
Private Sub RichTextBox1_SelChange()
    'if there is one font in the selection, then display
    'it on the status bar (multiple fonts return Null)
    If IsNull(RichTextBox1.SelFontName) Then
        StatusBar1.Panels(2).Text = ""
    Else
        StatusBar1.Panels(2).Text = RichTextBox1.SelFontName
    End If
    ...
End Sub
```

Progress Information

16

Again, I use the IsNull function to check to see if SelFontName property contains a Null value. SelFontName returns Null when the current selection contains two different font names. Because this would result in a runtime error, I check for Null before I assign the value, and simply clear the second panel if multiple names are found.

The status panels that display the time and date information in the program work automatically. You don't need to add any program code to run them.

One Step Further   Displaying Caps Lock and Num Lock Status

Take a minute now to experiment with a few other automatic formatting styles on the status bar. As I mentioned earlier in the lesson, you can use the Panel tab in the Property Pages dialog box to configure your panels to monitor several useful keyboard toggle states, including Caps Lock, Num Lock, Insert, and Scroll Lock.

❶ Right-click the status bar object, and then click the Properties command.
The Property Pages dialog box appears.

❷ Click the Panels tab.

❸ Click the right Panel Index arrow twice to move to index 3 (Time).

❹ Click the Style drop-down list box, and click the sbrCaps style (Caps Lock).

❺ Click the right Panel Index arrow to display the settings for the fourth panel (Date).

❻ Click the Style drop-down list box, and click the sbrNum style (Num Lock).

❼ Click OK to close the Property Pages dialog box.

With just a few mouse clicks, you've added Caps Lock and Num Lock information to the status bar. Now you'll run the program to see how they work.

Start button

❽ Click Start on the toolbar to run the RTFEdit2 program.

❾ Press the Caps Lock and Num Lock keys several times to check their toggle operation. The figure on the following page illustrates how the keys will appear on your status bar.

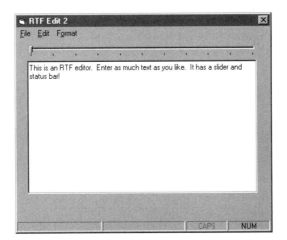

If you want to continue to the next lesson

● Keep Visual Basic running, and turn to Lesson 17.

If you want to quit Visual Basic for now

● On the File menu, click Exit.

 If you see a Save dialog box, click No. (You don't need to save your Caps Lock and Num Lock changes.)

Upgrade Notes: What's Different in Visual Basic .NET?

If you choose to upgrade to Visual Basic .NET in the future, you'll notice some new features related to the topics in this lesson, including the following:

■ The Visual Basic 6.0 Progress Bar control has the same name in Visual Studio .NET, although some of the methods and properties have changed. You can either continue using the Visual Basic 6.0 Progress Bar through the COM interface, or modify your existing code to incorporate the new control.

■ The Visual Basic 6.0 Slider control is now called TrackBar in Visual Studio .NET, and there are some new methods and properties to learn.

■ The Visual Basic 6.0 Status Bar control has the same name in Visual Studio .NET. Some of the methods and properties have changed.

Lesson 16 Quick Reference

To	Do this
Install the Windows Common Control	On the Project menu, click the Components command, click the Controls tab, and select the Windows Common Controls 6.0 entry.
Display a progress bar	Set the Visible property. For example: `ProgressBar1.Visible = True`
Hide a progress bar	Set the Visible property. For example: `ProgressBar1.Visible = False`
Update the progress of a progress bar	Set the Value property. For example: `ProgressBar.Value = curline%`
Set the maximum value for a slider object	Set the Max property. For example: `Slider1.Max = RichTextBox1.Width`
Set the rate of tick marks on a slider object	Set the TickFrequency property. For example: `Slider1.TickFrequency = Slider.Max * 0.1`
Move the slider with program code	Set the Value property. For example: `Slider1.Value = RichTextBox1.SelIndent`
Configure status bar panels at design time	Right-click the status bar object, click the Properties command, and use the Panels tab.
Set the text in a status bar panel at runtime	Use the Panels collection and the Text property. For example: `StatusBar1.Panels(1).Text = "myfile.txt"`
Display Caps Lock, Num Lock, Insert, and Scroll Lock keys in a status bar panel	Right-click the status bar object, click the Properties command, click the Panels tab, click the Style drop-down list box, and pick a predefined style.

17

Integrating Music and Video with the Multimedia MCI Control

ESTIMATED TIME
40 min.

In this lesson you will learn how to:

✔ *Play audio from a .wav file when your program starts.*

✔ *Run a video stored in an .avi file.*

✔ *Play music from an audio CD in an attached CD-ROM drive.*

In this lesson, you'll learn how to add music and video to your application with the Multimedia MCI control, an ActiveX control included with Microsoft Visual Basic Professional Edition. The *Multimedia MCI control* manages the recording and playback of multimedia files on MCI (media control interface) devices, such as audio CD players, VCRs, and videodisc players. The control also provides a handy set of compact disc–style buttons for playing and recording media in your programs. In this lesson, you'll use the Multimedia MCI control to play the most popular multimedia formats, including .wav files, .avi files, and audio CDs.

Playing Audio from .WAV Files

The Multimedia MCI ActiveX control is located in the Microsoft Multimedia Control 6.0 file (mci32.ocx). To use this control in your program, you add the control to your toolbox with the Components command on the Project menu, and then click the control and create the command bar interface for the tool on your form. The Multimedia MCI control consists of a series of command buttons that function automatically when a valid multimedia device is open and the control is enabled. The buttons are named Prev, Next, Play, Pause, Back, Step, Stop, Record, and Eject, respectively. You can add special features to these buttons by writing event procedures for specific button events. However, manually configuring the buttons usually isn't necessary. In most cases, you'll find that the default button settings play music and run videos very well.

The Multi-media MCI control provides several useful buttons.

The Multimedia MCI control has several uses. You can make the control visible at runtime (the default setting) and use the control to give the user a convenient method for managing an attached multimedia device, such as a VCR or audio CD player. Or you can make the control invisible at runtime by setting its Visible property to False. This method is most useful when you want to use the control to play sounds or run special effects in your program. I'll demonstrate both uses in this lesson.

The DeviceType Property

Before you can use the buttons in the Multimedia MCI control, you must open a valid multimedia device with the control's DeviceType property. This is typically accomplished by placing program code in the Form_Load event procedure, so that the control is automatically configured when the program starts. However, you can also change the DeviceType property while your program is running if you want the same control to manage several different multimedia devices.

The syntax for the DeviceType property is as follows:

```
MMControl1.DeviceType = DevName
```

where *DevName* is a string value representing one of the valid device types. For example, to specify a device capable of displaying .wav files (WaveAudio) you would specify the following string:

```
MMControl1.DeviceType = "WaveAudio"
```

The following table lists the multimedia devices currently supported by the Multimedia MCI control and the *DevName* arguments you should use in the DeviceType property for each:

Multimedia device	DevName	Description
Video (.avi files)	AVIVideo	Microsoft AVI format video
Audio CDs	CDAudio	Music CDs via attached CD-ROM drive
Digital tape	DAT	Attached digital tape (DAT) device
Digital video	DigitalVideo	Digital video data
Video	MMMovie	Multimedia movie format (displayed in window)
Video	Overlay	Frame overlay device (displayed in window)
Scanner	Scanner	Attached scanner
MIDI sequencer	Sequencer	MIDI sequencer data
Videotape	VCR	Attached videotape player/ recorder (displayed in window)
Videodisc	Videodisc	Attached videodisc player
Wave (.wav files)	WaveAudio	Microsoft Windows audio file
User defined	Other	User-defined multimedia type

The Command Property

After you identify the device you want to use with the DeviceType property, you can start sending MCI commands to the device with the Command property. The commands you can use conveniently match the names of each of the buttons on the Multimedia MCI control: Prev, Next, Play, Pause, Back, Step, Stop, Record, and Eject. In addition, you can also issue a few general-purpose MCI commands to the control, including Open, Close, Sound, Seek, and Save. The nice thing about using MCI commands is that you don't need to know much about the multimedia device that you're using to send the command. For example, you don't have to know how the data is stored on a CD-ROM drive to command the drive to start playing.

The Command property sends MCI commands to your multimedia device.

This program statement uses the Command property of the Multimedia MCI control to play the open multimedia device:

```
MMControl1.Command = "Play"
```

The PlayTune Program

Several commercially available programs (including Microsoft Windows) play an opening "theme song" when they first begin to entice the user. If you would like a .wav file that contains a song or audio track to play at startup, you can create this simple effect quickly with the Multimedia MCI control. The .wav file format (WaveAudio) is a common multimedia standard used by Microsoft to store audio information. Several commercially available audio applications (such as Sound Forge) can create and edit files in the .wav format. You'll also find several .wav files in the Windows operating system and in application suites like Microsoft Office.

Run the PlayTune program

Try running the PlayTune program now to play an "applause" .wav file with the Multimedia MCI control.

1. Start Visual Basic, and open the project named PlayTune.vbp located in the \Vb6Sbs\Less17 folder.

Start button

2. Click the Start button on the toolbar to run the program.

   Visual Basic displays the program's opening form and plays the applause.wav file with the Multimedia MCI control. The startup form may seem familiar by now—I used it in Lesson 9 to demonstrate how you can load an extra form to display introductory information about an application. However, in this context the startup form is only something nice to look at while the .wav file plays.

3. Click the Continue button on the form after the applause stops.

   Because this opening form is just a demonstration, the program stops here.

Now you'll take a look at the program code that produced this audio effect.

Examine the program code that plays .WAV files

The PlayTune program uses a Multimedia MCI control to play the applause.wav file when the form loads. However, it doesn't display the Multimedia MCI control itself. Instead, this example uses a Multimedia MCI control to create a special effect in a program without using the control's command buttons. To hide the Multimedia MCI control, I set its Visible property to False in the Properties window at design time.

1 Open the PlayTune program's Form_Load event procedure in the Code window.

You'll see the following program code:

```
Private Sub Form_Load()
    MMControl1.Notify = False
    MMControl1.Wait = True
    MMControl1.Shareable = False
    MMControl1.DeviceType = "WaveAudio"
    MMControl1.FileName = "c:\vb6sbs\less17\applause.wav"
    MMControl1.Command = "Open"
    MMControl1.Command = "Play"
End Sub
```

To play a "theme song" when you first start a program, you use the Form_Load event procedure to set the Multimedia MCI control's DeviceType property to WaveAudio (for .wav files), and then use the Command property to run the two MCI commands Open and Play. In addition to these essential properties, I set a few additional properties that prepare the Multimedia MCI control for typical operating events. These settings generally don't vary much from application to application. Note the following items:

- I set the value of the Notify property to False because I didn't want the Multimedia MCI control to notify me programmatically when the Open and Play commands were completed. (A value of True creates what is known as a callback event, a level of sophistication I don't need in this simple program.)

- I set the value of the Wait property to True because I wanted the control to wait until the upcoming Open command was completed before sending a Play command to the device.

- I set the Shareable property of the Multimedia MCI control to False so that other applications in the system could not access the open MCI device. (I don't want two applications playing different parts of the same audio file at once.)

▒ I set the FileName property to the path of applause.wav—the .wav file I
wanted to open and play. In most cases, you'll need to use the FileName
property to specify the media file that you want to use before you run
the Open command to open the device. An important exception is using
an audio CD in an attached CD-ROM drive. In this case, you don't need
to specify a filename because audio CDs don't use filenames to track
their content. With this medium, simply issuing the Open command
with the Command property will start the CD on the first track.

2 Open the Form_Unload event procedure in the Code window.

You'll see the following program code:

```
Private Sub Form_Unload(Cancel As Integer)
    MMControl1.Command = "Close"
End Sub
```

After you've finished using the Multimedia MCI control, you should issue
a Close command with the Command property to release the system
resources taken up by the multimedia device. The best place to close the
control is usually the Form_Unload event procedure, because this procedure
runs every time your application quits "normally" (that is, without crash-
ing). Using Close in Form_Unload addresses the user who prefers to exit the
application by clicking the Close button on the title bar, because that action
also triggers the Form_Unload event procedure.

Playing Video from .AVI Files

Another lively special effect that you can add to your program is full motion
video through .avi files. Files of type .avi follow a standard file format for storing video recordings with supporting audio. To configure the Multimedia MCI
control to play .avi files, you use the DeviceType, FileName, and Command properties as follows:

```
MMControl1.DeviceType = "AVIVideo"
MMControl1.FileName = "c:\vb6sbs\less17\michael.avi"
MMControl1.Command = "Open"
MMControl1.Command = "Play"
```

When you add these program statements to a program with an enabled Multimedia MCI control, the control will load and run the specified video file
(michael.avi, in this instance).

tip

When you start a video in the .avi format, it appears in its own windows and plays automatically. You don't need to create a special form for the video or control it programmatically.

The RunVideo Program

The RunVideo program demonstrates how you can use the Multimedia MCI control to run a video stored in .avi format from within a Visual Basic application. To make the program a little more useful, I added a common dialog object to the form so that you can open any .avi file on your system. If you don't have an .avi file handy, run the michael.avi file included in the \Vb6Sbs\Less17 folder. It presents a short video congratulating you on how well you've done so far in this programming course. (Technically, you shouldn't run this program until you're finished with the book, but try it now for a sneak preview!)

Start the RunVideo program

1   Open the RunVideo.vbp project located in the \Vb6Sbs\Less17 folder.

2   Click the Start button on the toolbar to run the program.

Start button

Visual Basic displays the form for the application:

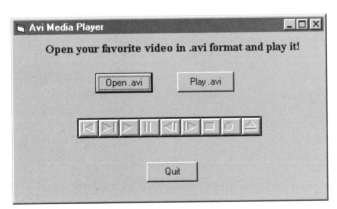

3   Click the Open .avi button on the form and use the Open dialog box to locate and open a suitable .avi file on your system.

If you want to see the video I recorded, open michael.avi in the \Vb6Sbs\Less17 folder. (Yes, that's me in the video!)

4   Click the Play .avi button on the form to run the video you've selected.

As shown below, a second window appears to display the video as it runs. If you're watching my video (a segment from my programming course *Learn Microsoft Visual Basic 6.0 Now*), you'll also hear me talking. Now try out a few of the buttons on the Multimedia MCI control while the video is running.

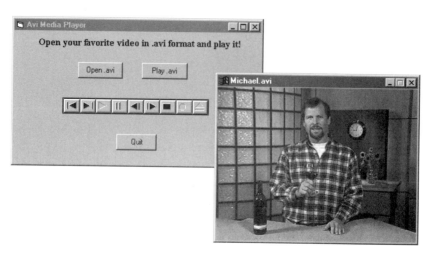

Cheers!

⑤   First, move the window holding the video if it's covering the form.

⑥   Now click the Prev button, the leftmost button on the Multimedia MCI control. The video restarts. (Click the Play button if it doesn't.)

⑦   Click the Pause button to stop the video temporarily.

⑧   Click the Play button to restart the video.

⑨   Click the Stop button to stop the video.

⑩   Click the Back and Next buttons to advance the video one frame backwards and forwards, respectively.

⑪   Finally, click the Play button again and let the video finish.

That's all there is to it! When you're viewing an .avi file, the Multimedia MCI control buttons work a lot like the buttons on your VCR.

⑫   Click the Close button on the .avi window to close the video.

⑬   Use the Open .avi and Play .avi buttons on the form to view additional .avi files on your system, if you like.

⑭   When you're finished, click the Quit button on the form to end the program.

Examine the program code to play an .AVI file

One of the most obvious differences between the two programs you've seen in this lesson is the role that the Multimedia MCI control plays in the user interface. In the PlayTune program, the control was made invisible by setting its Visible property to False. In the RunVideo program, the Multimedia MCI control was made visible by setting its Visible property to True (the default). With the True option, the user has access to the buttons on the control.

Take a few moments to examine the event procedures in the RunVideo program.

1 Open the Form_Load event procedure in the Code window.

Like the PlayTune program, the RunVideo program begins by initializing the Multimedia MCI control in the Form_Load event procedure. This time, however, the DeviceType property is set to AVIVideo to configure the control for .avi files:

```
Private Sub Form_Load()
    MMControl1.Notify = False
    MMControl1.Wait = True
    MMControl1.Shareable = False
    MMControl1.DeviceType = "AVIVideo"
End Sub
```

2 Open the cmdOpen_Click event procedure in the Code window.

The cmdOpen_Click event procedure runs each time the user clicks the Open .avi button on the form. The procedure uses a common dialog object to display an Open dialog box, and uses the Filter property to show only .avi files in the file browser. If the user clicks the Cancel button, the Errhandler: label terminates the loading operation by jumping over the Multimedia MCI control statements to the End statement. However, if the user selects a valid .avi file in the Open dialog box, the Multimedia MCI control immediately opens it by setting the FileName property to the path name of the file and by issuing the Open command with the Command property:

```
Private Sub cmdOpen_Click()
    CommonDialog1.CancelError = True
    On Error GoTo Errhandler:
    CommonDialog1.Flags = cdlOFNFileMustExist
    CommonDialog1.Filter = "Video (*.AVI)|*.AVI"
    CommonDialog1.ShowOpen
    MMControl1.FileName = CommonDialog1.FileName
    MMControl1.Command = "Open"
Errhandler:
    'If Cancel clicked, then exit procedure
End Sub
```

❸ Open the cmdPlay_Click event procedure in the Code window.

When the user clicks the Play .avi button on the form, the cmdPlay_Click event procedure issues the Play command to run the .avi file in its own window:

The Play command starts the video

```
Private Sub cmdPlay_Click()
    MMControl1.Command = "Play"
End Sub
```

❹ Open the cmdQuit_Click event procedure in the Code window.

The cmdQuit_Click event procedure ends the program and unloads the form from memory. This activity causes the Form_Unload event procedure to execute, which closes the open multimedia device and returns its resources to the system pool.

```
Private Sub cmdQuit_Click()
    End
End Sub

.

.

.

Private Sub Form_Unload(Cancel As Integer)
    MMControl1.Command = "Close"
End Sub
```

Follow these basic steps whenever you want to add video clips stored in .avi format to your application. You'll find them to be great tools for adding animation, step by step instructions, help information, or simply a personal touch to your program.

One Step Further   Playing Music from Audio CDs

As a final demonstration of the power of the Multimedia MCI control, I've included a third program in this lesson. The PlayCD program is an example of how you can play music stored on a standard audio CD from within your Visual Basic application. Adding music to your programs has obvious benefits. Remember, however, that the technique shown here requires that an audio CD be in the CD-ROM drive of your system. That may not always be practical or possible for your users. Still, there's nothing like playing your favorite tunes while you're at work!

Run the PlayCD program

① Open the PlayCD.vbp project located in the \Vb6Sbs\Less17 folder.

② Place an audio CD in the primary CD-ROM drive of your system.

③ Wait a moment to see if the CD begins to play by itself automatically.

On many systems, Windows will automatically recognize that the CD you've inserted is an audio CD and will start playing it with the CD Player accessory. If this happens, close the CD Player accessory so that you can test the PlayCD program.

Start button

④ Click the Start button on the toolbar to run the PlayCD program in Visual Basic.

The PlayCD form appears on the screen, featuring the Multimedia MCI control.

⑤ Click the Play CD command button on the form to open the audio CD device (CDAudio) with the Multimedia MCI control.

A red arrow and the words "Click play to start!" appear on the form. I added this detailed instruction to gently tell users to use the Play button to start the CD player. (This won't be obvious to everyone.) I created the arrow and text in Paintbrush. Then I used the cmdPlay_Click event's Picture property to load the bitmap into an image object on the form. I also display the contents of the image object from within the Play CD button's Click event procedure.

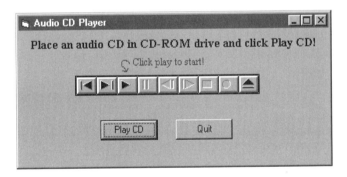

⑥ Click the Play button in the Multimedia MCI control.

The audio CD in the CD-ROM drive starts playing.

⑦ Use the buttons on the Multimedia MCI control to play different tracks on the CD.

⑧ When you're finished, click the Quit button on the form.

The music stops, and the program closes.

Examine the PlayCD program code

❶ Open the cmdPlay_Click event procedure in the Code window.

The cmdPlay_Click event procedure runs when the user clicks the Play CD button on the form. Rather than load the CDAudio device in the Form_Load event procedure, I chose to give my users the opportunity to read the instructions on the screen and put a CD in the drive after the program had started. You may want to take a closer look at two interesting items in this procedure. First, the device type I specified (CDAudio) does not require a filename for the compact disc media it plays. Rather, the CDAudio device simply jumps to the primary CD-ROM drive on the system and starts playing at the first track when a Play command is issued. Although some newer audio CDs do contain filename information, it is not required by the CDAudio device I currently have open. Second, note the last line in the event procedure, which sets the Visible property of the Image1 object to True. This is the program statement that displays the arrow and the text "Click play to start!" on the form.

```
Private Sub cmdPlay_Click()
    MMControl1.Notify = False
    MMControl1.Wait = True
    MMControl1.Shareable = False
    'specify CD Audio type (from CD-ROM drive)
    MMControl1.DeviceType = "CDAudio"
    MMControl1.Command = "Open"
    Image1.Visible = True
End Sub
```

❷ Open the MMControl1_PlayClick event procedure in the Code window.

As I mentioned earlier in the lesson, you can customize the behavior of the buttons on the Multimedia MCI control by adding program code to the button events associated with the control. In this event procedure, I have added a program statement that hides the red arrow and "hint" text ("Click play to start!") I placed on the form.

```
Private Sub MMControl1_PlayClick(Cancel As Integer)
    'hide instruction bitmap before playing CD
    Image1.Visible = False
End Sub
```

Note that the Image1.Visible property setting does not replace the Play command issued by the Play button. It simply runs before the Play command. In short, the button event procedures allow you to customize how each button on the Multimedia MCI control works without replacing its functionality. How you utilize this ability is up to you!

3 Open the cmdQuit_Click event procedure in the Code window.

The Quit command button stops the CD audio if it is still running, and terminates the program with the End statement. As I've discussed previously, the End statement causes the Form_Unload event to run and closes the open multimedia device.

```
Private Sub cmdQuit_Click()
    'stop CD audio if quit button clicked
    MMControl1.Command = "Stop"
    End
End Sub
```

```
Private Sub Form_Unload(Cancel As Integer)
    'always close device when finished
    MMControl1.Command = "Close"
End Sub
```

Congratulations! You've learned how to play .wav files, .avi files, and CD audio tracks with the Multimedia MCI control—three great ways to integrate multimedia functionality into your application.

If you want to continue to the next lesson

● Keep Visual Basic running, and turn to Lesson 18.

If you want to quit Visual Basic for now

● On the File menu, click Exit.

If you see a Save dialog box, click Yes.

Upgrade Notes:
What's Different in Visual Basic .NET?

If you choose to upgrade to Visual Basic .NET in the future, you'll notice some new features related to the topics in this lesson, including the following:

■ The first release of Visual Studio .NET does not contain a version of the Multimedia MCI control. However, you can use the Visual Basic 6.0 version through the COM interface in Visual Basic .NET successfully, provided you still have Visual Basic 6.0 installed on your system (or at least the Professional Edition ActiveX controls).

Lesson 17 Quick Reference

To	Do this
Add the Multimedia MCI ActiveX control to your toolbox	On the Project menu, click the Components command. Click the Controls tab, place a check mark next to Microsoft Multimedia Control 6.0, and click OK.
Specify a multimedia device	Use the DeviceType property of the Multimedia MCI control. For example, to specify the WaveAudio device to play .wav files, type: `MMControl1.DeviceType = "WaveAudio"`

Send an MCI command to the specified multimedia device	Use the Command property. For example, to open and play the multimedia device identified by the DeviceType property, type:
	
	`MMControl1.Command = "Open"`
	`MMControl1.Command = "Play"`

Hide the Multimedia MCI control at runtime	Use the Properties window to set the Multimedia MCI control's Visible property to False.
Display the Multimedia MCI control at runtime	Set the Multimedia MCI control's Visible property to True with the Properties window or program code.
Close the Multimedia MCI control and release system resources	Use the Close command with the Command property (typically placed in the Form_Unload event procedure). For example: `MMControl1.Command = "Close"`

Beyond Visual Basic: Using the Windows API

**ESTIMATED TIME
40 min.**

In this lesson you will learn how to:

✔ *Extend your programs by calling Microsoft Windows API functions.*

✔ *Use the API Viewer utility to insert function, constant, and type declarations.*

✔ *Use the GlobalMemoryStatus API to monitor memory usage on your system.*

In Lesson 18, you will extend your programs by using powerful functions in the Microsoft Windows API (application programming interface). Calling functions in the Windows API is often thought of as an "advanced" programming concept. However, after a few examples I think that you'll find the topic straightforward and useful. First, you'll explore the general scope of the Windows API and the calling conventions necessary to employ it. Next, you'll learn how to use Microsoft Visual Basic's API Viewer add-in to search for a specific API function and copy the necessary declaration to your project. Finally, you'll learn how to use the GlobalMemoryStatus API to check the memory usage on your computer. The basic skills you'll learn in this lesson will apply to most of the work you do with the Windows API in the future.

Inside the Windows API

So… what *is* this Windows API, anyway? As acronyms go, the Windows API has a decidedly mysterious ring to it. In fact, this ominous sounding entity is nothing but an oversized collection of functions that collectively perform the day-to-day tasks of the Microsoft Windows operating system. Windows applications and software development tools actively use these routines to perform typical computing tasks. For example, Visual Basic calls to the Windows API whenever it paints graphic images, saves a file, or allocates memory to a new application. More than 1000 functions are grouped in the Windows API. These functions are divided into several general categories: system services (routines in the kernel), the graphics device interface, Windows application management, multimedia, and so on. In practice, the Windows API is implemented as a collection of .dll files (dynamic link libraries) that are loaded at runtime to provide the necessary computing services for the programs that are active in the Windows operating system.

If the routines in the Windows API are simply functions, are they different from functions, such as UCase, Eof, and Format, that a Visual Basic programmer uses regularly? Well, not really. The only practical difference is that the Visual Basic functions are defined automatically in the Visual Basic development environment, while the Windows API functions require that you first declare them in your project via a standard module or event procedure. After this declaration, Windows API functions work much like built-in Visual Basic functions—you call them by name with the necessary arguments, and you receive a return value that you can process in your program to accomplish useful work.

The GlobalMemoryStatus Function

The Windows API function I'll use in this lesson is GlobalMemoryStatus, a function that returns useful information about the current memory usage in your computer. To declare the GlobalMemoryStatus function in a standard module (.bas file), you add a program statement to the top of the module that tells Visual Basic what the GlobalMemoryStatus function does and what type of arguments it requires. Like most programmers, I've broken this declaration into two lines with the line-continuation character (_) so that I can see it easily in the Code window. The GlobalMemoryStatus API function declaration looks like this:

A typical Windows API declaration.

```
Public Declare Sub GlobalMemoryStatus Lib "kernel32" _
    (lpBuffer As MemoryStatus)
```

Right away, you'll probably notice a few unusual things about this declaration. GlobalMemoryStatus is the name of the function in the Windows API library. When I call the GlobalMemoryStatus function in my program, I'll use this name to execute the function, and I'll include the arguments listed in parentheses at the end of the declaration statement. (This function requires only one argument, but some of the functions require several.) The parameter "kernel32" identifies the specific library I'm using, the 32-bit Windows API library associated with functions in the operating system kernel.

The name of the required argument is lpBuffer. The two-character prefix lp identifies the argument as a long integer pointer value, a memory address that identifies the location or *points* to the data I'll be using to gather information about system memory. The argument lpBuffer is not declared using one of Visual Basic's standard data types, such as Integer, String, or Boolean. Instead, it is declared using a user-defined type called MemoryStatus that contains eight numeric entries identifying the state of physical and virtual memory on the computer. The programmer who originally wrote this API function created the MemoryStatus type by using a struct (structure) statement in the C programming language. (I mention this because you'll occasionally see "struct" used when type declarations are discussed—most of the people who use the Windows API are C programmers familiar with a slightly different way of describing data types and function calls.)

Declaring Windows API functions in Visual Basic is somewhat cumbersome because you must include a type declaration for each user-defined type that is part of the API function you want to call. In this case, the GlobalMemoryStatus function requires the MemoryStatus type. And note: you need to place the declaration for the GlobalMemoryStatus function in the standard module. The MemoryStatus type declaration looks like this:

The MemoryStatus type holds the data gathered during the API call.

```
Public Type MemoryStatus
        dwLength As Long
        dwMemoryLoad As Long
        dwTotalPhys As Long
        dwAvailPhys As Long
        dwTotalPageFile As Long
        dwAvailPageFile As Long
        dwTotalVirtual As Long
        dwAvailVirtual As Long
End Type
```

A user-defined type is delimited in Visual Basic with the Public Type statement and the End Type keywords. The information between these two statements defines the name of the type and each of the type elements. The dw prefix before each element in this particular type declaration means "double word," or DWORD in the C programming language, a 4-byte (32-bit) integer value. In Visual Basic, you make this type declaration with the Long keyword, but you still retain the dw prefix because that's how the C programmer who wrote the original type declaration did it. The Long variable type (which is a really big integer value) is necessary because the numbers that you receive from the GlobalMemoryStatus function are measured in bytes and get very big in a hurry. For example, 32 MB of RAM (a typical amount of system memory) is equivalent to 33,554,432 bytes.

Before you call the GlobalMemoryStatus function, you must also dimension a public variable of the MemoryStatus type in your standard module, so that you can pass information to the GlobalMemoryStatus function and get the results. You can assign any name to the variable you declare. In my program, which you'll run shortly, I chose to call the variable memInfo:

Declare a variable to use the MemoryStatus type.

```
Public memInfo As MemoryStatus
```

Next, you need to prepare the memInfo variable that you declared for a call to the GlobalMemoryStatus function. GlobalMemoryStatus requires that the dwLength element of the MemoryStatus type contain the length (in bytes) of the MemoryStatus type. This may seems like an odd requirement because we know the length of MemoryStatus in advance; it's usually 32 bytes (eight 4-byte-long integers). However, functions in the Windows API typically require this information when they use pointers to access memory locations. (This syntax helps the function reserve the correct amount of memory for the function and allows for larger numbers in the future.) To assign this length programmatically, you use the following program statement either in the Form_Load event procedure or elsewhere in your code before you want to call the GlobalMemoryStatus function:

Determine the length of the user-defined type.

```
memInfo.dwLength = Len(memInfo)
```

In this statement, the Len function determines the entire length of the memInfo variable, which contains the MemoryStatus type. It then assigns that number to the dwLength element of the memInfo variable.

After initializing the dwLength element with the proper length information, you're ready to call the GlobalMemoryStatus function in your program. You do this by using the Call statement to identify the function and including the memInfo variable as an argument. (If you declared the GlobalMemoryStatus function in a standard module, you can place this statement in any event procedure in your project.)

Call the API.

```
Call GlobalMemoryStatus(memInfo)
```

After a call to the GlobalMemoryStatus API has been processed successfully by the Windows operating system, the memInfo variable will contain eight long integers with information about the current memory conditions in your computer. The dwLength element will still contain the same number (32 bytes), but the other elements in the type will now contain handy information about system memory. For example, the following statement uses the dwTotalPhys element to display the total amount of your system's physical memory (RAM) in a message box.

```
MsgBox memInfo.dwTotalPhys
```

Likewise, the following statement will display the total amount of your system's virtual memory in bytes. (Virtual memory is physical memory plus hard disk space used for temporary storage.)

```
MsgBox memInfo.dwTotalVirtual
```

Each time that you call the GlobalMemoryStatus function, the Windows operating system updates the type with a new snapshot of your memory usage—just the information you need to create a great memory usage utility for your desktop!

You've just had your first look at how a Windows API is used in a program, step by step. As you probably noticed, there are really only two essential techniques to master here. First, you need to include the proper function and type declarations in your program so that you can call the Windows API correctly. Second, you need to put up with some new terms and syntax that come from the C programming language. This terminology includes *pointer, DWORD, structure,* and several other terms that we didn't cover here. However, most of these terms have an equivalent Visual Basic programming concept, so you don't need to learn a completely new abstraction to call a Windows API.

So far, so good. But how do you find out what declarations, types, and constants you should use for the other 1000+ Windows APIs out there? Is all this information included in the online Help or in some giant book? Indeed, both of these documentation options are available to you. The MSDN Library includes a complete discussion of the 1000+ functions in the Windows API. Also, you can purchase a handy reference book from Ziff-Davis Press that lists the most useful Windows API functions for Visual Basic programmers (*Dan Appleman's Visual Basic 5.0 Programmer's Guide to the Win32 API*, ISBN 1-56276-446-2). However, before you run off to consult these useful references, practice using the API Viewer utility, an add-in tool that you can launch from the Add-Ins menu on the Visual Basic toolbar. With this slick utility, you can insert the declarations, constants, and types you need to use when calling any function in the Windows API.

Using the API Viewer Utility

To facilitate use of the functions in the Windows API, Visual Basic 6 includes a special text file called Win32api.txt that contains all the declarations, constants, and user-defined types you need to call Windows API functions from your Visual Basic project. Microsoft has structured this text file to work with the

API Viewer add-in so that you can quickly search for functions and insert the necessary code automatically. Try using the API Viewer now to add the declaration and type information you've just studied.

Install the API Viewer add-in

First, you'll create a menu command for the API Viewer add-in utility.

1 Start Visual Basic, and open a new standard project.

2 On the Add-Ins menu, click the Add-In Manager command.

The Add-In Manager dialog box appears, listing the extra utilities that you can add to the Add-Ins menu on the Visual Basic menu bar. An *add-in* is a special program designed to add functionality to your Visual Basic application. Visual Basic 6 includes several standard add-ins; you can also purchase add-in programs from third-party developers.

3 Double-click the VB 6 API Viewer add-in in the list box.

The word "Loaded" appears next to the add-in name, and a description appears in the Description window identifying the purpose of the utility. The Loaded/Unloaded check box is also checked. When a check mark appears in this box, the selected add-in appears on the Add-Ins menu for all projects until you remove it. Your Add-In Manager will look like this:

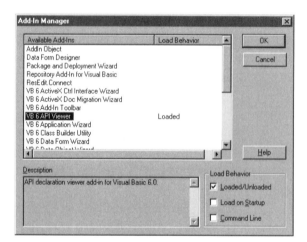

important

If you don't see the VB 6 API Viewer add-in, run the Visual Basic 6 setup program again, and install all add-in programs.

④   Click OK to add the API Viewer add-in to the Add-Ins menu.

Your Add-Ins menu will now have an API Viewer command.

Use the API Viewer to insert declarations

Now you'll practice searching for API functions with the API Viewer.

①   On the Add-Ins menu, click the API Viewer command.

The API Viewer appears on your screen. Now you'll need to locate the Win32api.txt file on your system. (The API Viewer can open any text file containing Windows API declarations. As future API collections become available, you'll be able to open them with this utility, too.)

②   On the API Viewer File menu, click the Load Text File command.

③   Browse to locate the Win32api.txt file on your system, and open it.

On most Visual Basic systems, you'll find this file in the C:\Program Files \Microsoft Visual Studio\Common\Tools\Winapi folder. If you don't have a folder with this name, use the Find command on the Windows Start menu to locate the file. (The file is also available on your Visual Basic Setup discs.)

tip

The Win32api.txt file is over 640 KB in size and can be a little slow to use. To convert the file to the Microsoft Jet database format for faster searching, choose the Convert Text to Database command on the File menu.

④   In the API Viewer text box, type **GlobalMemoryStatus**.

As you type, API names appear in the Available Items text box. By the time you're finished typing, GlobalMemoryStatus is the only item selected.

important

If your copy of the Win32api.txt file does not include the GlobalMemoryStatus function, try searching for the MemoryStatus function instead. Both functions perform the same task and are called with the same type argument (the MemoryStatus buffer). The Win32api.txt file is updated from time to time to incorporate changes and new naming conventions in the Windows and Windows NT operating systems.

5 Click Add to add the GlobalMemoryStatus function declaration to the Selected Items list.

The API Viewer will look similar to the following:

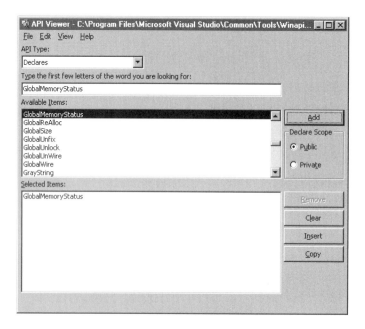

Now you'll add the MemoryStatus type declaration to the Selected Items list.

6 Click the API Type drop-down list box, and then click the Types item.

The API Viewer searches for the type declarations in the Win32api.txt file and displays the first entries in the Available Items list box. If you are prompted to save the Win32api.txt file as a database for faster access, click No. You can take this extra step if you find yourself using the Win32api.txt file often.

7 Delete the GlobalMemoryStatus function from the "Type the first few letters…" text box. Now type **MemoryStatus**, and click the Add button.

The MemoryStatus type declaration is copied to the Selected Items list. Now you'll copy both declarations to the clipboard so that you can insert them in a standard module in your Visual Basic program.

8 Click the Copy button.

The API Viewer copies both declarations to the Windows clipboard.

9 Minimize the API Viewer utility and maximize the Visual Basic development environment.

10 On the Project menu, click the Add Module command, and then click the Open button to open a new standard module in your project.

11 Verify that the insertion point is blinking in the Code window for the standard module. Then click the Paste button on the Visual Basic toolbar to insert the two declarations into the module.

Visual Basic adds the declarations to your standard module.

12 Break the first line into two lines with the underscore character (_) so that you can see the entire declaration in the Code window.

A good place to break the line is after the "kernel32" library name. Never break a line in the middle of a statement name or quotation.

13 Move the GlobalMemoryStatus declaration (now on two lines) below the MemoryStatus type declaration.

Your Code window will look like this:

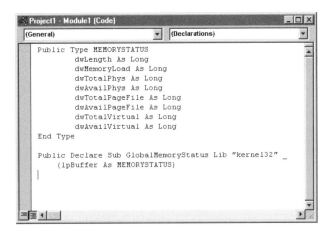

Moving the GlobalMemoryStatus declaration below the type declaration is necessary because the GlobalMemoryStatus declaration relies on the MemoryStatus type in its definition. If the type declaration follows the function declaration, Visual Basic will display an error message when you run the program.

14 Close the API Viewer utility that appears minimized on the Windows taskbar.

That's all there is to it! The API Viewer automatically copies all the information you need to run a Windows API function. Simply search for the API you need, and copy it to your project via the clipboard!

tip
Some API functions and types use constants in their declarations. Although I didn't demonstrate how to do so, you can also use the API Viewer to copy constant declarations from the Win32api.txt file to your project. Constants in the Win32api.txt file are similar to the constants you've already encountered in Visual Basic (like the vbYesNo constant you've used in message boxes to display the Yes and No buttons). To add the constant declarations by using the API Viewer utility, click Constants in the API Viewer's Type list box, type the constant name in the "Type the first few letters…" text box, and then copy the constant you need to your standard module.

Monitoring Memory Usage on Your Computer

Now that you've had some practice working with the GlobalMemoryStatus function, take a few minutes to run the FreeMem program I created with Visual Basic to showcase the GlobalMemoryStatus API. The FreeMem program graphically displays the total amount of physical and virtual memory used on your computer. This information is useful if you want to monitor how the RAM and hard disk space in your computer are being allocated to programs. If you learn that very little virtual memory is free, for example, you may want to make more disk space available for system memory. The FreeMem program also uses the GlobalMemoryStatus function to display the following details about your system's memory usage (in bytes):

- Total amount of physical memory (RAM) in your computer.
- Total amount of physical memory (RAM) free for allocation.
- Size of the current paging file.
- Amount of free memory in the current paging file.
- Total amount of virtual memory (RAM plus hard disk space) in your computer. The Windows Swap file controls this figure.
- Total amount of virtual memory (RAM plus hard disk space) free for allocation.

Try running the FreeMem program now to see how the memory in your system is being used.

Run the FreeMem program

❶ Open the FreeMem.vbp project in the \Vb6Sbs\Less18 folder.

When you are asked if you want to save your changes, click No. (I've already added all the API declarations you'll need in this project.)

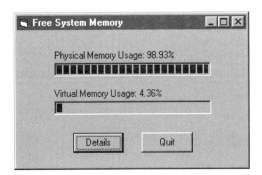

Start button

❷ Click the Start button on the toolbar to run the program.

The FreeMem program loads and uses the GlobalMemoryStatus API to gather information about the memory in your computer. After a moment, you'll see a result similar to the following:

FreeMem displays two fundamental memory statistics graphically: the total amount of physical memory used, and the total amount of virtual memory in the Swap file. The numbers are updated every three seconds by a timer object in the program. Two progress bar objects present the information visually and also as a percentage value.

tip

Does physical memory usage look high to you? Although it might seem unusual, don't be surprised if the percentage for physical memory (RAM) usage is nearly 100% on your computer. Even if you are running only one application (Visual Basic), the Windows memory manager will fill your computer's unused RAM with routines in the operating system, swap files, code from previously opened applications, useful .dll's, clipboard values, and so forth. A high usage percentage for physical memory is quite normal.

❸ Click the Details button on the form to display more specific information about the memory usage in your computer.

FreeMem opens a second form to display the details of the last call to the GlobalMemoryStatus API. You'll see information similar to the following:

The GlobalMemoryStatus API returns each of these values in the MemoryStatus type. Although the default measurement unit of the function is bytes, I've displayed the information in kilobytes (KB) to reduce eyestrain. (You can accomplish this by dividing each value by 1024.) Although the physical and virtual memory numbers are probably familiar to you by now, the paging file figures might require a little additional discussion.

A paging file is a block of virtual memory.

A *page* is a fixed-size block of memory associated with the Windows Swap file in virtual memory. This block of memory can be allocated to a program as it runs. The Windows memory manager keeps track of paging files in virtual memory so that the fastest physical memory can be allocated to the programs that were used most recently. Paging files also provide an additional benefit: they relieve the programmer from worrying about the exact location of the physical memory his or her program is using. The contents of a paging file can be located anywhere in the Window Swap file—in physical RAM, on the hard disk, or in another storage resource in the system. When one paging file fills up, the Windows memory manager opens up another one.

4   Click OK to close the Details form, and then click Quit to end the program.

Now you'll take a look at the program code that makes this application work.

Examine the FreeMem program code

1   Open the standard module (FreeMem.bas) in the Code window to see how the GlobalMemoryStatus function is declared.

You'll see the same program statements I've been discussing throughout this chapter: a MemoryStatus type that holds eight values about system memory, a declaration statement for the GlobalMemoryStatus API, and a declaration statement that creates a public variable named MemInfo of type MemoryStatus:

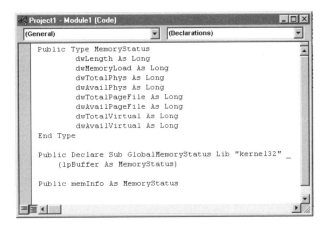

```
Project1 - Module1 [Code]
(General)                          (Declarations)
   Public Type MemoryStatus
           dwLength As Long
           dwMemoryLoad As Long
           dwTotalPhys As Long
           dwAvailPhys As Long
           dwTotalPageFile As Long
           dwAvailPageFile As Long
           dwTotalVirtual As Long
           dwAvailVirtual As Long
   End Type

   Public Declare Sub GlobalMemoryStatus Lib "kernel32" _
       (lpBuffer As MemoryStatus)

   Public memInfo As MemoryStatus
```

② Open the primary form (Form1) in the Code window and display the Form_Load event procedure to see how the GlobalMemoryStatus function is used.

You'll see the following source code:

```
Private Sub Form_Load()
    'Determine length of memInfo type
    memInfo.dwLength = Len(memInfo)
    'Call GlobalMemoryStatus API to set up progress bars
    Call GlobalMemoryStatus(memInfo)
    pgbPhysMem.Min = 0
    pgbPhysMem.Max = memInfo.dwTotalPhys
    pgbVirtMem.Min = 0
    pgbVirtMem.Max = memInfo.dwTotalVirtual
End Sub
```

As I described earlier, you need to set the dwLength element of the memInfo type to the length of the type before you call the GlobalMemoryStatus function for the first time. After assigning this number (32 bytes) with the Len function, I call the GlobalMemoryStatus API and then use the dwTotalPhys and dwTotalVirtual elements to set the maximum memory size of the two progress bars in my program. (To keep track of these progress bars, I've named them pgbPhysMem and pgbVirtMem.)

③ Open the Timer1_event procedure to see how the progress bars are updated with the amount of memory in use.

You'll see the following code:

```
Private Sub Timer1_Timer()
    Dim PhysUsed
    Dim VirtUsed
    'Call GlobalMemoryStatus API to get memory usage info
    Call GlobalMemoryStatus(memInfo)
    PhysUsed = memInfo.dwTotalPhys - memInfo.dwAvailPhys
    pgbPhysMem.Value = PhysUsed
    'Display memory usage with labels and progress bars
    lblPhysUsed.Caption = "Physical Memory Usage: " & _
        Format(PhysUsed / memInfo.dwTotalPhys, "0.00%")
    VirtUsed = memInfo.dwTotalVirtual - memInfo.dwAvailVirtual
    pgbVirtMem.Value = VirtUsed
    lblVirtUsed.Caption = "Virtual Memory Usage: " & _
        Format(VirtUsed / memInfo.dwTotalVirtual, "0.00%")
End Sub
```

Because the amount of memory in use is always changing, I wanted to update the display every few moments so that the user can see the changes first hand. (For example, try running the program and then closing an open application to see the numbers change.) The simplest way to update the display periodically is to use a timer object and set its Interval property to 3000 (three seconds). As long as my program runs, the Timer1_Timer event procedure will call the GlobalMemoryStatus function every three seconds and update the progress bars and labels. (Note that I subtracted available memory from total memory to get the percentage used.)

❹ Open the second form (frmDetails) in the Code window, and display the Form_Load event procedure to see how the details of the memory usage are displayed.

You'll see the following code:

```
Private Sub Form_Load()
    'Use memInfo type to display memory usage details
    lblTotalPhys.Caption = "Total physical memory (RAM): " & _
        memInfo.dwTotalPhys / 1024 & " KB"
    lblAvailPhys.Caption = "Free physical memory (RAM): " & _
        memInfo.dwAvailPhys / 1024 & " KB"
    lblTotalPage.Caption = "Total KB in current paging file: " & _
        memInfo.dwTotalPageFile / 1024
    lblAvailPage.Caption = "Free KB in current paging file: " & _
        memInfo.dwAvailPageFile / 1024
    lblTotalVirtual.Caption = "Total virtual memory: " & _
        memInfo.dwTotalVirtual / 1024 & " KB"
```

```
lblAvailVirtual.Caption = "Free virtual memory: " & _
    memInfo.dwAvailVirtual / 1024 & " KB"
End Sub
```

The frmDetails form is a second form I created in the program to display more detailed information about memory usage. I placed the program code to display the data in the Form_Load event procedure so that it would display the data as soon as the user clicked the Details button. Unlike the progress bars and labels on Form1, the Details form does not provide dynamic data, but simply a snapshot of current memory usage. Because I am using six labels to display this data on my form, I renamed the labels with the lbl prefix, and I included a description of their purpose so that I could keep them organized. Each element in the memInfo type displayed by the event procedure is divided by 1024 so that the information appears in kilobytes.

18

Using the Windows API

One Step Further   **Terminate Your Programs with Unload**

While you still have the FreeMem program open, take a moment to see how I terminate the program when the user clicks the Quit button on Form1.

● Open Form1's Command2_Click event procedure in the Code window.

You'll see the following source code:

```
Private Sub Command2_Click()
    Unload frmDetails       'unload both forms to quit
    Unload Form1
End Sub
```

Previously in this book, you've terminated your programs by using the End statement. This method is perfectly acceptable, but as you start working on more sophisticated programming projects (and begin reading more advanced books on Visual Basic programming), you will probably find that some Visual Basic programmers use the Unload statement to end their programs. The Unload statement itself shouldn't be new to you—we used it to close an open form in Lesson 8. As you may recall, Unload not only removes a form from the screen, but also releases the memory it was using. In addition, Unload can be used to terminate a program if it is used for the current (and only remaining) form in the open application. I followed this usage in the FreeMem program—Unload removes both frmDetails and Form1 from memory. Feel free to use this technique in your programs as a very professional-looking alternative to the End statement.

If you want to continue to the next lesson

● Keep Visual Basic running, and turn to Lesson 19.

If you want to quit Visual Basic for now

● On the File menu, click Exit.

   If you see a Save dialog box, click No.

Upgrade Notes:
What's Different in Visual Basic .NET?

If you choose to upgrade to Visual Basic .NET in the future, you'll notice some new features related to the topics in this lesson, including the following:

■ In Visual Basic .NET, calling Windows system services gets a lot easier thanks to a major new feature called the .NET Framework, a class library that lets you tap the power of the Windows operating system and accomplish many of the programming tasks that you need to carry out in your programs.

■ The .NET Framework is an underlying interface that becomes part of the Windows operating system itself. It is organized into classes that you can include by name in your Visual Basic .NET projects with the Imports statement. In Visual Basic .NET, you no longer need to use the API Viewer utility to call system services.

■ The System class in the .NET Framework contains most of the system services you'll need to call in your Visual Basic programs, including the services that check memory usage. The syntax for calling these services is much simpler than it is in Visual Basic 6.0. For example, you no longer need to conform to C programming language conventions or search through the Win32api.txt file for header information.

■ It is still possible to call Windows APIs directly in Visual Basic .NET, although the .NET Framework has significantly reduced the need to do so. Since Windows APIs are stored in static DLL files, you can call them directly through a mechanism called Platform Invocation Services. When you use this mechanism, you need to declare the API in Visual Basic .NET and call the function in a manner similar to how you have done it in this lesson.

Lesson 18 Quick Reference

To	Do this
Declare Windows API functions in your program	Copy the necessary function, type, and constant declarations to a standard module in your project. An excellent way to do this is to search for the function with the API Viewer add-in and copy the declarations via the Windows clipboard.
Determine the length of a user-defined type	Use the Len function. For example: `memInfo.dwLength = Len(memInfo)`
Call a Windows API function	Use the Call statement, and supply any necessary arguments. For example, to call the Global-MemoryStatus function, type: `Call GlobalMemoryStatus(memInfo)`
Access the elements in a type returned by a Windows API function	Specify the variable name associated with the type and the element name. For example, to assign the dwTotalPhys element of the memInfo variable (of type MemoryStatus) to the Max property of a progress bar, type: `pgbPhysMem.Max = memInfo.dwTotalPhys`
Terminate a program with the Unload statement	Use the Unload statement with the primary form in your program as an argument. For example: `Unload Form1`

PART 6

Internet Programming Fundamentals

Downloading Files with the Internet Transfer Control

In this lesson you will learn how to:

✔ *Download HTML documents from the World Wide Web.*

✔ *Transfer files over the Internet with FTP (file transfer protocol).*

✔ *Handle errors that occur during Internet transactions.*

ESTIMATED TIME
20 min.

In Part 6, you'll learn the essential programming techniques necessary to work with Web sites, protocols, and Dynamic HTML applications on the Internet. For a software developer, the Internet brings three opportunities for Web-aware applications. At the basic level, you can give your application the ability to download files and HTML documents from the Internet. This capability allows you to gather important information from remote locations, but it doesn't necessarily give you the ability to process it. (You might be downloading .zip files, for example.) At the next level, you can build your programs so that they are able to display HTML documents from the Web within your application. This level of support gives your users programmatic access to HTML documents through a browser, such as Microsoft Internet Explorer. Finally, you can use Microsoft Visual Basic and a special tool called the Dynamic HTML Page Designer to create Web applications (DHTML pages) that work with Internet servers on the Web. I'll introduce each of these programming techniques in Part 6.

In Lesson 19, you'll take your first steps on the Internet by learning how to download files with the Internet Transfer ActiveX control. Taking full advantage of the Internet is a complex topic, but you don't need to know all the details if you just want to pick a few files off your favorite Web site. In this lesson, you'll download files by using two widely used Internet protocols: HTTP (hypertext transfer protocol) and FTP (file transfer protocol). The Internet Transfer control is a straightforward tool that handles the file transfer details in a variety of contexts.

Downloading HTML Documents from the World Wide Web

If you're like most programmers, making your applications communicate with the Internet has become a high priority. Your company may use the Internet to transfer files to various locations around the world, or you may be routinely connected to a particular Web site that publishes documents and other information you need on a regular basis. If you want to make your Visual Basic applications minimally Web-aware, the first step is probably giving your users the ability to download files from a server computer to a client computer. A *server* is a computer running on the Internet that maintains or hosts a Web page and other services. A *client* is a computer with access to the Internet that requests information from a server. Client requests for information can originate from a browser program, such as Internet Explorer, or from a Visual Basic program.

To give your Visual Basic program (the client) the ability to request information from an Internet server, you can use the Internet Transfer ActiveX control included with Visual Basic Professional Edition. The Internet Transfer control is able to download files by using two of the most widely used protocols on the Internet: HTTP and FTP. HTTP is used primarily for transferring HTML (hypertext markup language) documents from servers on the Web. When you begin an Internet address in your Web browser with "http://" you're telling the server that you want to open a document with HTML formatting codes that your browser can understand and display. The Internet Transfer control can also use this protocol to download Web pages from servers on the Internet.

FTP is primarily used for transferring binary files or text files from special servers known as FTP servers or FTP sites. You can recognize FTP servers by the "ftp:/" prefix in front of the server name. A typical company will use its FTP site to transfer project files in .zip (compressed) format, and other binary files such as dynamic link libraries (.dll) and executable files (.exe). The Internet Transfer control can also manage FTP transactions (both downloading and uploading).

You can use the OpenURL method of the Internet Transfer control to download an entire file in one operation, or you can use the control to handle the specific, byte-by-byte details of a file transfer. The examples in the lesson will demonstrate the simpler OpenURL method, which downloads the entire file in one synchronous data stream. (In other words, Visual Basic won't execute additional program statements until the file transfer is complete.) The byte-by-byte technique is too detailed for most simple Internet-aware applications, but comes in handy when you're handling more demanding file transfers. To receive data in this way, use the Internet Transfer control's GetChunk method.

important

The Internet Transfer control is an ActiveX control that is included in Visual Basic Professional Edition and Enterprise Edition. Recall that to add a control to your toolbox, you click the Components command on the Project menu, place a check mark next to the control name (Microsoft Internet Transfer Control 6.0), and click OK.

Run the GetHTML program

Try running the GetHTML program now to see what you can do with the Internet Transfer control.

1. Start Visual Basic and open the GetHTML.vbp project in the \Vb6Sbs\Less19 folder on your hard disk.

Start button

2. Click the Start button on the toolbar to run the program.

   The user interface for the program looks like the figure on the following page.

   GetHTML is designed to download and save HTML documents that are located on the Web. Although GetHTML contains a text box that allows you to see the HTML code you are downloading, the program doesn't contain a browser that allows you to view the document as a Web page. (You'll learn how to display Web pages in Lesson 20.) However, you can view the downloaded HTML document offline with Internet Explorer or another browser.

   GetHTML contains another text box that allows you to locate the document you want to download by specifying the Internet address, a pathname also known as the *uniform resource locator* (URL). By default, the URL text box contains the Internet address for the MSNBC home page, but you can change this address to any Web page that you like.

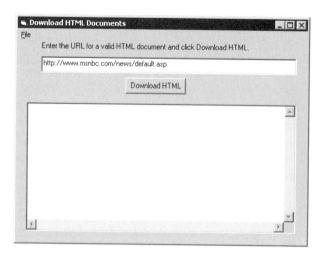

❸ Click the Download HTML button.

Visual Basic uses the Internet Transfer control to connect to the Internet and copy the specified HTML page to the text box. If you are not currently online, the Internet Transfer control will use your default Internet provider to open a connection to the Internet. (On my system, the Microsoft Network Sign In screen appears, and I need to enter a member ID and password to establish a connection.)

After a moment, your text box will contain HTML text from the MSNBC home page that looks similar to the illustration on the following page. The text box contains scroll bars so that you can examine the entire HTML document.

Rather than an attractive looking Web page, you'll see formatting codes or *tags* that appear in pairs of angled brackets. These tags include <HTML>, which signals the beginning of an HTML document, and <TITLE>, which determines what text appears in your browser's title bar when the document appears. The MSNBC home page is a very complex HTML document, with numerous tags, styles, and scripts. However, there is a reason behind each particular rhyme used here. Like the RTF standard you explored in Lesson 15, HTML is a text format delimited standard with many special tags that tell an HTML browser how to display the formatting and graphics in the document.

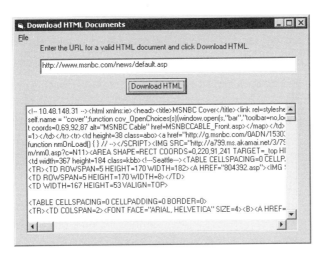

④ Click the File menu in the GetHTML program, and then click the Save As HTML command.

Visual Basic displays the Save As dialog box. (Your current folder may be different.)

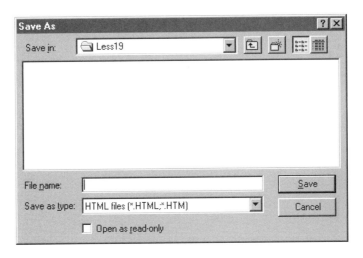

⑤ Navigate to the \Vb6Sbs\Less19 folder (if it is not currently open), and type **MSNBC** in the File Name text box.

6   Click the Save button.

Visual Basic saves the HTML document to disk with the .html extension.

7   Click the File menu in the GetHTML program, and click Exit.

Visual Basic closes the application.

Display your HTML document with Internet Explorer

Now you'll use Internet Explorer or another browser on your system to see what the MSNBC home page HTML document looks like as a Web page.

1   Start your Internet browser as you normally do.

I use Internet Explorer to browse the Internet. I start the browser by clicking the Start menu, pointing to Programs, pointing to the Internet Explorer folder, and clicking the Internet Explorer icon.

2   If you are prompted to connect to the Internet, click Cancel to work offline.

It is not necessary to connect to the Internet to view the document you have downloaded. It already resides on your hard disk.

3   Type **C:\Vb6Sbs\Less19\MSNBC.htm** in your browser's Address (URL) text box, and press Enter.

If you saved the MSNBC HTML document as directed in the previous section, your browser will load the MSNBC home page document from the \Vb6Sbs\Less19 folder. Your screen will look similar to the following:

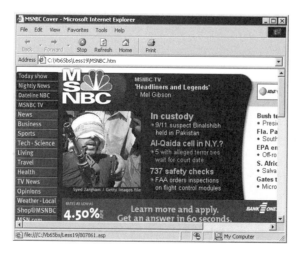

tip

If you're using a Netscape browser, display the HTML document by clicking the Open Page command on the Netscape File menu, clicking Choose File, navigating to the MSNBC HTML document you downloaded, and clicking Open twice.

Now, instead of intricate HTML formatting tags, you'll see the document you downloaded as a Web page. Although you're currently offline, you may see some blinking lights or graphic activity on this page. These are the result of special formatting that Microsoft has added to the Web page. In addition, notice that none of the hyperlinks on the Web page are currently active. The reason is that you've only downloaded a copy of the opening HTML document Microsoft provides on the MSNBC Web site, not a complete copy of their Web application with supporting files.

tip

Some HTML documents are self-contained files that hold all the resources they need to function in your browser. Others require additional supporting HTML documents, programs, and ActiveX controls that are located on the server.

❹ Take a few moments to examine the formatting on the MSNBC Web page, and then close your browser.

You'll use Internet Explorer again in Lesson 20, when you learn how to display HTML documents from within your Visual Basic application.

tip

To save money on connection charges, use this application to download Web pages that contain detailed information that you want to study closely. After you download the HTML document, disconnect from the Internet and view the page offline at your leisure!

Examine the GetHTML program code

Now that you've had a little experience working with HTML documents, take a look at the program code for the GetHTML program.

1 Open the Declarations section of Form1 in the Code window.

You'll see the following program code:

```
'declare a variable for the current URL
Dim strUrl As String
```

The Declarations section (the code above the first event procedure) is used to declare public variables that maintain their values in each event procedure on the form. In this declaration section, I've declared a public string variable named strUrl to hold the Internet address of the file on the Web that I want to download. I'll use this name again in the Command1_Click event procedure.

2 Display the Command1_Click event procedure in the Code window.

You'll see the following code:

```
Private Sub Command1_Click()
    On Error GoTo errorhandler
    strUrl = txtURLbox.Text
    'check for at least 11 characters ("http://www.")
    If Len(strUrl) > 11 Then
        'copy html document into text box
        txtNote.Text = Inet1.OpenURL(strUrl)
    Else
        MsgBox "Enter valid document name in the URL box"
    End If
    Exit Sub
errorhandler:
    MsgBox "Error opening URL", , Err.Description
End Sub
```

This event procedure copies the Internet address in the first text box (txtURLbox) to the public variable strUrl. Then it uses the Internet Transfer control to connect to the Internet and copy the HTML document specified. The critical statement is

```
txtNote.Text = Inet1.OpenURL(strUrl)
```

which uses the Internet transfer object's OpenURL method to download the file referenced by the strUrl variable and copy it to the second text box on the form (txtNote). If the transfer is not successful and an error is returned, the error handler displays the error with the Description property of the Err object. In this context, the most common errors are bad URL names (an invalid Internet address) or a time-out for the connection.

important

The Internet Transfer control has a SetTimeout property that sets the number of seconds an operation is allowed before a time-out occurs. (A *time-out* is an error produced by an excessive delay in the transaction.) I set this delay to 80 seconds in the program to allow users plenty of time to log on to their Internet service provider, but you can shorten this interval if you want. Note that if you try to exit your application before the time limit for a transaction has expired, Visual Basic will continue to wait for the specified interval before it closes the program.

❸ Display the mnuItemHTML_Click event procedure in the Code window.

You'll see the following program code:

```
Private Sub mnuItemHTML_Click()
'note: the entire file is stored in a string
CommonDialog1.DefaultExt = "HTM"
CommonDialog1.Filter = "HTML files (*.HTML;*.HTM)|*.HTML;HTM"
CommonDialog1.ShowSave        'display Save dialog
If CommonDialog1.FileName <> "" Then
    Open CommonDialog1.FileName For Output As #1
    Print #1, txtNote.Text  'save string to file
    Close #1                  'close file
End If
End Sub
```

This event procedure is executed when the user clicks the Save As HTML command on the GetHTML File menu. This routine simply saves the HTML document that you have downloaded into the text box as a text file, and adds the .htm filename extension if the user doesn't. (HTML documents are simply text files with formatting tags that have the .htm extension.) The procedure for opening and saving text is the same as the one that I discussed in Lesson 12.

❹ Display the mnuItemSave_Click event procedure in the Code window.

You'll see the code on the following page.

19

Downloading Files

```
Private Sub mnuItemSave_Click()
'note: the entire file is stored in a string
CommonDialog1.DefaultExt = "TXT"
CommonDialog1.Filter = "Text files (*.TXT)|*.TXT"
CommonDialog1.ShowSave        'display Save dialog
If CommonDialog1.FileName <> "" Then
    Open CommonDialog1.FileName For Output As #1
    Print #1, txtNote.Text  'save string to file
    Close #1                'close file
End If
End Sub
```

This event procedure is executed if you click the Save As Text command on the File menu. You didn't test this command when you ran the GetHTML program, but it operates just like the Save As HTML command. The only difference is that Save As Text adds the .txt extension to your document, which makes it appear as a text file in folder listings. However, the command does not remove the HTML formatting tags from your document (the routine simply changes the filename extension).

Now that you've had an introduction to downloading HTML documents with the Internet Transfer control, you'll try using the FTP protocol to copy files that are not formatted with HTML tags.

Transferring Files with FTP

As an alternative to downloading files with the OpenURL method, you can also use the Internet Transfer control's Execute method to copy files via a handful of useful FTP commands. FTP commands are codes that execute file system operations defined by the *FTP protocol*, a standard agreed to by Internet architects and developers. Useful FTP commands include GET (to download files), PUT (to upload files), SIZE (to determine the size of a file on an FTP site), and DIR (to list the files in the current FTP directory). In the following exercises, you'll examine how to use the GET command to download a text file from Microsoft Corporation's FTP site.

tip

To learn more about the FTP commands you can use with the Internet Transfer control, click the Index tab in the MSDN Library online Help, and type **FTP servers, arguments for Execute method**.

Run the FTP program

1 Open the FTP.vbp project in the \Vb6Sbs\Less19 folder on your hard disk. Click No if you are asked to save changes to the GetHTML program.

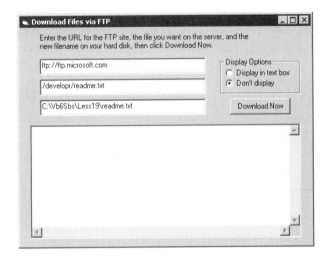

Start button

2 Click the Start button on the toolbar to run the program.

The FTP program starts, and your screen looks like the following:

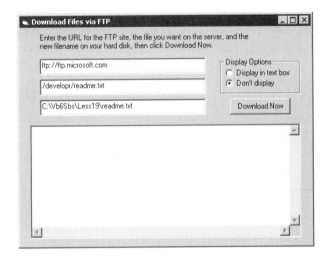

I designed GetHTML to download files from Internet FTP sites to my hard disk. The utility works with any type of file, and includes a pair of option buttons (Display and Don't Display) that let you choose whether to display the file after it has been downloaded. Certain files, like the disclaimer.txt file in the root directory of Microsoft's FTP site, are simple text files that are easily viewed in a Visual Basic text box. However, other file types, such as .zip, .exe, and .dll, are written in binary format and are not designed for display in a text box. (That's why this utility offers you a choice.)

3 Click the Display In Text Box option button, and then click Download Now.

The FTP program uses the Internet Transfer control to establish an Internet connection and to download the file you specified. (If you are not currently online, the Internet Transfer control will also open your Internet login screen and prompt you for your member ID and password.)

To give you a practical example of how the Execute method works, I specified the Microsoft FTP site and the readme.txt file, which should be on that site for the foreseeable future. However, if Microsoft moves the disclaimer.txt file after this writing, you'll see an error message when the

Execute method attempts to download the file. If this happens, specify a different filename on the Microsoft FTP site, or practice with another FTP site that you're familiar with.

important

The default settings of the FTP program also assume that you've installed the practice files in the default location. If the \Vb6Sbs\Less19 folder does not exist, specify a different folder in the destination text box (the third box from the top).

After a moment, your form will look like this:

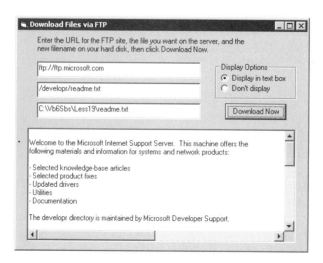

This program might function incorrectly if you use firewall software. Other versions of Microsoft Windows might also produce different results here.

4 Click the Download Now button again, without changing any of the paths in the text boxes.

The Internet Transfer control generates an error message because you didn't change the destination filename, and the download operation you requested would overwrite a file. You'll see the following message box:

⑤ Click OK to close the message box. Specify a new destination filename, and click Download Now again.

The program copies the file to the location you specified, and displays the contents of the disclaimer again in the text box.

⑥ If you know the address of another FTP site, specify it now in the first text box. Then type the name of the source file you want to copy in the second text box, and the destination pathname on your hard disk in the third text box.

Use your Internet browser, if necessary, to find the file you want. If you can, specify a binary file (like a .zip file) to see how the utility works with another format. (Be sure to click the Don't Display option button if you do, however.)

⑦ Click Download Now to download the file you specified.

⑧ When you're finished working with the FTP application, click the Close button on the program's title bar to exit.

Examine the FTP program code

The FTP program uses the Internet Transfer control's Execute method to download files from the specified FTP site, and the StateChanged event to detect the completion of the transfer and trap any errors that occur. You'll examine the program code now.

❶ Open the Declarations section of the FTP form in the Code window.

You'll see the following program code:

```
'Declare variables for URL, location of file on server,
'and destination pathname for file on hard disk
Dim strUrl As String          'URL is ftp site
Dim strSource As String
Dim strDest As String
```

Like the GetHTML program, the FTP program uses the Declaration section to declare public variables that will be used throughout the program. The strUrl string variable holds the Internet address of the FTP site; the strSource variable holds the pathname of the source file to copy on the FTP site; and the strDest variable holds the pathname of the destination file on the user's hard disk.

2 Open the Command1_Click event procedure in the Code window.

You'll see the following program code:

```
Private Sub Command1_Click()
'Connect to ftp site and copy file to hard disk
strUrl = txtURLbox.Text          'get URL from user
strSource = txtServerPath.Text 'get path to source file
strDest = txtLocalPath.Text      'get destination path
'Use Execute method and GET operation to copy file
Inet1.Execute strUrl, "GET " & strSource & " " & strDest
End Sub
```

This event procedure assigns the FTP address, source path, and destination path for the downloading operation to the three public variables in the program. The procedure then uses these variables as arguments for the Internet transfer object's Execute method. The syntax of the Execute method is a little tricky, because Execute itself must supply a string of arguments that conform to the conventions used when FTP commands are used on the Internet. The syntax of the GET command (which downloads files from an FTP site) looks like this:

```
GET sourcefile destinationfile
```

So, when used with the Execute method, the syntax for downloading a file is this:

```
Inet1.Execute strUrl, "GET " & strSource & " " & strDest
```

(I've used the concatenation operator to join together the strings and create the necessary spacing between them.)

3 Open the Inet1_StateChanged event procedure in the Code window.

You'll see the following program code:

```
Private Sub Inet1_StateChanged(ByVal State As Integer)
'This event is triggered when the control completes
'various tasks, such as connecting and logging errors
Dim strAllText As String 'dim two variables for
Dim strLine As String    'displaying text file
'When the transfer is complete or an error occurs,
'process the state appropriately
Select Case State
Case icError   'if there is an error, describe it
    If Inet1.ResponseCode = 80 Then 'file exists error
        MsgBox "File Exists! Please specify new destination"
    Else       'if not code 80, then show unknown error
        MsgBox Inet1.ResponseInfo, , "File transfer failed"
    End If
Case icResponseCompleted         'if ftp successful
    If Option1.Value = True Then 'display requested file
        Open strDest For Input As #1 'open in text box
        Do Until EOF(1)
            Line Input #1, strLine   'read each line
            strAllText = strAllText & strLine & vbCrLf
        Loop
        Close #1
        txtNote.Text = strAllText    'copy to text box
    Else  'if the user selects no text display (default)
        txtNote.Text = ""   'simply announce completion
        MsgBox "Transfer complete", , strDest
    End If
End Select
End Sub
```

The StateChanged event procedure is a very useful place to check the progress of downloading activities initiated by the Execute method. As you saw earlier, the Internet Transfer control's OpenURL method handles file transfers in a synchronous manner, waiting until the entire download is complete (or a time-out occurs) before proceeding with the next program statement. The Execute method is different—it handles file transfers *asynchronously*, meaning that it sends FTP commands to the FTP server and then continues executing the code in your program.

When you use the Execute method, you need to have some way of determining what happened to the command that your program sent to the FTP server. The mechanism in Visual Basic for monitoring what transpires is to write code in the StateChanged event procedure. This procedure is executed each time the Internet Transfer control detects a state change in the Internet connection it is monitoring. The StateChanged event procedure provides a special parameter named State, which includes a code indicating the most recent transmission event that has occurred in your connection. This code lets you use a Select Case structure to evaluate the different return values in the State parameter and to respond accordingly.

Take a moment to examine the icResponseCompleted case in the StateChanged event procedure. This segment runs when the GET operation is complete—that is, when the file has been successfully downloaded from the FTP site. When this happens, an If...Then...Else decision structure checks to see which option button is selected on the form and branches accordingly. If the first button (Display in Text Box) is selected, the file is opened again, and its contents are copied to the large text box object on the form. If not, the text box is cleared, and a message box announces the successful completion of the current FTP transfer.

The Execute method of the Internet Transfer control is an excellent tool for managing FTP transfers. If you use it, be sure that you also plan for the success or failure of the transfer with a StateChanged event procedure.

One Step Further   Handling Errors During Internet Transactions

As you learned in the preceding section, the StateChanged event procedure is a useful mechanism for detecting the completion of a file transfer initiated by the Execute method. You can also use the StateChanged event procedure to handle error conditions that arise when you use FTP commands and other methods and properties.

When an error occurs in your Internet connection, the Internet Transfer control sets the State parameter in the StateChanged event procedure to the constant "icError" (the number 11). If you check for the icError state in the StateChanged event procedure with a Case statement, you can trap any errors that occur and determine their exact cause by displaying the ResponseCode property of the Internet Transfer control. Normally, the ResponseCode property has a value of 0 (no error), but when the state is set to icError in the StateChanged event procedure, a special value is placed in the ResponseCode property to identify the error that has occurred.

● Open the Inet1_StateChanged event procedure in the Code window (if it is not still open) and scroll to the first Case statement in the procedure.

The icError case looks like this:

```
Case icError    'if there is an error, describe it
    If Inet1.ResponseCode = 80 Then 'file exists error
        MsgBox "File Exists! Please specify new destination"
    Else        'if not code 80, then show unknown error
        MsgBox Inet1.ResponseInfo, , "File transfer failed"
    End If
```

If icError evaluates to True, an error has occurred in the current Internet connection, and the user needs to be told what to do next. I chose to test specifically for a value of 80 in the ResponseCode property, which indicates that the destination file specified in the third text box already exists on the user's system. (Fortunately, the GET command won't overwrite destination files automatically; you get an error message instead.) If a value of 80 is detected, the program displays a message box with an appropriate warning, and the user can correct the problem. If an error condition other than a problem with the destination file exists, I use an Else clause to display the general message "File transfer failed," and then display the exact error warning with the ResponseInfo property. At runtime, ResponseInfo contains an explanatory text string that is similar in function to the message produced by the Description property of the Err object.

By adding an error trapping mechanism to your StateChanged event procedure, you can stop general connection errors from disabling your FTP application.

If you want to continue to the next lesson

● Keep Visual Basic running, and turn to Lesson 20.

If you want to quit Visual Basic for now

● On the File menu, click Exit.

If you see a Save dialog box, click No.

Upgrade Notes:
What's Different in Visual Basic .NET?

If you choose to upgrade to Visual Basic .NET in the future, you'll notice some new features related to the topics in this lesson, including the following:

■ The Visual Basic 6.0 Internet Transfer control is not included in the Visual Studio .NET toolbox. However, you can use Internet Transfer successfully through the COM interface in Visual Basic .NET if you still have the Visual Basic 6.0 Professional Edition controls installed on your system.

■ Most of the functionality of the Visual Basic 6.0 Internet Transfer control is available in Visual Basic .NET through the System.Net libraries of the .NET Framework. In other words, you can manage most file transfer operations on the Internet simply by calling library functions, rather than manipulating the methods and properties of a specific control that you add to a form.

Lesson 19 Quick Reference

To	Do this
Add the Internet Transfer ActiveX control to your toolbox	On the Project menu, click the Components command. Click the Controls tab, place a check mark next to Microsoft Internet Transfer Control 6.0, and click OK.
Copy an HTML document from the Web to a text box in your program	Use the OpenURL method of the Internet Transfer control. For example: `txtNote.Text = Inet1.OpenURL(strUrl)`
Download a file from an FTP site	Use the Execute method of the Internet Transfer control. For example: `Inet1.Execute strUrl, "GET " & strSource _ & " " & strDest`
Respond to state changes in your Internet connection	Write a Select Case decision structure that evaluates the State property in the Internet Transfer control's StateChanged event procedure.

Displaying HTML Documents with Internet Explorer

In this lesson you will learn how to:

✔ *Investigate the Microsoft Internet Explorer object model.*

✔ *View HTML documents from within your application.*

✔ *Use Internet Explorer events.*

**ESTIMATED TIME
40 min.**

In Lesson 19, you learned how to download files from within Microsoft Visual Basic programs by using the Internet Transfer control. With this useful tool, you can download almost any type of information from the Internet, including text files, HTML documents, executable files, compressed files (like .zip files), spreadsheets, and so on. In this lesson, you'll learn how to display HTML documents in your applications with the Internet Explorer object, a programmable component with properties, methods, and events that are available to every computer system that features a copy of the Internet Explorer software. As you investigate the Internet Explorer object model, you'll learn how to add the Internet Explorer object to your Visual Basic projects, and how to use Internet Explorer properties, methods, and events to display HTML documents. As you'll soon see, the Internet Explorer features a useful object model that is similar in many ways to the objects exposed by Microsoft Office applications. With Internet Explorer, you can display complex HTML documents and Web pages without writing the browser software yourself.

Getting Started with the Internet Explorer Object

Microsoft Internet Explorer is a general-purpose browser application that displays HTML documents located on the Internet or on your hard disk. Microsoft designed the Internet Explorer so that you could use it as an individual application (started from the Windows Start menu) or as a component object in a program of your own creation. Accordingly, Internet Explorer exposes its features as a collection of properties, methods, and events in a recognizable object model. You can investigate this object model by using the Visual Basic Object Browser and put its features to work in your programs.

The *Internet Explorer object* is not an ActiveX control included in Visual Basic Professional Edition. Instead, it is an object library that resides on all systems with an installed copy of Internet Explorer. (In other words, the Internet Explorer needs to be present in the system registry.) Because Microsoft uses the Internet Explorer to display Help files in many of its applications (including Visual Basic 6), you'll find the Internet Explorer object library on most systems that contain Microsoft software.

important

The version of Internet Explorer described in this lesson is 4.0 (the version shipped with Visual Basic 6). Core properties, methods, and events in the Internet Explorer object have not changed significantly between versions. However, be sure to check which version of Internet Explorer you are using before you start this lesson. If you have a version other than 4.0, use the Object Browser to verify that it contains the properties, methods, and events that you plan to use. Like the object libraries in Microsoft Office applications, the Internet Explorer object model is updated from time to time. Undoubtedly, future versions will be a little different (and richer in terms of features).

Adding the Microsoft Internet Controls Reference to Your Application

The first step in using the Internet Explorer object is adding a reference to the object library in your application. You accomplish this by using the References command on the Visual Basic Project menu, as shown in the following exercise. Practice adding a reference now, if you like, or simply note the steps for later use. (The program I include in this lesson already includes this reference, but you should practice adding it now if you want to investigate the object model later in this section.)

Include the Internet Explorer object in your project

❶ Start Visual Basic, and open a new, standard project.

❷ On the Project menu, click the References command.

❸ Scroll to the Microsoft Internet Controls (shdocvw.dll) reference, and then click the check box to the left of the reference name.

Your dialog box will look similar to this:

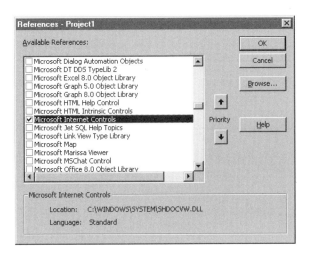

❹ Click OK to add the reference to your project.

Visual Basic adds the Internet Explorer object library to your project.

Investigating the Internet Explorer Object Model

Before you use the Internet Explorer object in a program, take a moment to examine its properties, methods, and events with the Visual Basic Object Browser. The Internet Explorer object is stored in a class named InternetExplorer, which is a member of the SHDocVw library (the Microsoft Internet Controls reference you just added to your project). Within the InternetExplorer class are the properties, methods, and events that you can use to display HTML documents in your programs. As you learned in Lesson 14, the Object Browser is your best source of information for an object library that is not shipped with Visual Basic. The Internet Explorer object library is a good case in point.

Use the Object Browser

Object Browser button

① Click the Object Browser button on the toolbar to display the Visual Basic Object Browser.

The Object Browser utility appears in a window.

> **tip**
>
> F2 is the keyboard shortcut for displaying the Object Browser. You can also open the Object Browser by clicking the Object Browser command on the View menu.

② In the Project/Library drop-down list box, click the SHDocVw library.

The Classes and Members list boxes display the elements of the SHDocVw library (the objects associated with Microsoft Internet Controls).

③ Scroll down in the Classes list box, and click the InternetExplorer class.

Your Object Browser will look similar to the following illustration:

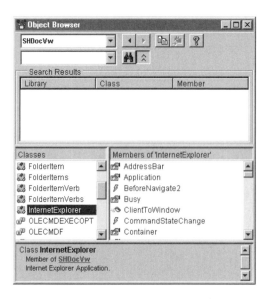

The properties, methods, and events of the InternetExplorer class appear in the Members list box on the right. You can click any of these members to see the syntax (and a short description) of each of the items that control how the Internet Explorer works. Try clicking a few of the properties, methods, and events now.

④ Click the Navigate method in the Members list box.

You'll see the following syntax description:

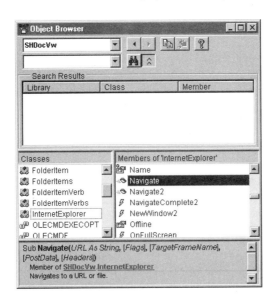

Navigate opens a URL.

The Navigate method opens the URL specified, which can be either an Internet address or an HTML document someplace on your system. The Flags argument specifies whether to add this URL to the Internet Explorer's history list or disk cache. The TargetFrameName, PostData, and Headers arguments describe how the HTML document should be opened and identified in the browser window. (The Flags, TargetFrameName, PostData, and Headers arguments are all optional.) Although it may appear complex, the Navigate method is very easy to use. In many cases, it's all you'll need to view an HTML document from within your application.

⑤ Click the LocationURL property in the Members list box.

The LocationURL property contains the pathname of the HTML document that is currently open in the Internet Explorer browser. If you want to keep track of each Web site a user visits in a computing session, you can use the Navigate method to copy the string in the LocationURL property to a text box or combo box after each successful connection to a Web page.

⑥ Click the NavigateComplete2 event in the Members list box.

The Internet Explorer object issues the NavigateComplete2 event when the Navigate method has been completed successfully and a new HTML document has been loaded into the browser window. We'll use this event in the "One Step Further" exercise later in this lesson to create a history list of visited Web sites.

> **tip**
> When Microsoft makes improvements to the Internet Explorer object model, it often creates updated versions of the existing properties, methods, and events with new (incremented) numbers appended to their names. By looking at the syntax and description entries for these new members, you can often determine what new arguments or features they support. This explains why you see Navigate and Navigate2 methods in the Internet Explorer 4 object library.

❼   Take a moment to explore other properties, methods, and events that look interesting with the Object Browser.

❽   When you're finished exploring the object model, click the Close button to quit the Object Browser.

Displaying HTML Documents

Displaying HTML documents with the Internet Explorer object requires just a few lines of program code in a Visual Basic application. First, you create an object variable in your application that represents the Internet Explorer object. Then you open the Internet Explorer application by setting the Visible property of that object variable to True. Next, you load an HTML document into the browser by issuing the Navigate method with a valid URL or local pathname as an argument. Here's what the process looks like with program code:

```
Set Explorer = New SHDocVw.InternetExplorer
Explorer.Visible = True
Explorer.Navigate "http://www.microsoft.com/"
```

In this example, I created an object variable named Explorer to represent the InternetExplorer class in the shdocvw.dll object library. If you want to use this object variable in every event procedure in your form, you should declare it as a global variable with the Public keyword in a standard module or in the Declarations section of your form.

To see how the Internet Explorer object works in a program, you'll run the ShowHTML demonstration that I created for this lesson. ShowHTML uses a combo box to present a list of favorite Web sites to the user, and uses the Internet Explorer's Navigate method to display whichever HTML document the user selects.

Run the ShowHTML program

Start button

1 Open the ShowHTML.vbp project in the \Vb6Sbs\Less20 folder.

2 Click the Start button on the toolbar to run the program.

Your form will look like the following:

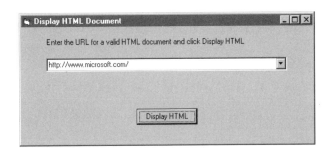

3 Click the Down arrow in the combo box on the form to display a list of favorite Web sites for Visual Basic programmers.

You'll see the following list of URLs:

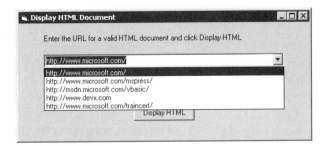

As you've probably noticed in your Internet browser, a combo box can be a handy control for presenting URLs to the user. In my Web applications, I usually try to display five or six URLs for users to choose from when they start their Web applications, and allow them to add their own favorites when they visit additional sites. The Internet addresses I've included here will connect you to a few sites that I think are of general interest to Visual Basic programmers. Feel free to use them, but note that one or two of the URLs may not be valid a year or two from now. (These things change rapidly.)

The following table lists the Web sites I present in the program:

Internet address	Description
http://www.microsoft.com/	Microsoft Corporation home page
http://www.microsoft.com/mspress/	Microsoft Press home page (with links for Visual Basic books)
http://msdn.microsoft.com/vbasic/	Microsoft Visual Basic Programming home page
http://www.devx.com/	Third-party resources for Visual Basic programming
http://www.microsoft.com/traincert/	Certification resources for Visual Basic

④ Click the Microsoft Visual Basic Programming home page (http://msdn.microsoft.com/vbasic/) in the combo box.

⑤ Click the Display HTML button.

Visual Basic opens Internet Explorer and loads the Microsoft Visual Basic URL into the browser. If you're not currently online, Internet Explorer prompts you for your internet service provider (ISP) member ID and password with a sign-in dialog box and connects you to the Internet. (If you connect to the Internet through a corporate network, you may have a different logon process.) After a moment, you'll see the Microsoft Visual Basic home page, which will look similar to the following illustration. (Your HTML document will contain more recent information.)

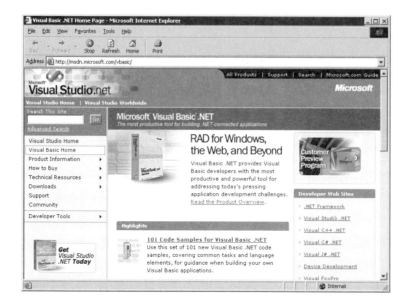

6 Maximize the Internet Explorer window if it is not already full-size, and then click one or two links of interest to you.

The Microsoft Visual Basic Programming home page is an excellent resource for late-breaking news about programming tools, tips, conferences, books, and other information about Visual Basic.

7 After you have finished reviewing the page, close the Internet Explorer window. If you are asked if you want to disconnect from the Internet, click No to remain connected.

8 Display the ShowHTML form again.

The ShowHTML program is still running, although it may have settled beneath a few other open applications by this point. If you don't see it, press Alt+Tab to display a list of currently open applications, and click Display HTML Document to bring the application to the forefront.

9 Pick another Web site from the combo box, and then click Display HTML to open it.

After you've had a look at my selections, open a few of your own favorite sites with the program.

10 Place the cursor in the combo box on the ShowHTML form, remove the current URL, and enter a URL of your own choosing. Then click Display HTML to open it.

In addition, you can use this tool to display HTML documents on your hard disk, if you wish.

11 After you've displayed three or four HTML documents, click the Close button on the ShowHTML program's title bar, and then close any open Internet Explorer windows on the task bar.

Now you'll take a look at the program code in the ShowHTML application that utilizes the Internet Explorer object.

Examine the Internet Explorer code in ShowHTML

1 Open the Declarations sections of the form in the Code window.

You'll see the following program code.

```
'Declare a variable for the current URL
Public Explorer As SHDocVw.InternetExplorer
```

Explorer is a public variable.

The ShowHTML program begins by declaring a public object variable named Explorer that will facilitate the program's connection to the Internet Explorer object library. The declaration references the InternetExplorer class in the shdocvw.dll file, which must be included in your project by using the References command on the Project menu.

2 Open the Command1_Click event procedure in the Code window.

You'll see the following program code:

```
Private Sub Command1_Click()
    On Error GoTo errorhandler
    Set Explorer = New SHDocVw.InternetExplorer
    Explorer.Visible = True
    Explorer.Navigate Combo1.Text
    Exit Sub
errorhandler:
    MsgBox "Error displaying file", , Err.Description
End Sub
```

The Command1_Click event procedure runs when the user clicks the Display HTML button on the form. This event means that the user either is satisfied with the default entry (http://www.microsoft.com/) and wants to display it or has specified another HTML document in the program's combo box to display. Accordingly, the event procedure sets an error handler to manage unexpected connection errors, and then creates a new Internet Explorer object. Next, it makes the Internet Explorer window visible and opens a document in the browser that corresponds to the user's selection in the combo box (a value currently held in the combo box object's Text property). At this point, the ShowHTML application runs in the background, while the user's attention is shifted to the now open Internet Explorer window, which manages the connection to the Internet (if necessary) and allows the user to view the selected Web site and click any existing hyperlinks on the page.

3 Open the Form_Load event procedure in the Code window.

You'll see the following program code:

```
Private Sub Form_Load()
'Add a few useful Web sites to combo box at startup
    'Microsoft Corp. home page
    Combo1.AddItem "http://www.microsoft.com/"
    'Microsoft Press home page
    Combo1.AddItem "http://www.microsoft.com/mspress/"
    'Microsoft Visual Basic Programming home page
    Combo1.AddItem "http://msdn.microsoft.com/vbasic/"
    'Third-party resources for VB programming
    Combo1.AddItem "http://www.devx.com"
    'Certification resources for VB
    Combo1.AddItem "http://www.microsoft.com/traincert/"
End Sub
```

When the ShowHTML program loads, the user is presented with a list of several "favorite" Web sites automatically. These URLs are presented in a combo box that I configured initially in the Form_Load event procedure by using the AddItem method. Feel free to add your own favorite URLs to this list by including additional AddItem statements—the combo box object includes scroll bars when necessary and can accommodate many entries.

<table>
<tr><td>One Step Further</td><td></td></tr>
</table>

One Step Further

Responding to Internet Explorer Events

In this lesson, you've manipulated the properties and methods of the Internet Explorer object to display HTML documents in a window. You can also take greater control of your browsing activities by responding to events that occur in the Internet Explorer object. As you may recall from previous lessons, each Visual Basic control has the ability to produce status announcements, or *events*, in the regular course of its operation. These events can include anything from a simple mouse movement in the Image control (the Drag event) to notification that a downloading activity is complete (the ResponseComplete event in the Internet Transfer control). The Internet Explorer object also produces events that you can respond to programmatically with event procedures. These include NavigateComplete2, DownloadBegin, DownloadComplete, TitleChange, DocumentComplete, and OnQuit.

If you want to use Internet Explorer events in your program, you first need to modify the statement in your program code that declares the Internet Explorer object variable. Events produced by external ActiveX components are not automatically listed in the Object drop-down list box of the Code window. However, you can include these events by using the WithEvents keyword when you make your object declaration. In the ShowHTML program developed in this lesson, you edit the declaration section of your form as follows:

```
'Declare a variable for the current URL
Public WithEvents Explorer As SHDocVw.InternetExplorer
```

WithEvents adds events to the Code window

After you use the WithEvents keyword, the Explorer object appears automatically in the Object drop-down list box in the Code window. When you select the Explorer object, its events appear in the Procedure drop-down list box. You can then select each event that you want to control and build an event procedure for it. You'll see how this works in the ShowHTML program.

Use the NavigateComplete2 event

In this exercise you'll write an event procedure that adds the URL for the current Web site in the Internet Explorer to the combo box object in the ShowHTML program.

1 Save the ShowHTML form as **MyHtmlHist.frm,** and then save the ShowHTML project as **MyHtmlHist.vbp.**

2 Display the Code window, and scroll to the Declarations section of the program, located at the top of the program listing.

3 Add the WithEvents keyword to the Internet Explorer object declaration after the Public keyword.

Your object declaration should look like this:

```
Public WithEvents Explorer As SHDocVw.InternetExplorer
```

4 Click the Object drop-down list box in the Code window and click the Explorer object.

5 Click the Procedure drop-down list box in the Code window and click the NavigateComplete2 event.

The parameters for the Explorer_NavigateComplete2 event procedure appear in the Code window.

6 Type the following statement in the event procedure:

```
Combo1.AddItem Explorer.LocationURL
```

Your procedure should now look like this:

```
Private Sub Explorer_NavigateComplete2(ByVal pDisp _
        As Object, URL As Variant)
    Combo1.AddItem Explorer.LocationURL
End Sub
```

The complete HtmlHist.vbp project is also available on disk in the \Vb6Sbs\Less20 folder.

The NavigateComplete2 event occurs when the Internet Explorer object has successfully loaded the specified document into the browser. This event only occurs when the document has been loaded successfully—an invalid Web page or URL will not trigger the event. As a result, watching for the NavigateComplete2 event is a useful way to keep track of the Web documents you've recently loaded. If you use the LocationURL property of the Explorer object, you can build your own history list of HTML documents. In this example, I've simply added the URL for the document to the combo box on the form, so you can easily revisit the site with a mere mouse click. However, you also could store this information permanently by writing the URL to a file or a database.

Start button

❼ Click the Save button on the toolbar to save your changes.

❽ Click the Start button on the toolbar to run the program.

❾ Click one of the Web sites listed in the combo box and click the Display HTML button.

❿ After the connection is established, click some of the hyperlinks on the site to jump to a few new URLs.

⓫ Click the Display HTML Document program icon on the taskbar, and click the combo box again.

The new sites you visited will appear at the bottom of the list, as shown in the following illustration:

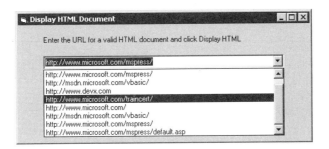

Experiment with the NavigateCompleted2 event by visiting a few more Web sites and adding them to the combo box.

⓬ When you're finished, close the Internet Explorer windows you have open. Then click the Close button on the HtmlHist application's title bar.

You're finished working with HTML in this lesson. Nice job!

If you want to continue to the next lesson

● Keep Visual Basic running, and turn to Lesson 21.

If you want to quit Visual Basic for now

● On the File menu, click Exit.

If you see a Save dialog box, click Yes. (You want to save your changes to the MyHtmlHist project you just created.)

20

Displaying HTML Documents

Upgrade Notes:
What's Different in Visual Basic .NET?

If you choose to upgrade to Visual Basic .NET in the future, you'll notice some new features related to the topics in this lesson, including the following:

- The version of Internet Explorer that was shipped with the first release of Visual Basic 6.0 was Internet Explorer 4. Internet Explorer 6.0 is included with the initial release of Visual Basic .NET. Both versions are largely compatible, so if you wrote Visual Basic 6.0 programs that used earlier versions of Internet Explorer, you should have little trouble compiling them under Visual Basic .NET and the new version of Internet Explorer.

- To use Internet Explorer features in a Visual Basic .NET program, you need to add a reference to the Microsoft Internet Controls object library (SHDocVw) using the Add Reference command on the Project menu. Because the Microsoft Internet Controls object library is based on COM specifications, Visual Studio will create a "wrapper" for the library containing the necessary types and classes for the component.

Lesson 20 Quick Reference

To	Do this
Add a reference to the Internet Explorer object library to your program	On the Project menu, click the References command and place a check mark in the box to the left of the Microsoft Internet Controls (shdocvw.dll) entry.
Investigate the Internet Explorer object model	Click the Object Browser button on the toolbar to open the Object Browser, select the SHDocVw library in the Project/Library drop-down list box, select the InternetExplorer class, and click individual members of the class for more information about the syntax for each property, method, and event.
Start Internet Explorer in your program	Declare an object variable of the SHDocVw type, and set its Visible property to True. For example: `Set Explorer = New SHDocVw.InternetExplorer` `Explorer.Visible = True`
Display a Web site with the Internet Explorer object	Use the Navigate method. For example: `Explorer.Navigate "http://www.microsoft.com/"`
Access the events of an external object (such as Internet Explorer)	Declare your object by using the WithEvents keyword. For example: `Public WithEvents Explorer As SHDocVw.InternetExplorer`

Displaying HTML Documents 20

21

Designing Dynamic HTML Pages for the Web

**ESTIMATED
TIME
40 min.**

In this lesson you will learn how to:

✔ *Get started with Dynamic HTML programming.*

✔ *Create a Web page with the DHTML Page Designer.*

✔ *Add text formatting, ID attributes, and SPAN tags to your
document.*

✔ *Insert a hyperlink to open additional HTML pages.*

✔ *Create a supporting HTML page in Microsoft Word 97.*

In Lesson 20, you learned the fundamental concepts of HTML and how to display HTML documents in a Microsoft Visual Basic application with a Microsoft Internet Explorer object. In this lesson, you'll learn how to build your own HTML applications with the new DHTML Page Designer included with Microsoft Visual Basic Professional Edition. *Dynamic hypertext markup language* (DHTML) is a sophisticated Internet technology based on the Microsoft component object model (COM) specification and documents produced by the World Wide Web Consortium. Although a complete description of DHTML is beyond the scope of this book, the DHTML Page Designer lets you begin creating Web applications even if you have little or no experience in Internet programming or Web page design. Invest a few hours in Lessons 21 and 22, and see if Dynamic HTML is for you!

Inside Dynamic HTML

Dynamic HTML is a Microsoft technology included in Internet Explorer versions 4.01 and later. With DHTML, you can create an HTML-based application that uses Internet Explorer to display a Web application's user interface and to process many of the computing requests traditionally handled by an Internet server. The application you create is stored as an HTML file and a dynamic link library (DLL) on the "client side" of an Internet or intranet connection. In other words, DHTML technology allows you to build Web applications that provide access to Internet servers but still reside physically on the end user's computer. This distributed "dynamic" approach makes DHTML programs more responsive than traditional Web applications that reside on the server, because DHTML programs don't rely on a distant computer to route information, store data, and process requests. In a DHTML application, the local browser handles many routine computing tasks, changes a page's layout, and executes the code behind DHTML pages without calling the server to refresh the data. This increases application speed, reduces the workload on Web servers, and (in many cases) allows end users to work offline with Internet or intranet data that they have already downloaded.

The DHTML Page Designer helps you create Web applications.

Visual Basic 6 Professional Edition includes a special editing component called the *DHTML Page Designer* that allows you to integrate Dynamic HTML into your Visual Basic applications. With the DHTML Page Designer, you can create your own Web applications from scratch, or you can customize existing HTML pages by adding DHTML features. As a programming language, DHTML is best thought of as an extension of Microsoft Visual Basic Scripting Edition (a version of Visual Basic for Internet development), but it also has much in common with the Visual Basic language you've been learning in this book. DHTML is not completely compatible with Visual Basic because it must remain compatible with earlier HTML standards, especially the object model used in earlier versions of Internet Explorer. As a result, certain Visual Basic controls, properties, methods, events, and keywords are not supported by Dynamic HTML. In Lessons 21 and 22, you'll explore a few of these important differences. More importantly, you'll also learn how to integrate your existing Visual Basic knowledge into Internet applications. Although Dynamic HTML is a new type of programming, the DHTML Page Designer smoothes many of the language's peculiarities by presenting HTML concepts in a familiar object model and the conventional Visual Basic development environment.

A New Programming Paradigm

What are the important differences between Visual Basic and DHTML programming? To begin with, DHTML features a slightly different programming paradigm from Visual Basic's. While Visual Basic uses forms as the primary user interface for an application, DHTML presents information to the user via one or more HTML pages with supporting program code. You can create these pages in a

DHTML Program Development, Step by Step

Because the DHTML Page Designer runs inside the Visual Basic programming environment, the overall DHTML development process is very similar to that of building a traditional Visual Basic application. Here are the steps you need to follow:

1 Start Visual Basic, and open a new DHTML Application project.

2 In the Project window, open the Designers folder, click the DHTMLPage1 item, and then click the View Object button.

3 Resize the DHTML project window so that it is large enough to hold your Web page.

4 Add text, DHTML toolbox elements, and ActiveX controls to your Web page as desired.

5 Format text with the formatting tools, and assign ID tags to any textual elements you want to reference with program code.

6 Write event procedures for any user interface elements that require them.

7 Add additional Web pages to the project with the Add DHTML Page command on the Project menu, and add text, controls, and event procedures as described in steps 4 through 6.

8 Save the project with the Save As command on the File menu.

9 Run the project by clicking the Start button on the Visual Basic toolbar, and be sure to test each feature. (You'll need Internet Explorer 4.01 or later on your system to run the program.)

10 If you want to distribute your application, compile the project with the MakeDHTMLProject.dll command on the File menu. Then deploy your application by running the Package And Deployment Wizard located in the Visual Studio 6.0 Tools folder on the Windows Start menu.

Dynamic HTML Pages

21

separate HTML editor (such as Microsoft Word or Microsoft FrontPage), or you can create them from scratch in the DHTML Page Designer included with Visual Basic. Another difference is related to the filename endings associated with the two languages: HTML pages are stored in .htm files, and Visual Basic forms are stored in .frm files.

On an HTML page, program-mable controls are called "elements."

Like a form, an HTML page can include text, graphic images, buttons, list boxes, ActiveX controls, and other objects that are employed to process input and display output. However, the basic set of controls you use to create an HTML page is not the same as the one in the Visual Basic 6 toolbox. Instead, the DHTML Page Designer features a toolbox with slightly different programmable objects called *elements* that perform tasks in the user interface according to the rules spelled out in the HTML specification. Each of these elements has its own unique methods, properties, and events, which are different from the ones you've used with Visual Basic objects. For example, although the DHTML Button element looks and operates much like the Visual Basic CommandButton control, it runs the Button1_onclick event procedure when it is clicked, rather than the Command1_Click event procedure. In Lesson 22, you'll learn more about adding DHTML elements and event procedures to your Web application.

Getting Started with the DHTML Page Designer

The best way to learn how to create a Dynamic HTML application is to get some hands-on practice using the DHTML Page Designer. In this section, you'll open the Page Designer in Visual Basic and create an HTML page with formatted text that will serve as the basis for your Internet application. The program you'll create will be an HTML version of the Lucky 7 slot machine game from Lessons 2 and 10 that runs under Internet Explorer. (The name of the project this time around will be WebLucky.vbp.) You'll add the text and formatting codes for the HTML application in this lesson, and the toolbox controls and event procedures in Lesson 22.

Open a new DHTML application

Follow these steps to start Visual Basic and open a new DHTML application in the DHTML Page Designer:

1 Start Visual Basic.

2 In the New Project dialog box, click the DHTML Application icon and click Open.

When you use the DHTML Application icon to open a new project, Visual Basic loads the DHTML Page Designer and configures the compiler to create an ActiveX dynamic link library (.dll). An ActiveX .dll is a file that provides objects and computing resources to an HTML page that issues Dynamic HTML commands. (Your Visual Basic program code is stored in this .dll.)

When the Page Designer opens, your screen will look like this:

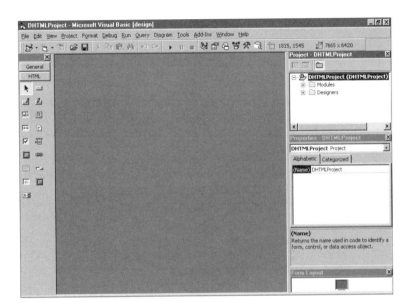

❸ Open the Designers folder in the Project window.

The default HTML page in the project (DHTMLPage1) appears in the Designers folder. A *designer* is an individual HTML page that contains the text, controls, and other elements of your application's user interface. (In Microsoft terminology, a designer is a special tool that creates a part of your Visual Basic application. In this book, you'll use designers to create DHTML application and ActiveX data objects.) If you want to include more than one HTML page in your application, you can add additional designers to the Designers folder with the Add DHTML Page command on the Project menu.

View Object button

❹ Click the DHTMLPage1 designer in the Designers folder, and then click the View Object button in the Project window.

Visual Basic displays the DHTML Page Designer in the programming environment. Because the Page Designer doesn't open full-sized by default, you should enlarge it now and reduce the amount of space taken up by the Project, Properties, and Form Layout windows.

21

Dynamic HTML Pages

5 Position the mouse over the left edge of the Project window until the mouse pointer changes to the sizing pointer, and then drag the window border to the right to reduce the amount of space it takes up in the programming environment.

Now you'll enlarge the DHTML Page Designer.

6 Position the mouse over the lower-right corner of the Page Designer. When the mouse pointer changes to the sizing pointer, enlarge the Page Designer so that it looks similar to the following illustration:

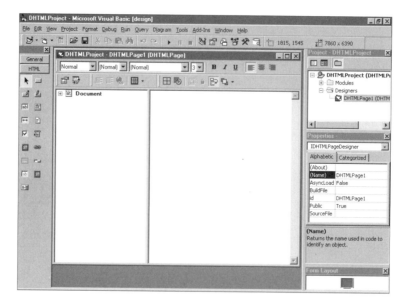

7 Take a moment to identify the major editing tools in the Page Designer.

The default page, DHTMLPage1, appears in the right pane of the Page Designer. (The page is currently blank.) In the left pane is a *tree view* description of the HTML code in your document. As you add text, controls, and formatting effects to your HTML page, the styles you select and the tools you use are reflected in a hierarchical structure in this pane.

Above the two panes in the Page Designer is the formatting toolbar, which contains buttons that format, position, and edit the elements on your HTML page. You'll use several of these buttons in this lesson. To the left of the Page Designer is a toolbox containing the intrinsic DHTML controls that you can add as programmable elements to your HTML pages. In addition to these DHTML controls, you can also add ActiveX controls, including the controls you've been experimenting with in Visual Basic 6 Professional Edition.

Now you're ready to add some text to your first HTML page.

Add text to an HTML page

Although controls and special formatting effects often add excitement to HTML pages on the Web, the bread and butter of a well-designed HTML application is usually an informative textual interface. In the following steps, you'll add the textual elements for the Lucky 7 program to the HTML page in the right pane of the Page Designer.

1 Click the HTML page (the page on the right side) in the Page Designer.

A blinking cursor appears at the top of the HTML page, and a tree view diagram of your document opens in the left pane of the Page Designer.

2 Type the following text into the HTML page, following the instructions in [brackets] to get the spacing exactly right:

Lucky 7 Game [Enter] [Enter] [Enter]
0 [Space] [Space] [Space] **0** [Space] [Space] [Space] **0** [Enter]
Wins: [Enter]
About Lucky 7

For each [Enter] instruction, press the Enter key. For each [Space] instruction, press the Spacebar once. When you're finished, your HTML page should look like the illustration on the following page.

tip

You're never required to know specific HTML formatting tags when you use the Page Designer in Visual Basic. However, you'll see HTML tags in the tree view pane from time to time to give you more information about how your document is organized.

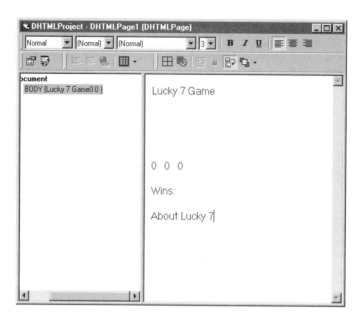

Notice that the BODY tag in the tree view pane now lists the initial contents of the HTML page you're working on. In HTML, the BODY tag contains instructions that control the basic graphical appearance and behavior of the contents of the Web page.

Format text in the Page Designer

In DHTML, *styles* replace the individual formatting tags that were used origi- nally in HTML to format individual text elements on a Web page. (The HTML formatting tags still exist, but the Page Designer hides them in a .dsx file for your project.) A *style* is a collection of properties that control the appearance of ele- ments in a DHTML document. Style sheets can apply a style to a single element or a group of elements. In addition, you can apply multiple styles to each element on the page (such as a heading style and a hyperlink style).

In the following steps, you'll format the text you typed earlier in the Lucky 7 application with formatting styles from the Page Designer toolbar.

1   Select the **Lucky 7 Game** text at the top of the HTML page.

Before you can change the style of text in the Page Designer, you need to select it.

2   Click the Style drop-down list box in the upper-left corner of the Page Designer, and point to the Heading 1 style.

Your screen will look like the illustration on the following page.

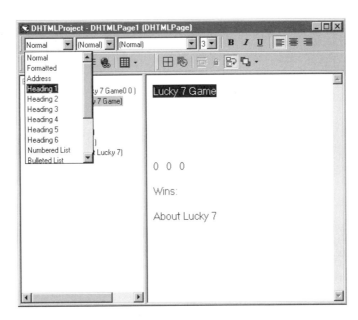

3 Click the Heading 1 style to format the **Lucky 7 Game** text in the Heading 1 style.

The Page Designer applies the Heading 1 style to the text, which enlarges it like this:

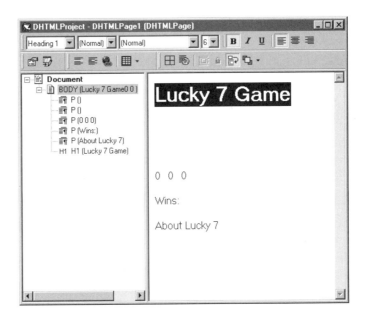

tip
Page Designer styles are similar to the styles provided by Microsoft Word and other word-processing applications.

Now you'll practice using a few more styles on your HTML page.

4 In the tree view pane, click the first blank paragraph—P()—in the document, and format it with the Heading 2 style. (If you don't see the P() tags, click the plus symbol next to the BODY element in the tree view pane, and then select the first P() tag and format it with the Heading 2 style.)

In addition to selecting text on an HTML page, you can also select and format individual lines from the tree view pane. After you click the Heading 2 style, the Page Designer enlarges the font. (However, because the line is blank, the only noticeable effect is a small increase in the spacing between the lines.)

5 Click the next blank paragraph P() in the document, and format it with the Heading 2 style.

Notice that as you apply formatting styles to the text elements in your document, the Page Designer identifies the formatting selection with a two-character code (H1, H2, and so on) and moves them to the bottom of the tree view pane. (If you've worked with HTML before, these heading tags will be familiar to you.)

6 Select the three zeros in the document (**0 0 0**), and format them with the Heading 1 style.

7 Select the **Wins:** text in the document, and format it with the Heading 3 style.

8 Select the **About Lucky 7** text (at the bottom of the HTML page), and format it with the Heading 4 style.

Your HTML Page will look like the illustration shown at the top of the following page.

That's all there is to it! By using formatting styles, you can add a precise and consistent look to your HTML pages that can be duplicated over and over again.

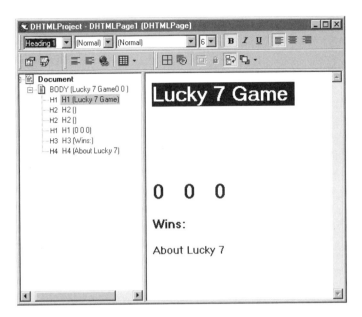

tip

In addition to the default formatting styles you've just explored, you can use the Font Size and Font Name drop-down list boxes in the Page Designer to adjust the font attributes on your HTML page. You can also use the Bold, Italic, and Underline buttons on the toolbar to adjust the font style, and the Left, Center, and Right buttons to adjust the alignment of text on the page.

Create SPAN tags to isolate individual characters

When you write DHTML applications in Visual Basic, a common task is using property settings to change the content of individual words or characters on a Web page. For example, you might want to update a number that announces the number of visitors to a Web site in a given month, or a number that identifies the quantity of a particular product remaining in inventory. If you know which words or characters you want to isolate with Visual Basic code when you are creating your HTML page, you can use the Page Designer to enclose the string with SPAN tags. In some situations you may not see these tags in your HTML document, but they will exist "behind the scenes" in the Page Designer, and you'll see them recorded in the tree view pane.

Follow these steps to delimit the three zeros in the Lucky 7 application with SPAN tags, so that you can replace them with random numbers later in an event procedure.

Wrap Selection In SPAN button

❶ Select the first **0** in the document, and then click the Wrap Selection In SPAN button on the Page Designer toolbar.

You may use either the keyboard or the mouse to select the text. (You'll probably find it easier to use the keyboard to select text if the characters you're selecting are surrounded by blank spaces.)

❷ Select the second **0**, and click the Wrap Selection In SPAN button on the Page Designer toolbar again.

❸ Select the third **0** in the document, and click the Wrap Selection In SPAN button for the final time.

Notice that a plus (+) symbol has now appeared next to the text tag in the tree view pane, indicating the presence of the SPAN tags you just created.

❹ Click the plus symbol in the tree view window to view the SPAN tags.

You'll see three SPAN indications in the formatting tree:

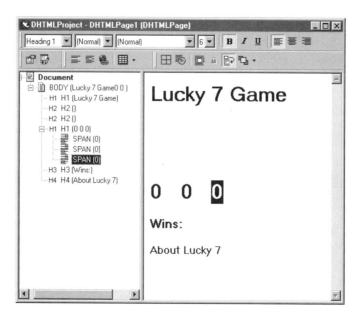

Now that you have isolated each of the random number placeholders in your document, you can manipulate them individually with program code.

tip

In addition to offsetting elements on your HTML page with SPAN tags, you can also link paragraphs together by using DIV tags. A DIV tag is handy when you want to format several elements with the same style in one comprehensive operation. Because everything within a DIV tag maintains the same formatting attributes, DIV can be a powerful way to coalesce information on a Web page. The toolbar button for the DIV tag, located next to the SPAN button, is labeled Wrap Selection In <DIV> . . . </DIV>.

Assign ID attributes with the Properties window

In a Visual Basic program, each object in your application's user interface has a unique name that the compiler uses to process runtime events. For example, the first text box object on a form is named Text1, the second is Text2, and so forth. In a Dynamic HTML application, each element on a page must also have a unique name or *ID attribute* if you want to manipulate it with program code. Each attribute you assign to the various elements on your page functions as the element's object name in your DHTML application.

Follow these steps to assign ID attributes to each textual element on your HTML page.

❶ Click the **Lucky 7 Game** heading in the tree view pane (the H1 tag).

❷ Open and enlarge the Properties window if it is currently not visible or if it is obscured by another window.

❸ Click the text box next to the ID entry in the Properties window, type **LuckyHead**, and press Enter.

The Page Designer sets the ID attribute of the selected text to LuckyHead. Although you won't programmatically control this head in this DHTML application, it's good programming practice to name each of the paragraphs that you're using.

❹ Click the second heading in the tree view window (the first blank line in the document), and change its ID attribute to Blank1 with the Properties window.

❺ Click the third heading in the tree view window and change its ID attribute to Blank2.

❻ Click the fourth heading (containing all three numbers) and change its ID attribute to Num.

The Num attribute (like a collection name) applies to all three numbers. However, you can also assign individual IDs to the strings designated by SPAN tags.

⑦   Click the first SPAN number, and assign it the ID Num1.

⑧   Click the second SPAN number, and assign it the ID Num2.

⑨   Click the third SPAN number, and assign it the ID Num3.

⑩   Click the Wins heading, and assign it the ID Result.

Your HTML page will look like this:

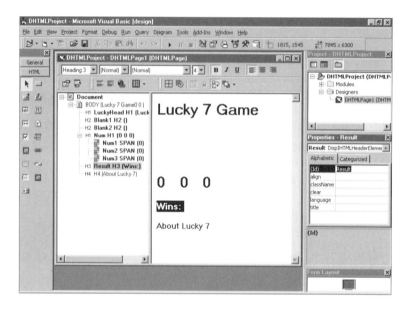

The last text heading (About Lucky 7) doesn't need an ID attribute right now. You'll format it as a hyperlink in the next exercise.

Create a link to another HTML page

If your Web application will feature more than one HTML page, a handy formatting tool you'll want to remember is the Make Selection Into Link button, located on the Page Designer toolbar. The Make Selection Into Link button formats the selected text as a *hyperlink*, which will load a new HTML page into Internet Explorer to replace the current one when the user clicks the link. After you format a text selection as a hyperlink, you can specify the desired connection (either a URL or a local pathname) by using the textual element's *href property* in the Properties window.

Follow these steps to format the About Lucky 7 text as a hyperlink:

①   Click H4 (About Lucky 7) in the tree view pane to select the final head on the page.

Before you can format text on your HTML page as a hyperlink, you need to select it.

Make Selection Into Link button

2 Click the Make Selection Into Link button on the Page Designer toolbar.

The selected head is formatted as a hyperlink in the right pane.

3 Now click a different line in the HTML document.

When the cursor moves away from the line containing the hyperlink, the hyperlink formatting (blue text and underline style) becomes visible, and a plus (+) symbol appears in the tree view pane.

4 Click the plus symbol in the tree view pane to see the ID attribute for the hyperlink (Hyperlink1).

5 Click the Hyperlink1 tag in the tree view pane to display the hyperlink's properties in the Properties window.

6 Scroll to the href property in the Properties window, and click the text box to the right of the property.

Your screen will look like this:

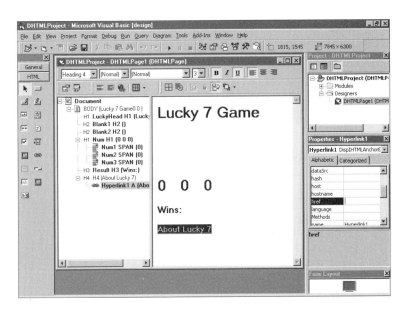

7 Type **c:\vb6sbs\less21\lucky.htm** in the href property entry for the hyperlink, and press Enter.

Lucky.htm is an HTML document you'll create in the next section ("One Step Further"). However, the Visual Basic Page Designer won't check now to see if the document exists or not. (It just checks at runtime.)

That's it! You've created all the text entries in the Lucky 7 Web application, and you've practiced formatting content, creating SPAN tags, assigning ID attributes, and creating hyperlinks. These skills will serve you well as you create your own DHTML applications in the future.

Save the WebLucky project

Now you'll save the project you've created under the name **MyWebLucky.vbp**.

① On the File menu, choose the Save Project As command.

② Type **MyWebLucky** when you are prompted for the name of your project (.vbp) file.

③ Type **MyWebLucky** when you are prompted for the name of your designer (.dsr) file.

A *designer file*, used here for the first time, is a special file that contains your HTML page and all of its formatting and controls.

④ Type **MyWebLucky** when you are asked to name your code module (.bas) file.

In a DHTML application, the .bas file contains functions that manage PutProperty and GetProperty operations—mechanisms for saving and retrieving important data on a Web page when the browser shifts from one page to the next. (You'll learn more about these functions in Lesson 22.)

Run the DHTML application

Now that your DHTML application is safely stored on disk, you'll run it with Internet Explorer.

tip
The WebLucky.vbp project is available on disk in the C:\Vb6Sbs\Less21 folder. You can open this folder if you didn't create the MyWebLucky application in this lesson, or if you want to compare your work against the original version.

Start button

① Click the Start button on the Visual Basic toolbar to run the MyWebLucky program (or WebLucky, if you chose to load it from disk).

The first time you run this application, you may see a Project Properties dialog box that looks like the illustration on the following page.

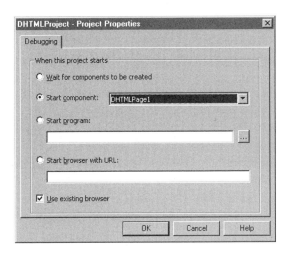

This box is simply asking you if you want to begin your application by loading the HTML form you just created in the Page Designer. The correct HTML component is specified already, so simply click OK if you see this dialog box now.

Visual Basic loads Internet Explorer and displays your DHTML application. In Internet Explorer version 4.01, the program looks like this:

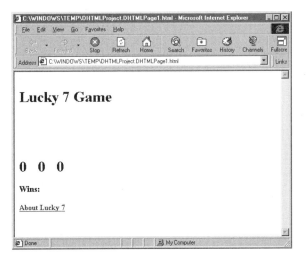

Typically, you'll see a few minor formatting differences in the way Internet Explorer presents your HTML page. At this point, your application is only halfway done, so you're not able to interact with the program, but you can see how the browser displays the formatting and hyperlink effects you've created.

> **tip**
> Did you notice the strange pathname in your browser's Address text box? When Visual Basic compiles your DHTML application in memory, it creates a temporary file on your hard disk to store the program while it runs. The path you see is simply the temporary storage location Visual Basic is using to store the file.

② Click the Close button on the Internet Explorer's title bar to close the Internet Explorer.

The Internet Explorer closes, but your application is still running because Internet Explorer is simply a browser, not the originator of the program.

③ Click the End button on the Visual Basic toolbar to stop the DHTML application.

After a moment, the program closes, and the Page Designer reappears in the programming environment.

One Step Further   Creating HTML Documents in Microsoft Word

As you learned earlier in this lesson, you can create Dynamic HTML pages inside Visual Basic with the DHTML Page Designer, or you can create HTML documents with an external editor or word processor and then incorporate the files directly into your programming project. As you'll learn in the next lesson, the DHTML Page Designer is extremely handy if you want to create advanced formatting effects with DHTML controls and third-party ActiveX controls. However, if you're simply entering text in your HTML documents, it sometimes makes more sense to create your HTML document in an outside editor first, and then to incorporate it into your project.

If you have Microsoft Word 97, Microsoft Word 2000, Microsoft Word XP, or a later version of Word on your system, you can use it as an HTML document editor without entering your own HTML code. (Word creates HTML codes automatically when you save documents in a certain way.) If you have a recent version of Microsoft Word on your system, try using it now to create a simple HTML Help file that describes the operation of the MyWebLucky application.

Use Word to create the Lucky.htm Help file

❶ Minimize the Visual Basic development environment, and start Microsoft Word on your computer.

I start Microsoft Word by pointing to the Start menu, pointing to the Programs folder, and clicking the Microsoft Word icon.

❷ When Word starts and a new, blank document appears, type the following text and format it as shown.

Lucky 7 Game

The Lucky 7 Game is a DHTML application developed for the book *Microsoft Visual Basic Professional 6.0 Step by Step, Second Edition*, by Michael Halvorson (Microsoft Press, 2003). (View the document with Microsoft Internet Explorer version 4.01 or later.) To learn more about how this application was created, read Lessons 21 and 22 in the book.

Playing instructions:

Object: To display a 7 in a group of three random numbers.

Odds: A 7 will appear at least once in approximately 28 out of 100 spins.

Your Word document will look like this when you're finished:

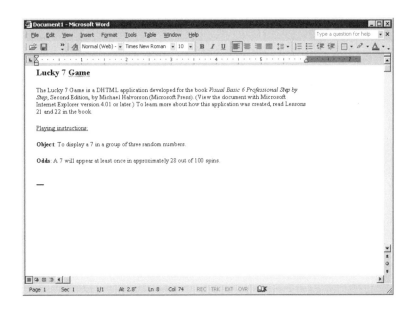

Now you'll save this document as an HTML file so that it can be displayed by the WebLucky application.

❸ On the Word File menu, click the Save As Web Page command. (In Word 97, this command is called Save As HTML.)

❹ When the Save As dialog box appears, specify the C:\Vb6Sbs\Less21 folder, and type **MyLucky** as the name of your HTML file.

Word will convert the file to HTML format and save it in the Less21 folder.

You may be asked if you want to continue without saving the file in Word format (to preserve formatting that can't be converted to HTML) or if you want to connect to the Web to download newer versions of the Web authoring tools. Click Yes to the first and No to the second. (You haven't used any formatting that can't be converted, and you don't want new tools now.)

❺ On the Word File menu, click the Exit command to quit Word.

Now you'll run the WebLucky program again to see how it works with an active hyperlink.

❻ Maximize Visual Basic.

important

If you have been following these instructions exactly, you'll need to change the href property of the Hyperlink1 object to C:\Vb6Sbs\Less21\MyLucky.htm before you run the WebLucky program, so that it opens the HTML file that you just created. I sent the href property to C:\Vb6Sbs\Less21\Lucky.htm (which you can also use) because I wanted you to be able to simply load and run the programs in this chapter. However, if you went to the trouble of creating MyLucky.htm, you might as well use it!

Start button

❼ Change the href property for the Hyperlink1 object if necessary, and then click the Start button on the Visual Basic toolbar to run the DHTML program.

❽ When the WebLucky page appears in the Internet Explorer, click the About

Lucky 7 hyperlink to display the linked page.

After a moment you'll see the output in Internet Explorer.

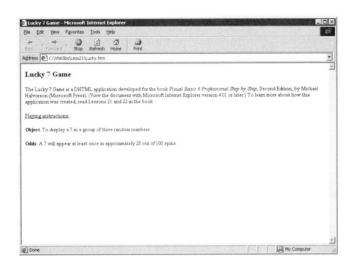

⑨ Click the Back button to return to the WebLucky HTML page.

⑩ Click the Close button on the Internet Explorer title bar.

⑪ Click the End button on the Visual Basic toolbar.

Using Microsoft Word (or another HTML editor or word processor) is often a helpful supplement to the DHTML Page Designer in Visual Basic. If you have such a program, you may want to use it to full advantage in your development efforts.

If you want to continue to the next lesson

● Keep Visual Basic running, and turn to Lesson 22.

If you want to quit Visual Basic for now

● On the File menu, click Exit.

If you see a Save dialog box, click Yes.

Upgrade Notes:
What's Different in Visual Basic .NET?

If you choose to upgrade to Visual Basic .NET in the future, you'll notice some new features related to the topics in this lesson, including the following:

- Visual Basic .NET offers a new Internet programming model called Web Forms, which is part of a technology called ASP.NET. Web Forms is a replacement for WebClasses and the DHTML Page Designer you are using in Visual Basic 6.0, which is powerful but admittedly quite different from the Windows Forms Designer you use when creating standard Windows applications.

- Visual Basic .NET now has two forms designers and two separate toolboxes with controls for each type of form. The Web Forms Designer is distinct from the Windows Forms Designer, although both offer similar controls and support drag-and-drop programming techniques. Because the Web Forms Designer is part of Visual Studio .NET, it is available to Visual Basic .NET and Visual C# .NET programmers.

- Web Forms applications in Visual Basic .NET are designed to be displayed by Internet browsers, such as Internet Explorer. The controls on Web Forms are visible in the client's Web browser (in other words, on the end-user's computer), but the functionality for the controls resides on the Web server that hosts the actual Web application.

- Web Forms programming is only supported in Visual Basic .NET on computers that have Windows 2000 or Windows XP Professional installed, along with a copy of Microsoft Internet Information Services (IIS), the Microsoft FrontPage 2000 Server Extensions, and the .NET Framework libraries.

- Microsoft recommends that Visual Basic 6.0 developers keep their DHTML solutions in Visual Basic 6.0 for the time being. Migrating them to Visual Basic .NET is possible but not simple. However, if you create new Web applications, you'll definitely want to use the Web Forms feature in Visual Basic .NET because the development process is much simpler.

Lesson 21 Quick Reference

To	Do this
Create a new DHTML application	Start Visual Basic, click the DHTML Application icon in the New Project dialog box, and click Open.
Display the DHTML Page Designer	Open a new or existing DHTML application in Visual Basic, open the Designers folder in the Project window, click the DHTML page you want to open, and then click the View Object button.
Add text to a DHTML page	Click the right pane in the Page Designer to move the insertion point to the open DHTML page, and then type text using the keyboard.
Format text on a DHTML page	Select the text you want to format, and then click a formatting style in the Styles drop-down list box on the Page Designer toolbar.
Create SPAN tags to make individual characters on a DHTML page programmable	Select the characters you want to isolate on the DHTML page, and then click the Wrap Selection In SPAN button on the Page Designer toolbar.
Assign ID attributes to text on a DHTML page	Click the text block you want to name in the Page Designer's tree view pane, and then type a unique ID attribute in the ID property in the Properties window.
Format text on a DHTML page as a hyperlink	Click the text block you want to format as a hyperlink in the tree view pane, and then click the Make Selection Into Link button on the Page Designer toolbar.
Save the components in a DHTML project	Choose the Save Project As command on the File menu and name your project components as directed.
Run a DHTML application	Click the Start button on the Visual Basic toolbar.
Create a HTML document in Microsoft Word 97	Start Word, type the text of your document, and choose the Save As HTML command on Word's File menu.

22

Adding Elements and ActiveX Controls to DHTML Pages

**ESTIMATED TIME
50 min.**

In this lesson you will learn how to:

✔ Use Dynamic HTML toolbox elements to process input on a Web page.

✔ Use ActiveX controls to enhance DHTML pages.

✔ Write event procedures for DHTML events.

✔ Use the DHTML Property Bag to store and retrieve important information.

✔ Compile your application as an HTML file and .dll.

In Lesson 21, you learned how to use the DHTML Page Designer to create a basic DHTML application with text elements, formatting, and a hyperlink. In this lesson, you'll learn how to add both intrinsic DHTML toolbox elements and ActiveX controls to your Web page, and you'll learn how to customize these objects with event procedures. In addition, you'll use the Property Bag to let key information on your Web page persist between page loads, and you'll learn how to compile your project as an HTML file with supporting .dll and other files.

Getting Started with Toolbox Elements

As you learned in the last lesson, the DHTML Page Designer includes a toolbox with DHTML controls, or *elements,* that you can use to enhance your Web page's user interface. These toolbox elements are not the same as the Microsoft Visual

Basic intrinsic controls, although they have many similarities. The DHTML toolbox elements create objects in accordance with HTML programming standards so that Microsoft Internet Explorer can display the Web pages that use those standards. DHTML toolbox elements provide different properties and methods from those of Visual Basic controls, and they also respond to different events. Finally, DHTML controls are optimized for operation on the Web, where size and speed are key factors. The following illustration identifies the elements in the DHTML toolbox:

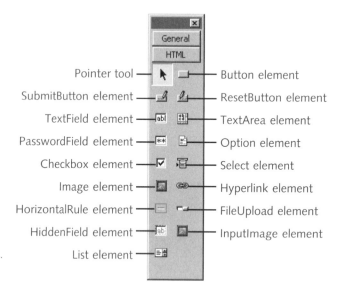

tip

The Visual Basic toolbox lets you switch back and forth between DHTML toolbox elements and Visual Basic toolbox controls. (Although the intrinsic Visual Basic controls are not available in a DHTML application, ActiveX controls in your Visual Basic toolbox are available.) To switch back and forth between elements and controls, click the HTML and General buttons in the toolbox, respectively. (Note that the HTML button moves to the bottom of the toolbox when the standard controls are visible.)

Documenting the DHTML Toolbox

Before you start using the toolbox elements in a DHTML application, spend a few moments exploring what the elements do. Although you won't be experimenting with every toolbox element in this lesson, the following summary will give you the information you need to get started on your own. For more information about how the toolbox elements are used in a DHTML application, type **HTML Intrinsic Controls** in the Index tab of the MSDN Library online Help.

Button

The Button element creates a command button on a Dynamic HTML page. The Value property holds the text that appears on the button, and the OnClick event procedure is executed each time the user clicks the element. The Button element is typically used during data entry on a form, to calculate new values, or to close Web pages.

SubmitButton

The SubmitButton element also creates a command button on a DHTML page. However, the SubmitButton is typically used to pass the information on a Web page to a back-end process, such as an Internet server. When this data is passed to the back-end process, the information entered through input elements is sent as text. The Value property holds the text that appears on the button, and the OnClick event procedure is executed each time the user clicks the element.

ResetButton

Like the Button element, the ResetButton element appears on a DHTML page as a command button object. However, the ResetButton element clears all the text fields on the current page. (It is typically used to clear a Web page used for data entry.) The Value property holds the text that appears on the button, and the OnClick event executes when the element is clicked.

TextField

The TextField element creates a single-line text box on a DHTML page that can receive textual input at runtime. This text box element works a lot like the TextBox control in Visual Basic. The Value property holds the text that appears in the text box. You can define this property at design time with the Properties window, or read the property at runtime to determine what the user typed. The TextField element executes the OnSelect event when the contents of the text box are selected, and the OnChange event when the text in the text box is changed.

TextArea

The TextArea element creates a larger text box on a DHTML page that allows multiline input and output. If necessary, the TextArea element features scroll bars to provide access to hidden lines. The Value property holds the text that appears in the text box. You can define this property at design time with the Properties window, or read the property at runtime to determine what the user typed. The Rows property lets you set the height of the element in lines, and the Cols property lets you set the width of the element in characters. Like the TextField element, the TextArea element executes the OnSelect event when the contents of the text box are selected, and the OnChange event when the text in the text box is changed.

PasswordField

The PasswordField element creates a text box on a DHTML page that hides or *masks* a password or other sensitive information that the user is entering. PasswordField is an appropriate element to use whenever you need to keep input away from intruding eyes. Like the TextField element, the Value property in the PasswordField element holds the text that appears in the password box. You can specify a hidden, default password at design time by setting the Value property with the Properties window, or you can read the Value property to receive the user's password at runtime. The PasswordField element executes the OnSelect event when the contents of the password box are selected, and the OnChange event when the text in the password box is changed.

Option

The Option element creates an option button, or *radio button,* on a DHTML page. In Visual Basic, you create a group of mutually exclusive option buttons (a set that allows only one selection at a time) by placing each button inside a Frame control on the form. However, the DHTML Page Designer has no Frame control. To group option buttons together on a DHTML page, you must use the Properties window. In the Properties window, first you set the Name property of each button to the same value, and then you set the ID property of each button to a unique ID attribute. The Checked property causes one button in the group to be selected by default, and the OnClick event is executed when the user clicks an individual button element.

Checkbox

The Checkbox element is used to add a check box to a DHTML page. Unlike a Visual Basic check box, the DHTML Checkbox element does not include a built-in label that describes the check box. (You need to add the label by typing text on the DHTML page.) The Checked property determines the current state of the check box. Set Checked to True to place a check mark in the box, or to False to remove the check mark. The OnClick event is executed when a check box element is clicked.

Select

The Select element adds a drop-down list box, or *combo box,* to a DHTML page. It is similar to the ComboBox control in Visual Basic. The Size property determines the number of items that are visible at one time in the combo box, and the Selected property causes an item to be selected by default. When the Select element is changed at runtime, the OnChange event is executed. To add items to a Select combo box at design time, right-click the Select element on the page, click the Properties command, and use the Property Page for the Select element to add list items.

Image

The Image element is used to add a standard graphic image to a DHTML page. To load an image into the element at design time or runtime, set the Src property with the pathname of the graphic you want to load. You can also use the Title property to display pop-up text when the user clicks the Image element on the page.

Hyperlink

The Hyperlink element is used to create a link to another HTML page in your application. To specify the name of the HTML document or URL that you want to link to, set the href property from the Properties window. Note that the text that appears in the formatted hyperlink on your page is not controlled by the Hyperlink element, but by the associated text element on the page. (You can adjust this by editing the hyperlinked text directly on the DHTML page.) You can also control exactly how the Hyperlink element jumps to another HTML document by writing code for the Hyperlink element's OnClick event.

HorizontalRule

The HorizontalRule element adds a horizontal line to the DHTML page. You can adjust the thickness of the line with the Size property, and the color of the line with the Color property. You can also set the length of the line with the Width property.

FileUpload

The FileUpload element adds a text box and a command button to the DHTML page that users can use to upload a file from their local hard disk to an Internet server. Users can either type the pathname in the text box, or they can click the Browser button to open a dialog box that allows them to search for the file on their system. The OnClick event is executed when a user clicks the FileUpload element, and the OnSelect event is executed when text is selected in the text box.

HiddenField

The HiddenField element adds a text box to the DHTML page that cannot be seen by the user. This text box is useful as a temporary storage location for data in your program (for example, a password that you want to verify). In addition, you can use the HiddenField element to pass information to an Internet server when the Submit operation is executed. The Value property holds the content of the hidden text, and can be set at design time or runtime.

InputImage

The InputImage element adds a picture to the DHTML page. The Src property specifies the pathname or URL of the image that appears in the image box. In addition to this basic functionality, the InputImage element allows the user to click the loaded image as a mechanism for input. For example, a DHTML programmer could load a map into the InputImage control and track the particular (x, y) location that the user clicks on the map.

List

The List element is used to add a scrolling list box to a DHTML page. The List element is similar to the ListBox control in Visual Basic. The Size property determines the number of items that are visible at one time in the combo box, and the Length property controls the height of the ListBox. When the Select element is changed at runtime, the OnChange event is executed, and the Value property contains the item selected. To add items to a List element at runtime, right-click the List element on the page, click the Properties command, and use the Property Page for the List element to add list items.

Creating and Customizing Elements

The process of physically creating DHTML toolbox elements on a Web page is almost identical to creating objects on a Visual Basic form with the toolbox. You can insert a DHTML toolbox element in three ways:

- By clicking the element icon in the toolbox and dragging it to the right pane of the Page Designer

- By clicking the element icon in the toolbox and drawing it on the right pane, as you would on a Visual Basic form

- By double-clicking the toolbox icon. (This creates a default element on the page automatically.)

You can resize toolbox elements with the sizing pointer just as you would resize a control on a Visual Basic form. If you want to move a toolbox element, you can do so simply by pressing the arrow keys on your keyboard. (If you move an element off the screen, it will be invisible to the user but still active.) You can position elements absolutely on the page or relative to other elements and the browser window. The Absolute Position Mode button on the Page Designer toolbar toggles these location modes.

tip
Absolute positioning means that the element you place on the page will appear in the exact location you have specified. Relative position allows an element to move in relation to neighboring elements if the page is resized.

At design time, you can customize your toolbox elements by setting properties from the Properties window. The available properties vary depending on the type of element you're using. Some toolbox elements contain Property Pages that you can customize by right-clicking the element, clicking the Properties command, and filling out the Property Pages dialog box. To delete a toolbox element, click the element name in the tree view pane and press Del.

Adding Elements to the WebLucky Application

In this section, you'll practice using toolbox elements by adding an Image element and a Button element to the WebLucky project, a DHTML application you started working on in Lesson 21. When you're finished customizing the

Elements and ActiveX Controls   22

program, you'll have a utility that displays random numbers when you click the Spin button. If one or more sevens appears on the page, your win will be announced by the sound of applause (produced by the Multimedia MCI control and a .wav file).

Rename the files in your DHTML application

If you want to work on a new version of a DHTML application, you need to rename the project (.vbp), designer (.dsr), and module (.mod) files first.

1   Start Visual Basic, and open the WebLucky.vbp project in the C:\Vb6Sbs\Less21 folder.

You'll save this project under a new name in the Less22 folder to protect the original version. (If you want to continue working with the MyWebLucky project you created in Lesson 21 rather than the version I created for you, open the MyWebLucky project now instead, and rename its files.)

2   On the File menu, click the Save Project As command.

3   Browse to the C:\Vb6Sbs\Less22 folder, and then type **MyDHTML7** and press Enter.

Visual Basic creates a copy of the WebLucky project file in the Less22 folder. Now you'll save the DHTML page under a new name.

4   Open the Designers folder in the Project window, and click the DHTMLPage1 designer.

5   On the File menu, click the Save WebLucky.dsr As command.

6   In the Save File As dialog box, type **MyDHTML7** and press Enter.

7   Open the Modules folder in the Project window, and click the modDHTML module.

8   On the File menu, click the Save modDHTML As command. (Your module may have a different name.)

9   In the Save File As dialog box, type **MyDHTML7** and press Enter.

Whenever you save an existing DHTML application under a new name, simply follow this three-step process: rename the project (.vbp) file, the designer (.dsr) file, and the module (.mod) file.

> **tip**
> In addition to project (.vbp), designer (.dsr), and module (.mod) files, a DHTML application includes a .dsx file with HTML codes for the designer you're using, and a .dca file with HTML code and other binary information.

Delete a text element on the page

In the Page Designer, you can delete any item by right-clicking it in the tree view pane or design pane and choosing the Delete command. This is a useful ability to have when you are editing DHTML pages. (Now and then you'll want to delete an element and start over again.)

Follow these steps to delete the first blank line (Blank1) on the page:

1 Click the Blank1 element in the tree view pane.

 The element is selected.

2 Right-click the Blank1 element and select Delete from the shortcut menu.

 The text element is deleted permanently from the page.

> **important**
> Be careful when deciding whether to delete an element from a DHTML page. The Page Designer has no Undo feature to reverse your decision!

Add an Image element to the page

Your first enhancement to the MyDHTML7 program will be adding an Image element to the page you've created for the slot machine game. The Image element will display a stack of coins when the program runs.

1 Double-click the Image element in the toolbox.

Image element

> **tip**
> If you're unsure which toolbox element is the Image element, hold the mouse over one or two likely candidates to see their names in a tooltip pop-up window.

The Page Designer places an Image element in the DHTML form, as shown in the following illustration:

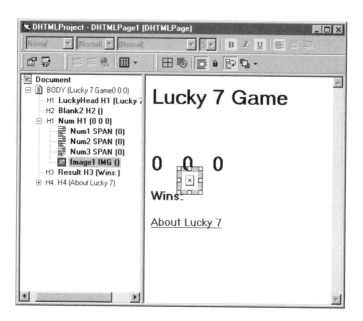

You can also create an Image element by clicking the element in the toolbox and dragging over the page with the mouse. However, double-clicking the toolbox element and resizing is usually the easiest approach. Notice that the Page Designer also inserted a name and description of the Image element into the tree view pane. (It might appear at a different location on your machine.)

❷ Press the Up and Left arrow keys until the Image element is between the Lucky 7 Game title and the three zeros.

The best way to move selected elements on a DHTML page is to move them with the arrow keys. You can specify fine movements by holding down the Ctrl key and pressing an arrow key. Your screen should look like the figure on the next page.

tip

You can resize the Image element with the mouse, but you'll probably find using the Width and Height properties much easier.

In its default state, the Image element will display an image full-sized on the page. However, you can configure the Image element to display a graphic at a particular size by setting the element's Width and Height properties from the Properties window. In this program, you'll keep the Image element at its default size to display a Windows metafile that fills up the Internet Explorer window at runtime. Note that unlike the image in the first Lucky 7 program you built, the coin stack in this program will always be visible.

Save Project button

❸ In the Properties window, scroll to the Border property, and click the text box to the right of the property.

❹ Type **0** in the Border property and press Enter to ensure the Image element does not display a border.

❺ Click the Save Project button on the Visual Basic toolbar to save your changes.

Button element

Add a Button element to the page

Now you'll add a Button element to the DHTML page to start the slot machine and display three random numbers.

❶ Double-click the Button element in the toolbox.

The Page Designer adds a Button element to your page and creates a new entry for the button in the tree view pane.

❷ Use the Right and Down arrow keys to move the button to the right side of the page, across from the Wins label.

Your page should look like this:

❸ Restore the Properties window, scroll down to the Value property, and delete the text in the Value property box (currently Button1).

The Value property holds the text that appears on the Button element. To change the text, update the Value property.

❹ Type **Spin** in the Value property box, and press Enter.

The text in the Button element changes to Spin, and your Property window looks like the following illustration:

Your Button element is now ready for program code. You'll add this after you add the Multimedia MCI ActiveX control to the page.

Adding ActiveX Controls to a DHTML Page

Although you can't use intrinsic Visual Basic toolbox controls in a DHTML application, you can add ActiveX controls to a DHTML page. The Page Designer manages these controls by placing <OBJECT> tags around them in the HTML code for your application. In most cases, the traditional properties, methods, and events supported by the original ActiveX control are available to you, with a few interesting limitations. (For example, you can't use the Visible property for ActiveX controls, because HTML pages don't use the Visible property the same way that Visual Basic forms do.) In addition to the standard collection of properties, methods, and events provided by ActiveX controls, you also have access to a few additional attributes from the HTML specification for your controls, including ClassID, CodeBase, CodeType, ID, and so on. These extra properties allow you to exploit the advanced attributes of HTML page elements, while still using the core functionality provided by the ActiveX control.

The ability to add ActiveX controls to DHTML applications is a great benefit to Visual Basic programmers. It lets you enhance your Web pages by using all the interesting Professional Edition ActiveX controls that you've been working with in this book. In the following exercise, you'll add the Multimedia MCI ActiveX control to your DHTML application to play an applause.wav file whenever a user hits the jackpot.

Add an ActiveX control to the toolbox

Before you can use an ActiveX control on your DHTML page, you must add it to the Visual Basic toolbox. ActiveX controls are stored in the General pane in the toolbox, which you can access by clicking the General button in the toolbox.

❶ On the Project menu, click the Components command.

Scroll down the list, and click the check box next to the Microsoft Multimedia Control 6.0 entry.

❷ Click OK to add this ActiveX control to your toolbox.

The Multimedia MCI control appears on the toolbox in the General pane, as shown in the illustration on the following page. (Notice that the intrinsic Visual Basic controls are currently dimmed, because they are unavailable to DHTML applications.)

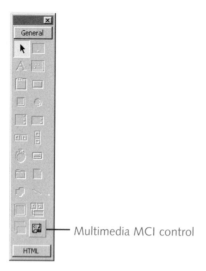

Multimedia MCI control

Now you're ready to add the ActiveX control to your application.

Create a Multimedia MCI control on the page

ActiveX controls are drawn on a DHTML page just like other controls. Because these controls do not have a Visible property, you'll need to drag them off the left margin if you don't want them to be visible when your program runs. (This "hides" the control when the DHTML page is displayed in the browser.) Note also that certain ActiveX controls with no user interface, such as the Common Dialog ActiveX control, are invisible on the page at design time as well as at runtime. You can set the properties for invisible or hidden controls by selecting them in the tree view pane.

Follow these steps to add the Multimedia MCI control to your application:

1 Double-click the Multimedia MCI control in the toolbox.

The Page Designer creates a new control in the middle of the page and adds an entry for the control to the tree view pane. Your page will look like the illustration on the next page.

2 Press the Left arrow key until the Multimedia MCI control has moved off the left edge of the page.

Moving the control out of view makes it invisible. (To move it back into view, simply click the control in the tree view pane, and hold down the Right arrow key.)

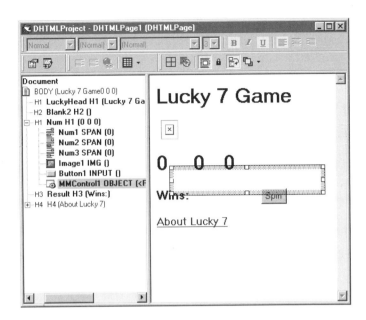

❸   Click the Save Project button on the Visual Basic toolbar to save your changes.

You'll configure the Multimedia MCI control and enable it to play the .wav file with program code in the following exercises.

Creating Event Procedures for DHTML Elements

You can programmatically control the elements and ActiveX controls on your DHTML page with event procedures and carefully chosen program code in much the same way as in a Visual Basic application. With a few important exceptions, the Visual Basic statements, functions, and keywords you've been using in this book will also work in DHTML event procedures. The biggest difference you'll encounter when writing DHTML event procedures is that many of the event names and object names have changed, so it takes a little practice to get your bearings. However, familiar structures like If...Then...Else, For...Next, and Do...Loop are all the same.

In this section, you'll build event procedures for two events that execute, or "fire," as your DHTML application runs. One is the DHTMLPage_Load event, which runs when your page is loaded into the Internet Explorer browser. The other is the Button1_onclick event, which runs when the user clicks the Spin button to display three random numbers.

tip

HTML programmers often say that an event "fires" when it is executed or called in a DHTML program. For example, "The Button element *fired* the onclick event when Bob clicked the Spin button." I mention this because the verb "fired" is often used in the DHTML online Help and in other resources for Internet programming.

Create the DHTMLPage_Load event procedure

In this exercise, you'll create the DHTMLPage_Load event procedure, which runs each time your DHTML page is loaded by the browser. This event procedure is generally equivalent to the Form_Load event procedure in Visual Basic, except for the fact that the DHTMLPage_Load event procedure is run each time the page is refreshed by the browser. (As you'll see below, you should keep this fact in mind when you write your code.)

*View Code
button*

1   Click the View Code button in the Project window to display the Code window.

2   Click the Object drop-down list box in the Code window, and then click the DHTMLPage object.

The event procedure for the DHTMLPage_Load event procedure appears in the Code window.

3   Type the following program code:

```
'Set underline style for heading
LuckyHead.Style.textDecorationUnderline = True
'Set color style of numbers to blue
Num.Style.Color = "blue"
'Seed random number generator (for truly random spins)
Randomize
'Display coin stack
Image1.src = "c:\vb6sbs\less22\coins.wmf"
'Configure and open Multimedia MCI control
MMControl1.Notify = False
MMControl1.Wait = True
MMControl1.Shareable = False
```

```
MMControl1.DeviceType = "WaveAudio"
MMControl1.FileName = "c:\vb6sbs\less22\applause.wav"
MMControl1.Command = "Open"
'Use GetProperty function to determine if any
'previous wins exist in the Property Bag (a storage
'location that persists during HTML page load and
'unload operations). With this code you can save
'the number of wins between jumps to the "About
'Lucky 7" hyperlink or other Web pages.
Result.innerText = "Wins: " & GetProperty(Document, "Wins")
```

④   Fix any obvious typing mistakes or syntax errors detected by Visual Basic.

⑤   Click the Save Project button on the Visual Basic toolbar to save your additions.

Exploring the DHTMLPage_Load Code

The event procedure that runs when the DHTML page is loaded into the browser accomplishes several important tasks. First, the code formats the LuckyHead element with the underline style to set it off visually on the page. (LuckyHead looks like an object, but it is really a textual element that you named "LuckyHead" with the Id property in the Properties window.) Likewise, I set the color of the numbers on the page to blue by using the Num ID, the Style attribute, and the Color property. I set these two properties to show you how to use program code to customize textual elements on a page.

The Randomize statement in the DHTMLPage_Load event procedure initializes or "seeds" the random number generator with a random number from the system clock. This ensures that each spin will result in a set of truly random numbers (not numbers in a set pattern). (You learned about the Randomize statement and seeding in Lesson 2.) The next statement loads the coins.wmf metafile into the Image element on the form by setting the element's Src property to the path of the graphic on my hard disk. Unlike the ImageBox control in Visual Basic, the Image element is set at runtime, not at design time.

The third set of program statements in this event procedure configures and opens the Multimedia MCI control for use. Lesson 17 describes how to program the Multimedia MCI control; the important thing to note here is that I've set the DeviceType property to WaveAudio (sound information stored in a .wav file), and I've set the FileName property to applause.wav to access this particular sound file. The actual applause sound is not played until the user hits the jackpot, a situation identified by the Button1_onclick event procedure that you'll write in the next section.

The Property Bag is a temporary storage location. The final set of program statements references a global value named Wins in the DHTML application's Property Bag to see if the player has scored any previous wins during the game. A *Property Bag* is a temporary storage container that exists outside of the current DHTML page. You can store information in the Property Bag by using the PutProperty function. When you call this function, you specify the value you want to store, and you assign it a variable name that you can use to retrieve the information. To retrieve this value later, you issue the GetProperty function and specify the name of the value you want. In the DHTMLPage_Load event procedure, I check the current position of the Wins value and display it on the page with the innerText property described below. Notice that the GetProperty function doesn't produce a result the first time the page is loaded. However, as the game progresses, this function preserves the number of wins if the user jumps to the About Lucky 7 hyperlink or to another Web page.

Create the Button1_onclick event procedure

Now you'll build the event procedure that runs when the Button element is clicked on the DHTML page.

1   Open the Object drop-down list box in the Code window, and click the Button1 object.

The Button1_onclick event procedure appears in the Code window.

2   Type the following program code:

```
'Declare local variable x for wins (copied to
'Property Bag between spins)
Dim x
'Pick three random numbers
Num1.innerText = Int(Rnd * 10)
Num2.innerText = Int(Rnd * 10)
Num3.innerText = Int(Rnd * 10)
'If any number is 7, display coin stack and beep
If Num1.innerText = 7 Or Num2.innerText = 7 Or _
    Num3.innerText = 7 Then
      'If we have a winner, play .wav file (applause.wav)
      MMControl1.Command = "Prev"   'rewind if necessary
      MMControl1.Command = "Play"   'play .wav file
      'and increment the win count in the Property Bag
      x = GetProperty(Document, "Wins")
      Result.innerText = "Wins: " & x + 1
      PutProperty Document, "Wins", x + 1
End If
End Function
```

❸ Fix any syntax errors detected by Visual Basic.

❹ Click the Save Project button on the toolbar to save your event procedure.

Exploring the Button1_onclick Code

The Button1_onclick event procedure runs when the user clicks the Spin button on the DHTML page. This routine has much in common with the Spin routine you used in Lessons 2 and 10 to produce random numbers for the Lucky 7 game. First, the event procedure declares a local variable named x to hold the number of wins stored in the Property Bag. Because x is a local variable, it is reset each time this event procedure runs. (The event procedure copies the total wins to date into the x variable with the GetProperty function.)

Use innerText to change text on the page.

Random numbers between 0 and 9 are generated by the Rnd function, truncated by the Int function, and copied onto the page by the innerText property of the Num1, Num2, and Num3 elements, respectively. (When you assigned the Num1, Num2, and Num3 IDs to the three text boxes on the page in Lesson 21, you made them programmable objects in your program code.) The innerText property modifies a textual element by substituting the text argument you specify for the existing text on the page. The innerText property only works with strictly textual elements; if you also want to insert HTML tags to format the text in a certain way, use the innerHTML property instead.

The innerText property can also represent the value of an element. I use this functionality in the If statement that checks to see if one of the random numbers placed on the page is a seven:

```
If Num1.innerText = 7 Or Num2.innerText = 7 Or _
    Num3.innerText = 7 Then
```

If a seven does appear, I use the Prev (previous) and Play arguments in the Multimedia MCI control to play the applause .wav file, which announces the victory. (I use the Prev argument to rewind the media player if the sound has been played before.) After starting the applause, I use the GetProperty function to copy the Wins value to the local variable x. Then I increment the Wins count on the form in the Result element. Finally, I copy the incremented Wins count back to the Property Bag with the PutProperty function:

```
PutProperty Document, "Wins", x + 1
```

Note that the PutProperty and GetProperty functions are declared in a standard module included by default in all DHTML projects (modDHTML). If you're interested in how these functions manage information in the Property Bag, take a moment to examine the code for the functions in the Code window. (Open the Modules folder in the Project window, click the modDHTML module, and then click View Code.) You can also put your own general-purpose functions and Sub procedures in this standard module.

The DHTML7 application is located in the \Vb6Sbs\Less22 folder.

Run the MyDHTML7 application

Now you'll run the MyDHTML7 application to see how your application looks and runs in the Internet Explorer browser.

Start button

❶ Click the Start button on the Visual Basic toolbar to start Internet Explorer and load the DHTML page.

Visual Basic needs to compile a few components in your application, so it takes a moment or two to load. (Click OK if you're asked to choose a start component.) You'll see the following:

❷ Click the Spin button until one or more sevens appears on the page.

When you hit the jackpot, the applause .wav file starts. (To hear the sound, you'll need to have speakers attached to your computer. Be sure to turn these on, and turn up the volume if you don't hear anything.) Your page should look like the figure on the next page.

important

If Internet Explorer displays a message at this time warning you that a control on the Web page might be unsafe, click Yes to allow the control to keep working. This behavior is caused by the MCI Multimedia control playing sounds.

③ Click several more times to build your Wins total to five or six.

Each time that a seven appears, another win is added to your total. (The information is being saved under the Wins name in the Property Bag.)

④ Click the Refresh button on the Internet Explorer toolbar to refresh the screen and execute the DHTMLPage1_Load event procedure.

After a moment, the page appears again with the proper number of wins.

⑤ Finally, click the hyperlink in the program, and then click the browser's Back button to verify that the correct Wins count is listed when the page is refreshed. (Click the letter "A" in the hyperlink if it doesn't work right away.)

tip

For more information about how this hyperlink was created, consult Lesson 21.

⑥ When you're finished experimenting with the MyDHTML7 application, click the Close button on Internet Explorer's title bar, and then click the End button on the Visual Basic toolbar.

Your DHTML program stops, and the Page Designer reappears in the development environment.

Elements and ActiveX Controls 22

One Step Further   Compiling a DHTML Application

A DHTML application consists of an HTML file, a dynamic link library (.dll), and a collection of support files. A DHTML application is compiled in the same way that any Visual Basic project is compiled—by choosing the Make command on the File menu. After the compilation, the DHTML application is called an *in-process component*, and it can be run in Internet Explorer on your own computer, on a corporate intranet, or over the Internet. If you choose to distribute your application, you need to run the Package and Deployment Wizard to build physical installation disks or Internet deployment files that contain your application and the necessary support files and controls. The Package and Deployment Wizard is located in the Microsoft Visual Studio 6.0 Tools folder, which is located in the Microsoft Visual Basic 6.0 folder on the Windows Start menu.

In the following practice exercise, you'll use the Make command to compile an HTML page and a .dll for the MyDHTML7 project.

Compile your project

❶   On the File menu, choose the Make MyHTML7.dll command.

Visual Basic displays the Make Project dialog box:

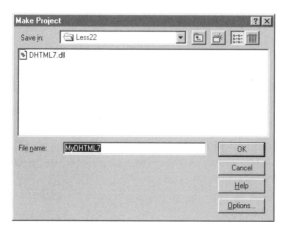

tip

To view advanced compiling options for your application, click the Options button in the Make Project dialog box.

2 Specify the C:\Vb6Sbs\Less22 folder (if it is not already selected), and then click OK to begin the compilation.

After a moment, you are prompted for the name of the HTML file that will load your project into Internet Explorer.

tip

You are prompted only once for the HTML filename. If you want to change this compilation location in the future, modify the BuildFile property of your page's designer (the IDHTMLPage1 object).

3 Specify the C:\Vb6Sbs\Less22 folder (if it is not already selected), type **MyDHTML7.htm,** and press Enter.

Visual Basic completes the compilation and places the files in the folder you specified. If you want to continue preparing your application for distribution to other users (via floppy disk or Web site), run the Setup and Deployment Wizard now.

tip

For more useful information about distributing DHTML files, search for **Deploying DHTML Applications** in the Index tab of the MSDN Library online Help.

If you want to continue to the next lesson

● Keep Visual Basic running, and turn to Lesson 23.

If you want to quit Visual Basic for now

● On the File menu, click Exit.

If you see a Save dialog box, click Yes.

Elements and ActiveX Controls 22

Upgrade Notes:
What's Different in Visual Basic .NET?

If you choose to upgrade to Visual Basic .NET in the future, you'll notice some new features related to the topics in this lesson, including the following:

■ Visual Basic .NET offers a new Internet programming model called Web Forms, which is part of a technology called ASP.NET. Web Forms is considered a replacement for the DHTML programming techniques you have been learning in this lesson and Lesson 21, although DHTML programming is similar in many ways to Web Forms programming.

■ Although many of the Web Forms controls have the same names as the Windows Forms controls in Visual Basic .NET or the DHTML controls in Visual Basic 6.0, the controls aren't identical. For example, Web Forms controls have an ID property, rather than a Name property.

Lesson 22 Quick Reference

To	Do this
Add a toolbox element to your DHTML page	Click the element icon in the toolbox and drag it over the DHTML page in the Page Designer. *or* Double-click the element icon in the toolbox.
Delete a toolbox element from a DHTML page	Click the element name in the tree view pane and press Del.
Add an Image element to a page	Double-click the Image element in the toolbox.
Add a Button element to a page	Double-click the Button element in the toolbox.
Move a toolbox element on a page	Press the arrow keys, or drag the element with the mouse.
Hide an element at runtime	Press the Left arrow key until the element moves off the left margin of the page.
Configure a toolbox element with property settings	Open the Properties window and change the desired property setting.

Lesson 22 Quick Reference

To	Do this
Add an ActiveX control to the toolbox	On the Project menu, click the Components command, and then place a check mark next to the control you want to add.
Write an event procedure for an element	Double-click the element on the page to open the Code window, specify the event you want to customize in the Procedure drop-down list box, and write your program code.
Load a graphic into the Image element at runtime	Use the element's Src property. For example: `Image1.src = "c:\vb6sbs\less22\coins.wmf"`
Change the text in a textual element at runtime	Use the innerText property. For example: `Num1.innerText = Int(Rnd * 10)`
Format the text in an element at runtime	Use the element's property settings. For example: `Num.Style.Color = "blue"`
Save a value in memory while other pages are loaded and unloaded	Use the PutProperty function to store the value in the DHTML Property Bag. For example: `PutProperty Document, "Wins", x + 1`
Retrieve a value from memory and copy it to a DHTML page	Use the GetProperty function to retrieve the value from the DHTML Property Bag. For example: `x = GetProperty (Document,"Wins")`
Run a DHTML application in Visual Basic	Click the Start button on the toolbar. *or* Press F5.
Compile a DHTML page and DLL	On the File menu, click the Make command.
Deploy a DHTML application via setup disks or the Internet	Click the Windows Start menu, point to the Programs folder, point to the Microsoft Visual Basic 6.0 folder, point to the Microsoft Visual Studio 6.0 Tools folder, and click the Setup and Deployment Wizard.

Elements and ActiveX Controls 22

PART 7

Advanced Database Programming

Managing Data with the FlexGrid Control

**ESTIMATED
TIME
30 min.**

In this lesson you will learn how to:

✔ *Create a FlexGrid spreadsheet and use it to display database records on a form.*

✔ *Sort database records by column.*

✔ *Search an entire database for key terms and highlight the results.*

In Part 7, you'll continue your exploration of database programming by focusing on several essential database tools and techniques in Microsoft Visual Basic 6 Professional Edition. In Lesson 13, you learned how to use the Data control to display database fields on a form, and how to add, delete, and search for records with program code. In this lesson and the following one, you'll learn how to display database information with the FlexGrid control, and how to work with a new database technology called ActiveX Data Objects (ADO).

In this lesson, you'll practice using the FlexGrid ActiveX control to create a spreadsheet, or *grid*, on a Microsoft Visual Basic form. The *FlexGrid ActiveX control* can be used to display grids with any type of tabular data: text, numbers, dates—even graphics. However, in this lesson you'll focus on using FlexGrid to display the fields and records of two Microsoft Access databases: Students.mdb and Biblio.mdb. The FlexGrid control translates the fields and records of a database table into columns and rows on a spreadsheet, respectively. You can perform many typical spreadsheet operations with FlexGrid, including selecting cells, resizing columns, aligning headings, and formatting text. You'll start by filling a simple FlexGrid control with text, selecting text, and setting a few formatting options. Next, you'll move on to binding the FlexGrid control to a database, displaying database tables, sorting records, and searching globally for user-defined text strings.

Using FlexGrid as a General-Purpose Spreadsheet

FlexGrid is an ActiveX control included with Microsoft Visual Basic Professional and Enterprise Editions. Before you can use FlexGrid in a project, you need to add it to your project's toolbox by selecting the Microsoft FlexGrid 6.0 control (msflxgrd.ocx) with the Components command on the Project menu. The FlexGrid control provides many of the traditional organizational benefits of a spreadsheet grid. You can use it to create invoices, calculate taxes, manage accounting ledgers, track parts lists and inventories, and so on. In addition, Microsoft designed FlexGrid to be a *bound control,* capable of displaying database information from a Data control that is also located on the form. If you want to display database information quickly in its original table format, FlexGrid is the tool for you.

tip

Visual Basic 6 Professional Edition also includes a companion spreadsheet control named the *Hierarchical FlexGrid ActiveX control* (mshflxgd.ocx). This control is used in the same way as the FlexGrid control and exposes the same core set of properties, methods, and events. However, the Hierarchical FlexGrid control can only be bound to the ActiveX Data Objects (ADO) control, not the intrinsic Data control in the Visual Basic toolbox. The adjective "hierarchical" means that the control can display *hierarchical recordsets*—recordsets created from more than one table in a database.

Understanding Rows and Columns

The spreadsheet grid produced by the FlexGrid control is a form containing a table with horizontal rows and vertical columns. By default, the top row and the left-most column are reserved for row and column titles and are displayed with a shaded background. You use the Rows property to set the number of rows in the table, and the Cols property to set the number of columns. The following illustration shows a form containing a FlexGrid table with 8 rows and 5 columns:

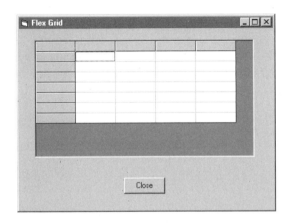

The tabular data in a FlexGrid control is manipulated like a two-dimensional array. The first dimension of the table is a row number, and the second dimension of the table is a column number. For example, the cell in the upper-left corner of the grid is referenced by the address 0, 0 (row 0, column 0).

To place a value in a FlexGrid cell, you set the TextMatrix property and specify a cell location and a value. You may specify any numeric or string data type. For example, to place the word "Bob" in cell 3, 1 (row 3, column 1), you would type the following program statement:

Add text to cells with the TextMatrix property.

```
MSFlexGrid1.TextMatrix(3, 1) = "Bob"
```

To assign the number 1500 to cell 2, 1 (row 2, column 1), you would use the following syntax:

```
MSFlexGrid1.TextMatrix(2, 1) = 1500
```

Inserting Graphics in Cells

You can also add graphics to FlexGrid cells with the Set statement, the CellPicture property, and the LoadPicture function. The valid graphics types are icon (.ico), bitmap (.bmp), and Windows metafile (.wmf). For example, the following program statement displays the Coins.wmf metafile in the selected cell on the grid:

Add graphics with the CellPicture property.

```
Set MSFlexGrid1.CellPicture = _
    LoadPicture("c:\vb6sbs\less22\coins.wmf")
```

When you add a graphic to a cell, the FlexGrid control doesn't resize the cell automatically to display it. However, you can manually adjust the height and width of a cell by using the RowHeight and ColWidth properties and specifying a measurement in twips for each. For example, the following statements widen the first row and the first column of the grid to 2000 twips. The numbers in parentheses represent the current row and column, respectively.

```
MSFlexGrid1.RowHeight(1) = 2000
MSFlexGrid1.ColWidth(1) = 2000
```

Placing these statements directly above the Set statement that loads your graphic into the CellPicture property will enlarge the cell sufficiently to display the entire graphic.

tip

When you resize one cell in the grid, you resize that cell's entire row and entire column.

Selecting Cells

As with most spreadsheets, you need to select cells in the FlexGrid control before you can format them. In the FlexGrid control, you can select individual cells or a *range* (a contiguous block) of cells with program code. To select an individual cell, simply set the Row property to the row you want to select, and set the Col property to the column you want to select. The selected cell will be at the intersection of the row and the column you specified. For example, to select cell 1, 1 on the grid, use the following program statements:

Select cells with the Row and Col properties.

```
MSFlexGrid1.Row = 1
MSFlexGrid1.Col = 1
```

To select a range of cells, you need to specify a starting and ending point for the selection. The starting point is the cell you last selected with the Row and Col properties (row 1, column 1 above). The ending point of the selection is identified by the RowSel and ColSel properties. For example, the following program statements select a contiguous block of 8 cells (cell 2, 2 to cell 5, 3) on the FlexGrid control:

```
MSFlexGrid1.Row = 2
MSFlexGrid1.Col = 2
MSFlexGrid1.RowSel = 5
MSFlexGrid1.ColSel = 3
```

On your form, the selection just described will look like the following figure:

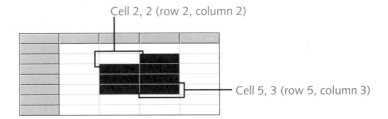

Cell 2, 2 (row 2, column 2)

Cell 5, 3 (row 5, column 3)

Finally, if you plan to format a range of cells, you need to include the following program statement after you make the selection:

```
MSFlexGrid1.FillStyle = flexFillRepeat
```

The flexFillRepeat value allows the FlexGrid control to format more than one selected cell at a time. (The default value, flexFillSingle, allows only one cell to be formatted at a time.) After this statement, you're ready to begin formatting selected cells individually or in ranges.

tip

You can also involve the user in the selection process if you want. For example, you could allow the user to select a group of cells on the FlexGrid control, and then click a button to change the text style of the selected cells to bold. You can control how the grid is accessed by users at runtime by setting the SelectionMode property to one of three options: flexSelectionFree (regular selection), flexSelectionByRow (selection by rows only), or flexSelectionByColumn (selection by column only).

23

The FlexGrid Control

Formatting Cells

The FlexGrid control provides many of the standard cell formatting features you'll find in a commercial spreadsheet application. These include properties for bold, italic, and underline formatting; text alignment in columns; font name and size; and foreground and background colors. The following table lists the most important formatting options available to you. You'll practice setting many of these properties later on in this lesson.

Eight cell formatting properties.

Property	Example
CellFontBold	`MSFlexGrid1.CellFontBold = True`
CellFontItalic	`MSFlexGrid1.CellFontItalic = True`
CellFontUnderline	`MSFlexGrid1.CellFontUnderline = True`
CellAlignment	`MSFlexGrid1.CellAlignment = flexAlignRightCenter`
CellFontName	`MSFlexGrid1.CellFontName = "Courier New"`
CellFontSize	`MSFlexGrid1.CellFontSize = 14`
CellForeColor	`MSFlexGrid1.CellForeColor = "red"`
CellBackColor	`MSFlexGrid1.CellBackColor = "blue"`

Adding New Rows

When you use the FlexGrid control to create invoices, accounting journal entries, and other tabular items, you'll find it useful to add new rows to the bottom of the spreadsheet. You can accomplish this with the AddItem method. The AddItem method works for the FlexControl just as it does for the ListBox and ComboBox controls. You specify the item you want to add, separating the information in each column with a tab character (the vbTab constant). For example, to add a new row to the bottom of a FlexGrid control with part information (beginning in the second column), use the following code:

Add rows with the AddItem method.

```
Dim Row As String
Row = vbTab & "Soccer ball" & vbTab & "W17-233" & vbTab & "34.95"
MSFlexGrid1.AddItem Row
```

As shown in the figure on the following page, such a statement would create a new row with part information for a soccer ball.

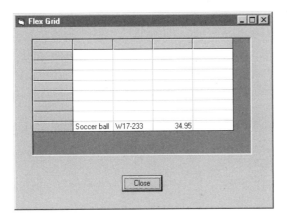

Use a FlexGrid control to track sales data

Now that you've acquired some background with the properties and methods of the FlexGrid control, you'll practice using it to create a two-quarter sales table that tracks sales by region.

1 Start Visual Basic, and open a new, standard project.

2 Enlarge the Project Container and Form windows so that you have plenty of room on your form to display a spreadsheet with several rows and columns.

3 On the Project menu, click the Components command, and then click the Controls tab.

The ActiveX controls that have been registered in your system registry appear in the Components dialog box.

4 Place a check mark next to the Microsoft FlexGrid Control 6.0 entry, and click OK.

Visual Basic adds the FlexGrid control to your toolbox.

5 Click the FlexGrid control in the toolbox, and create a large flex grid object on your form.

FlexGrid control

6 Double-click the CommandButton control in the toolbox.

A default-sized command button object appears on your form.

7 Drag the command button object below the flex grid object.

8 Use the Properties window to change the Caption property of the command button object to "Add Rows".

9 Use the Properties window to change the Cols property of the MSFlexGrid1 object to 4.

The Cols property contains the number of columns that will appear in your flex grid object. (You can change this value at runtime with program code.) Your form will look similar to the following:

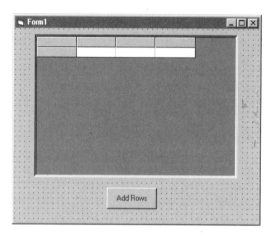

Write the FlexGrid program code

In this exercise you'll write the program code that creates a sales table in the flex grid object.

1 Double-click the form to open the Form_Load event procedure in the Code window.

2 Type the following program code:

```
With MSFlexGrid1    'use shorthand "With" notation
'Create headings for Columns 1 and 2
.TextMatrix(0, 1) = "Q1 1999"
.TextMatrix(0, 2) = "Q2 1999"
'Select headings
.Row = 0
.Col = 1
.RowSel = 0
.ColSel = 2
'Format headings with bold and align on center
.FillStyle = flexFillRepeat 'fill entire selection
.CellFontBold = True
.CellAlignment = flexAlignCenterCenter
'Add three entries for first row
```

```
.TextMatrix(1, 0) = "International"   'title column (0)
.TextMatrix(1, 1) = "55000"          'col 1
.TextMatrix(1, 2) = "83000"          'col 2
End With
```

The program statements in this event procedure are executed when Visual Basic starts the program and loads the first form into memory. These statements demonstrate several techniques for entering and managing information in a flex grid object: placing text in individual cells, selecting a cell range, formatting the range in bold type, and aligning the text in each cell in the range on center.

Of particular interest here is the With statement (introduced in Lesson 11), which allows you to forgo the drudgery of typing in the MSFlexGrid1 object name each time you want to access one of its properties or methods. Remember that each time you use a With statement in this way, as a short-hand notation, you must conclude the routine that follows it with an End With statement.

❸ Next, click the Object drop-down list box in the Code window, and select the Command1 object.

❹ In the Command1_Click event procedure, type the following program code:

```
With MSFlexGrid1
'Add four entries to table with each click
.AddItem "North" & vbTab & "45,000" & vbTab & "53,000"
.AddItem "South" & vbTab & "20,000" & vbTab & "25,000"
.AddItem "East" & vbTab & "38,000" & vbTab & "77,300"
.AddItem "West" & vbTab & "102,000" & vbTab & "87,500"
End With
```

The program statements in this event procedure are executed when the user clicks the Add Rows button on the form. The AddItem method creates a new row in the flex grid object and fills the first three columns with data. The vbTab constant marks the beginning of a new column in the table.

❺ On the File menu, click the Save Project As command. Save your form as **MySaleGrid.frm** and your project as **MySaleGrid.vbp.**

Run the MySaleGrid program

Now you'll run the program to see how the FlexGrid control displays tabular data.

Start button

❶ Click the Start button on the toolbar.

The program loads and displays the flex grid object with two column headings and one row of data. (These entries and formatting selections were defined by the Form_Load event procedure.)

The SaleGrid.vbp project is available on disk in the \Vb6Sbs\Less23 folder.

2   Click the Add Rows button.

Visual Basic adds four rows of sales data to the table. (These cells were created by the AddItem method in the Command1_Click event procedure.) Your form will look like the following illustration:

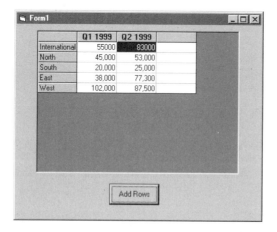

3   Click the Add Rows button two more times.

Visual Basic adds eight more rows to the table. Scroll bars appear on the right side of the table to let you access the rows that are no longer visible.

4   Continue adding rows if you like, and use the scroll bars to access them. When you're finished, click the Close button on the form's title bar.

The program terminates.

Using FlexGrid to Display Database Records

As you've probably noticed, adding table entries one at a time to a FlexGrid control can be a little cumbersome. However, connecting the FlexGrid control to a properly configured Data control on your form makes the powerful text management capabilities of FlexGrid really apparent. Like other bound controls, the Data control is connected to the FlexGrid control via a property setting. In this case, you set the FlexGrid's DataSource property to the name of the Data control on your form. When you establish this connection, the flex grid object fills with database records automatically.

In the following exercise, you'll open and run the DataGrid program, which demonstrates how you can display database records on a form by using the

FlexGrid control. The DataGrid program displays database records as a table and provides access to them with scroll bars. In addition, the program demonstrates two operations that are especially handy with large databases: a sort function that sorts database records by column, and a search function that searches an entire database for keywords and highlights them. The DataGrid program is an extension of the Courses.vbp project developed in Lesson 13, which lets the user add, delete, and find records in a Microsoft Access database called Students.mdb. In the DataGrid program, you also have the options of displaying your database table as a grid and creating new views with the sort and search functions.

Run the DataGrid program

1 Open the DataGrid.vbp project in the C:\Vb6Sbs\Less23 folder.

If you are asked to save any changes to the MySaleGrid project, click Yes.

Start button

2 Click the Start button to run the DataGrid program.

Visual Basic loads the DataGrid form, which is similar to the DelRec.frm user interface you created in Lesson 13. The new Grid View button on the form is used to open a second form containing a flex grid object.

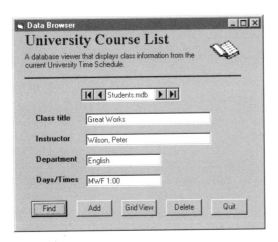

3 Click the Grid View button.

Visual Basic opens the second form (GridView.frm) and uses the flex grid object to display the Students table in the Students.mdb database. Your form will look like the figure on the following page.

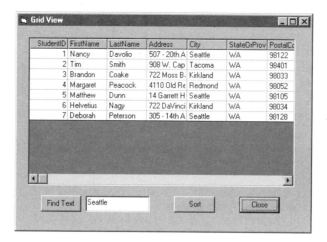

The flex grid object automatically loads database records from the Students.mdb database in this program—no program code is used to copy the individual rows from the database.

4 Move the mouse pointer to the top row of the flex grid object, between the Address and City headers.

The mouse pointer changes into a resizing pointer. When the FlexGrid control's AllowUserResizing property is set to 1 - flexResizeColumns, the user can change the width of the columns in the spreadsheet.

5 Use the resizing pointer to increase the width of the Address column.

The column increases in size and displays more data. In most cases, you'll want to give your users this viewing convenience.

Now try using the sort and search features.

6 Click the Sort button on the Grid View form.

The flex grid object sorts the rows in the spreadsheet alphabetically by comparing each cell in the LastName column. (I chose this column as the sorting key in the program code, as you'll see later.) As in the figure on the next page, it's easy to see the results of the sort because the first column (StudentID) still preserves the original creation order of the entries (although they are jumbled about now).

tip

The true, internal order of the Students.mdb database has not changed with this sorting operation—only the contents of the flex grid spreadsheet have changed. The link between the Data control and the FlexGrid control is one-way, so the changes you make in the flex grid object do not update the database.

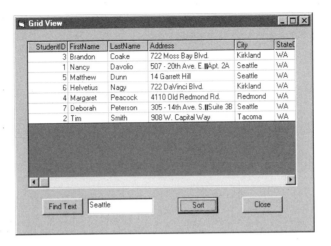

❼ Click the Find Text button on the Grid View form.

Visual Basic searches the spreadsheet for the text in the find text box (currently "Seattle", a default value I put in the text box). After a moment, each cell that contains the Seattle text is highlighted with bold formatting.

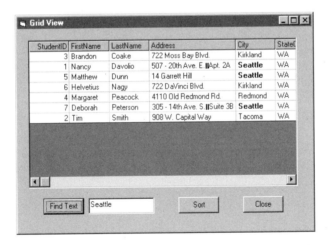

If you watch closely when you click the Find Text button, you might see a progress bar object appear briefly at the bottom of the screen to track the search progress. I added this to give users visual feedback during long searches (those involving thousands of records), but because this database is so small, it comes and goes pretty fast. You'll see this progress bar again in the "One Step Further" exercise, when you search for text in the giant Biblio.mdb database.

8 Click the text box on the form, delete the current contents (Seattle), type **an**, and click the Find Text button.

This time Visual Basic highlights four cells that contain the text string "an". Because I'm using the InStr function, I am also able to detect partial hits for my search. (In other words, this search will highlight words that contain the letters "an", such as Nancy.)

9 Click the Close button on the Grid View form, and then click the Quit button on the Data Browser form.

The program closes, and the development environment returns.

Advanced Sort and Search Operations

The DataGrid program can sort and search the entire contents of a database table, because of several handy features of the FlexGrid control and a few concise event procedures. Sorting is handled by the FlexGrid's Sort property, which sorts a table based on one or more key columns and a directional sorting argument. Searching requires a little more program code, but is handled in a straightforward manner by two nested For...Next loops and an InStr function that compares each cell to the search string. You'll see how these event procedures work in the following exercise.

Explore the DataGrid program code

1 Open the Form2 Code window and display the cmdSort_Click event procedure.

You'll see the following program code:

The Sort property starts a sort.

```
Private Sub cmdSort_Click()
    'Set column 2 (LastName) as the sort key
    MSFlexGrid1.Col = 2
    'Sort grid in ascending order
    MSFlexGrid1.Sort = 1
End Sub
```

This simple event procedure uses two program statements to sort the entire contents of the database in the flex grid object. The first statement sets the second column as the comparison key for the sort. I chose the LastName field because it is traditionally used to order lists, but any column in the database table could be chosen. The sort itself is executed by the Sort property, which takes an integer argument from 0 to 9 indicating the direction of the sort. I chose argument 1 (generic ascending), which means that the control sorts the cells in alphabetical order, and tries to guess if the cell contains a number or a string before the sort begins. Other popular options include 2 (generic descending), 3 (numeric ascending), and 4 (numeric descending). In numeric sorts, strings are converted to numbers (their ASCII equivalents) before the sort begins.

2 Open the cmdFindText_Click event procedure in the Code window.

You'll see the following program code:

```
Private Sub cmdFindTxt_Click()
    'Select entire grid and remove bold formatting
    '(to remove the results of previous finds)
    MSFlexGrid1.FillStyle = flexFillRepeat
    MSFlexGrid1.Col = 0
    MSFlexGrid1.Row = 0
    MSFlexGrid1.ColSel = MSFlexGrid1.Cols - 1
    MSFlexGrid1.RowSel = MSFlexGrid1.Rows - 1
    MSFlexGrid1.CellFontBold = False

    'Initialize ProgressBar to track search
    ProgressBar1.Min = 0
    ProgressBar1.Max = MSFlexGrid1.Rows - 1
    ProgressBar1.Visible = True

    'Search the grid cell by cell for find text
    MSFlexGrid1.FillStyle = flexFillSingle
    For i = 0 To MSFlexGrid1.Cols - 1
        For j = 1 To MSFlexGrid1.Rows - 1
        'Display current row location on ProgressBar
        ProgressBar1.Value = j
            'If current cell matches find text box
            If InStr(MSFlexGrid1.TextMatrix(j, i), _
            Text1.Text) Then
                '...select cell and format bold
                MSFlexGrid1.Col = i
                MSFlexGrid1.Row = j
                MSFlexGrid1.CellFontBold = True
            End If
        Next j
    Next i
    ProgressBar1.Visible = False 'hide ProgressBar
End Sub
```

The cmdFindText_Click event procedure runs when the user clicks the Find Text button on Form2. The purpose of the routine is to compare each cell in the flex grid object with the search text in the Text1 text box, and to change the cell formatting of any matching cells to bold. The event procedure first clears any existing bold formatting from the flex grid object by selecting the entire spreadsheet and changing its CellFontBold property to False. Then the procedure initializes the progress bar object to display graphical output at the bottom of the screen while the search continues (the progress bar is filled once for each column in the table).

The flex grid search itself is accomplished by two For...Next loops: one loop to step through each row in the table, and one loop to step through each column. The loop then uses the TextMatrix property and the InStr function to compare the current loop position (j, i) with the find text string (Text1.Text). If a match is found, the CellFontBold property sets the text formatting in the cell to bold.

3 Close the Code window.

You've finished looking at the DataGrid program code.

DataGrid Property Settings

Before you leave the DataGrid program, take note of a few important property settings for the objects on Form2 (GridView.frm). They demonstrate the close connection between the flex grid object and the data object.

Flex grid object   The FixedCols property is set to 0 to suppress the heading column on the spreadsheet. (The Students data table doesn't use it.) The first row and column of the flex grid is gray-shaded by default, but you can remove the shading by setting the FixedCols or FixedRows property to 0.

Data object   The DatabaseName property of this object is set to C:\Vb6Sbs \Less03\Students.mdb, and the RecordSource property is set to Students. The Visible property is set to False to hide the user interface to the control. This project has two Data controls that point to the same database (which is totally legitimate in Visual Basic). You can also have the Data controls point to different databases, as you'll see in the "One Step Further" exercise.

One Step Further   **Searching the Biblio.mdb Database**

The DataGrid program provided a useful demonstration of the concepts in this lesson. Before you move on to the next lesson, I thought you might like to see how the FlexGrid control works with really big databases. When you write your own database applications, it's always a good idea to "stress test" your database tools before you put them to work on complex, mission-critical data sources.

Try revising the DataGrid program now to work with the Biblio.mdb database, an Access database containing over 10,000 records and several complex tables. To demonstrate how you can access two different databases from one project, you'll leave the data object on Form1 connected to the Students.mdb database, but you'll change the data object connection on Form2 to Biblio.mdb.

Use the FlexGrid control to display Biblio.mdb records

1 Display Form2 in the DataGrid.vbp project, and select the data object on the form.

(The DataGrid project should still be loaded in the development environment. If it is not, load it now from the C:\Vb6Sbs\Less23 folder.)

2 In the Properties window, change the DatabaseName property of the Data1 object to C:\Vb6Sbs\Extras\Biblio.mdb.

3 In the Properties window, click the RecordSource property of the Data1 object, and then click the Titles record.

The Titles record contains a large collection of books about computer programming.

4 Double-click the Sort button on Form2 to open the cmdSort_Click event procedure in the Code window.

5 In the line that assigns the Col property to set the key column for the sort, change the 2 to a **0**.

You want to use the first column in the table (Titles) as the key for the sort. The program statement should look like this:

```
MSFlexGrid1.Col = 0
```

Now you'll run the program.

Start button

6 Click the Start button on the toolbar.

Visual Basic displays the first form in your program, which opens the Students.mdb database and fills several bound text boxes with data.

7 Click the Grid View button.

Visual Basic loads the Biblio.mdb database in the flex grid object and displays it.

8 Use the resizing pointer to widen the first column of the flex grid object.

Your form will look similar to the following figure:

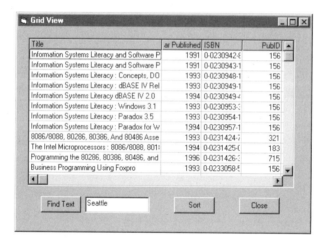

9 Click the Sort button to sort the table using the first column for the comparison.

After a moment, the database is sorted alphabetically. Your form looks like this:

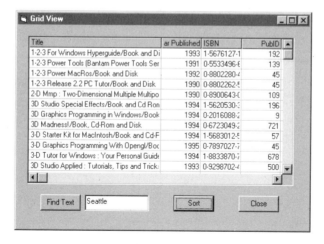

⑩ Now delete the text in the text box, type **Book**, and click the Find Text button.

The search begins, and you can see several cells in the first column with bold formatting. The progress bar at the bottom of the screen gives you graphical feedback for the lengthy operation, which involves checking over 80,000 cells. (The progress bar fills once per column.) After several moments (depending on the speed of your computer), the flex grid will complete its global search task and the scroll bars will be available for use. Your form will look like this:

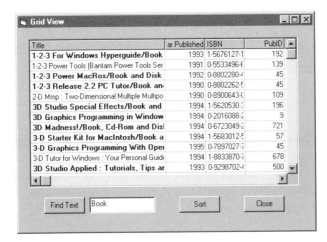

⑪ Take a few moments scrolling through the database—you've just scanned a lot of text!

⑫ When you're finished, click the Close button on Form2, and then click the Quit button on Form1.

If you want to continue to the next lesson

● Keep Visual Basic running, and turn to Lesson 24.

If you want to quit Visual Basic for now

● On the File menu, click Exit.

If you see a Save dialog box, click No to discard your changes to DataGrid.

Upgrade Notes:
What's Different in Visual Basic .NET?

If you upgrade to Visual Basic .NET in the future, you'll notice some new features related to the topics in this lesson, including the following:

- In Visual Basic 6.0, there are several grid controls that you can use to display database information on a form, including FlexGrid, Hierarchical FlexGrid, and DataGrid. In Visual Basic .NET, the DataGrid control is the only spreadsheet-style control that is provided to display database records.

- The DataGrid control in Visual Basic .NET works exclusively with ADO.NET data sources. The DataGrid control is connected, or bound, to database information through the DataGrid's DataSource and DataMember properties.

- There are several differences between the DataGrid control in Visual Basic .NET and the FlexGrid control included with Visual Basic 6.0. One important improvement is that the Visual Basic .NET DataGrid control doesn't require data-specific commands because all the data access functionality is handled by the underlying .NET data adapter and dataset object. Several familiar properties and methods have also changed, but all-in-all you'll probably appreciate the improvements.

Lesson 23 Quick Reference

To	Do this
Add the FlexGrid ActiveX control to the toolbox	On the Project menu, click the Components command, and then click the Controls tab. Place a check mark next to the Microsoft FlexGrid Control 6.0 entry, and click OK.
Assign text to a FlexGrid cell	Use the TextMatrix property. For example, to place the word "Bob" in cell 3, 1 (row 3, column 1), type the following: `MSFlexGrid1.TextMatrix(3, 1) = "Bob"`

Insert a graphic in a cell	Use the CellPicture property. For example:
	
	`Set MSFlexGrid1.CellPicture = _`
	`    LoadPicture("c:\vb6sbs\less22\coins.wmf")`

Lesson 23 Quick Reference

To	Do this

Select a cell	Use the Row and Col properties together. For example, to select cell 1, 1 (row 1, column 1), type:
	```MSFlexGrid1.Row = 1```
	```MSFlexGrid1.Col = 1```

Format the current selection with bold type	Use the CellFontBold property. For example: ```MSFlexGrid1.CellFontBold = True```

Add a new row	Use the AddItem method, and separate cell columns with the tab character (vbTab). For example:
	```Dim Row As String```
	```Row = "Soccer ball" & vbTab & "W17-233"```
	```MSFlexGrid1.AddItem Row```

Sort the contents of a flex grid object by column	Use the Col property to set the sort key, and then set the Sort property with a direction argument. For example:
	```MSFlexGrid1.Col = 2 'column 2 for key```
	```MSFlexGrid1.Sort = 1 'ascending order```

Search an entire flex grid object for text in a text box object	Use the InStr function inside two For...Next loops. For example:
	```For i = 0 To MSFlexGrid1.Cols - 1```
	``` For j = 1 To MSFlexGrid1.Rows - 1```
	``` If InStr(MSFlexGrid1.TextMatrix(j, i), _```
	``` Text1.Text) Then```
	``` [code to execute if match found]```
	``` End If```
	``` Next j```
	```Next i```

23

The FlexGrid Control

LESSON

24

Exploring ActiveX Data Objects

ESTIMATED TIME 50 min.

In this lesson you will learn how to:

✔ *Install and use the ActiveX Data Object (ADO) control.*

✔ *Write program code to manage ADO transactions.*

✔ *Create your own ActiveX data objects with the Data Environment Designer.*

In this lesson, you'll get your feet wet with a powerful database technology from Microsoft called *ActiveX Data Objects (ADO)*. You'll learn how to install and use the ADO ActiveX control, how to display database fields and records on your form with bound controls, and how to write program code that manages ADO transactions. In addition, you'll learn how to create your own ActiveX data objects by using a special tool called the Data Environment Designer. These skills will help you manage stand-alone Microsoft Access databases, corporate intranet databases, and distributed database objects on the World Wide Web.

Inside ADO

ADO is Microsoft's newest technology for working with information in relational and nonrelational databases. (Relational database management systems manipulate information in tables, but not all data sources follow this model.) ADO does not completely replace the existing database technology—Data Access Objects (DAO)—that you've been working with in this book, but it does extend DAO programming into new areas. ADO is based on Microsoft's latest data access paradigm called OLE DB, which has been specifically designed to provide access to a wide range of business data sources, including traditional relational database tables, e-mail systems, graphics formats, Internet resources, and so on. ADO requires less memory than DAO, so it is more suitable for networked computer systems that experience heavy traffic and high transaction rates.

Four Database-Programming Paradigms

Microsoft has offered four different database-programming paradigms to Visual Basic programmers over the years. The first three are supported by Visual Basic 6, and the fourth is new in Visual Basic .NET. Master these acronyms for small talk at your next cocktail party!

DAO The Data Access Objects (DAO) paradigm was the first object-oriented interface that allowed programmers to manipulate the Microsoft Jet database engine. The Jet database engine is a technology used to access the fields and records in Microsoft Access tables and other data sources. DAO is still popular and effective for single-system database applications and small to medium-size workgroup networks.

RDO The Remote Data Objects (RDO) paradigm is an object-oriented interface to Open Database Connectivity (ODBC) sources. RDO is the object model used by most database developers who work intensively with Microsoft SQL Server, Oracle, and other large relational databases.

ADO The ActiveX Data Objects (ADO) paradigm has been designed as the successor to DAO and RDO, and it has a similar object model. In ADO, programmable objects represent all the local and remote data sources available to your computer. You can access these data objects in Visual Basic 6 Professional Edition by using the ADO control, by binding data objects to intrinsic and ActiveX controls, by creating DHTML applications, and by using the new Data Environment Designer.

ADO.NET The ADO.NET paradigm is Microsoft's newest database programming model and the standard data technology for all the tools in the Visual Studio .NET programming suite, including Visual Basic .NET. ADO.NET has been designed to seamlessly integrate Web data, meaning that it uses the same method for accessing local, client-server, and Internet-based data sources. ADO.NET also uses XML as its internal database format, so it is somewhat easier to use ADO.NET with existing Internet data sources. However, you only need to consider ADO.NET if you upgrade to Visual Basic .NET.

Microsoft recommends that Visual Basic programmers use ADO when they create new database applications in Visual Basic 6, and has included several features specifically designed to support ADO in Microsoft Visual Basic 6 Professional Edition. ADO is closely related to ADO.NET, Microsoft's newest database programming technology, which is an important part of Visual Studio .NET. However, I recommend that you explore ADO only after you have gained a firm understanding of the fundamental database programming concepts discussed already in this book: using the intrinsic Data control, displaying data with bound controls, managing fields and records with event procedures, using a FlexGrid control to display and sort records, and so forth. When you upgrade to ADO, you'll be looking at database information in an entirely new way.

Using the ADO ActiveX Control

The simplest way to experiment with ADO is to use the new ADO ActiveX control to display the fields and records in an Access database on a form. Following the ADO paradigm, the ADO control does not include a DatabaseName property that lets you connect directly to a database file on your computer. Instead, the ADO control contains a ConnectionString property that lets you connect to an ActiveX data source on your computer. A series of dialog boxes help you make this connection, and you can customize the process by building new ActiveX data objects from existing data sources with the Data Environment Designer. (You'll learn how to do this later in the lesson.)

Once you understand the practical differences between ADO and DAO connections, you'll find the ADO control to be quite similar to the intrinsic Data control. In this section, you'll learn how to add the ADO control to your toolbox, how to set the ConnectionString property, and how to display database records on your form with a few bound controls. You'll also master the fundamentals of ADO program code.

Install the ADO control

The ADO control is an ActiveX control that you need to add to your toolbox before you can use it in a program. You'll install the ADO control in this exercise.

1. Start Visual Basic, and open a new standard project.
2. On the Project menu, click the Components command, and then click the Controls tab.
3. Scroll down the list to the Microsoft ADO Data Control 6.0 item, and click the check box next to it.

4 Click OK to add the control to your toolbox.

Visual Basic adds the ADO control, as shown in the following illustration:

Now you'll create an ADO object on your form to display a few records from the Students.mdb database.

Create an ADO object and bound controls

ADO control

1 Click the ADO control in the toolbox, and create a small rectangular ADO object on your form.

When you release the mouse button, Visual Basic creates an ADO object. Your form will look like this:

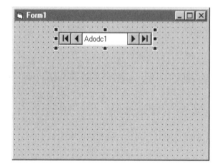

Like the Data control you used in Lessons 3 and 13, the ADO control creates a database navigation control with four arrows. At runtime, when the object is visible and connected to a suitable database, you can click the first left arrow to move to the first record in the database, and the last right arrow to move to the last record in the database. The inner arrows allow you to move to the previous and next database records, respectively.

> ## tip
> You can change the title text displayed in the ADO data object by selecting the ADO object, opening the Properties window, and modifying the Caption property.

Now you'll add two text box controls to the form to display the LastName and PhoneNumber fields in the Students.mdb database.

TextBox control

2 Click the TextBox control in the toolbox, and create a text box object below the ADO object. After you create the first object, click the TextBox control again and create another one beside it.

Your form will look like this:

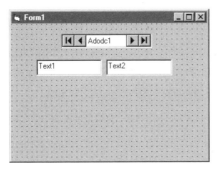

Creating a Data Source Name

If you were using the Data control now, you'd simply set the DatabaseName property of the Data control to the pathname of a valid database on your system to link to the database. However, the designers of ADO have asked you to take one more preliminary step in the name of future flexibility. You need to describe the database record you want to link to by creating an ActiveX Data

Object. You have three options when you create data objects: you can create an OLE DB file; you can create an ODBC Data Source Name (DSN) file; or you can build an OLE DB connection string. The Data Environment Designer is designed specifically to help you create ActiveX Data Objects. (You'll try this later in the lesson.) However, you can also create the necessary files by using the ADO control's ConnectionString property.

In the following exercise, you'll establish a connection to the Students.mdb database with the ADO control's ConnectionString property. To facilitate the connection and provide the necessary ActiveX data objects, you'll create an ODBC Data Source Name file.

tip

You only need to create a Data Source Name (.dsn) file once for each data source you plan to use. After that, you can use the file over and over again to reference the same data tables.

Set the ConnectionString property

1 Click the ADO object on your form, open the Properties window, and click the button in the ConnectionString property field.

A Property Pages dialog box appears, as shown in the following illustration:

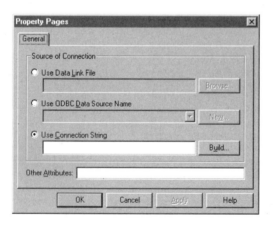

2 Click the second option button in the list (Use ODBC Data Source Name).

You'll create a Data Source Name file that references the Students.mdb database. You'll be able to use this file now and in the future.

3 Click the New button to the right of the Use ODBC Data Source Name option button.

You'll see the following dialog box (the first in a series):

This dialog box asks how you intend to share the database you're accessing in this Visual Basic program. The top selection (File Data Source) signifies that your database will be made available to users on other computers (via a network or the Internet). This option allows you considerable flexibility, but is not necessary for single-system database applications.

The second option (User Data Source) means that the database resides on the physical machine you're working on now, and that it will be used only by you (a person with your username). You'll choose the second option in this lesson, because you're creating a simple demonstration for yourself only.

The third option (System Data Source) means that the database resides on the computer you're working on, and should be made generally available to other people who use your computer and are logged in under different usernames (a popular work arrangement on some Windows workstations).

4 Click the second option button (User Data Source), and then click the Next button.

As shown in the figure on the following page, you'll be prompted for the database driver you want to use when making the connection to your database. A number of formats are supported.

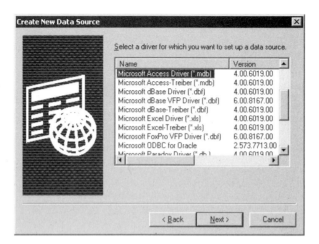

5   Select the Microsoft Access Driver, and then click the Next button to continue.

Visual Basic summarizes the selections you have made, and asks you to click the Finish button to continue configuring your Data Source Name file.

6   Click the Finish button.

A new dialog box appears, named ODBC Microsoft Access Setup. This dialog box lets you name your Data Source Name file, select the database you'll be connecting to, and customize your connection.

7   Type **Student Records** in the Data Source Name text box.

Student Records is the name you'll use later when you're prompted for a DSN file in the Property Pages dialog box.

8   Click the Select button, browse to the C:\Vb6Sbs\Less03 folder, click the Students.mdb database, and click OK.

Your dialog box will look like the following figure:

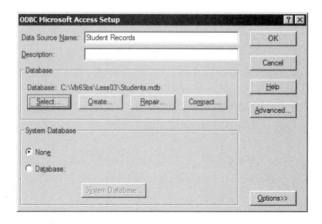

9   Click OK to close the dialog box.

The Property Pages dialog box reappears. You just created a new DSN file, so your only remaining task is to select the DSN from the drop-down list box below the Use ODBC Data Source Name option button.

10   Click the ODBC Data Source Name drop-down list box, and click the Student Records item.

11   Click OK in the Property Pages dialog box to finalize your connection.

The Property Pages dialog box closes, and the entry DSN=Student Records appears in the Properties window next to the ConnectionString property.

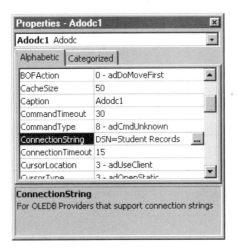

That wasn't so bad, was it? Although creating a Data Source Name file takes a few extra steps, the process allows you substantial latitude in customizing how each database connection is configured and established. When you start managing complex databases with Visual Basic, you'll appreciate the flexibility and consistency Data Source Names provide.

Now you'll put your database connection to work by binding database fields from the ADO object to your two text boxes.

Bind ADO data to text box objects

1   With the ADO object (adodc1) still selected in the Properties window, scroll down to the RecordSource property, and click the button to the right of the RecordSource property name.

You'll see the Property Pages dialog box again, and this time the RecordSource tab is visible. In ADO programming, you have access to more than just database tables in your database connections. You can also reference stored procedure objects and text objects in your data sources. In ADO, the ActiveX objects you use are called *commands*. In this exercise, you'll select the Table command type, which gives you access to the tables in the Students.mdb database and a few other table objects provided by ADO.

2 Click the Command Type drop-down list box, and select 2 - adCmdTable.

Using the DSN file, Visual Basic opens the Students.mdb database and loads the table names in the Table Or Stored Procedure Name drop-down list box.

3 Click the Table Or Stored Procedure Name drop-down list box, scroll down the list, and select the Students table.

Your Property Pages dialog box will look like this:

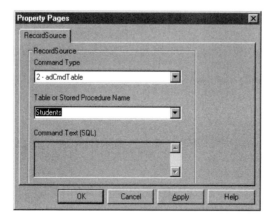

4 Click OK to finalize your RecordSource selection.

The table name Students appears in the Properties window next to the RecordSource property.

5 Click the Text1 object in the Properties window. Set its DataSource property to Adodc1, and its DataField property to LastName.

6 Click the Text2 object in the Properties window. Set its DataSource property to Adodc1, and its DataField property to PhoneNumber.

As you learned in earlier lessons, linking intrinsic toolbox controls or ActiveX controls to a data object on a form in this way is called *binding* the data to controls.

Now you'll run the program you have created.

Run the ADO control demo

Start button

1 Click the Start button on the toolbar.

The text boxes fill with data from the first record in the Students.mdb database. Your form looks like this:

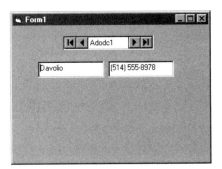

➋ Click the inner-right arrow (Next) in the ADO object a few times.

Each time you click the Next arrow, the LastName and PhoneNumber fields for a new record appear on the form.

➌ Click the inner-left arrow (Previous) in the ADO object.

The fields for the previous record appear on the form.

➍ Click the outer-right arrow (Last) in the ADO object.

The ADO object displays the fields for the last record in the database.

➎ Click the outer-left arrow (First) in the ADO object.

The fields for the first record appear again.

➏ When you're finished experimenting with the ADO object, click the Close button on the Form1 title bar.

The development environment reappears.

➐ On the File menu, click the Save Project As command. Save your form under the name **MyAdoCtrl.frm,** and your project under the name **MyAdoCtrl.vbp.**

Now that you've explored the basics of using ActiveX data objects, it's time to investigate a meatier topic—writing ADO program code.

Writing ADO Program Code

Event procedures that manage ActiveX data objects are the core of a database application that exploits the ADO paradigm. The methods, properties, and events exposed by ActiveX data objects using the ADO control are similar in many ways to the methods, properties, and events you processed with the Data control in Lesson 13. For example, you manipulate information in both paradigms through recordsets, which hold the current database information you are manipulating.

In the following exercise, you'll enter ADO program code into a skeleton program I wrote called AdoData. The AdoData program is a modification of the

AdoCtrl program you built earlier in this lesson. In its revised form, AdoData allows the user to browse through database records with new Next and Previous command buttons, and it allows you to double-click a field name in a list box and copy all the records in the database that match that field to a text file. (For example, you can copy all the LastName fields to a text file with one double-click.) I've created the complete user interface for you in the project—you just need to enter the program code.

Create the MyAdoData program

Open button

① Click the Open Project button on the Visual Basic toolbar.

If you are prompted to save your changes, save them to the MyAdoCtrl project.

② Open the AdoForm.vbp project located in the C:\Vb6SbS\Less24 folder.

③ On the File menu, click the Save AdoForm.frm As command, type **MyAdoData**, and press Enter.

Saving the form and project under a new name preserves the original files, in case you want to try the exercise again later.

④ On the File menu, click the Save Project As command, type **MyAdoData**, and press Enter.

Your form will look like the following:

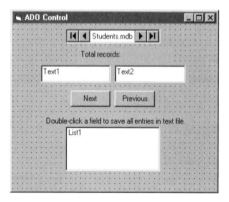

The form still has an ADO object and two text boxes, but I've added a new list box object and two label objects.

⑤ Double-click the Next command button on the form to open the Command1_Click event procedure in the Code window, and enter the following program code between the Sub and End Sub statements:

```
'If not already at last record, move to next
If Not Adodc1.Recordset.EOF Then
    Adodc1.Recordset.MoveNext
End If
```

This simple routine checks the EOF property and advances the ADO object to the next record with the MoveNext method if the current record is not the last record in the database. By checking the EOF (end of file) property before the move, you avoid the runtime error that would occur if the ADO control tried to move past the last record.

The ADO control is represented in this routine by the Adodc1 object, which is connected to the Students table in the Students.mdb database. As a member of the Adodc1 object, the Recordset property holds the Students table in memory and provides access to its data and commands. This recordset is not the actual data in your table, but a copy of the data that your application works with at runtime. A recordset may be an exact copy of a table, or it may be the result of a query or other selection activity.

6 Open the Command2_Click event procedure in the Code window, and type the following program code between the Sub and End Sub statements:

```
'If not already at first record, move to previous
If Not Adodc1.Recordset.BOF Then
    Adodc1.Recordset.MovePrevious
End If
```

This event procedure programs the Previous button to move back one record when the user clicks it. If the BOF (beginning of file) property evaluates to True, the routine skips the MovePrevious method, because attempting to move to the previous record when the first record is visible would cause a runtime error.

7 Open the Form_Load event procedure in the Code window, and type the following code between the Sub and End Sub statements:

```
'Populate list box with field names
For i = 1 To Adodc1.Recordset.Fields.Count - 1
    List1.AddItem Adodc1.Recordset.Fields(i).Name
Next i
'Display total number of records
Label1.Caption = "Total records: " & _
    Adodc1.Recordset.RecordCount
```

The Form_Load event procedure performs two tasks. It adds each field name in the Students table to the list box object (List1), and it displays the total number of records in the database with the first label object (Label1). Both tasks are accomplished by a careful use of the ADO object's properties.

I use the Fields collection to get both a count of the fields and the names of individual items. You can access the fields in a table by using an index with the Fields object name. For example, Fields(2) represents the second field in the table. With a For...Next loop that runs once for each field in the database, I copy the name of each field into the list box object so that the user can select it later by double-clicking it.

I use the RecordCount property to display the total number of records on the form. This value lets users know how many records will be written to disk if they choose to double-click field names in the list box object. To keep this value manageable, I have limited the Students.mdb database to seven records. (The user may want to think twice before writing the 10,000 fields from the Biblio.mdb database to a text file!)

8 Open the List1_DblClick event procedure in the Code window.

9 Type the following program statements between the Sub and End Sub statements:

```
'Create constant to hold text file name
Const myFile = "c:\vb6sbs\less24\names.txt"
'Open file for Append (to support multiple fields)
Open myFile For Append As #1
Print #1, String$(30, "-")    'print dashed line
Adodc1.Recordset.MoveFirst    'move to first record
x = List1.ListIndex + 1       'get item clicked
'For each record in database, write field to disk
For i = 1 To Adodc1.Recordset.RecordCount
    Print #1, Adodc1.Recordset.Fields(x).Value
    Adodc1.Recordset.MoveNext
Next i
'Print success message and close file
MsgBox Adodc1.Recordset.Fields(x).Name & _
    " field written to " & myFile
Close #1
Adodc1.Recordset.MoveFirst
```

Save button

10 Click the Save Project button on the Visual Basic toolbar to save your changes.

The List1_DblClick event procedure handles the actual saving process by creating a text file on disk called Names.txt. First the routine declares a constant to hold the pathname to the file. Then it opens the file in Append mode so that more than one field can be stored in the file without overwriting the previous transaction. I use the MoveFirst method to move the recordset to the first record in the table. Then I determine the field that the user double-clicked in the list box by adding 1 to the ListIndex property and assigning it to the x variable. ListIndex is a useful property that contains the number of the item selected in a list; I increment this number because I need to compensate for the fact that list boxes start with an index value of zero (0).

The actual field value is written to disk with the following program statement:

```
Print #1, Adodc1.Recordset.Fields(x).Value
```

As you learned earlier, the Name property of the Fields collection contains the name of the selected field. This time, I'm using the Value property to access the actual text stored in the field itself. The Print statement writes this value to the text file on its own line. This operation is repeated for each matching field in the database.

Now you'll run the program to see how the ADO code works.

Run the AdoData program

1 Click the Start button on the toolbar.

Start button

The ADO object opens the Students.mdb database and displays its fields in two text boxes and a list box. The current record count (7) is also displayed, as shown in the following figure.

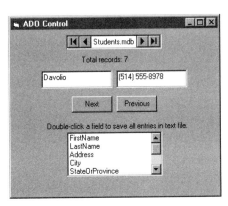

2 Click the Next button to display the next record in the database.

3 The Next button displays the next record, just as the inner right arrow did on the ADO control.

④ Click the Previous button to display the first record again.

The Previous button works just as the inner left button does on the ADO control. Now try double-clicking the list box to write a few fields to disk.

⑤ Double-click the LastName field in the list box.

The ADO object opens the Names.txt file in the C:\Vb6Sbs\Less24 folder, and copies seven last names from the Students.mdb database to this file. After the copy operation is completed, you see the following message box:

⑥ Click OK, and then double-click the Address field in the list box.

The addresses are written to disk, and a message box again notifies you about the transaction.

⑦ Click OK, and click the Close button on the form's title bar.

You're done running the MyAdoData program.

The AdoData program is on disk in the \Vb6Sbs\Less24 folder.

⑧ If you like, open the Names.txt file in the C:\Vb6Sbs\Less24 folder on your hard disk and examine the text file you created with the LastName and Address fields.

In Microsoft Word, the file looks like this:

Congratulations! You've taken several important steps in learning to work with ADO recordsets and event procedures.

tip

To learn more about the ADO object model, open the Object Browser and examine the properties, methods, and events exposed by the MSAdodcLib library.

Building ActiveX Data Objects with the Data Environment Designer

Earlier in this lesson, you created a Data Source Name (DSN) file that connected the Students.mdb database to the ADO control. The ActiveX data objects provided by this file allowed you to construct event procedures that displayed and extracted fields from the Students table in the database. You can also build your own custom ActiveX Data Objects with a new utility in Visual Basic 6 Professional Edition called the *Data Environment Designer*. The Data Environment Designer lets you create object commands that can customize and reorganize database tables, fields, and records in powerful new ways. The following illustration shows the relationship between data sources, ADO command objects, and a program that uses ADO resources. (A Microsoft Access command object is currently selected—only one of the available connection options.)

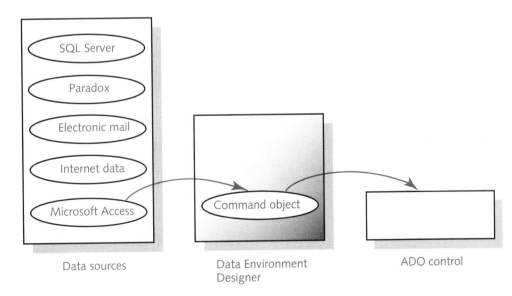

Data sources   Data Environment Designer   ADO control

As a final exercise, you'll create a custom ActiveX data object with the Data Environment Designer.

Create a custom data environment

To create a custom data environment containing ActiveX data objects for your application, you follow these steps:

1   On the Visual Basic Project menu, click the Add Data Environment command. Visual Basic adds a Data Environment Designer to your project. This special data management component allows you to create new ActiveX data objects and to use them in your project. The Data Environment Window is shown in the following figure:

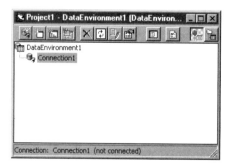

The Data Environment window features a generous display area that lets you view your current connections and ADO commands. Connection1 is the database connection that you just established when you selected the Student Records DSN. This connection allows you to fine-tune how the tables, fields, and records in the Students.mdb database are accessed.

2   In the Data Environment Window, right-click Connection1 and then select Properties from the context menu.

The Provider tab of the Data Link Properties dialog box appears, which allows you to select the provider that you want to use to access your data.

3   On the Provider tab be sure that Microsoft OLE DB Provider For ODBC Drivers is selected and then click Next.

As shown in the following figure, the Connection tab is displayed, which prompts you for the source of your data.

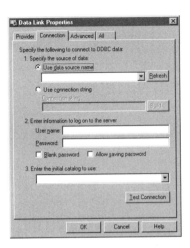

④ Click the Use ODBC Data Source Name option button (if it is not already selected), click Student Records in the drop-down list box, and then click OK.

You created the Student Records DSN earlier in this lesson.

Add Command button

⑤ Click the Add Command button on the Data Environment toolbar.

⑥ The Add Command button creates a new ActiveX data object in the Data Environment. To set the unique attributes of this data object, right-click Command1 in the Data Environment Window and select Properties from the context menu.

⑦ Type **InstructorTable** in the Command Name text box.

InstructorTable will be the name of your recordset object when you use this ADO command later.

⑧ Click the drop-down list box to the right of the Database Object option button, and click the Table type.

By selecting Table, you are telling the Data Environment that you want to create a table object.

⑨ Click the Object Name drop-down list box, and click the Instructors table.

The Data Environment displays a list of all the tables in the Students.mdb database, and highlights Instructors when you click it. Your dialog box will look like the figure on the following page.

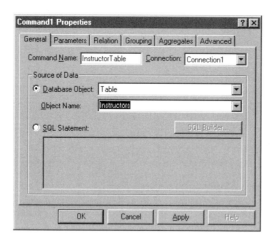

10 Click OK to create the InstructorTable command in the Data Environment.

11 Click the plus sign next to the InstructorTable command to expand the table and see its fields.

Your Data Environment will look similar to the following figure:

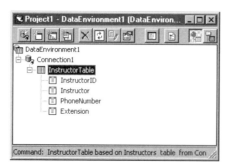

You have just created a new ActiveX data object that you can use in this project or in any other project to which you add this Data Environment Designer. The Data Environment Designer is stored in a special file with a .dsr extension (DataEnvironment1.dsr by default). You'll practice saving this file to disk now so that you can use it in other projects.

12 Open the Project window, and click the DataEnvironment1 designer.

Your Project window will look like this:

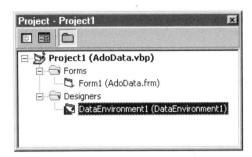

Like DHTML Designers, Data Environment Designers are listed in the Designers folder, and can be saved or deleted with menu commands.

⑬   On the File menu, click the Save DataEnvironment1 As command.

⑭   Type **Instruct,** and press Enter.

If you are told that this file already exists on your system, choose a new name to protect the original version.

tip
    •

If you want to remove the Instruct.dsr designer from your project at a later time, click the Instruct.dsr designer in the Project window and click the Remove Instruct.dsr command on the Project menu. If you want to add a designer to a project, click the Add File command on the Project menu and specify the designer.

One Step Further

Referencing ADO Commands in Your Application

Like the ActiveX data objects exposed by the ADO control, the ADO commands held in Data Environment Designers can be used in bound controls and event procedures. For example, in the project you just created, you can select the Data-Environment1 object by using the DataSource property in a text box object.

Exploring ADO   24

Similarly, you can access ADO commands with program code. For example, to move to the next record in a database table by using the DataEnvironment1 object you created above, you would type

```
DataEnvironment1.rsInstructorTable.MoveNext
```

The InstructorTable command has the rs prefix here because it refers to the record-set maintained by the current Data Environment Designer, DataEnvironment1. Note that this command is roughly equivalent to the MoveNext statement that you wrote earlier for the ADO control:

```
Adodc1.Recordset.MoveNext
```

In this case, however, you are referencing the Instructors table in the Students.mdb database with a custom ActiveX data object that you built with the Data Environment Designer. In many cases, referencing data through your own ActiveX data objects will make your programs clearer and more adaptable to the needs of diverse data sources. Take some time experimenting with ActiveX data objects, and put them to work in your own applications.

Congratulations! You've completed the *Microsoft Visual Basic Professional 6.0 Step by Step* programming course. Skim through the lessons you've completed, and assess the journey you've taken. Learning to write effective Visual Basic applications requires many skills. Among them are a thorough understanding of intrinsic toolbox controls and ActiveX components; the ability to set and manipulate an object's methods, properties, and events; the capacity to write clean, reusable program code; and the vision to design an effective user interface. Each lesson in this course has emphasized these principles. You'll find that you can immediately apply the skills you've learned in the simple examples presented here to more sophisticated Visual Basic applications in the real world.

important

Please open and run the Michael.avi video located in the Less17 folder. (Start Windows Explorer, use the browser to locate the C:\Vb6Sbs\Less17 folder, and double-click the Michael.avi file.) I'd like to propose a toast!

The secret to becoming a professional Visual Basic developer is writing programs that push your knowledge of Visual Basic to its limits and require you to learn more. As you seek to expand your programming skills, I recommend that you consult the online and printed resources listed in Appendix B, Where to Go for More Information. If you're interested in migrating your applications to Visual Basic .NET, see Appendix A, Upgrading Visual Basic 6 Programs to Visual Basic .NET.

Upgrade Notes: What's Different in Visual Basic .NET?

If you choose to upgrade to Visual Basic .NET in the future, you'll notice some new features related to the topics in this lesson, including the following:

- In Visual Basic .NET, the ActiveX Data Objects (ADO) data access model has been replaced by the ADO.NET data access model, a database technology based on ADO+. ADO.NET is an improvement because it offers a wider range of data access possibilities than its predecessors, including the ability to seamlessly manipulate XML data sources.

- When you use ADO.NET to access data in Visual Basic .NET, you don't use the ADO control you've been using in this lesson. Instead, you use the Server Explorer tool in the Visual Studio .NET development environment to establish a connection to the database, create a data adapter to extract specific information from the database (such as the results of an SQL SELECT statement), and then you create a dataset object to represent the database information in your program.

- To display data on a form in a Visual Basic .NET application, you add controls to the form and then bind them to the data connection you've established with the Server Explorer, data adapter, and dataset. You then write event procedures to display and manipulate the data—just like in Visual Basic 6.

- Here's another fine point: In Visual Basic 6, ADO database information is represented in a program by the Recordset object. In Visual Basic .NET, ADO.NET data is represented by the dataset object, an image of a portion of the database that you want to work with. However, the dataset object is not the actual database, but a disconnected image of it.

- ADO.NET data access is possible in Visual Basic .NET in both Windows Forms and Web Forms. The seamless implementation is a major advantage of Visual Basic .NET.

Lesson 24 Quick Reference

To	Do this	Button
Add the ADO control to the toolbox	On the Project menu, click the Components command, and click the Controls tab. Place a check mark next to the Microsoft ADO Data Control 6.0 item, and click OK.	
Create an ADO object on a form	Click the ADO control in the toolbox, and drag the mouse on the form.	
Connect an ADO object to a data source	Click the ADO object on the form, and open the Properties window. Click the button in the ConnectionString property text box, and specify a valid Data Source Name (DSN) in the dialog box.	
Select a data table (recordset) in the ADO object	Click the ADO object on the form, and open the Properties window. Click the RecordSource property text box, and pick a table from the list.	
Bind objects on your form to an ADO object	Click the object you want to bind (for example, a text box object). Then open the Properties window, and set the object's DataSource property to the name of the ADO object. Specify the field you want to display with the DataField property.	
Write ADO program code	Open an event procedure in the Code window, identify the ActiveX data object you want to use, and specify a valid method or property. For example, to scroll to the next record in the current recordset that is held in the Adodc1 object, type Adodc1.Recordset.MoveNext	
Learn more about the ADO object model Browser	Open a project that contains an ADO control or object reference, and then click the Object Browser command on the View menu. In the Library drop-down list box, click MSAdodcLib, and use the Object to explore the methods, properties, and events in the ADO object model.	
Open the Data Environment Designer	On the Project menu, click the Add Microsoft Data Environment 6.0 command.	

Lesson 24 Quick Reference

To	Do this	Button
Create new ActiveX data objects (ADO commands)	Click the Add Command button in the Data Environment, and configure the object with the Command1 Properties dialog box.	
Save a Data Environment Designer containing ActiveX data objects	Open the Project window, and click the designer you want to save in the Designers folder. On the File menu, click the Save DataEnvironment1 As command.	
Use an ActiveX data object contained in a Data Environment Designer in program code	Specify the designer name, the ADO command name with an "rs" (recordset) prefix, and the method or property you want to use. For example: `DataEnvironment1.rsMyTable.MoveFirst`	

24

Exploring ADO

Upgrading Visual Basic 6 Programs to Visual Basic .NET

In this appendix you will learn how to:

✔ *Evaluate Visual Basic 6 programs for compatibility with Visual Basic .NET.*

✔ *Locate Internet resources for migrating applications.*

✔ *Watch the Visual Basic .NET Upgrade Wizard upgrade a Visual Basic 6 program to Visual Basic .NET.*

This book teaches Visual Basic 6 programming techniques from scratch and assumes no additional development experience with Microsoft tools. However, now that a newer version of Visual Basic is available—Microsoft Visual Basic .NET— you may be wondering to what extent these two development systems are compatible, and what steps you will need to follow if you want to convert Visual Basic 6 programs to Visual Basic .NET. In particular, what resources and tools are available that can actually assist in this upgrading or *migration* process?

This appendix identifies a few resources for analyzing your Visual Basic 6 programs and upgrading Visual Basic 6 programs to Visual Basic .NET. You'll learn some of the major features of Visual Basic 6 that are no longer supported in Visual Basic .NET, the strategies Microsoft recommends for migrating Visual Basic 6 applications, and the location of useful Internet resources that document the upgrading process in greater detail. You'll also learn how to use the Visual Basic Upgrade Wizard (a tool supplied with several editions of Visual Basic .NET), which can automatically convert part or all of your Visual Basic 6 application to Visual Basic .NET.

Assessing Visual Basic 6 Programs for Compatibility

Visual Basic .NET is a significant revision to the Visual Basic programming language and to Windows programming in general. This change brings numerous advantages: a revised Visual Basic language syntax, which emphasizes clear and maintainable code; the new .NET Framework class libraries, which add additional functionality and eliminate the hassle of calling Windows APIs; real object-oriented programming features, including inheritance; the new ADO.NET database programming model, which provides access to truly distributed data sources; and new controls in the Toolbox, including the Web Forms controls for Internet programming. However, these new features come at a cost—not all Visual Basic 6 code is supported in Visual Basic .NET, and in many cases you'll need to extensively revise existing Visual Basic 6 programs to make them compatible with Visual Basic .NET.

The decision is up to you—you can upgrade your existing Visual Basic 6 code or you can continue to maintain some of it in Visual Basic 6, which Microsoft will continue to sell and support through 2007. For each Visual Basic 6 application, you have three choices:

1   Leave your programs in Visual Basic 6 format. Microsoft continues to support Visual Basic 6 and will do so for the foreseeable future. Additional information is currently available at the following Microsoft (MSDN) Web address: http://msdn.microsoft.com/vbasic/support/vb6.asp

2   Upgrade part of your Visual Basic 6 program (for example, one or more components), and interoperate with COM components created using Visual Basic 6.

3   Upgrade the entire Visual Basic 6 program to Visual Basic .NET.

Your decision will depend on the goals of your project. If your Visual Basic 6 application is basically complete, if you are in maintenance mode, or if your program relies on some older components that can not easily be updated, you may wish to leave the program in Visual Basic 6 format. If your application is still in development, if it will make particular use of XML or Web pages, or if it will utilize distributed data sources, upgrading the program to Visual Basic .NET will likely be cost effective.

Upgrade Issues

Microsoft has collected a list of unsupported or problematic features in Visual Basic 6 that will require special consideration when you upgrade your application to Visual Basic .NET. Some of those unsupported features include

- **OLE Container Control** This ActiveX control is not supported in Visual Basic .NET, and no replacement is available.

- **Dynamic Data Exchange** Dynamic Data Exchange (DDE) methods are no longer supported. Applications that depend on DDE should be revised to use another method of interapplication communication, such as the SendMessage API.

- **DAO or RDO Data Binding** Data binding to a DAO or an RDO data source is not supported in Visual Basic .NET. The Data control and the RemoteData control are no longer available in Visual Basic .NET. Applications that rely on DAO or RDO data binding should either be updated to use ADO in Visual Basic 6 or should use ADO.NET after upgrading to Visual Basic .NET.

- **Visual Basic 5 Projects** Visual Basic 5 projects should be upgraded to Visual Basic 6 projects before upgrading to Visual Basic .NET. To upgrade to Visual Basic 6, open the project in Visual Basic 6 and choose to upgrade controls. Then save the project in Visual Basic 6 before upgrading to Visual Basic .NET.

- **ActiveX DHTML Page Applications** These are client-side Web technologies and cannot be automatically upgraded to Visual Basic .NET. They should be left in Visual Basic 6. These applications interoperate well with Visual Basic .NET technologies; you can navigate from an ActiveX DHTML page application and a Web Forms page and back.

- **ActiveX Documents** Like ActiveX DHTML page applications, ActiveX documents cannot be automatically upgraded to Visual Basic .NET. Similarly, you can navigate from an ActiveX document to an ASP.NET Web page and back; you can leave these applications in Visual Basic 6.

- **Property Pages**   These are not supported in Visual Basic .NET because the Windows Forms property browser is very flexible and can display and edit any classes, unlike the Visual Basic 6 property browser. You should implement the properties on property pages as standard control properties.

- **User Controls**   User controls created with Visual Basic 6 can be used in Visual Basic .NET. Currently, modifications to user controls should be done in Visual Basic 6.

- **WebClasses**   Visual Basic 6 WebClasses cannot be upgraded to Visual Basic .NET Web Forms. WebClasses can interoperate with Visual Basic .NET Web technologies— however, you can navigate from a Visual Basic 6 WebClass to an ASP.NET application or from an ASP.NET application to a Visual Basic 6 WebClass.

- **Visual Basic Add-ins**   Because Visual Basic .NET uses the Visual Studio IDE, the object model for extensibility is significantly different from that of Visual Basic 6. Add-ins will need to be rewritten in Visual Basic. NET. The advantage in doing so is that the add-in will then be available to all languages.

- **Graphics**   The Visual Basic 6 forms graphics methods, such as Line or Circle, cannot be automatically upgraded by the Visual Basic Upgrade Wizard.

- **Drag-and-Drop Functionality**   Drag-and-drop functionality cannot be automatically upgraded by the Visual Basic Upgrade Wizard.

- **Variants**   Visual Basic .NET no longer supports the Variant data type in Visual Basic 6. When an application is upgraded using the Visual Basic Upgrade Wizard, the Variant data type is converted to Object.

- **Windows APIs**   It is still legitimate to call the Windows API directly in a Visual Basic .NET application, but many existing API calls are no longer necessary due to the increased functionality of the .NET Framework class libraries. Existing calls to the Windows API in Visual Basic 6 applications may need to be revised, although direct calls are still permissible.

Internet Resources for Migration

Microsoft has assembled numerous resources on the Web to make the process of upgrading existing code easier, or at least more straightforward. The following

Web site contains useful information for assessing existing Visual Basic 6 applications and converting them to Visual Basic .NET:

http://msdn.microsoft.com/vbasic/techinfo/articles/upgrade/default.asp

On this site, you'll find white papers about various aspects of upgrading Visual Basic 6 applications, technical sessions (multimedia presentations) describing important migration tools and issues, and checklists for planning the conversion process. This site is updated periodically, so monitor it on a regular basis if you are in the process of upgrading one or more Visual Basic 6 applications to Visual Basic .NET.

Upgrade Steps

If you decide that upgrading your existing Visual Basic 6 applications to Visual Basic .NET is your best choice, here are the steps recommended by Microsoft:

1   Install Visual Basic 6 and Visual Basic .NET on the same computer.

    Installing Visual Basic 6 isn't a requirement, but if the project to be upgraded uses controls or components that don't have an upgrade equivalent in Visual Basic .NET, you may encounter additional upgrade errors and warnings.

2   Compile and run your application in Visual Basic 6 first to ensure it works correctly.

3   Run the Visual Basic Upgrade Wizard to upgrade.

4   Review the upgrade report and upgrade comments and make any necessary modifications.

Using the Visual Basic Upgrade Wizard

Some editions of Visual Studio .NET include a special program called the Visual Basic Upgrade Wizard that can assist you in upgrading your Visual Basic 6 applications to Visual Basic .NET. The Visual Basic Upgrade Wizard isn't a complete solution for migrating Visual Basic 6 applications; the tool can handle most repetitive code changes and can even swap .NET controls for Visual Basic 6 controls on forms, but in all but the most trivial applications, you'll have some hand coding to do when the wizard is complete.

The Visual Basic Upgrade Wizard starts automatically when you try to load a Visual Basic 6 application in Visual Studio .NET. It creates a new Visual Basic .NET project for the original application, and then migrates as much code as possible. When the wizard cannot upgrade a feature, it adds comments to the program code identifying issues that you will need to address later. The wizard also

A

Upgrading to .NET

creates an upgrade report listing general issues related to the migration, and any problems it wasn't able to fix.

The following exercise demonstrates how the Visual Basic Upgrade Wizard works. In the example, I'll open and upgrade the Visual Basic 6 project named Alarm.vbp, which I created near the end of Lesson 7. The Alarm project uses a Timer control, TextBox controls, and Button controls to create a personal appointment reminder that notifies users when it is time for an important meeting. Because the program doesn't use any unsupported features, the upgrade is relatively straightforward. Within Visual Basic 6, the Alarm project looks like this:

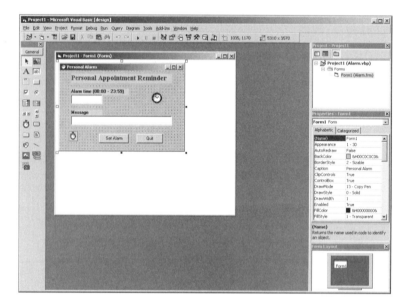

note

You can complete the following steps only if you have Microsoft Visual Basic .NET installed on your computer. However, I think it is useful to observe a sample upgrade session even if you don't have Visual Basic .NET, so you can evaluate for yourself how simple the migration process is.

Upgrade the Alarm project

1   Start Visual Studio .NET and open the Alarm.vbp project in the c:\vb6sbs\appa folder.

Visual Studio recognizes that Alarm.vbp is a Visual Basic 6 project, and starts the Visual Basic Upgrade Wizard to upgrade the project to Visual Basic .NET. You'll see this dialog box:

A

Upgrading to .NET

note

Visual Basic .NET Standard Edition doesn't include the Visual Basic Upgrade Wizard. If your edition of Visual Studio .NET doesn't include the Visual Basic Upgrade Wizard, a message box will be displayed indicating that Visual Basic 6 migration isn't supported.

As the dialog box indicates, the Visual Basic Upgrade Wizard assists in the migration process by creating a new Visual Basic .NET project for the Visual Basic 6 application, copying form and class files to the project and converting them to the new format, and issuing an upgrade report that identifies additional work items. The upgrade report is added to the Visual Basic .NET project so that it easy to locate and read.

2   Click Next to start the conversion.

The wizard asks you some questions about the format of your project and its component contents. Your screen will look like the dialog box on the following page.

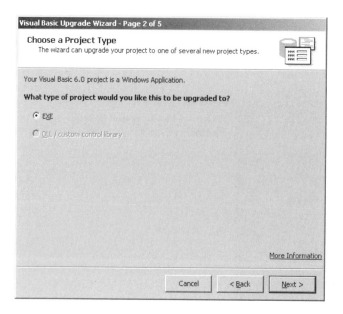

In this example, EXE format was selected by default for the Alarm application, because the tool is an application program and not a DLL (dynamic link library).

3   Click Next to continue the upgrade process.

The wizard prompts you for a location for the new Visual Basic .NET project. The default folder is a subfolder within your original project folder, as shown in this dialog box:

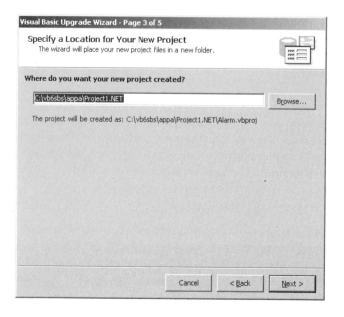

4   Change the new project path to **c:\vb6sbs\appa\my alarmvb.net**

This will place the upgraded Visual Basic .NET project in a new folder named My AlarmVB.NET in the appa folder.

5   Click the Next button, and then click Yes if you are prompted to create a new folder.

6   Click Next again to begin the upgrade process.

The Visual Basic Upgrade Wizard invokes the upgrade engine and steps through the Alarm project's form and code to convert the controls to .NET controls, to update the program code to conform to Visual Basic .NET specifications, and to create an upgrade report. The upgrade report is saved in HTML format and is named _UpgradeReport.htm.

After several minutes, the wizard closes and the new Visual Basic .NET project appears in the Visual Studio development environment. The new project's contents are listed in Solution Explorer.

View Designer button

7   If the form isn't visible, select Alarm.vb in Solution Explorer and click the View Designer button.

Your screen will look like this:

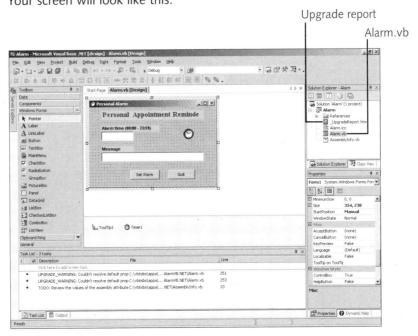

If you compare this figure to the first one in this appendix (the Alarm project loaded in Visual Basic 6), you'll notice a few characteristics of the Visual Basic Upgrade Wizard. First, although the wizard accurately sized the form and its objects, the fonts used on the form aren't an exact match, and will need to be adjusted in Visual Studio .NET to display the proper user interface. Second, the Visual Basic 6 controls were upgraded to .NET controls. The Label and TextBox controls were upgraded to their equivalent .NET versions. The CommandButton controls are now Button controls, even though they still have the "Command" name. The Image control showing the clock was upgraded to a .NET PictureBox control. Visual Studio .NET doesn't have an Image control, and graphic files are now displayed using just the PictureBox control. The Timer control was upgraded to the .NET version and it now appears in the component tray.

Finally, the wizard has added a ToolTip control to the component tray below the form. In Visual Basic 6, many controls had a ToolTipText property to display a tool tip for an individual control. Visual Studio .NET has a different mechanism to display tool tips and uses a single ToolTip control to manage tool tips for all the controls on a form. Since many Visual Basic 6 controls had the ToolTipText property even if it was empty, the Visual Basic Upgrade Wizard adds it as a matter of course to upgraded Visual Basic 6 projects.

8   Double-click the _UpgradeReport.htm file in Solution Explorer.

Visual Studio displays the formatted upgrade report, giving you an opportunity to review the issues that remain in the migration of this application.

9   If necessary, close the Toolbox to get more space, and then open the Global Issues and Alarm.vb sections by clicking the plus sign (+) for each section to read the detailed report.

Your screen will look like this:

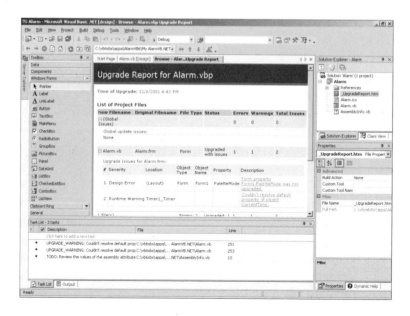

The upgrade report describes any upgrade issues. For example, the PaletteMode property for the form wasn't upgraded and the default property for the Timer1 object couldn't be resolved. If you click on the Description hyperlinks, additional documentation about the issue is displayed.

View Code button

10 Click Alarm.vb in Solution Explorer and click the View Code button to display the Alarm code in the Code Editor.

Near the top of the Code Editor, you'll see a collapsed Upgrade Support section. This section includes code to assist Visual Basic 6 compatibility. As you scan through the program code, you'll see comments that flag potential issues, as shown here:

Upgrade Support section

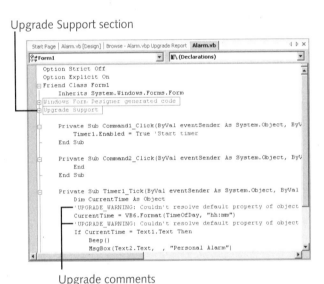

Upgrade comments

These upgrade comments describe the issue, and if you scroll the Code Editor to the right, the comments typically contain a hyperlink for additional documentation. For example:

```
'UPGRADE_WARNING: Couldn't resolve default property of object
   'CurrentTime. Click for more:
   'ms-help://MS.VSCC/commoner/redir/redirect.htm?keyword="vbup1037"'
```

Realizing that some upgrade problems might be confusing, Microsoft has engineered the Visual Basic Upgrade Wizard to insert hyperlinks to where there is more information.

Upgrading to .NET

Run the upgraded Alarm project

The upgraded Alarm project is located in the c:\vb6sbs\ appa\alarmvb.net folder.

1   Click the Start button on the Standard toolbar.

A Save File As dialog box appears asking for a location and name for the Alarm solution file.

2   Click Save to accept the default name of Alarm.sln in the AlarmVB.NET folder.

The Personal Alarm form appears! Even though the upgrade included warnings, it didn't include errors that required modifications to the code.

3   Type a time in the Alarm Time text box that is a couple minutes in the future. Specify the time using a military format, where 1:00 pm is specified as 13:00.

4   Type a short message in the Message text box, such as **Upgraded to Visual Basic .NET!**, and click the Set Alarm button.

Patiently wait for the time to expire and you should see your message appear.

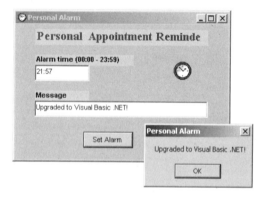

5   Click OK, and then click Quit to close the program.

In this simple case, the Visual Basic 6 project was upgraded, and didn't require modifications to run. However, most upgrades will require some modifications to compile and run without error. You will also typically need to make some user interface adjustments and perform careful testing to ensure the program works as it did under Visual Basic 6. In my opinion, the benefits of upgrading most projects using the Visual Basic Upgrade Wizard outweigh the potential disadvantages, but you'll need to assess this for your own projects on a case by case basis. For more information about the new features in Visual Basic .NET, see "Visual Basic 6 vs. Visual Basic .NET" near the front of this book.

Where to Go for More Information

In this appendix you will learn how to:

✔ *Search Web sites for information about Visual Basic 6.*

✔ *Locate additional books about Visual Basic programming.*

This book has presented beginning, intermediate, and advanced Visual Basic programming techniques with the aim of making you a confident software developer and Windows programmer. Now that you have experimented with many of the tools and features in Visual Basic 6, you are ready for more advanced topics and the full breadth of the Visual Studio development suite. If you have your sights set on a career in Visual Basic programming, you may also wish to test your proficiency by preparing for a certified exam in Visual Basic development. In this appendix, you'll learn about additional resources for Visual Basic 6 programming, including helpful Web sites on the Internet, a source for certification information, and books that you can use to expand your Visual Basic programming skills.

Visual Basic Web Sites

The Web is a boon to programmers, and definitely the fastest mechanism for gathering information about Visual Basic 6 and related technologies. In the following section, I list several of the Web sites that I use to learn about new products and services related to Visual Basic 6. As you use this list, note that the

Internet address and contents of each site change from time to time, so things may not appear exactly as I have described. Considering the constant ebb and flow of information on the Internet, it is also a good idea to search for "visual basic" or "visual studio 6" from time to time to see what new information is available. You may also want to investigate a few Visual Basic .NET Web sites, to see how the features and tools in Visual Basic 6 stack up against the newest version of Visual Basic.

http://msdn.microsoft.com/vbasic/

The Microsoft Corporation Visual Basic home page is the best overall site for documentation, breaking news, conference information, and product support for Visual Basic 6 and Visual Basic .NET. This site will give you up-to-date information about the entire Visual Basic product line, and will let you know how new operating systems, applications, and programming tools affect Visual Basic development. From the Visual Basic home page you can also click on support links for the remaining Visual Studio tools.

http://www.devx.com/

DevX is a commercial Web site devoted to numerous Windows development topics and issues, including Visual Studio and Visual Basic programming. Discussion groups among professional Visual Basic 6 and Visual Basic .NET programmers provide peer-to-peer interaction and feedback for many development issues. In addition, the DevX Marketplace offers books, controls, and third-party tools for sale. Look here for independent information about the merits of upgrading to Visual Basic .NET, for example.

http://www.microsoft.com/mspress/

The Microsoft Press home page offers the newest books on Visual Basic 6 and Visual Basic .NET programming from Microsoft Press authors. Check here for new books about Microsoft Visual C++ and Microsoft Windows programming as well. You can also download freebees and send mail to Microsoft Press.

http://www.microsoft.com/trainingandservices/

The Microsoft Corporation Web site offers resources for software training and services, including testing and certification. Over the last few years, many Visual Basic programmers have found that they can better demonstrate their development skills to potential employers if they pass one or more certification examinations and earn a Microsoft certified credential, such as the MCP (Microsoft Certified Professional), MCSE (Microsoft Certified Systems Engineer), or MCSA (Microsoft Certified Systems Administrator). Visit this Web site to learn more about your certification options.

http://communities.microsoft.com/newsgroups/

Here you'll find newsgroup communities for many Microsoft development products, including Visual Basic 6, Visual Basic .NET, and the remaining tools in the Visual Studio family. Currently, useful newsgroup communities are listed under the keywords "vb," "vb.6," "vb.controls," "vb.3rdparty," "dotnet," "vsnet," and "vstudio."

Books for Visual Basic 6 Programming

Books about Visual Basic programming provide in-depth sources of information and self-paced training that Web sites can supplement but not replace. As you seek to expand your Visual Basic programming skills, I recommend that you consult the following sources of printed information (listed here by category). Note that this isn't a complete bibliography of Visual Basic 6 titles, but a list that is representative of the books available in English near the end of 2002.

Visual Basic 6 Programming

Programming Microsoft Visual Basic 6.0, by Francesco Balena (Microsoft Press, ISBN 0-7356-0558-0).

Desktop Applications with Microsoft Visual Basic 6.0 MCSD Training Kit For Exam 70-176, by Microsoft Corporation (Microsoft Press, ISBN 0-7356-0620-X).

Teach Yourself Visual Basic 6 in 21 Days, by Greg Perry (Sams, ISBN 0-672-31310-3).

Beginning Visual Basic 6, by Peter Wright (Wrox Press, ISBN 1-861001-05-3).

Programming Components with Microsoft Visual Basic 6.0, Second Edition, by Guy Eddon and Henry Eddon (Microsoft Press, ISBN 1-57231-966-6).

Programming Distributed Applications with COM and Microsoft Visual Basic 6.0, by Ted Pattison (Microsoft Press, ISBN 1-57231-961-5).

Web Programming with Visual Basic 6

Web Database Development Step by Step, by Jim Buyens (Microsoft Press, ISBN 0-7356-0966-7).

Professional Visual Basic 6 Web Programming, by Wrox Team (Wrox Press, ISBN 1-861002-22-X).

Database Programming with Visual Basic 6

Beginning Visual Basic 6 Database Programming, by John Connell (Wrox Press, ISBN 1-861001-06-1).

Mastering Database Programming with Visual Basic 6, by Evangelos Petroutsos (Sybex, ISBN 0-7821-2598-0).

ADO Programming in Visual Basic 6, by Steven Holzner (Prentice Hall, ISBN 0-13-085857-9).

Database Access with Visual Basic 6, by Jeffrey P. McManus (Sams, ISBN 0-672-31422-3).

Professional Visual Basic 6 Databases, by Charles Williams (Wrox Press, ISBN 1-861002-02-5).

Visual Basic for Applications Programming

Microsoft Excel 2002 Visual Basic for Applications Step by Step, by Reed Jacobson (Microsoft Press, ISBN 0-7356-1359-1).

Excel 2002 Power Programming with VBA, by John Walkenbach (Hungry Minds, ISBN 0-7645-4799-2).

Microsoft Access 2002 Visual Basic for Applications Step by Step, by Evan Callahan (Microsoft Press, ISBN 0-7356-1358-3).

Books for Visual Basic .NET Programming

If you are looking for more printed information about upgrading to Visual Basic .NET, the following books may be useful to you:

Microsoft Visual Basic .NET Step by Step, by Michael Halvorson (Microsoft Press, ISBN 0-7356-1374-5).

Upgrading Microsoft Visual Basic 6.0 to Microsoft Visual Basic .NET,
  by Ed Robinson, Michael Bond, and Ian Oliver (Microsoft Press, ISBN
  0-7356-1587-x).

Programming Microsoft Visual Basic .NET, by Francesco Balena
  (Microsoft Press, ISBN 0-7356-1375-3).

Coding Techniques for Microsoft Visual Basic .NET, by John Connell
  (Microsoft Press, ISBN 0-7356-1254-4).

Practical Standards for Microsoft Visual Basic .NET, by James D.
  Foxall (Microsoft Press, ISBN 0-7356-1356-7).

Beginning Visual Basic .NET Databases, by Wrox Author Team (Wrox
  Press, ISBN 1-8610-0555-5).

B

More Information

Index

N

T

W

About the Author

Michael Halvorson is the author or coauthor of 25 computer books, including *Microsoft Visual Basic .NET Step by Step, Microsoft Office XP Inside Out, Learn Microsoft Visual Basic 6 Now, and Microsoft Word 97/Visual Basic Step by Step*. Michael earned a bachelor's degree in Computer Science from Pacific Lutheran University in Tacoma, Washington, and master's and doctoral degrees in History from the University of Washington in Seattle, Washington. He was employed at Microsoft Corporation as a technical editor, acquisitions editor, and localization manager from 1985 through 1993. Michael currently spends his time developing innovative software solutions for Microsoft Office and Microsoft Visual Basic and teaching European history courses at colleges in the Pacific Northwest.

Photo by Kim Halvorson

Antique Stereoscope

A stereoscope creates the illusion of depth in a two-dimensional photograph called a stereograph, consisting of two separate photographs, each taken from a slightly different angle. When viewed through a stereoscope, the two images are received separately but fuse in the viewer's brain into a single, three-dimensional image. In the late 19th century, before radio and television, stereoscopes were an immensely popular form of entertainment in Europe and North America. Photographers of stereoscopic images traveled around the world to create stereographs of popular tourist attractions and to document important events. Enthusiasts purchased cards featuring stereographs of famous events or sights and viewed them through stereoscopes in their own homes. By the 1930s, stereoscopes had declined in popularity. In 1939 German-born American inventor William Gruber and American businessman Harold Graves revived public interest in stereographs when they introduced the View-Master, a portable stereoscope that displays many different color stereographs mounted on a revolving disk called a reel.*

At Microsoft Press, we use tools to illustrate our books for software developers and IT professionals. Tools very simply and powerfully symbolize human inventiveness. They're a metaphor for people extending their capabilities, precision, and reach. From simple calipers and pliers to digital micrometers and lasers, these stylized illustrations give each book a visual identity, and a personality to the series. With tools and knowledge, there's no limit to creativity and innovation. Our tagline says it all: *the tools you need to put technology to work.*

*Microsoft ® Encarta ® Reference Library 2002. © 1993-2001 Microsoft Corporation. All rights reserved.

The manuscript for this book was prepared and submitted to Microsoft Press in electronic form. Text files were prepared using Microsoft Word XP. Pages were composed by Microsoft Press using Adobe PageMaker 6.52 for Windows, with text set in Sabon and display type in Syntax and Syntax Black. Composed pages were delivered to the printer as electronic prepress files.

Interior Graphic Artist

Joel Panchot

Principal Compositors

Kerri DeVault, Dan Latimer

Principal Copy Editor

Cheryl Penner

Indexer

Bill Myers

Go beyond

knowing how Visual Basic works to learning how to write professional-level Microsoft .NET code.

U.S.A. **$59.99**
Canada $86.99
ISBN: 0-7356-1254-4

Most books about Visual Basic use abstract snippets of code to illustrate the language's syntax, data structures, and controls. But even if you know the language, it's sometimes difficult to see how to put these elements together to write a complete program. This practical handbook of software construction covers the vital details about the latest version—Microsoft® Visual Basic® .NET, with its integrated development environment (IDE), complete support for XML, and ASP.NET Web-development functionality, including Web Forms and XML Web services. Whether you're a beginner or a self-taught programmer, a professional looking for a refresher in coding techniques, or a programmer coming from another language, this is the Visual Basic book for you.

microsoft.com/mspress

Get the plain facts on
how to upgrade your code
from Visual Basic 6.0 to Visual Basic .NET
efficiently with proven methods
direct from the source—Microsoft.

U.S.A. **$59.99**
Canada $86.99
ISBN: 0-7356-1587-X

Microsoft® Visual Basic® .NET offers remarkable power and flexibility, with richer object models for data, forms, transactions, and more. But you must upgrade your applications—sometimes with major modifications—before they'll compile and run in the Microsoft .NET environment. Get the in-depth technical details you need to upgrade code efficiently to the .NET version with this reference, which is dedicated entirely to the upgrade process. Learn about new functionality in Visual Basic .NET such as inheritance, multithreading, drag-and-drop XML Web services, RAD programmability for servers, the new forms package, and more. Examine side-by-side examples of code in Visual Basic 6.0 and Visual Basic .NET. Learn to evaluate projects to determine which ones can benefit most from an upgrade to Visual Basic .NET and which can function best in a mixed-code environment. Along the way, you'll find out everything you need to take full advantage of the epic shift to Visual Basic .NET.

microsoft.com/mspress

Get a **Free**
e-mail newsletter, updates,
special offers, links to related books,
and more when you

register on line!

Register your Microsoft Press® title on our Web site and you'll get a FREE subscription to our e-mail newsletter, *Microsoft Press Book Connections.* You'll find out about newly released and upcoming books and learning tools, online events, software downloads, special offers and coupons for Microsoft Press customers, and information about major Microsoft® product releases. You can also read useful additional information about all the titles we publish, such as detailed book descriptions, tables of contents and indexes, sample chapters, links to related books and book series, author biographies, and reviews by other customers.

Registration is easy. Just visit this Web page and fill in your information:

http://www.microsoft.com/mspress/register

Microsoft

- -

Proof of Purchase

Use this page as proof of purchase if participating in a promotion or rebate offer on this title. Proof of purchase must be used in conjunction with other proof(s) of payment such as your dated sales receipt—see offer details.

Microsoft® Visual Basic® 6.0 Professional Step by Step,
Second Edition
0-7356-1883-6

CUSTOMER NAME

Microsoft Press, PO Box 97017, Redmond, WA 98073-9830

MICROSOFT LICENSE AGREEMENT

Book Companion CD

IMPORTANT—READ CAREFULLY: This Microsoft End-User License Agreement ("EULA") is a legal agreement between you (either an individual or an entity) and Microsoft Corporation for the Microsoft product identified above, which includes computer software and may include associated media, printed materials, and "online" or electronic documentation ("SOFTWARE PRODUCT"). Any component included within the SOFTWARE PRODUCT that is accompanied by a separate End-User License Agreement shall be governed by such agreement and not the terms set forth below. By installing, copying, or otherwise using the SOFTWARE PRODUCT, you agree to be bound by the terms of this EULA. If you do not agree to the terms of this EULA, you are not authorized to install, copy, or otherwise use the SOFTWARE PRODUCT; you may, however, return the SOFTWARE PRODUCT, along with all printed materials and other items that form a part of the Microsoft product that includes the SOFTWARE PRODUCT, to the place you obtained them for a full refund.

SOFTWARE PRODUCT LICENSE

The SOFTWARE PRODUCT is protected by United States copyright laws and international copyright treaties, as well as other intellectual property laws and treaties. The SOFTWARE PRODUCT is licensed, not sold.

1. **GRANT OF LICENSE.** This EULA grants you the following rights:

   a. **Software Product.** You may install and use one copy of the SOFTWARE PRODUCT on a single computer. The primary user of the computer on which the SOFTWARE PRODUCT is installed may make a second copy for his or her exclusive use on a portable computer.

   b. **Storage/Network Use.** You may also store or install a copy of the SOFTWARE PRODUCT on a storage device, such as a network server, used only to install or run the SOFTWARE PRODUCT on your other computers over an internal network; however, you must acquire and dedicate a license for each separate computer on which the SOFTWARE PRODUCT is installed or run from the storage device. A license for the SOFTWARE PRODUCT may not be shared or used concurrently on different computers.

   c. **License Pak.** If you have acquired this EULA in a Microsoft License Pak, you may make the number of additional copies of the computer software portion of the SOFTWARE PRODUCT authorized on the printed copy of this EULA, and you may use each copy in the manner specified above. You are also entitled to make a corresponding number of secondary copies for portable computer use as specified above.

   d. **Sample Code.** Solely with respect to portions, if any, of the SOFTWARE PRODUCT that are identified within the SOFTWARE PRODUCT as sample code (the "SAMPLE CODE"):

      i. **Use and Modification.** Microsoft grants you the right to use and modify the source code version of the SAMPLE CODE, *provided* you comply with subsection (d)(iii) below. You may not distribute the SAMPLE CODE, or any modified version of the SAMPLE CODE, in source code form.

      ii. **Redistributable Files.** Provided you comply with subsection (d)(iii) below, Microsoft grants you a nonexclusive, royalty-free right to reproduce and distribute the object code version of the SAMPLE CODE and of any modified SAMPLE CODE, other than SAMPLE CODE, or any modified version thereof, designated as not redistributable in the Readme file that forms a part of the SOFTWARE PRODUCT (the "Non-Redistributable Sample Code"). All SAMPLE CODE other than the Non-Redistributable Sample Code is collectively referred to as the "REDISTRIBUTABLES."

      iii. **Redistribution Requirements.** If you redistribute the REDISTRIBUTABLES, you agree to: (i) distribute the REDISTRIBUTABLES in object code form only in conjunction with and as a part of your software application product; (ii) not use Microsoft's name, logo, or trademarks to market your software application product; (iii) include a valid copyright notice on your software application product; (iv) indemnify, hold harmless, and defend Microsoft from and against any claims or lawsuits, including attorney's fees, that arise or result from the use or distribution of your software application product; and (v) not permit further distribution of the REDISTRIBUTABLES by your end user. Contact Microsoft for the applicable royalties due and other licensing terms for all other uses and/or distribution of the REDISTRIBUTABLES.

2. **DESCRIPTION OF OTHER RIGHTS AND LIMITATIONS.**

   - **Limitations on Reverse Engineering, Decompilation, and Disassembly.** You may not reverse engineer, decompile, or disassemble the SOFTWARE PRODUCT, except and only to the extent that such activity is expressly permitted by applicable law notwithstanding this limitation.

   - **Separation of Components.** The SOFTWARE PRODUCT is licensed as a single product. Its component parts may not be separated for use on more than one computer.

   - **Rental.** You may not rent, lease, or lend the SOFTWARE PRODUCT.

   - **Support Services.** Microsoft may, but is not obligated to, provide you with support services related to the SOFTWARE PRODUCT ("Support Services"). Use of Support Services is governed by the Microsoft policies and programs described in the user manual, in "online" documentation, and/or in other Microsoft-provided materials. Any supplemental software code provided to you as part of the Support Services shall be considered part of the SOFTWARE PRODUCT and subject to the terms and conditions of this EULA. With respect to technical information you provide to Microsoft as part of the Support Services, Microsoft may use such information for its business purposes, including for product support and development. Microsoft will not utilize such technical information in a form that personally identifies you.

- **Software Transfer.** You may permanently transfer all of your rights under this EULA, provided you retain no copies, you transfer all of the SOFTWARE PRODUCT (including all component parts, the media and printed materials, any upgrades, this EULA, and, if applicable, the Certificate of Authenticity), **and** the recipient agrees to the terms of this EULA.

- **Termination.** Without prejudice to any other rights, Microsoft may terminate this EULA if you fail to comply with the terms and conditions of this EULA. In such event, you must destroy all copies of the SOFTWARE PRODUCT and all of its component parts.

3. **COPYRIGHT.** All title and copyrights in and to the SOFTWARE PRODUCT (including but not limited to any images, photographs, animations, video, audio, music, text, SAMPLE CODE, REDISTRIBUTABLES, and "applets" incorporated into the SOFTWARE PRODUCT) and any copies of the SOFTWARE PRODUCT are owned by Microsoft or its suppliers. The SOFTWARE PRODUCT is protected by copyright laws and international treaty provisions. Therefore, you must treat the SOFTWARE PRODUCT like any other copyrighted material **except** that you may install the SOFTWARE PRODUCT on a single computer provided you keep the original solely for backup or archival purposes. You may not copy the printed materials accompanying the SOFTWARE PRODUCT.

4. **U.S. GOVERNMENT RESTRICTED RIGHTS.** The SOFTWARE PRODUCT and documentation are provided with RESTRICTED RIGHTS. Use, duplication, or disclosure by the Government is subject to restrictions as set forth in subparagraph (c)(1)(ii) of the Rights in Technical Data and Computer Software clause at DFARS 252.227-7013 or subparagraphs (c)(1) and (2) of the Commercial Computer Software—Restricted Rights at 48 CFR 52.227-19, as applicable. Manufacturer is Microsoft Corporation/One Microsoft Way/Redmond, WA 98052-6399.

5. **EXPORT RESTRICTIONS.** You agree that you will not export or re-export the SOFTWARE PRODUCT, any part thereof, or any process or service that is the direct product of the SOFTWARE PRODUCT (the foregoing collectively referred to as the "Restricted Components"), to any country, person, entity, or end user subject to U.S. export restrictions. You specifically agree not to export or re-export any of the Restricted Components (i) to any country to which the U.S. has embargoed or restricted the export of goods or services, which currently include, but are not necessarily limited to, Cuba, Iran, Iraq, Libya, North Korea, Sudan, and Syria, or to any national of any such country, wherever located, who intends to transmit or transport the Restricted Components back to such country; (ii) to any end user who you know or have reason to know will utilize the Restricted Components in the design, development, or production of nuclear, chemical, or biological weapons; or (iii) to any end user who has been prohibited from participating in U.S. export transactions by any federal agency of the U.S. government. You warrant and represent that neither the BXA nor any other U.S. federal agency has suspended, revoked, or denied your export privileges.

DISCLAIMER OF WARRANTY

NO WARRANTIES OR CONDITIONS. MICROSOFT EXPRESSLY DISCLAIMS ANY WARRANTY OR CONDITION FOR THE SOFTWARE PRODUCT. THE SOFTWARE PRODUCT AND ANY RELATED DOCUMENTATION ARE PROVIDED "AS IS" WITHOUT WARRANTY OR CONDITION OF ANY KIND, EITHER EXPRESS OR IMPLIED, INCLUDING, WITHOUT LIMITATION, THE IMPLIED WARRANTIES OF MERCHANTABILITY, FITNESS FOR A PARTICULAR PURPOSE, OR NONINFRINGEMENT. THE ENTIRE RISK ARISING OUT OF USE OR PERFORMANCE OF THE SOFTWARE PRODUCT REMAINS WITH YOU.

LIMITATION OF LIABILITY. TO THE MAXIMUM EXTENT PERMITTED BY APPLICABLE LAW, IN NO EVENT SHALL MICROSOFT OR ITS SUPPLIERS BE LIABLE FOR ANY SPECIAL, INCIDENTAL, INDIRECT, OR CONSEQUENTIAL DAMAGES WHATSOEVER (INCLUDING, WITHOUT LIMITATION, DAMAGES FOR LOSS OF BUSINESS PROFITS, BUSINESS INTERRUPTION, LOSS OF BUSINESS INFORMATION, OR ANY OTHER PECUNIARY LOSS) ARISING OUT OF THE USE OF OR INABILITY TO USE THE SOFTWARE PRODUCT OR THE PROVISION OF OR FAILURE TO PROVIDE SUPPORT SERVICES, EVEN IF MICROSOFT HAS BEEN ADVISED OF THE POSSIBILITY OF SUCH DAMAGES. IN ANY CASE, MICROSOFT'S ENTIRE LIABILITY UNDER ANY PROVISION OF THIS EULA SHALL BE LIMITED TO THE GREATER OF THE AMOUNT ACTUALLY PAID BY YOU FOR THE SOFTWARE PRODUCT OR US$5.00; PROVIDED, HOWEVER, IF YOU HAVE ENTERED INTO A MICROSOFT SUPPORT SERVICES AGREEMENT, MICROSOFT'S ENTIRE LIABILITY REGARDING SUPPORT SERVICES SHALL BE GOVERNED BY THE TERMS OF THAT AGREEMENT. BECAUSE SOME STATES AND JURISDICTIONS DO NOT ALLOW THE EXCLUSION OR LIMITATION OF LIABILITY, THE ABOVE LIMITATION MAY NOT APPLY TO YOU.

MISCELLANEOUS

This EULA is governed by the laws of the State of Washington USA, except and only to the extent that applicable law mandates governing law of a different jurisdiction.

Should you have any questions concerning this EULA, or if you desire to contact Microsoft for any reason, please contact the Microsoft subsidiary serving your country, or write: Microsoft Sales Information Center/One Microsoft Way/Redmond, WA 98052-6399.